THE SOUND OF POETRY / THE POETRY OF SOUND

THE
SOUND
OF
POETRY
THE
POETRY
OF
SOUND

EDITED BY MARJORIE PERLOFF AND CRAIG DWORKIN

THE UNIVERSITY OF CHICAGO PRESS / CHICAGO AND LONDON

Marjorie Perloff is professor of English emerita
at Stanford University and author of many books,
including *Wittgenstein's Ladder* and *The Futurist
Moment,* both also from the University of
Chicago Press.

Craig Dworkin is associate professor of English
at the University of Utah and the author of, most
recently, *Language to Cover a Page: The Early
Writtings of Vito Acconci.*

The University of Chicago Press, Chicago 60637
The University of Chicago Press, Ltd., London
© 2009 by The University of Chicago
All rights reserved. Published 2009
Printed in the United States of America

18 17 16 15 14 13 12 11 10 09

1 2 3 4 5

ISBN-13: 978-0-226-65742-4 (cloth)
ISBN-13: 978-0-226-65743-1 (paper)

ISBN-10: 0-226-65742-6 (cloth)
ISBN-10: 0-226-65743-4 (paper)

Portions of the introduction are reprinted from
PMLA (May 2008) and appear here in revised,
expanded form. Reprinted by permission of
the copyright owner, The Modern Language
Association of America.

A slightly different version of the chapter by
Susan Howe appeared in *Souls of the Labadie
Tract,* copyright © 2007 by Susan Howe.
Reprinted by permission of New Directions
Publishing Corp.

Library of Congress
Cataloging-in-Publication Data

The sound of poetry, the poetry of sound / edited
by Marjorie Perloff and Craig Dworkin.
    p. cm.
Includes index.
    ISBN-13: 978-0-226-65742-4 (cloth : alk. paper)
    ISBN-13: 978-0-226-65743-1 (pbk. : alk. paper)
    ISBN-10: 0-226-65742-6 (cloth : alk. paper)
    ISBN-10: 0-226-65743-4 (pbk. : alk. paper)
    1. Sound poetry.   I. Perloff, Marjorie.
II. Dworkin, Craig Douglas.
    PN1525.S66   2009
    809.8′14—dc22

                                2009020245

⊗ The paper used in this publication meets
the minimum requirements of the American
National Standard for Information Sciences—
Permanence of Paper for Printed Library
Materials, ANSI Z39.48-1992.

CONTENTS

INTRODUCTION:
THE SOUND OF POETRY/THE POETRY OF SOUND

The Sound of Poetry

An onomatopoeic expression automatically entails the specification of what
is being described. A pattering sound cannot come from a block of wood.
But when I was listening to [Peter Ablinger's Berlin sound] recordings, I sometimes couldn't tell whether a sound was coming from thunder or a sheet of
metal. I wanted to represent the sound, not the person who was producing it,
nor its metaphorical significance. It took me quite some time to come up
with a solution: My solution was not to find a solution, but rather to enter into
the crevice between sound and language and make countless little notes.

YOKO TAWADA, "The Art of Being Nonsynchronous"

The Sound of Poetry / The Poetry of Sound had its origin in the Presidential
Forum and related workshops and special sessions held at the Modern Language Association annual convention in 2006. Our organizing theme was
prompted by two fairly simple and self-evident propositions. The first is that
poetry (the word comes from the Greek *poiesis,* a making or creation; in Medieval Latin, *poetria,* the art of verbal creation) inherently involves the structuring of sound. As Roman Jakobson put it, "Poetry is not the only area where
sound symbolism makes itself felt, but it is a province where the internal
nexus between sound and meaning changes from latent into patent and manifests itself most palpably and intensely."[1] The second proposition — or more
properly conundrum — is that however central the sound dimension is to any
and all poetry, no other poetic feature is currently as neglected. Indeed, the
discourse on poetry today, largely fixated as it is on what a given poem or set of

poems ostensibly "says," regards the sound structure in question — whether the slow and stately *terza rima* of Shelley's "Ode to the West Wind" or the phonemic/morphemic patterning of monosyllabic words like "cat," "top," "pit," "pot." and "foot" in the "free verse" of William Carlos Williams's "As the cat . . . " — as little more than a peripheral issue, a kind of sideline. At the same time — and here "the poetry of sound" comes in — the many exhibitions of sound art, performances of sound poetry, and studies of sound mediation in the case of radio, television, performance art, and the digital environment suggest that what the Japanese-German writer Yoko Tawada calls "the crevice between sound and language" has never been more challenging to explore.

What accounts for the large-scale indifference to sound structure in the current discourse on poetry? One problem, it would seem, is that "scientific" prosodic analysis, as practiced by linguists and rhetoricians over the past few decades, has relied on an empiricist model that allows for little generalization about poetic modes and values: the more thorough the description of a given poem's rhythmic and metrical units, its repetition of vowels and consonants, its pitch contours, the less we may be able to discern the larger contours of a given poet's particular practice, much less a period style or cultural construct. Then, too, conventional prosodic studies cannot allow for the difference individual performance makes, much less for variants of individual and culturally determined reception.

Still, linguistic studies of prosody, however specialized, have done much less to dampen the interest in poetic sound than has the continuing dominance of romantic lyric theory, with its equation of "poetry" and "lyric," coupled with an understanding of "lyric" as *the* mode of subjectivity — of self-reflexiveness, the mode in which a solitary "I" is overheard in meditation or conversation with an unnamed other. Harold Bloom, who referred to such lyric as "the romantic crisis poem," insisted in his *Agon* that "from 1744 [the death of Alexander Pope] to the present day the best poetry internalized its subject matter, particularly in the mode of Wordsworth after 1798. Wordsworth had no true subject except his own subjective nature, and *very nearly all significant poetry since Wordsworth . . . has repeated Wordsworth's inward turning.*"[2] The representation of "inwardness" demanded, in its turn, that the reader would pay the closest possible attention to a given poem's figurative language. Here the paradigmatic study remains Paul de Man's "Lyric and Modernity," in *Blindness and Insight*. De Man, who uses the terms *lyric* and *poetry* interchangeably, casts his eye on such tropes as prosopopoeia, metaphor, and catachresis, so as to show that in Mallarmé's lyric, "language is representational and allegorical at the same time," that indeed Mallarmé "remains a representational poet as he remains in fact a poet of the self, however impersonal, disincarnated, and ironical this self may become."[3]

"Lyric and Modernity" dates from 1969, Bloom's *The Anxiety of Influence* from 1973 and *Agon* from 1982. In the decades that followed — decades in which literature departments turned increasingly to Cultural Studies and Postcolonialism — the lyric paradigm, when it was invoked at all, remained the same. As recently as 2008, a "state of the art" collection of essays published in *PMLA* called *The New Lyric Studies* tacitly accepted the premise that poetry equals lyric, with its corollaries that poetry is distinguished from prose by its lineation and that the domain of lyric is subjectivity, however displaced or ironized.[4] Oren Izenberg's "Poems out of Our Heads," for example, argues that "poetry is an extraordinary kind of thinking." Examining Emily Dickinson's "I think I was enchanted" as an exemplar of the role *qualia* ("the subjective or phenomenal aspects of conscious experience" as defined by recent philosophers of mind) can play in poetry, Izenberg concludes that in this and related poems, Dickinson is "addressing — by means of form — the ontological *problem* of constitutively first-person experiences, precisely by worrying the epistemological problem of third-person access to first-person states."[5]

What does the word "form" mean in this sentence? Presumably, Izenberg is referring to Dickinson's figurative language: "the overloaded and overdetermined significance of Dickinson's metaphors encourage us to attend to the fact that the primary modality of change attested to in this poem is not of *kind* at all . . . but rather of *scale* or *quality:* small things seen as large, dark things seen as bright."[6] Suggestive as this reading of Dickinson is, one is left wondering what is exclusively "poetic" about Dickinson's epistemology. Doesn't, say, Proust's *À la recherche du temps perdu*, concern itself with the "ontological *problem* of third-person access to first-person states"? Conversely, what would Izenberg make of Yeats's short lyric poem "A Deep-sworn Vow"? :

Others because you did not keep
That deep-sworn vow have been friends of mine;
Yet always when I look death in the face,
When I clamber to the heights of sleep,
Or when I grow excited with wine,
Suddenly I meet your face.[7]

This little love poem "says" no more than "I can't get you out of my mind!" and says it using such well-worn phrases as "deep-sworn vow," "look death in the face," "clamber to the heights of sleep," and "excited with wine." The poem's interest depends less on what Izenberg refers to as its "hermeneutic payoff" than on the role rhythm, repetition, and especially rhyme play in making new a well-worn motif of love poetry — indeed, in creating meaning. The six-line *abcabc* ballad stanza, with its slow, stately four-stress lines and open vowel sounds, is made strange, first by the strong reverse stress in the opening word "Óthers" and then by the drumbeat internal rhyme on "keep" and "deep-sworn," looking ahead to "sleep" in line 4. But the real coup is reserved for the poem's conclusion. The continuity of the "when . . . " clauses of lines 3–5 suddenly gives way, the expected rhyme for "face" (place? race? lace? erase?) failing to materialize. Instead of rhyme, repetition: it is "face" itself that returns and sends us back to line 3, suggesting that "your face" — a "face" the lover evidently cannot have — is equivalent to "look[ing] death in the face" in the third or nonrhyming line.

It is a great tour de force, but one needs to read "A Deep-sworn Vow" in the context of Yeats's other poems to understand what repetition, whether verbal or phonemic — and its absence — can do. In a neighboring poem from *The Wild Swans at Coole* called "Memory," "face" recurs, now linked to those unnamed "Others" with whom the poet took up so as to distract himself; face" is here linked to their passing "charm." But "charm," rhyming inexactly with "form" in the poem's rhyme scheme, has the word "harm" inside it, and "harm" is precisely what the poet's unrequited love has brought him. And from here it is just a step to the insistent question, in "Easter 1916," "And what if excess of love / Bewildered them till they died?"

Indeed, the common practice of reading lyric poems in isolation — what we might call the anthology syndrome — presents a rather skewed view of the poetic process. We don't, after all, judge novelists by single chapters, or dramatists by single scenes. But the contributors to *New Lyric Studies* exemplify their particular theories of the lyric by citing individual cases. These include Robert Frost's "Spring Pools" (Jonathan Culler), C. P. Cavafy's "Dareios" (Stathis Gourgouris), Herman Melville's "The Portent" (Virginia Jackson), Tennyson's "Break, Break Break" (Yopie Prins), and the already mentioned Dickinson's "I Think I Was Enchanted" (Oren Izenberg). But not just any short poem. For, as it turns out, all the exemplary lyrics discussed in this collection belong to the hundred-year period between 1830 and 1930.[8]

Such anachronism is hardly an accident, it being the case that the "new poetry" of the past century simply fails to accord with the "new lyric" paradigms as presented here and elsewhere. From Rimbaud's *Illuminations* and Mallarmé's *Un coup de dés* to Gertrude Stein's *Tender Buttons* and Pound's *Cantos,* to Susan Howe's *Articulations of Sound Forms in Time* and Christian Bök's *Cyborg Opera,* both of the latter discussed by their respective authors in this volume, the word *poetry* cannot be understood as equivalent to "the lyric," much less the postromantic lyric. Indeed, generic classification has become much less important than the *poeticity* of the language itself.

To understand this shift, it will be useful to begin with etymology. The word *lyric,* the *Oxford English Dictionary* tells us, comes from the Greek *lyra* (lyre) and originally designated "a poem composed to be accompanied by the lyre."[9] A related term is the Chinese word for poem, *shi:* the first anthology of Chinese poems, the *Shi jing* (Classic of Poetry) compiled after 600 B.C. and attributed to Confucius, contained folk, courtier, and dynastic songs, as well as ceremonial hymns, originally sung or chanted.[10] Indeed, the coupling of words and musical accompaniment has been a hallmark of lyric from ancient times (Sumerian, Hebrew, Greek) to the beginnings of print culture in the Renaissance, reaching a kind of apogee in such forms as the early medieval Arabic *ghazal* and *qasida* and, somewhat later, the *planh, chanso, pastorela,* and *alba* composed by the Provençal troubadours. "After 1400," writes J. W. Johnson, "the lyric and music became increasingly dissociated, as evidenced by the rise of such primarily melodic forms as the madrigal, glee, catch, and round, which subordinated the words to the music. Despite the efforts of later writers who were primarily poets and not composers, such as Swinburne, Hopkins, and Yeats, the lyric since the Renaissance has remained a verbal rather than a musical discipline, and the traces of its melodic origin have become largely vestigial."[11] The Oulipo poet-theorist Jacques Roubaud discusses this transformation in "Poetry and Orality," the polemic prelude to this collection:

> The breaking of the bond between word and sound, which occurred during the fourteenth century, brought about a new *double form* called *poetry.* This form would combine the words of a language in writing and in speech such that they would be indissociable.
>
> That other form which brings word and sound together has by no means disappeared; we call it *song.*
>
> A song is not a poem and a poem is not a song.

The new "double form" Roubaud speaks of—the words of a language as represented in writing (visual) coupled with their oral performance (aural) — was normative until the romantic period, when, as Johnson notes, the drive began to define lyric poetry by reference to its secondary (i.e., non-musical) qualities:

> Among the best known and most often cited proscriptions regarding the lyric are that it must (1) be brief (Poe); (2) "be one, the parts of which mutually support and explain each other, all in their proportion harmonizing with, and supporting the purpose and known influence of metrical arrangement" (Coleridge); (3) be "the spontaneous overflow of powerful feelings" (Wordsworth); (4) be an intensely subjective and personal expression (Hegel); (5) be an inverted action of mind upon will (Schopenhauer); or (6) be "the utterance that is overheard" (Mill).[12]

To which Johnson responds, "Though the attributes of brevity, metrical coherence, subjectivity, passion, sensuality, and particularity of image are frequently ascribed to the lyric, *there are schools of poetry obviously lyric which are not susceptible to such criteria*" (my emphasis). Milton's *L'Allegro* and *Il Penseroso* fail the brevity test; Elizabethan love sonnets the test of impassioned subjectivity, and most twentieth-century free-verse poetry obviously does not exhibit "metrical coherence." Indeed, what is surely the most famous poem written in English in the twentieth century, *The Waste Land*, defies all of the above, except possibly "particularity of image," and even that particularity is ironized and complicated by the poem's elaborate tissue of quotations, allusions, foreign phrases, and colloquial speech patterns, as in the pub dialogue in "The Game of Chess." But then the chief model for *The Waste Land* was not a "lyric" poem at all but Pope's mock epic *The Rape of the Lock,* which is, among other things, one of the great source books for poetic devices — from the rhetorical figures of antithesis, parallelism, zeugma ("Or stain her honour, or her new brocade"), and mock-cataloguing ("Puffs, Powders, Patches, Bibles, Billet-doux") to the metrical art of the heroic couplet and the use of sound figures from anaphora to witty rhyming, as in this address to Queen Anne:

> Here Thou, great ANNA! whom three Realms obey,
> Dost sometimes Counsel take — and sometimes Tea.

Or this sly comparison:

> One speaks the Glory of the *British Queen,*
> And one describes a charming *Indian* screen.[13]

"The irreducible denominator of all lyric poetry," Johnson himself concludes, "must, therefore comprise those elements which it shares with the musical forms that produced it. Although lyric poetry is not music. . . . it retains
structural or substantive evidence of its melodic origins, and this factor serves
as the categorical principle of poetic lyricism."[14] This definition reasonably
stresses the structuring of sound, rather than subjectivity or emotion or metrical coherence, as "irreducible denominator" of lyric, but some important
qualifications are in order. First, as Jacques Roubaud notes, the "structural
evidence" of "melodic origins" is, of course, the poem's visual representation
in writing, and that visual representation — how it looks in the book, on the
page, or, more recently, on the screen — is central to its understanding. Second, the "structural or substantive evidence of melodic origins" applies not
only to "the lyric" but to other poetic genres as well. Surely no one would deny
that *The Rape of the Lock* or Byron's *Don Juan* qualify as poetry, even if theirs
is mock-epic or satiric poetry. In our own century, some of the most important poems have incorporated prose, as in William Carlos Williams's *Spring
and All,* or even, in the Pound tradition, pictogram and diagram, as in Louis
Zukofsky's *"A"* or, more recently, Christian Bök's *Crystallography.*

Third — and this is the fascinating issue Craig Dworkin addresses
below — Johnson's phrase "melodic origins" makes little sense at a time when
"music" itself is anything but "melodic." In the age of John Cage or Iannis
Xenakis, *lyric,* with its traditional connotations of "melodic," may thus no
longer be the best term to use in our discourse about poetry. Indeed, from
Jackson Mac Low's *The Pronouns,* available both as printed text and as CD
performance, to Ian Hamilton Finlay's poem-sculptures at Little Sparta
(Scotland), to Haroldo de Campos's *Galáxias,* written in a highly stylized
"musical" prose, the term *poetry* has come to be understood less as the lyric
genre than as a distinctive way of organizing language — which is to say, the
language art. Poetic language is language made strange, made somehow extraordinary by the use of verbal and sound repetition, visual configuration,
and syntactic deformation. Or again, it is language perhaps quite ordinary
but placed in a new and unexpected context, as in Kenneth Goldsmith's
found text *The Weather* or Yoko Tawada's "second-language" poem-essays in
Sprachpolizei und Spielpolyglotte. "Do not forget," cautioned Wittgenstein,
"that a poem, although it is composed in the language of information, is not
used in the language-game of giving information."[15] Once this is understood,
the semantics of a given poem can no longer be separated from its sound.

The Sound of Poetry / The Poetry of Sound, many of whose contributors are themselves poets, begins with a section on sound translation, whose first essay, Susan Stewart's "Rhyme and Freedom," provides the groundwork for the others in its typology and aesthetic of rhyme in poetry across centuries and cultures. In the "free verse" climate of the twentieth century, Stewart notes, rhyme may no longer be fashionable, but it is not about to disappear:

> Given the power of rhyme schemes of all kinds to lend particular semantic and visual weight to the place of unrhymed words, we might see the development of free verse as an unrhymed pause in the greater scheme of rhyme's poetic history. Far from a constraint, rhyme endows us with certain freedoms — among them: the vernacular, including the locality of the poem itself, released from the standard; the monolingual in dialogue with the multilingual; sound opened up by vision, and sound released from meaning entirely; expectation released into surprise; and pattern drawn from the oblivion of time. Rhyme is perfect, imperfect, total, and partial at once. To follow Dante, why, in making poems or any other art form, not allow "as much liberty as may be desired"?

Rhyme, as translators know only too well, is impossible to translate: the many versions of Baudelaire, for example, take into account the need to invent alternate sound patterns that might compensate for the emphatic echo of rhyme in closural position. Is the *poetic,* then, the dimension of a given poem that is untranslatable? Or is the poet-translator Leevi Lehto, who has translated countless poets into the language of his "minor literature" — Finnish — right in positing that today translation is unavoidable, that English as a second or nth language, babelized and mongrelized, now dominates the field? Yunte Huang's analysis of Pound's free and often homophonic translations of Chinese into English would seem to support Leevi's point. But Richard Sieburth and Rosmarie Waldrop, themselves illustrious translators of German and French poetry, are more optimistic: there is, both posit, a way to render language A in terms of B — sometimes "translating" a procedure used rather than the words themselves — but it is a demanding project, requiring much artistry as well as trial and error. Then, too, some poets are more translatable than others. Both Sieburth and Waldrop describe their own practice: Sieburth, his translation of Maurice Scève's Renaissance sonnet — or rather *dizain* — sequence *Délie,* and Waldrop, her recent translations of her German contemporary Ulf Stolterfoht's *Fachsprachen.* And in this scheme of things, fiction is not immune from the challenge. Gordana Crnković discusses the "poetic" dimension of postmodernist narrative prose, a dimension too often ignored by translators. Crnković 's example is the Serbo-Croatian novel *Derviš i smrt* (Dervish and Death, 1966) by Meša Selimović . In its first American translation (1996), Crnković posits, the role of sound and syntax in the generation of meaning simply disappears. What, then, is the status of the "translation"?

In our global culture, such issues can no longer be peripheral. In a media culture, they are further complicated by new conjunctions of verbal and visual, verbal and sonic, the poet's "voice" and its representations in different media. And further, as my coeditor Craig Dworkin suggests below, sound is itself a slippery word, one that, vis-à-vis its traditional other — sense — has always carried antonymic meanings.

Marjorie Perloff

The Poetry of Sound

The relation of sound to poetry has always been triangulated, implicitly or explicitly, by an equally nebulous third term: sense. The relation is ambiguous and shifting, because "sound" — especially in the context of poetry — belongs to that species of homographs which produce their own antonyms.[16] On the one hand, sound — defined by *The Oxford English Dictionary* (*OED*) as "the audible articulation corresponding to a letter or word" — has been understood as distinct from linguistic meaning: "the sound must seem an echo to the sense," as Pope famously put it.[17] Furthermore, that distinction is often pushed to a full-fledged antonymy, so that sound is understood as being, by definition, diametrically opposed to meaning: a "mere audible effect without significance or real importance" as the *OED* puts it. John Locke underscores that opposition in a passage from his *Essay concerning Human Understanding:* "for let us consider this proposition as to its meaning (for it is the sense, and not the sound, that is and must be the principle or common notion)" (§18). Or, more famously, in Shakespeare's phrasing: "a tale told by an idiot, full of sound and fury, signifying nothing" (*Macbeth* V, v). At the same time, however, sound can also denote precisely the signifying referent of language: "import, sense, significance" (*OED*). Indeed, rather than posing an alternative to meaning, sound in poetry has been heard as conveying meaning in its own right. "In human speech," Leonard Bloomfield asserts, "different sounds have different meanings."[18] Jan Mukařovský concurs: "'Sound' components are not only a mere sensorily perceptible vehicle of meaning but also have a semantic nature themselves."[19]

At once the antithesis of meaning and the very essence of meaning, sound in poetry articulates the same problems that have attended early twentieth-century definitions of the category of "poetry" itself, reflecting the identical logic at a fractal remove. From the Prague School to Ludwig Wittgenstein to Tel Quel, modern philosophers of language have described poetry — which is to say, literary language broadly conceived or simply "verbal art," in Roman Jakobson's eventual phrasing — as a kind of text that deviates from conventionally utile language by self-reflexively foregrounding elements other than the referentially communicative. Poetry, in these accounts, calls attention to structures such as sound while damping the banausic, denotative impetus of language.[20]

The ratios thus form a curious recursion: sound is to sense as poetic language is to conventional language, but the relation of sound and sense, understood in this way, is nested within the category of the poetic. Taken as the opposite of sense, sound, in the formalist economy, encapsulates the logic of the poetic. One among the material, palpable, quantifiable facets of language, sound contrasts with the ideas conveyed by the referential sign. Behind the Slavic formalists, we might of course also think of Ferdinand de Saussure's attempt to define signs not as the relation of names and things but rather as the coupling of the "concept" indicated by the signified and the *image acoustique* (sound shape) of the signifier. And further behind Saussure, as the quotes from Pope and Shakespeare attest, lies the intuitive sense that one can perceive aspects of language without comprehending its message. More complicated still, however, the *mise-en-abîme* of sound and poetry can also reflect (back on) the communicative side of the equation. The relationship between material sound and referential meaning is often understood to be itself referential. The two key words in Pope's declaration, for instance, both bind sound to mimetic appearance: "sound must *seem* an *echo* to the sense." Sound, in this understanding, thus also encapsulates the operation of meaning. The same is true when sound is taken to be expressive in its own right and thought to "have a semantic nature" in itself.

Simultaneously bridging and sequestering, sound has accordingly been understood as both the defining opposite of meaning and the very essence of meaning. This duplicity is due in part to the inadequacy of the vague term "meaning," but it also comes into play because of the belief — implicit in Pope's formulation — that the value of a poem lies in the relation between sound and sense. A mediocre term paper called "The Poetry of Sound," available for purchase on the internet, states the basic position (if rather ineptly):

> Poems usually begin with words or phrase which appeal more because of their sound than their meaning, and the movement and phrasing of a poem. Every poem has a texture of sound, which is at least as important as the meaning behind the poem.[21]

All of the contributors to the present volume would agree with the general statement; indeed, one of the grounding premises for the forum and workshops in which these essays originated was that the sound of poetry was — in all senses of the word — significant. The question, of course, is exactly *how* sound comes to be important in poetry. This is the place neither for a history of the poetics of sound nor for a careful parsing of the theoretical variations on the topic, but I do want to note the extent to which literary theorists have been both certain about the central importance of sound to poetry and unable to exactly specify the nature of that importance. Roman Jakobson is typical:

> No doubt verse is primarily a recurrent "figure of sound." Primarily, always, but never uniquely. Any attempts to confine such poetic conventions as meters, alliteration, or rhyme to the sound level are speculative reasonings without any empirical justification.[22]

He goes on to quote Alexander von Humboldt: "there is an apparent connection between sound and meaning which, however, only seldom lends itself to an exact elucidation, is often only glimpsed, and most usually remains obscure." The essays in the second half of this book turn their attention to elucidating those connections.

Susan Howe's personal narrative of writing *Articulation of Sound Forms in Time,* appropriately, begins with precisely the glimpsed and obscure, two ocular terms that may be ironic in Humboldt's sentence, with its vocabulary of appearance and elucidation, but that are all to the point for Howe's synæsthetic argument that voice and print are inseparable; "font-voices summon a reader into visible earshot," she writes, imagining the "blank space" of the page as an essential "quiet" that "articulates poetry." Howe focuses on sound as mere audible effect without coherent meaning or ordered structure: a "nonsense soliloquy" of "tumbled syllables" and "allophone tangle[s]" in a "vocalized wilderness" of "phonemic cacophony." Such inchoate sounds are a recurrent theme for Howe throughout her writing, but they also provide a formal model for the skewed, overprinted, partially legible or canceled lines that make the look of her poetry so distinctive.

Howe's conflation of voice and print provides an ideal test case for Johanna Drucker's argument that the visual and the aural do not always overlap and indeed cannot ever be perfectly congruent, because the different codes used to sort linguistic material — some audible and some visual — mobilize fundamentally different kinds of cognition. While Drucker focuses on the visual, on what is "not sound," her arguments about the graphic features of texts illuminate the sound features of texts as well, since the two codes, though distinct, operate in the same fundamental way. Lacking "absolute values," Drucker argues, "graphic codes and other material features are not static, inherent, or self-evident"; rather, they are "provocations" to readers. Drucker, on this important point, is in accord with Benjamin Harshav's arguments about the expressivity of sound patterns. For Harshav, the relation between poetic sound and sense is a back-and-forth process of recursive feedback. No sound pattern, in his view, is inherently meaningful; sibilants, for instance (to take his central example), have been understood as representing both silence and noise. However, once a reader identifies the presence of a sound pattern, certain referential statements from the poem — what one might think of as the conventional meaning of its "message" — are transferred onto that pattern, which in turn loops back to reinforce and foreground particular themes in the message.[23] Brian Reed, in his wide-ranging essay on the medium of poetry, makes a similar point, arguing like Drucker that the given structures of texts (whether visual, bibliographic, aural, et cetera) provide opportunities for authors and audiences to exploit, détourne, or rebel against them. "The poem," Reed writes, "has something to do with sound, of course — one can scan it metrically, for instance, or talk about its intonation and tone — but it remains less vocalized than vocalizable." Focusing on the limits of the vocalizable, Ming-Qian Ma's theoretical analysis of what the Russian futurists termed *zvukopis,* or "visual noise," brings Howe, Drucker, and Reed into direct dialogue. Contra Drucker, Ma proposes that the audible and the visual are indeed translatable, asking — like Reed — what it would mean to read the kinds of paratextual writing presented along with a poem but not considered to be part of a poem: "geometric figures, scientific schemata, technical charts, mathematical notations" (Ma); "page numbers, line numbers, annotations, illustrations, choice of font" (Reed). Like Howe,

Ma proposes that the visually obscure cannot only be read but also actively invite and demand a voice: the "random drawings, obscure forms, fuzzy shapes, chaotic aggregates, and the like, which, confusing in representational intention and seemingly informationless in content, appear to be inarticulate or reticent."

Other contributors take a less semiotic approach, arguing that sense can be sounded only in a historicized space, with particular bodies at specific cultural moments. Indeed, as several of the authors show, this is true of even the most abstract or seemingly meaningless sounds. Steve McCaffery's essay investigates Hugo Ball's *Lautgedichte,* poems that are composed, like Christian Bök's *Cyborg Opera,* by "arranging words, not according to their semantic meanings, but according to their phonetic valences" (Bök). McCaffery argues that even if purely phonetic arrangements of sound do not cohere into standard words or avail themselves of conventional grammars, they nonetheless cannot be understood — even as abstract asemantic arrangements of sound — until heard against the background of their cultural and biographical contexts. Similarly, in his explication of the poetics of radio in Jean Cocteau's *Orphée,* Rubén Gallo listens carefully to the seemingly meaningless sounds of the film's mysterious radio transmissions, in which nonsensical snippets of surrealist poetry initially appear to be no more comprehensible than the beeps, whines, whistles, and "howling of secondary waves" with which they are presented. As Gallo shows, these sounds do indeed make sense when heard in the historical context — political as well as technological — of early radio. Similarly, Yoko Tawada's account of dubbing locates the meaning of sounds in the culturally coded bodies that produce them; the same sounds are understood differently when heard in different contexts, where the speakers can be seen and their bodies scrutinized. Like Gallo, Tawada focuses on electronic recording media, the film and tape that capture individual performances. Those performances are the subject of Charles Bernstein's essay on the institutional archiving of poetry readings, which similarly insists on the unique inscriptions made by individuals whose cultural positions are audible in their accents, aspects of voice that mark class, geography, gender, and race. Kenneth Goldsmith — who relies on audio tape and electronic recording to produce many of his own poems — attends, like Tawada, to patterns of silence and vocal discrepancies. Through his witty collage of quotations, Goldsmith listens in on the ability of recording media to both open and record unsounded gaps between noise and the body. For Goldsmith, meaning arises from the patterns of sound that are not consciously heard: the pauses and spaces that make speech audible; the phatic back-channel fillers and voiced pauses that punctuate messages (all the *ums* and *ahs* and *uh-huhs*); and those audible units, from rhyme to syllable to breath phrase, that can organize otherwise undifferentiated flows of speech sound. For all of these writers, sound is never either inherently noise or message; instead, sound and sense are located at the intersection of social bodies in particular spaces.

Such contextual approaches to literary sound deviate dramatically from the traditional "empiricist models" that Marjorie Perloff has cited above. Alan Galt's *Sound and Sense in the Poetry of Theodor Storm,* for an example of one such model, attempts to scientifically demonstrate that the musical qualities of poetry "may be defined in terms of phonological 'skew,' i.e., deviation from the normal proportional distribution of sounds in poetic language."[24] Galt (using a slide rule, no less) tabulated all of the phonemes in Storm's collected poetry, some 78,965 consonants and 43,641 vowels, according to his count.[25] The outcome is almost 'pataphysical, combining a sober scientific tone with absurd results and evoking nothing so much as the phonemic dictionaries of Velimir Khlebnikov.[26] Galt determines that the phoneme /l/, for instance, evinces

> Positive skews in love poems and in narratives; strong positive skews in "tender" and "musical" poems. Negative skews in poems of family and home, nostalgia, and humor, with a negative skew for "non-musical" poems which is just below the level of significance. This phoneme certainly distinguishes, in Storm's verse, between "musicality" and its opposite, and its presence can evidently also contribute to a feeling of "tenderness."[27]

The phoneme /u/, similarly, reveals "positive skews in nature poems, political poems, and in 'musical' poems. Negative skews in poems of age and death, and in humorous and occasional poems. Evidently this is a determiner of 'musicality.'"[28] And so on. Meaning, in Galt's account, is inseparable from sound, even as the significance of sound is imperceptible, recognizable only at the level of massive statistical analysis. Form, here, is indeed an extension of content: "a group of poems which share the same theme or content tends to show a phonological 'skew' which is broadly characteristic of that group."[29]

While Galt's work may have greater affinities with avant-garde poetry than with conventional literary criticism, I call attention to it because his sort of focus on "musicality" is another point at which the essays included in this volume differ from traditional scholarship. James McNeill Whistler famously opined that "music is the poetry of sound," and poetry, in turn, has often been characterized as musical: "lower limit speech," as Louis Zukofsky ran his calculus, "upper limit music."[30] Sarah Stickney Ellis wrote, in the early nineteenth century:

> Sound is perhaps of all subjects the most intimately connected with poetic feeling, not only because it comprehends within its widely extended sphere, the influence of music, so powerful over the passions and affections of our nature; but because there is in poetry itself, a cadence — a perceptible harmony, which delights the ear while the eye remains unaffected.[31]

Ellis's argument echoes in John Hollander's entry "Music and Poetry" in the *Princeton Encyclopedia of Poetry and Poetics,* which states that both poetry and music "move to affect a listener in some subrational fashion, just as both are in some way involved in the communication of feeling rather than of knowledge."[32] That involvement of music in poetry is of particular significance, moreover, because it bears on our understanding of the lyric. According to J. W. Johnson's entry in the *Princeton Encyclopedia,* as Perloff notes above, lyric poetry "may be said to retain most pronouncedly the elements of poetry which evidence its origins in musical expression . . . the musical element is intrinsic to the work intellectually as well as aesthetically."[33] Indeed, "the irreducible denominator of all lyric poetry," according to Johnson, must be "those elements which it shares with the musical forms that produced it. Although lyric poetry is not music, it is representational of music in its sound patterns."[34]

The problem, of course, is what might be meant by "music," a term no more stable or well defined than "lyric." Music, in this context, is often taken to mean merely euphonious language, a mid-nineteenth-century sense of harmony and melodic line that "delights the ear." This definition, in fact, makes music a synonym for sound itself, one of the denotations of which is "used with implications of richness, euphony, or harmony" (*OED*). But "music" of course encompasses a range of works far more expansive than the classical and romantic imagination of the pleasant, mellifluous, or affecting. We might still define the lyric in terms of music, but what if the music represented by the lyric were Erik Satie's *Vexations,* a few bars of fragmentary melody meant to be repeated 840 times in succession? Or György Ligeti's *Poème symphonique,* scored for one hundred carefully wound metronomes? Or John Cage's *Music for Piano,* composed by enlarging the imperfections found when a sheet of staff paper is scrutinized under a magnifying glass?

Or the game pieces of John Zorn, or the stochastic compositions of Iannis Xenakis, or David Soldier's orchestra of Thai elephants, or any number of works that Ellis would likely not have recognized as music at all?

"Music," in this expanded field, may no longer be especially useful for defining poetry, but as several of the contributors to this volume show, it may be a productive tool for understanding poetry and for thinking in new ways about what poetry might aspire to do. Nancy Perloff's insightful parallel history of sound poetry and avant-garde composition makes a clear case for the extent to which an expanded definition of music can expand the definition of poetry. In the musical field exemplified by John Cage's double deconstruction of both "silence" and "noise" as well as "noise" and "music," sound remains central to music, even as it "discards lyricism." Christian Bök's essay on his own bravura athletic sound poetry similarly argues for the degree to which poetic practice can be expanded by enlarging the scope of what we consider "musical": techno, electronica, beat-boxing, the soundtracks to video games, the noise of power tools. "In order to explain avant-garde sound poems through the trope of music," Bök explains, "poets of today may have to adopt a genre better suited to express our millennial anxieties in an era now driven by the hectic tempos of our technology." My own contribution to the volume takes tempo and technology as a starting point, listening to the electronic music of Alvin Lucier in order to better understand how the stutter can function as a formal structuring device for literature. Recovering the importance of sound and music for the strikingly visual poetry of the Brazilian concrete poets, Antonio Sergio Bessa documents an earlier instance of Bök's call to adopt a sufficiently modern music adequate to the aspirations of a self-consciously modern poetry. Noting the importance of harmonic (rather than melodic) structures to Décio Pignatari, as well as Augusto de Campos's debt to Anton Webern's notion of atonally emotive *Klangfarbenmelodie* (not to mention samba and bossa nova), Bessa demonstrates that "in several texts written in the early 1950s by the Noigandres poets, collectively and individually, one finds repeated references to sound, particularly the emerging new music of composers like Pierre Boulez, Guido Alberto Fano, and Karlheinz Stockhausen." Likewise, Hélène Aji rereads the visual texts of Jackson Mac Low in light of his involvement with Cage and twentieth-century music, with particular attention to the innovations in scoring and aleatory compositions noted in Nancy Perloff's historical sketch.

Rethinking the nature of sound, as Nancy Perloff explains, led to new understandings of music in the twentieth century, and rethinking the nature of music, as these essays evince, can lead to new understandings of poetry. Or, to paraphrase David Antin's aphorism on the connection between modernism and postmodernism: from the music you choose, you get the lyric you deserve.

Craig Dworkin

PRELUDE: POETRY AND ORALITY

JACQUES ROUBAUD

Translated by Jean-Jacques Poucel

I

@ 1. In order to speak of oral poetry I must necessarily speak of written poetry.

@ 2. Let me then begin at the beginning: the notion of poetry on which I'll stake my claims here does not emerge until after the fall of the *trobar*.

@ 3. The trobar, or the art of the troubadours, finds expression in the *canso*, a form that unites word and sound.

@ 4. The trobar indissolubly interlaces a particular language and its music. The Provençal term for this craft is *entrebescar*.

@ 5. The breaking of the bond between word and sound, which occurred during the fourteenth century, brought about a new *double form* called *poetry*. This form would combine the words of a language in writing and in speech such that they would be indissociable.

@ 6. That other form which brings word and sound together has by no means disappeared; we call it *song*.

@ 7. A song is not a poem and a poem is not a song.

@ 8. The words of a song deprived of their sounds may constitute a poem; or not. The words of a poem put to music may constitute a song; or not.

@ 9. It's an insult to poetry to call it song. It's an insult to song to call it poetry.

II

@ 10. From the fourteenth to the end of the nineteenth century the form *poetry* maintained its existence and autonomy in relation to other types of language arts: philosophy, rhetoric, literature, and so on.

@ 11. Poetry exists in language and in poems. A poem is the union of four forms.

@ 12. *A quartet of forms and a score.*

@ 13. I think a poem has two internal and two external aspects.

@ 14. *Two external aspects:* the written form, the oral form. Both are fixed (the oral as well as the written) and constitute the *score.* Of course, there are many possible executions of the oral form, performances; just as there are many possible executions of the written form, written performances. The score is the coupling of these two external forms of a poem. For me, they both always exist (though one perhaps only virtually). Plus, their relationship is always antagonistic, which is good (this conflict helps constitute the rhythmic component of poetry).

@ 15. *Two internal aspects:* the wRitten form (*wRitten:* a term coined out of necessity for this purpose; orally the homonym of written) and the aural form (aural: holds the same homonymic relation with oral as wRitten does with written). Internal to what? To the person receiving the poem. The reader is included in defining poetry as a quartet of forms.

@ 16. The external aspects of a poem are interpersonal. They are transmissible to practically anyone who speaks and reads the language in which a given poem is composed. The internal aspects are personal. They are in the mind of the reader-listener; essentially nontransmissible from one person to another; they are always in movement within memory: movement of images, of thoughts. Ultimately, the external written form is idle, but not the internal mental page that constitutes the wRitten form.

@ 17. There's no poem without reading. And in the interior reading, as in the external aspects, one form confronts the other; they collide.

@ 18. A poem cannot be reduced to its external aspect alone. If it has not entered a single mind, a poem does not yet exist.

@ 19. In addition, the very constitution of a poem as an object of language also depends on the fact that there remains an irreducible variability of interior readings among a wide variety of people. It's perhaps banal to remark that there are always differences in the way any linguistic enunciation is received and interpreted from one person to another. But in modes of speech other than poetry, meaning must be considered public, ideally transmissible; that which is not transmissible is not part of the meaning. In the case of poetry, it's the exact opposite — which is not to say that poems do not contain a transmissible meaning; if there is one, it's there as a surplus.

III

@ 20. In France, during the period that culminates at the end of the nineteenth century, all four aspects are in harmony: *meter* and *rhyme* guarantee a relatively easy passage from the page to the ear, from virtual seeing to virtual hearing.

@ 21. But these dynamics change with the assault against traditional form, the rhymed alexandrine in France, the *ipen* (iambic pentameter) in English-speaking countries. From then onward Poetry distinguishes itself via *breaking the line,* and quite differently from the way that technique is used in prose. It's a fairly weak constraint and requires in oral performance some attempt to mark the end of lines.

@ 22. Until the 1960s in France, the (masked) persistence of certain funda-mental traits of traditional verse (essentially, the coincidence of line breaks and syntactical units) allows the previous dynamics between oral and written poetry to remain unchallenged. It's the golden age of SFV (standard free verse). Denis Roche, however, dismantles that soft "consensus" and forces "free verse" to enter a period of turbulence.

@ 23. Meanwhile (in the 1950s and '60s), American poetry recovers its lost orality (from Allen Ginsberg to Robert Creeley) and invents OFV (oral free verse), which successfully realizes the formal ideal of free verse (accomplishing what the Surrealists had failed to do in their "breaking the line"): their line break has a *fundamentally oral* nature. What's written is entirely subordinated. This OFV is ubiquitously present thirty or forty years later. And it's steeped in an almost universal blindness on the part of

American poets with respect to the particularities of written form in poems (cause for a rude awakening for quite a few French poets when confronted with translations of their poems that totally disregard all that is implicitly understood as obsessive flourish: typesetting, line spacing, the role of white space, and so on).

@ 24. In poetry, as in many things, the influence of the United States takes no time to make its impression. And the predictable result has been the decline of OFV (much like the degradation of the English language into a commercial mumbo jumbo).

IV

@ 25. Many years ago, when examining modern poetry from a formal viewpoint, at least in most so-called Western languages, I gleaned that a single form of poetry dominated. It's versified in a uniform manner and can be used universally. It's what I have termed international free verse, or IFV.

@ 26. Description of IFV: Parallel to other forms of global homogenization (economic, financial, musical, ideological, fashion sense, gastronomic, and so on) during the last quarter century, and under the obvious influence of poetry written in American English (an involuntary but real side effect of the domination that highly militarized state exerts over all others), verse has suffered its own homogenization. Free verse, as written in French by the Surrealists and their followers, was still far too dependent on the history of French verse, defiantly standing against the memory of alexandrine verse. IFV, however, is unfettered by such trappings.

@ 27. To be brief, like SFV, the IFV is written and characterized by page settings that differ from those used in prose, but with line breaks that "prudently" adhere to syntactic structures.

@ 28. The excessive line-on-line enjambments common among American poets until the 1960s are severely condemned by IFV.

@ 29. I'm not even speaking about disarticulations à la Denis Roche (breaking the line in the middle of a word, for example).

@ 30. IFV is generally found in short poems or sequences of poems.

@ 31. IFV is verse with a universal vocation: it's easy to translate and can be practiced at least in all Western languages, and probably in all the languages of the world.

@ 32. As opposed to the French Surrealists' free verse, it owes little or nothing to the measures and rhythms of the traditional prosody of the languages it so enthusiastically colonizes. Hence: No more provincial slavery!

@ 33 In order to examine the oral presentation of IFV (its written presentation can be seen in magazines and books) at the international poetry festivals (or festivals featuring poetry) that I have attended over the past few years, I decided to listen to the largest possible number of readings and, when I had a copy of the written text or a translation into one of the languages I can more or less understand, I would follow what was happening on the page (though some phenomena require no advanced understanding of the words). Here is what I've concluded:

@ 34. Nearly every single reader — a multinational poet in this context — solves the problem of how to read his or her poems out loud in an extremely simple way. They read them exactly *as if they were reading prose.* It's obvious that there are several ways of orally (and aurally) reconstituting what the written score of a poem provides. One of them could be the manner I've just described (though I don't see what it has to recommend it, unless you're following the written text of the poem; and little even then). (It would be far more interesting to do this with metrical verse, or rhymed metrical verse, in front of an audience aware of the laws of prosody.)

@ 35. But in reality, there isn't the slightest intentionality in this herd-like practice of reading. It's quite simply the way everyone does it. Things should be done as usual, nothing should be strikingly different from this new universal law. This also has consequences for the writing of such poems.

@ 36. There's one *slight exception* — a certain number of poets (I'm tempted to say, especially American ones, but my investigations have not advanced far enough to be categorical) make a clear distinction from prose: they emphasize the ends of their lines by raising their voices slightly (like actors at the Comédie Française in the 1950s). In this way, we're assured that it's poetry we're hearing.

@ 37. The absolute rule about what can be said in a poem written in IFV is *accessibility*. Not only must the poem in IFV contain no difficulties of comprehension or of linguistic construction, it must also avoid anything particularly striking, unless it's lexical (and in a tone acceptable in a travel agency), and it must certainly not adopt the incomprehensible manner in which traditional poetry used to chop up and divide what it had to say. Hence the total rejection of anything formal, the domination of narrative verse, of ethical exclamations (limited to subjects recognized by CNN), and so on . . . it's easy to see what the consequences of such limitations are.

@ 38. In such a context, why maintain the distinction between poetry and prose as limited by the distinction between verse and nonverse? But the fact remains (still in this context) that it's unseemly to drop the visual elements that characterize IFV. Why is this?

@ 39. You may object that if you are invited to an international poetry festival, then you must in some way distinguish yourself as a poet, and that the simplest exterior sign that is most easily recognizable to all organizers of international festivals is, of course, the use of IFV; you'd be right. But I think there's more to it than that: the very existence of this modest way for poetry to survive (extremely modest: except when there's some exceptional political context, audiences for any given poet are meager) is linked to what I have already termed (in a different context) *a ghost-effect*. The overall devaluation of poetry provokes a pitiful attention to its few places of survival. It becomes something decorative, a way for the "cultured" (so long as the proceedings do not cost them more than a tiny fraction of what they'd pay to see an opera or exhibition) to prove the height of their culture. But if, and only if of course, the poets are serious and well behaved. So their poetry must be serious and well behaved too.

@ 40. Within these formal boundaries you can say anything that is feminist, multiculturalist, antiracist, anti anti-personnel-mine-ist, you can Chernobylize at length, or burble on about peace and your grandmother, so long as no one suspects you of playing "formal games" or of being "difficult," which would be "elitist," "nondemocratic" and probably in breach of the rights of man and an insult to NGOs.

@ 41. In the realm of IFV, form becomes increasingly secondary. This tendency is particularly manifest in public readings. I have listened to tons of them over the past ten years: the dominant tendency is to read "as if it were prose." This tendency is present and on the rise among American poets too. Of course, more often than not these so-called poems are quite simply short prose texts. And since it's rather tricky to relate a full narrative in a short text, poetry risks becoming nothing more than "short prose."

@ 42. To conclude this point, IFV is the essential form of SIP (standardized international poetry), whose servants are POWs (poets of the world).

V

@ 43. The drift of IFV toward "short prose" is but one modality of poetry's extinction.

@ 44. Others abound. Denis Roche, who toiled at dismantling free verse, belonged to a self-proclaimed avant-garde, the Tel Quel group. One of its goals was to eradicate poetry and replace it with what would be called *le texte*.

@ 45. That onslaught had no lasting effects (with the possible exception of a yet more modern version: *post-poetry*). Nonetheless, there's a tendency to reinforce the growing marginalization of poetry within the contemporary context, to accelerate its loss of "market share" in the commerce of so-called cultural products (poetry is vanishing from bookstores, publishing catalogues, and the purportedly literary segments of newspapers or television programs), by theorizing its erasure, by openly rejecting its traditional techniques, now dismissed as passé, and finally by replacing poetry with something else, as if to extend "TelQuelism" into the twenty-first century. It's an energetically pursued tendency, one that is easily granted space in newspapers (at least in theory).

@ 46. Where one once read the slogan "Poetry is Dead," one now reads "Poetry is Elsewhere." That is, elsewhere than in poems as I have described them and as they continue to be written.

@ 47. Of course, the meaning of "Elsewhere" is variable. For Dominique de Villepin, the former prime minister of France, it means EUROPE. For others, it means the SUNSET. Some argue, and more affirmatively, that it means SONG, ROCK AND ROLL, and so on.

@ 48. The so-called arts sections of newspapers increasingly promote elaborate and carefully thought-out strategies opposing the survival of poetry-form as I have described it. Take, for example, RAP . . .

@ 49. Or SLAM; of late, the French practitioners of these arts have extolled their desire to be crowned the "real poets" of the twenty-first century.

@ 50. And finally there's PERFORMANCE POETRY. Developed in France (and elsewhere) from the 1950s onward, this brand now enjoys some currency in the press after more than fifty years of being ignored. This sudden show of favor is part of the same strategy, *the erasure of poetry*.

@ 51. Just about anything may be encountered in the guise of "performance poetry": music, declamation, theatrical bits, acrobatics, "primal screams," and so on. And all of it presented with an utter scorn for the written word.

@ 52. Which is entirely understandable: if one were to commit to paper what normally constitutes this type of "poetry" — assuming it contains words from any given language — we would be in the presence of an absolutely mediocre text. Reading it would be deadly boring.

@ 53. I have nothing against these activities. In the best cases, they make for a high-quality *spectacle*. But why call these events "poetry" as opposed to something else? Why not simply call them a PERFORMANCE?

@ 54. I think the reason is clear: to benefit from the *aura* still associated with the word POETRY, to ride the coattails of what I call the GHOST-EFFECT of poetry.

VI

@ 55. I am not a prophet. It's possible that what I call poetry will disappear (except among the belated few), vanish into prose, or be replaced by "performance." There is, however, at least one group of writings, initiated nearly half a century ago, in which the link between the oral and the written is thriving and aligned with the counted and rhymed tradition. I am referring to *writing under constraint* as it's practiced by OULIPO. It has as much to offer prose and "performance" as it does poetry. In a paradoxical reversal of the "crise de vers" at the turn of the nineteenth century, Oulipian practice tends to submit prose to poetry.

PART I / TRANSLATING SOUND

RHYME AND FREEDOM / SUSAN STEWART

orange, chimney, breadth, circle, desert,
monarch, month, virtue, wisdom

> English words that "cannot be rhymed at all" listed in the
> *Princeton Encyclopedia of Poetry and Poetics*

As for the organisation of rhymes, in so far as they are used in the frons or the
cauda, it seems that as much liberty as may be desired must be allowed..

DANTE, *De vulgari eloquentia*

Two lines of poetry came to me one day in the form of a paradox: *"There
is a kind of leaving when you arrive / even though it's the place you've come
from."* And, as I continued to write, *arrive* became *alive,* and *from* grew into
none, and I found myself composing in terza rima, as each new stanza followed with increasing insistence and increasing ease. What drove this insistence and ease? It was, it seems, a sense of living voice — to arrive "alive" in a
poem that, in fact, turned out to be an elegy. The dangling preposition in the
second line already seemed to have framed the poem as spoken, rather than
written. Perhaps every elegy can't help being concerned with aliveness and its
own living speech in the face of a death, but to begin by writing and then to
find yourself in speech can be the difference between death and life for any
poem, and rhyme, along with other intelligible repetitions of sounds, is often
the symptom or indication that the poem is quickening. If, however, a poem
remains predominately writing, never coming alive to voice and to sounds as
voiced, it will remain only a sketch for a work.

In the case of this poem that emerged to be concerned with the shedding succession of generations, inherited memories, and the differences between closed and open kinds of knowledge, it wasn't difficult to see how terza rima seemed to "fit" the theme. Or was it the other way around? Was — is — terza rima there waiting, an opening to a certain means of shaping inchoate feelings and experiences into form? Later, as I looked at that first line, I realized that "a kind of leaving when you arrive" is exactly what terza rima does. As the second rhyme of a stanza "arrives," the middle-line end word "leaves" to form its own new pair in the ensuing stanza.

When any artist sets to work, various forces of contingency and necessity are at play, some conscious, others unconscious, some available to analysis and others not, or perhaps not yet. At the start, all the elements are assembled. As I began what turned out to be my elegy, I had the initial phrase. Until such a mark or note is struck, and then the next and the next, the form is replete with any number of choices, and each choice then exercised is dense with its relation to what otherwise could have been. Each determination thereby leaves behind a trace of alternatives; like the trail of filings left by a burin, and the sounds of similar words that went unchosen linger for a while. Before all these successive determinations reach the finality of form, the maker has an experience of expanded insight and increased powers of judgment that can be described as resonant.

Artistic freedom reaches its apogee when intention approaches the rich cognitive moment on the brink of realized structure. Because structures of this kind are historical, and those who make and apprehend them historical beings, it is inadequate to describe this as a moment of pure willfulness. Yet certainly whatever freedom the will might possess is available at this point of possibility without resolution. Rhyming is at once both intended and compulsive, an art practice that makes full use, by means of sound, of these possibilities for resonance and saturation. As Hegel noted, "what belongs peculiarly to lyric is the ramified figuration of rhyme which, with the return of the same sounds of letters, syllables, and words, or the alternation of different ones, is developed and completed in variously articulated and interlaced rhyme-strophes."[1] In other words, it is not only that stanzas demand rhymes, but also that rhymes create stanza structures; lyric process is propelled by the sounded repetition of sameness and difference, of rhymes thrown forward as both moving line and anchor.

How is it, then, that as early as Aristotle's denigration of mere verse in the *Poetics,* and especially under modernist theories of free verse, rhyming has been viewed by many as both a purely formal device and a kind of restraint?[2] When the first modernists speak of free verse, their preoccupation is usually meter, but they often include rhyme as one of those features of verse from which poets have been "freed." In one of the earliest statements on free verse, in the pages of *The Egoist* in 1914, Richard Aldington argued against "the old rhymed, accented verse." There he wrote: "The old accented verse forced the poet to abandon some of his individuality, most of his accuracy and all his style in order to wedge his emotions into some preconceived and childish formality; free verse permits the poet all his individuality because he creates his cadence instead of copying other people's, all his accuracy because with his cadence flowing naturally he tends to write naturally and therefore with precision, all his style because style consists in concentration, and exactness which could only be obtained rarely in the old forms."[3] "Old" here may convey mostly an all-round fatigue with Victorian poetry, "childish formality" may refer particularly to Algernon Swinburne's obsessive rhythms. Even so, it's worth considering some of the ideas expressed in this long sentence as more than a reaction to immediate precursors, for Aldington's approach hasn't disappeared as a way of framing rhyme's relation to poetic freedom.

Aldington indicates that the "individuality" of the poet has some basis in a "natural flow" that nevertheless also has a "precision." In this regard, the end of poetry is, for him, to free the poet from the cadences of the poetry of the past. Aldington recognizes that "there is a tyranny of novelty as there is a tyranny of antiquity,"[4] but he believes that some essential individuality characterizes free verse. Is it true that fixing individuality would free the poet? Wouldn't this result instead in a reification of voice or style? And would relying on nature herself as a source of rhythms necessarily open up the possibilities of the poet's invention? In fact, Aldington's test for effective free verse lines is the degree to which they conform to the grammar, not of nature, but of ordinary speech: he constantly singles out inverted syntax as "inaccurate" and unnatural. Yet there is nothing natural about ordinary English syntax. And rhythm is not meter.

Our English word *rhyme* does come from Latin and Greek *rithmus* or *rhythmos,* and surely the natural flow Aldington mentions is based in organic life in such a way that our speech rhythms are only a small instance of rhythm as a force in nature, indeed a force in the cosmos. Solar pulses, the ebb and flow of tides, those circadian rhythms that affect our sleeping and waking as heliotropic beings are only some of the rhythms to which we are subjected. Rhythm indeed may be a necessary, if not sufficient, condition of human life, for the embryonic heart begins to beat eighteen to twenty-one days after conception; at that point there is no blood to pump, no function for the heart to serve, but if the beat stops, the embryo dies.[5] What does this rhythm have to do with syntax? A periodic sentence of the kind Aldington himself has written has a certain prose rhythm, and that rhythm inevitably must grow out of the human experience of rhythms of all kinds, but there is nothing about syntax that makes it the basis of natural rhythm. To hope to free rhythm from meter, as such early proponents of free verse as Aldington and Pound did, is to return to a real, rather than ideal, relation to nature. Yet it is hardly to create a condition of freedom, for natural rhythms are a contingent force everywhere in our existence, bearing down upon and transporting us as surely as we have breathing lungs and beating hearts.[6]

The Old English word *rim* has a complex etymology indicating, among other meanings, counting or reckoning, as well as covering with "rime" or hoarfrost; it reminds us that meter is a determinative and ideal pattern placed over rhythm. Pure repetition of course is never possible. Even within the logical realms of mathematics and physics, the temporal situation of the beholder fragments the possibility of such perfect isomorphism. Yet meter admits the possibility of organizing the language in ways that may include, and may also go beyond, the spoken language, and meter can function as an abstract grid even as it is never totally realized. Syllables have a life in meter that they cannot have in the actual ordinary practice of spoken phonemes — a fact exploited beautifully, for example, in the sprung rhythms of Gerard Manley Hopkins. Consider the opening lines of his 1885 sonnet "(The Soldier)." If they were written as a prose argument, they would look like this:

> Yes. Why do we all, seeing of a soldier, bless him? Bless our redcoats, our tars? Both these being, the greater part, but frail clay, nay but foul clay. Here it is: the heart, since, proud, it calls the calling manly, gives a guess that, hopes that, makes believe, the men must be no less. It fancies, feigns, deems, dears the artist after his art.

Hopkins writes them, however, like this:

> Yes. Whý do we áll, séeing of a / soldier, bless him? bléss
> Our redcoats, our tars? Both / thése being, the greater part,
> But frail clay, nay but foul clay. / Hére it is: the heart,

Since, proud, it calls the calling / manly, gives a guess
That, hopes that, mákesbelieve, / the men must be no less;
It fancies, feigns, deems, dears / the artist after his art.

Hopkins had written in his journals that hexameter lines such as these would not work in English without splitting down the middle. Here, in a poem he wrote while serving as confessor to the Cowley Barracks at Oxford, he uses that very effect, emphasized by his placing of a virgule in each line, to lay out a set of fissures: the see in seeing, the red in redcoats, the be in being, the call in calling, the man in manly, the makes in makesbelieve, the art in artist. Reading down his diacritical marks — *why all see / bless // these // here // makes // dears* — the emphasized monosyllables are like an x-ray of the conventional syntax whereby soldiers are blessed and thereby endowed with certain attributes. This syntax is in tension with the dense language of the poem that remains unmarked: the frail and foul clay out of which this art is made; the sacrifice that "dears," exemplified at the volta between the octave and sestet by "Mark Christ our King." The simple, exact *abbaabbacdcdcd* rhyme scheme (bless / art / heart / guess / less / art / smart / express / through / bliss / do / kiss / too / this) contrasts the enveloped, protective, structure of the octave's blessing to the march-like duality of the sestet's two rhyme words, designed to emphasize the soldier's own point of view.

To ask what is obviously a rhetorical question: which admits of more freedom of expression, the regular prose syntax here, or the poetic line, with its complex interplay of end rhyme, internal alliteration and consonance, split phrasing, and re-marked syllables? Aldington makes it clear that "cadence" or rhythm is what is un-"wedged" from the "preconceived and childish formality" of traditional meters, yet just how preconceived, if not childish, is traditional meter? Even if a rhyme scheme is anticipated, the unfolding consequences of its manifestation can be full of surprises, particularly surprises of content and perspective.

Nevertheless, despite an apparently universal tendency for rhyming to be part of the process of language learning, most of the world's languages do not use poetic rhyme.[7] Chinese poetry has had a continuous history of using rhyme since 1000 B.C., but the ingenious prosody of biblical Hebrew did not turn to rhyme; secular Hebrew poetry developed a system of rhyme words based on consonant/vowel units only as it came under the influence of Arab poetics during the medieval period. Ancient poetry, especially Greek poetry, in the West rarely used rhyme, and when it did, rhyme was often a feature of ridicule or comedy, as in the rhyming speech of the drunk Hercules in Euripides' *Alcestis:*

> brotois hapasi katthanein opheiletai,
> kouk esti thnêtôn hostis exepistatai
> tên aurion mellousan ei biôsetai:
> to tês tukhês gar aphanes hoi probêsetai,
> kast' ou didakton oud' halisketai tekhnêi.

Here is Richard Aldington's own 1930 translation of these lines, which, perhaps not surprisingly, do not rhyme:

> Know the nature of human life? Don't think you do. You couldn't. Listen to me. All mortals must die. Isn't one who knows if he'll be alive to-morrow morning. Who knows where Fortune will lead? Nobody can teach it. Nobody learn it by rules.[8]

The slightly tipsy veering quality of the Greek lines is complete lost in this flat and broken-up rendition.

Rhyme appears as a dominant feature of poetry in the West only with the gradual substitution of accent for quantity in poetic measures, and the strongest influences upon Western rhyme come from Irish and Arabic poetry. *Homeoteleuton,* the repetition of words that end alike, regardless of stress or quantity, was frowned upon by most classical and medieval rhetoricians, especially with regard to unstressed syllables, and the fact that most words of more than one syllable adhered to the Latin rule of penultimate stress meant that few words could be rhymed.[9] But the hymns of Hilary of Poitiers and Saints Ambrose and Augustine in the third and fourth centuries begin a syncretic tradition of using both assonance and end rhyme, and the Latin hymn is indebted to Irish verse forms. Old Irish depended upon an alliterative accentual line similar to that found in German poetry. For a time Old Irish poets simultaneously practiced both this accentual verse and a syllabic line based on irregular speech rhythms with an end-line rhyme in a fixed meter; eventually, in Middle Irish verse, the syllabic system prevailed. The vernacular traditions of Irish poetry, known in print through monastic inscriptions from the fifth century forward, were in this sense a repository of a great array of techniques: accentual and syllabic verse; alliteration, internal rhyme, and end-rhyme, and a complex system of metrical requirements for rhyme.[10] In the rhyming couplets of the sixth-century Latin hymn "Dies irae" (Day of Wrath) of Saint Columba (521–97) we find similar practices:

Regis regum rectissimi
prope est dies domini,
dies irae et vindictae,
tenerarum et nebulae,
diesque mirabilium
tonitruorum fortium,
dies quoque angustiae,
maeroris ac tristitiae,
in quo cessabit mulierum
amor et desiderium,
hominumque contentio
mundi huius et cupido.[11]

The end-rhymed couplets play on a cumulative and receding pattern of sound like a wave, with the most variation at either end: *aabbccbbccdd*. More subtly, the multisyllabic rhymes also cluster toward the middle at *ccb*(2)*b*(2). The end rhymes are offset by initial assonance and much internal rhyme, although there is no use, as there might be in Irish, of binding alliteration or any metrical parallelism in the rhyming words.

It is surely one of the ironies of literary history that a powerfully refined ancient Irish system of rhyming converged in the Latin hymn with an earlier classical tradition of discounting rhyme. Caesar's *Gallic Wars* contains the first Western record of the social context of such Irish rhyming practices, including an account of the professorial duties of the Druids.[12] Druid scholar/poet/priests instructed young men in verses for a period as long as twenty years so that they might acquire the sacred and juridical knowledge encoded in meter and rhyme. In addition to rules of line length and syllabic patterns, this Celtic poetics, also practiced by Goidelic, Brittonic, and Welsh poets, established what are known as generic rhymes — rhymes based on identical vowel sounds, certain nasal clusters, and clusters of consonants, particularly *g-d-b, dd-l-r, -gh-f-w*.[13]

The Germanic languages, including Old English, because of their emphasis on fore-stressed words, developed alliteration as the primary structural feature of their poetry. In the Romance languages, where word stress is not generally as strong as phrase stress and the pronunciation of vowels is relatively fixed, it is difficult not to rhyme.[14] Rhyme as we know it in the West came to the fore in the period 1100–1300 by means of troubadour verse and the evolution of an emphasis on sound in the *dolce stil nuovo*. But the question of whether rhyme originated in this period is controversial. There is much agreement that the rhyming practices of Arabic poetics were an influence on the flowering of Occitan verse forms, yet older scholarship indicated an influence of Arabic poetics on Western prosody much earlier through similarities between Zoroastrian sacred texts and early Christian rhyme practices.[15]

The eroticization of rhyme and the aesthetic category of sweet words flourish in the late medieval period along with other developments in the arts, including the perspectivalism of Giotto, which relies upon viewing from a particular set of conditions, such as the aerial or bird's-eye view. At this moment the erotic and cognitive powers of art seem intensified by the development of techniques that require inhabiting multiple perspectives and anticipated patterns. Ezra Pound notes, for example, that a *canzon* of Arnaut Daniel beginning "L'aura amara" praised by Dante depended upon holding seventeen rhymes in mind at once.[16] Gestures of withholding and release, calculation and surprise, typify a poetics eroticized by its courtly love context where the metaphorical and imaginative had as much power as the literally realized and where the deferred pleasures of the aesthetic held sway.[17]

Yet despite their fellowship as Imagists, Aldington rejected Pound's medievalism tout court, arguing that "complicated accented metres were invented by the Provençals, who, as a rule have nothing to say and say it badly."[18] Such a broad condemnation perhaps does not even merit answering, but consider this little poem, heir to the troubadour tradition and addressed to rhyming poets ("A Diversi Rimatori"), by the poet friend of Dante Alighieri, Dante da Maiano:

> Provedi, saggio, ad esta visione,
> e per mercé ne trai vera sentenza.
> Dico: una donna di bella fazone,
> di cu' el meo cor gradir molto s'agenza,
> mi fé d'una ghirlanda donagione,
> verde, fronzuta, con bella accoglienza:
> appresso mi trovai per vestigione
> camicia di suo dosso, a mia parvenza.
> Allor di tanto, amico, mi francai,

che dolcemente presila abbracciare:
non si acontese, ma ridea la bella.
Così, ridendo, molto la baciai:
del più non dico, ché mi fé giurare.
E morta, ch'è mia madre, era con ella.[19]

Published in Dante Alighieri's *Rime* as number 39, this sonnet was written, like most of da Maiano's work, as a piece of coterie poetry.[20] It compresses a remarkable amount of action and thought into its brief compass. The shift between possessive pronouns (*meo [cor]* / *mia [parvenza]* / *mia [madre]*) and passive verbs (*mi fé, mi trovai, mi francai, mi fé [giurare]*) adds to the drama of possession and transformation. The rhyme scheme's transition at the volta from *abababab* to *cdecde* signals as well the change from the kissing couple to the presence of a third figure — the poet's dead mother.[21] A psychoanalytic treatise could be written about this development, but for now suffice it to say that it would be impossible to render the action of this poem into free verse without giving up a great deal; the braided garland, the twined lovers, the echoing *b* and *ci* sounds of kissing (*baciare*), the toll-like sounding of *bella, bella, bella,* into *ella,* the ghostly triangulation of the third figure and third sound — all would be lost entirely.

The schemes of troubadour lyrics and the poetry of the *dolce stil nuovo* rely on rhyme patterns as much as accent. Nevertheless, free verse can use rhyme and remain free of the relatively fixed meters of earlier poetry, as it did in Irish and as it has in English verse at least since John Skelton's work at the turn of the sixteenth century. Indeed, the Skeltonic two- to three-beat line, with patterns of increasing and subsiding density of rhyme, seems as close as one could come to a merging of the compulsions of rhythm and emotion of the kind Aldington praises as exclusively new in the "intensity and concentration" of such modernist poems as H.D.'s "Gods of the Sea." Here is Skelton's "Mistress Margaret Hussey," written in 1495, revised and first published in 1522–23, and one lyric of a ten-lyric cycle, *The Garland of Laurel,* written for the women attending the court of the countess of Surrey:

Merry Margaret,
As midsummer flower,
Gentle as falcon
Or hawk of the tower
With solace and gladness,
Much mirth and no madness,

All good and no badness;
So joyously,
So maidenly,
So womanly
Her demeaning
In every thing,
Far, far passing
That I can indite,
Or suffice to write
Of Merry Margaret
As midsummer flower,
Gentle as falcon
Or hawk of the tower.
As patient and still
And as full of good will
As fair Isaphill,
Coriander,
Sweet pomander,
Good Cassander,
Steadfast of thought,
Well made, well wrought,
Far may be sought
Ere that ye can find
So courteous, so kind
Merry Margaret,
As midsummer flower,
Gentle as falcon
Or hawk of the tower.

At this moment of initial separation of English poetry from the alliterative verse that prevailed before it, we see certain changes literally being wrought by rhyme. The alternating rhymes of the refrain seem to collapse into the insistent trochaic rhymes of the exposition. Here is an inversion of our usual expectation that refrains will rhyme or sing the closures of the more discursive lines of a poem. There is a compulsion to Skelton's falling meters, underlined by the insistent rhymes, just as his rising meters seem to call up or slow the motion of his poems. In "Mistress Margaret Hussey" rhyme pairs separated by unrhymed lines turn into unseparated trios, then unseparated pairs again: Margaret /

flower / falcon / tower; gladness / madness / badness; joyously / maidenly / womanly; demeaning / everything / passing; indite / write; Margaret / flower / falcon / tower; still / will / Isaphill; Coriander / pomander / Cassander; thought / wrought / sought; find / kind; Margaret / flower / falcon / tower. These moments of intense rhyming are matched by exact, epideictic details: the trio rhymes list adjectival nouns and adverbs that swirl around the person of Margaret Hussey as the poet barely is able to "indite" and "write," and "find" her "kind." Spinning proper names and metaphorical terms, the poet's naming practices effect the turns and metamorphoses of praise by something akin to uttering spells. Rhyme is in the end the main reason Skelton can make such bold observations about Margaret Hussey and other ladies-in-waiting.

A striking feature of the history of rhyme is that even when, as in our own era, rhyming does not dominate poetry, the use of rhyme, continuing or renewed, does not acquire an archaic cast. Milton's introductory remarks to the reader of *Paradise Lost* described rhyme as follows: "Rime being no necessary Adjunct or true Ornament of Poem or good Verse, in longer works especially, but the Invention of a barbarous Age to set off wretched matter and lame Meter." He went on to say that "only in apt Numbers, fit quantity of Syllables, and the sense variously drawn out from one Verse into another, not in the jingling sound of like endings" was a "fault avoided by the learned Ancients."[22] Classicist that he was, Milton was well aware that ancient poetry rarely rhymed. Nevertheless in neoclassicism rhyming couplets return to become the dominant verse form.[23]

Analogously, despite the triumph of free verse in modernism and in contemporary works by poets as varied as the Northern Irish lyricists Paul Muldoon and Ciaran Carson, the American Language poet Charles Bernstein, and the Milanese love poet Patrizia Valduga, rhyme takes precedence over many other aspects of poetic form. Rhyme returns as inevitably as, well, rhyme and the seasons that in many ways it emulates. If it disappears only to reappear in the practice of poetry, perhaps this is yet another level of the relation of rhyme to the aesthetics of interval and surprise. Rhyming is based in aural coincidences that themselves depend upon noncoincidence in time and space. If most poets can't help but rhyme at times by accident and passively, such a practice can also awaken an intention to rhyme; whether working in, as the troubadours put it, a "closed" or an "easy" style, the poet who rhymes along the way finds himself or herself in a sound world of echoes and resonances.

A natural cycle of rhyme and in rhyme was described by Emerson in his essay *The Poet*: "A rhyme in one of our sonnets should not be less pleasing than the iterated nodes of a seashell, or the resembling difference of a group of flowers. The pairing of the birds is an idyl . . . a tempest is a rough ode without falsehood or rant; a summer, with its harvest sown, reaped and stored is an epic song, subordinating how many admirably executed parts. Why should not the symmetry and truth that modulate these, glide into our spirits, and we participate the invention of nature?"[24] Sound vibrations and color vibrations in fact do seem to have some correlation,[25] and rhyme can be a feature of visual experience as much as an auditory one. When Emerson speaks of the "resembling difference of a group of flowers," he could have in mind the abstractions of the color wheel or the way each spring, the yellows of daffodils, narcissus and forsythia are followed by the purples of crocuses and hyacinths, tulips and lilacs. This resembling difference is a feature of the numerical rhyme that underlies the appearance of the Fibonacci sequence in the seed heads of sunflowers and coneflowers; the fractal geometry of the chambered nautilus and pine cones, various twins and multiples in the living world, and the convergent evolution of similar species in different contexts. It is indeed possible to use the word *rhyme* to describe certain senses of rotation and repetition in time, as when we note coincidences or have a sense of déjà vu. Our temporal powers of retrospection and projection depend upon abilities to hold in mind and attend to aural likenesses.

Emerson's list of principles — resembling difference, iteration, pairing, sequence, symmetry, and ultimately invention under the pressure of truth — also indicates some of the relations rhyming holds to simile and what Emanuel Swedenborg, Charles Baudelaire, and Emerson himself have thought of as correspondences in the most general sense. Swedenborg wrote that "order and the world are in an imperfect state when they do not harmonize; and in such degree imperfect, as they fall short of harmony."[26] And in *Representative Men*, Emerson wrote of Swedenborg's theories of correspondence:

> These grand rhymes or returns in nature, — the dear, best-known face startling us at every turn, under a mask so unexpected that we think it the face of a stranger, and carrying up the semblance into divine forms, — delighted the prophetic eye of Swedenborg; and he must be reckoned a leader in that revolution, which, by giving to science an idea, has given to an aimless accumulation of experiments, guidance and form and a beating heart.[27]

Emerson's idea that "we participate the invention of nature," however, surely stems as well from Aristotle's contention that poiesis as making is a means of discovery of our relation to nature. For Aristotle, all art as perfected form is an improvement upon nature, penetrating to nature's principles.[28] What, then, does poetic rhyme — that is, rhyme that is both intended and received — draw on and complete? If rhyme is a feature of nature, or at least of our temporal perception of nature, rhyme also is an ever-present feature of language, if not of poetry. Rhyme offers a particular kind of pattern, one that is only partly determinative. Unlike rhythm, which may exist as pure haptic or tactile feeling, rhyme comes with acoustical, if not always semantic, content; and unlike meter, which remains ideal, rhyme is always realized or manifested. There is a certain balance between the will and contingency that is effected in rhyming and that is a recurring theme of poetic treatises on rhyme. As we follow, for example, the intermittent discussion of rhyme in the text that provides the epigraph on rhyme and freedom for this essay, Dante's *De vulgari eloquentia,* we see a frequent play between describing rhyme as "weaving" (*texere*) and as "echo" (*eco*); the dynamic between activity and passivity, the production and reception of sounds could not be more starkly set forward.[29]

The willed production of sound always is in tension with the involuntary aspect of hearing. Yet in rhyme, the production of sound can seem involuntary and hearing can be attuned to particular intervals. It was this compelling attention, a feature of all repetitive form, that Wordsworth believed helped us endure painful feeling in poetry's content, and he especially singles out the power of rhyme in this regard: "The end of Poetry is to produce excitement in co-existence with an overbalance of pleasure. . . . Now the co-presence of something regular, something to which the mind has been accustomed in various moods and in a less excited state, cannot but have great efficacy in tempering and restraining the passion by an intertexture of ordinary feeling . . . there can be little doubt but that more pathetic situations and sentiments, that is, those which have a greater proportion of pain connected with them, may be endured in metrical composition, especially in rhyme, than in prose."[30] In his treatise *The World as Will and Idea,* Arthur Schopenhauer further emphasized the mesmerizing power of rhyme when he described our "consent" to recurring sound. As he described it, such consent involves a strange combination of willingly following and blindly agreeing that takes place prior to judgment — a "power of convincing" independent of all reasons.[31] Even as it is often an effect of conscious will, or, as we say, a "scheme," rhyme seems to come to us from somewhere else, from some outside that may be deeply inside, in the sense that it is unconscious or, perhaps, simply compulsive.

The "I can't help myself" aspect to rhyming behavior can be found in babies' babbling and the verbal dueling in many cultures, including contemporary hip-hop and rap music practices of rhyming. Because vowels are acoustically more alike than consonants, any vowel can be in slant rhyme with any other, and whereas the differentiation of phonemes that creates intelligible sounds is the task of everyday speech, the ever-present possibility of alliteration, consonance, assonance, and the vast array of other kinds of rhymes is always latent in speech and serves such functions as stabilizing the forms of irregular verbs.[32] There is a family resemblance in this sense between rhyme and punning, for as puns join multiple meanings within one morpheme, and so make the integrity of a morpheme as a unit of meaning literally break apart, so does rhyming show that proximity in sound has little consequence for proximity of semantics.[33]

Rhyme is in this sense always a showcase for the arbitrary nature of the sign and limits our efforts to dominate meaning; rhyming draws us beyond ourselves with its potential for aural pleasure, which, when one is trying to concentrate on univocal meaning and syntactical sequence, can be something like aural pain. Here is the basis of the tension between rhyme and syntax, a tension at the heart of the modernist rejection of rhyme. This disparity is also the reason why syntax motivated by the requirements of rhyme will seem unnatural. Rhyme punctuates and concentrates, it does not flow.[34]

Although rhyming is part of the language of the crib, most people are able to notice and use nonadjacent rhymes for the first time between the ages of five and seven; other phonological skills appear at this age, and this is of course also most often the age of the onset of reading, whether children are learning to read a language with a fairly transparent orthography, such as Italian, or a fairly opaque one, such as English.[35] One of the most suggestive aspects of the role of rhyming in language learning is that rhyming seems to precede, or help facilitate, phonological awareness per se.[36] When words are grouped by "phonological neighborhood," such as *brat, rot, at, rat,* adults have some difficulty recognizing individual words, but such density actually leads to better word recognition in infants and young children.[37] Rhyme returns readers to the scene of distinguishing words from one another, of hearing them fully as both different from and similar to other words. In attending to rhyme in poems, we are deeply engaged in an art made of words, and we literally renew our sense of them.

Without ascribing any particular value or teleology to the dialectic that is implied, we could say that poetic rhyme mediates the relation between the purely felt that is rhythm and the purely rational that is meter. Its relation to semantics remains both under- and overdetermined, for rhyme can endow meaning with greater depth or empty it of its syntactical or context-bound force. Rhyme introduces a realm of conscience and anticipation in poiesis that is particular to human experience, one that indicates a preference for variation and pattern at once. As the perception of rhyme is at once retrospective and proleptic, rhyming requires awareness in ways that the physical possession of rhythm does not. Rhythm is lulling; in contrast, rhyme, like meter, requires identification and attention; everything counts, including pauses and silences.[38] But meter happens at a constant rate of marks, while rhyme is an effect at a distance. To this extent, rhyme can serve as an interruption or counter to rhythm.

"Rhyme shmyme, I never use the stuff," a poet colleague said to me when I mentioned I was writing this essay. His very reply echoes the everyday use of what we call in English "close rhyme" (in German *schlagreim,* "hammer rhyme") as a mnemonic that somehow has a skepticism built in. When we hear rhyme shmyme, helter-skelter, fender bender, double trouble, mishmash, hoity-toity, flimflam, dingdong, or such ancient examples as hoi poloi and holy moly, we are in the realm of instant parody. The reason for that, it seems, is the universal principle that the closer rhymes appear as adjacent pairs, the stronger the sound play and lesser the stability of meaning in individual words. These mnemonics are literal models of equivocation; the second term modifies and weakens the force of the first as our attention is drawn to sound alone.[39] Poets use adjacency in a range of ways beyond rhyme, but it is memorable when rhyming words are stacked very close to one another in a poem, as they are in John Donne's "Song": "And swear / Nowhere / Lives a woman true, and fair."[40] Envelope stanzas, such as *abba,* foreground the possibilities of hearing the differences between consecutive and nonadjacent rhyme pairs and thereby require two kinds of suspension in the listener.[41]

Making rhymes involves separating marked and unmarked utterances, yet pause does not effect it, and rhyme is neither universal nor precisely language specific. Poetic rhyme is a record of the living language, more particularly the poet's living language at a moment of relation between languages and poetic practices; it is thus both more local and more universal than any given language's storehouse of rhymes. Those third- and fourth-century Latin hymns mentioned above that work under both quantitative and qualitative systems of meter are a practice where diverging traditions meet.[42] The variable initial, internal, and terminal rhymes of Hebrew liturgical poetry in the fourth century and the free-floating rhymed strophes of early eleventh-century Iberian Arabic poetry are further examples of syncretic rhyming practices. Whereas Chaucer's rhymes tend, like those French rhymes upon which they were modeled, to be full or "perfect" for the most part, from the time of Spenser forward similar, rather than identical, sounds are used. Sidney's *Defense of Poetry* suggests that rhyme is an ornament, adding a pleasing melody and harmony to a work.[43] Other writers, such as the prosodist George Saintsbury, have been concerned with rhyme as a punctuating device in rhythm.[44]

Moments of intense rhyming activity seem to coincide with the meeting of dialects and languages — the melting pot of troubadour culture, the macaronic verse of medieval scholasticism, Dante's turn between Latin and the Tuscan vernacular, Chaucer's encounter with Romance languages, Spenser's with Irish. We find other polyglot practices in Pushkin's use of Turkish rhyming words in his poems of 1829[45] and the Greek, French, German, and English rhymes of Pound and Eliot. The freezing and melting that typify erotic poetry in the West also seem to characterize the social life of rhymes. Rhymes fix sounds inflexibly at the ends of lines or freeze a local pronunciation like a fossil. Yet rhyme seems also to flourish in situations where dialects and languages meet and to form a record of how pronunciation is constantly changing by means of living language.

The larger history of rhyme has yet to be written, but perhaps, as we saw in the example of Druid poetics and possible Zoroastrian origins for many Western rhyme schemes, it will reveal close connections to a history of the ritual or magical manipulation of objects. As Aristotle noted, sensation continues even after an organ has ceased to sense it; he uses the analogy of the motion of any object that has been thrown even after the thrower no longer touches it. Both rhyming and juggling are prominent in sixth-century Ireland, thirteenth-century Provence, and in the street performances and hip-hop forms of our own era, and in all these practices we see a separation, or breaking up, of bodily purposiveness in the service of an external form or outline that establishes a domain with its own internal power — the power of the intrinsic art work, or a space of sacred attention, or both.[46]

Rhyme tends to overcome alliteration once words drop their unstressed endings. But, as we have seen, rhyme does not have to show up at the ends of words or the ends of lines. And if it doesn't, the ends of lines are of course marked by measure, or ratio, or reason alone. Lines without rhyme, or reason in this sense, have to have some other means of ending — perhaps a dogma of "breath" or a simple adherence to prose syntax. Nevertheless, line-end rhyme

seems linked broadly to the kinds of paralinguistic marking we find in clapping, stamping, and clicking speech play in many cultures, from the clicking
markers nursing mothers use in Chinese nursery rhymes to the recent fad for
singing Happy Birthday in American restaurants with each phrase marked by
a collective hand clap.[47] Clapping and stamping indeed emphasize the relation between our bodily symmetry and symmetrical sounds. Like nonsense
phonemes, these motions of the hands, feet, and tongue can be considered a
secondary level of rhythmic punctuation; once rhyme accrues around phonemes that are also morphemes, it becomes an indispensable and attached
dimension of the poem's meaning. We could argue inversely that nonsemantic forms of punctuated sound become meaningful as they appear in poems.
This is yet another way that poiesis keeps us ahead of the existing possibilities
of a language, giving us the freedom to create meanings where there are none
and deny them where they may seem to appear. When words are used at once
linguistically and paralinguistically, separations between speech and sound
do not hold and the performative power of words is strengthened.

Line-end rhyme thus often involves subduing or suppressing rhymes that
occur elsewhere in the line, as hearing univocal meaning involves subduing
or suppressing both rhymes and puns in the spoken language in general. We
could conclude that a rhyme is a rhyme only if it is heard as one, but we
can also think of rhymes as a vector of arbitrariness and sound for its own
sake that is always latent in any utterance. Perhaps a desire for emphasis or
semantic reinforcement, or for a practice that makes perfect, underlies a dog's
multiple barks, a bird's repertoire of more than one song, animal warning
cries that continue even after a danger is gone. But the repetition of sound in
human rhymes also is conducive to memory; as George Santayana wrote in
his study of the cognitive claims of memory, a memory does not sink back
into old experience but rather recovers knowledge by means of the awakening of affect or sentiment, and the rhymes of any work create such an affec-
tive field.[48]

We have only to think of rhyme's relation to the production of sound
in music to have some clearer sense of this power to create effects across
temporal distance. To hear external objects ring, chime, or otherwise produce sounds against one another, we must hold them next to each other, rub
them against each other, or pluck or otherwise play them. But to create those
sounding external objects that are rhymes, whether we are producing them
or receiving them, we need only use our aural memory. The physical sound
itself is not lost into space; rather it can be called back or summoned by the

next instance of the complementary sound, and we need only do this three times to establish a pattern that makes it all the easier to go on to play variations on that sound.

Remembering and anticipating the progress of a piece of music depends upon certain structural devices in the same way that remembering and anticipating rhymes does. For a rhyme to be held over so many lines, so great a distance, it also must resonate beyond its adjacent sounds. Rhyming practices, by varying between opening and closing consonant sounds and internal vowel sounds, give words interiors and exteriors; because there are many more similarities between vowels than between consonants, rhyme also moderates and distinguishes those sounds. Similarly, the so-called unrhymed or unmarked end words of a poem can acquire a particular semantic cast simply because they do not rhyme: we are all familiar with the let-down effect of the World War I poets' use of such unrhymed words at closing. Consider as well how in the first two ballad stanzas of the "And Did Those Feet" passage of Blake's *Milton,* the lack of rhyme between *time* and *God* and *Divine* and *here* comes to outweigh the rhymes of *green* and *seen* and *hills* and *mills:*

> And did those feet in ancient time
> Walk upon England's mountains green?
> And was the holy Lamb of God
> On England's pleasant pastures seen?
>
> And did the Countenance Divine
> Shine forth upon our clouded hills?
> And was Jerusalem builded here
> Among these dark satanic mills?

Analogously, the slant rhymes of Emily Dickinson's "A Narrow Fellow in the Grass" (rides / is; seen / on; sun / gone) underline the intermittent exact rhymes of *corn* and *morn* and *bone* and *alone,* as the latter pair also stand in stark contrast at the close of the poem to the easy meeting of the singular syllable *me* with the several syllables of *cordiality:*

> A narrow fellow in the grass
> Occasionally rides;
> You may have met him, — did you not,
> His notice sudden is.

The grass divides as with a comb,
A spotted shaft is seen;
And then it closes at your feet
And opens further on.

He likes a boggy acre,
A floor too cool for corn.
Yet when a child, and barefoot,
I more than once, at morn,

Have passed, I thought, a whip-lash
Unbraiding in the sun, —
When, stooping to secure it,
It wrinkled, and was gone.

Several of nature's people
I know, and they know me;
I feel for them a transport
Of cordiality;

But never met this fellow,
Attended or alone,
Without a tighter breathing,
And zero at the bone.

The poem's geometry of barefoot meeting is made of lines and circles: lines that open into circles (like zero at the bone) and circles that open the spaces between lines (like the path of a cylindrical snake through a patch of grass). In this poem Dickinson also uses a device that seems close to "close rhyme," and yet, so far as I know, we have no term for it: the pairing of identical letters. Our letters, after all, are made of circles, parts of circles, and lines. Here are the words of the poem that have one or more such pairings: *narrow, fellow, grass, occasionally, sudden, grass, spotted, feet, boggy, floor, too, cool, barefoot, passed, stooping, feel, fellow, attended.* If we then look at the doubled letters themselves — *rr ll ss cc ll dd ss tt ee gg oo oo oo oo ss oo ee ll tt* — we can see that they begin with a rr[o]ll and culminate in a chorus of serpentines and oo circles that have emerged from the grass-like ll's before they [ha]lltt.

Given the power of rhyme schemes of all kinds to lend particular semantic and visual weight to the place of unrhymed words, we might see the development of free verse as an unrhymed pause in the greater scheme of rhyme's poetic history. Far from a constraint, rhyme endows us with certain freedoms — among them: the vernacular, including the locality of the poem itself, released from the standard; the monolingual in dialogue with the multilingual; sound opened up by vision, and sound released from meaning entirely; expectation released into surprise; and pattern drawn from the oblivion of time. Rhyme is perfect, imperfect, total, and partial at once. To follow Dante, why, in making poems or any other art form, not allow "as much liberty as may be desired"?

orange/strange, chimney/skinn'd knee, breadth/heath, circle/girdle, desert/death's hurt, monarch/my ark, month/menthe, virtue/eschew, wisdom/his dome

IN THE BEGINNING WAS TRANSLATION / LEEVI LEHTO

Let me start by quoting my "official statement" concerning my translation of Charles Bernstein's "Besotted Desquamation," a poem that can be seen as consisting of twenty-seven sections, with all the words in each individual section sharing the same initial letter.[1]

> When I sat down to translate the poem into Finnish, I was disappointed, confused even, to find that the words my dictionary suggested for replacement seemed to begin with just about any letter. . . . I began . . . to have doubts as to the very fundaments of the profession of translation. I mean, how can we imagine to translate anything, when we cannot even get the first letters right? Eventually, I think I did find a problem to the solution. What I did was to put the original away — for good, I never looked at it again. . . . I then proceeded, not to translate, not even to rewrite, but to write the poem, exactly the way Charles had done before me.

We are evidently dealing with poetic sound in translation here. For most of us, I believe, it wouldn't even make sense to speak about translating poetry without accounting for the sound. On the other hand, it doesn't exactly make sense to speak about "translating sound" either. Perhaps more meaningfully we could speak of *transferring* the sound — but then, should we succeed in this, we would be back to the original.

Let me make two observations:

First, I want to refer to sound as a certain *material* dimension of language[2] — and that in more than one way. I've always liked M. H. Abrams's remark that the sound in Keats's poetry is partly determined by the physical pleasure of reciting it.[3] The specific sound of a poem or a poet usually represents a *new* material dimension inside a natural language.

49

Two. The differences between languages are, "in the last instance," material ones. Think of Walter Benjamin's well-known essay "The Task of the Translator," where he distinguishes between "intention" (common to all languages) and "the mode of intention" (where they differ).[4] In my view, Benjamin's example — the difference between the German word *Brot* and the French word *pain,* both meaning "bread" — refers, in the last instance, to their material dissimilarity. His central argument would hold even if the words' "semantic" connotations in each of their languages were exactly the "same" (which they — because not stable — can never be).

In his essay, Benjamin makes the case for the translator's task being to effect "an echo" of the foreign (or source) language in the target one, as part of creating what he calls "the pure language." On this latter, difficult concept I will content myself with noting that if anything, "*pure* language," for Benjamin, represents the greatest confidence in proliferating the *impure.* If the original poem already effects a new material dimension in its own language, translation in turn will unfold yet another one that is not, strictly speaking, situated in either of the languages. This way, Benjamin's solution to the "problem" of babelization is — more babelization.

In fact, in the history of translating poetry, Benjamin's method has been in wider use than is usually recognized. Here, I like to cite the example of transferring English, German, and French metrical patterns into Finnish poetry during its so-called traditional period (1880–1950). Blank verse, for instance, is ill suited to Finnish where the stress always falls on the first syllable of the word; however, instead of the impossible task of showing "how Shakespeare would have written should his native language have been Finnish," the Finnish translators went to great lengths to invent new prosodies, foreign to the "natural language," to enable the Finns to grasp, as an echo, the dynamics of Shakespeare's poetical thinking. Quite Benjaminian, in fact.

Another, somewhat contrary, example. In Finland, it is customary to think that translating Eliot, in the wake of his winning the Nobel Prize, triggered what is known as the modernist period of Finnish poetry — a 1950s phenomenon. In fact, those early translations very much ignored Eliot's prosody, making him into a strongly textual poet writing almost exclusively in free verse. Furthermore, the Finnish modernists can be seen as having *reacted against* the poetics of these translations, rather than simply as having been influenced by them. A double process of misprision that again seems to fall nicely in the frame of the Benjaminian model.

As these examples suggest, I tend to see translation — and the translation of poetic sound in particular — as part of a larger dynamics of cultural development and interaction. In a sense, I don't think of translation as having anything to do with interlingual communication, and I'm all for inverting the currently dominant paradigm in which the languages are seen as something primary, translation as a secondary, ensuing "problem." To me, "in the beginning was translation."[5] Translation, not languages per se, forms the *basis* of cultures — meaning, among other things, that translation is always also (already) political.

Let me illustrate this point by means of a historical contrast. In his classic essay on "the methods of translation," Friedrich Schleiermacher, another German theoretician of translation, writing a hundred years before Benjamin, was markedly conscious of precisely this cultural dimension.[6] For him, translating the Greek and Roman classics was closely connected to the task of elevating the German language to the level of its "historical task." In our present global language situation, dominated as it is by the rise of national states and corresponding national languages, this sound Schleiermachian intuition has come to be replaced by a naive conception of a "democratic" "equality" of languages. Translation has come to be seen as "transferring contents" between languages — something that in turn necessarily affects what comes to be written in the first place (though, of course, there's no such thing as "writing in the first place").

Inspired by Schleiermacher, but rejecting (or inverting) the cultural hegemonism inherent in his position, my alternative view on the *politics of poetic sound in translation* would conform to the linguistic reality of a world that, under this surface of unproblematically transferred cultural contents, is more and more characterized by a (in my view) positive babelization and, as its most dynamic element, an increasing Cacophony of Sounds. Instead of a simplified schema of transferred cultural content, it would concentrate on the factual overlapping of languages with their peculiar dynamics and power structures, admitting some linguistic formations to be more "important" than others, but also ready to react to the structures of suppression and dominance between them. It would emphasize misunderstandings and misprisions and as such be against all language communities and language-based models of identification — models that, incidentally, tend to rely on sound, as epitomized by the example of the middle-aged, educated couple from Boulder, Colorado, who once told my wife how there was nothing special about their place of domicile, except that it seemed to be the only place in the whole world where English was spoken without any noticeable accent . . .

Let me conclude by three programmatic recommendations, all related to sound in translation.

Stressing the primacy of translation does not rule out the possibility that "original works" may contribute to the realization of the pure (read impure) language. I'm interested in this possibility in the frame of what I see as the real, dominant lingua franca of our world, one that, surprisingly, seems still to lack its literature — English spoken as second (or *n*th) language. My first recommendation is for creating and expanding this literature, a new poetry of Barbaric English, sure to contribute to the proliferation of sound in English.[7]

Second, I like Schleiermacher's joke that attempting to show how a "language A poet" would have written in language B — the conventional view of translation — is like producing an image of what the author would have looked like should his/her mother have conceived her with a different father.[8] The result may be interesting as such, but the question is: to whom? In 1994, I published John Ashbery's *Flow Chart* in my Finnish. While I do not regret this, I perhaps wouldn't do it again — the young Finnish poets of today are sufficiently versed in English to misunderstand Ashbery in the original. Instead, I would think that my version of Ashbery with a different father (like those by others) would be of interest to his native English readers. Actually, one can only wonder why Ashbery, a poet so widely translated, is still waiting to be translated into his native tongue. A volume of such translations, as an addition to the soundscape of the New York School tradition of poetry, could be on my list of future editing projects.

Third, though I don't believe in "untranslatability" as such, I would not deny the importance of works attempting to create it. A work like *Eunoia* by Christian Bök — a radical lipogram where, in each chapter, only one vowel is allowed at a time — is important, among other things, because of its challenge to translatability (it too would be best translated without even glancing at the original). I recently started working on a related project, a book of three hundred pages where I'd use the vowels of the first Finnish novel, *Seitsemän veljestä* (The Seven Brothers), by Aleksis Kivi — all of them, in the order they appear in Kivi's work, and no other vowels but them. In a sense, this would be a work for the Finns only. But even this text would not be untranslatable — being, among other things, itself a translation of the work by Kivi and, well, one where I'd finally get at least half of the letters right.

CHINESE WHISPERS / YUNTE HUANG

Finally the rumors grew more fabulous than the real thing.

JOHN ASHBERY, "Chinese Whispers"

Trying to undermine the credibility of Marco Polo, a critic once said that the travelogue of the famous medieval Merchant of Venice "sounds like a Chinese whisper translated from Persian."[1] To Marco Polo's debunkers, who have tried to prove that he actually never went to China, what gives him away is not his forgetting to mention the Great Wall of China or the custom of tea drinking. It is, above all, the strangeness of his language. For instance, the names of places, persons, and objects in the book are often heard in their Persian, Mongol, or Turkish sounds, but not Chinese. The foreignness of proper names seems to suggest that Marco Polo was a forger who got his tales of wonder by hearsay, giving the lie to the term "Chinese whisper."

In a game of Chinese Whispers, also known as the telephone game, broken telephone, or Russian Scandals, players line up in a circle and whisper in sequence to their immediate neighbor so that no one else can hear. The player at the beginning of the line thinks of a phrase and whispers it as quietly as possible to her/his neighbor. The neighbor then passes on the message to the next player to the best of his or her ability. The passing continues in this fashion until the phrase reaches the player at the end of the line, who calls out the message he or she received. If the game has been "successful," the final message will bear little or no resemblance to the original, because of the cumulative effect of mistakes along the line.[2]

What lies at the heart of the game of Chinese Whispers is the notion of the unreliability of hearsay, as John Ashbery puts it in the epigraph quoted above. But why "Chinese"? What's so Chinese in the "Chinese Whispers"? Here I will not try to track the cultural, or rather cross-cultural, history of the game, a history that suggests the entangled routes of Orientalism, exoticism, and Cold War propaganda. Rather, to me as a translator and scholar of translation, such a game of hearsay seems more like an instance of sound or homophonic translation: what's specifically Chinese in the Chinese Whispers is the very word "Chinese" itself, which is derived homophonically, through hearsay, *possibly* from the Chinese term *Chin,* a dynasty in ancient China; or *possibly* from *si,* the Chinese term for "silk." I emphasize the word "possibly" because it speaks to the very nature of homophonic translation, the unreliability and elusiveness of sound.

The question of sound in the domains of linguistics, music, and economics has become increasingly important in the age of empires and globalization. As Jacques Attali points out in *Noise: The Political Economy of Music,* "For twenty-five centuries, Western knowledge has tried to look upon the world. It has failed to understand that the world is not for the beholding. It is for hearing. It is not legible, but audible."[3] In the same vein, Kublai Khan, in Italo Calvino's *Invisible Cities,* wants to *hear* about the cities within the vast domain of his empire. The Great Khan understands that he may have conquered the visual space, but cities can be invisible because they exist in the soundscape, which is much more elusive, defying the spatial logic of the imperial power. Sound does not respect space. In the context of such politicized sound, I want to explore the poetics of homophonic translation and the ways in which it facilitates the global flows of signs, signals, local names, global currencies, and so on.

When I was growing up in China, my grandmother was a Buddhist, and she was semiliterate, which means she could recognize some Chinese words — let's say a few hundred out of the approximately four thousand needed to make her a competent reader. At one time, she was reading the Diamond Sutra every day as part of her devotional practice. Her version of the Sutra, it turns out, was a partially homophonic translation from Sanskrit. There were a lot of words, names, terms, that would look and sound Chinese but make no sense in Chinese. Since the amount of her Chinese vocabulary was not really enough to enable her to read the whole text, let alone comprehend, my grandmother would often ask me to teach her how to pronounce this or that Chinese character in the text. After I told her how to sound out those words, she would just go on with her "reading" without asking what those words meant, which seemed quite odd to me at the time.

Now that I'm teaching poetry to university students, I've encountered the opposite, equally odd phenomenon: when reading Pound's *Cantos* or Stein's *The Making of Americans,* they always ask what this and that means and do not want to read the words aloud. They often come to class with the notion that sounding out a poem may be nice and cool, but it really has little to do with the intrinsic "meaning" of the poem. Whenever they say that, I tell them, "Maybe you should talk to my grandma."

I'm not writing to defend my grandmother; her position is easily defensible or comprehensible in the context of some religious practices where the sonic components of the corpus of sacred and liturgical texts take precedence over their semantic meaning. Such a reading does not take as its goal the uncovering of symbolic meanings through an interpretive approach, but instead it suggests that the revealed sacred words must be continually affirmed and accepted in oral performance rather than regarded as merely a statement of facts and norms. Here we can think of analogies or parallels with Jerome Rothenberg's idea of "total translation," where the translation "exists absolutely in the present without recourse to the historical contextuality."[4] Or Bronislaw Malinowski's famous essay "The Meaning of Meaningless Words and the Coefficient of Weirdness," a study of the Trobriand language of magic in which "there is no desire to explain — there is solely the desire to experience."[5] Or Charles Olson's "projective verse," especially his distinction between "language as the act of the instant and language as the act of thought about the instant."[6]

All these appeals to the evocative, experiential, and enactive modes of language would explain nicely the practice of homophonic translation. But I want to focus on a technical feature of homophonic translation: the way in which it changes every word to a proper name and invokes the indexical rather than symbolic or even iconic power of a sign. Here I would like to expand the definition of homophonic translation to include all instances of textual reproduction that direct attention to the acoustic dimensions of language, ranging from the narrow sense of homophonic translation, such as Louis Zukofsky's *Catullus,* to Ezra Pound's use of foreign words in his poetry and translation, and even to Jorge Luis Borges's *Pierre Menard,* where the so-called reconstruction of *Don Quixote* is merely word-for-word copying. In the world of literacy, Pierre Menard's case is one of copying; but in the world of orality, it's a perfect example of repetition, recitation, and hence an absurd case of zero-degree homophonic translation.

Let me pick the middle ground in this widened range of homophonic translation and use Pound as an example to explain what I mean by the notion that sound translation changes the words in question into proper names. Take a look at these concluding lines from Pound's translation of Li Po's "The River–Merchant's Wife" in his *Cathay* (1915):

> If you are coming down through the narrows of the river Kiang,
> Please let me know beforehand,
> And I will come out to meet you,
>   As far as Cho-fu-Sa.[7]

The Chinese original for "Cho-fu-Sa," *chang feng sha,* can be translated literally and semantically, as Wai-Lim Yip and others have done, into "Long Wind Sand." Marjorie Perloff, in her recent essay on Pound as a nominalist, suggests insightfully that Pound prefers the more exotic "Cho-fu-Sa" to the plain "Long Wind Sand" because the former looks more like a proper name, and "proper names are part and parcel of Pound's Imagist, and later Vorticist doctrine, with its call for 'direct treatment of the thing' and the new method of 'luminous detail.'"[8] The same goes for another case in a *Cathay* poem, where Pound uses Ko-jin to translate a simple noun phrase, "old acquaintance":

> Ko-jin goes west from Ko-kaku-ro,
> The smoke-flowers are blurred over the river.[9]

For Perloff, such a use of foreign and foreignizing tags is not just a simultaneously authenticating and distancing device. Pound's preference for proper names, Perloff suggests, is really an indication of his nominalism, a doctrine that "denies the existence of abstract objects and universals . . . holding that all that really exists are particulars, usually physical objects."[10]

While agreeing with Perloff's interpretation, I want to add that Pound's nominalist work is achieved not just by converting words to icons or real visual objects, as we have often been taught to appreciate with regard to Pound's visual poetic matrix, but also, more importantly, by converting words to indices, to proper names as sound objects that are concrete, particular, and foreign.

It is important to remember that, in his tripartite system of signification — icon, index, and symbol — Charles Sanders Peirce includes the proper name in the category of the index, whose relation to the Dynamic Object, or the signified, is one of contiguity: an index is "a sign determined by its Dynamic Object by virtue of being in a real relation to it. Such is a Proper

Name . . . ; such is the occurrence of a symptom of a disease."[11] As indexes, proper names are words that are foreign to any language, because they are not semantically constrained by the internal sense relation of any language as symbols are.

The best example I can give is Richard Nixon's "the great Great Wall." When Nixon visited China in 1972, his Chinese host took him to see the Great Wall. The first thing Nixon said upon arrival was "What a great wall!" Once a proper name, "Great Wall" has lost its semantic constraints to be "great"; it can still be called the "Great Wall" even if it has become a small wall. Or someone whose last name is "Goodman" doesn't really have to be a good man at all. Or my last name "Huang," which in Chinese means yellow, doesn't really have to mean that I'm yellow, even though in this case I happen to be yellow, which oddly makes my name redundant. A word, insofar as it is valued as an arbitrary sign, depends on its context, which includes its syntactic contact with other words. But as a proper name, the word is freed from the conventional system of signification, from the demand of making sense in the same way as arbitrary signs do, and hence it becomes a foreign word, presentable in any language but belonging to none.[12]

If we look back at the two examples from Pound, "Cho-fu-Sa" and "Ko-jin," we can see or hear that homophonic translation has liberated the original Chinese words from their conventional obligations or relations to other Chinese words as arbitrary signs within a system of language, and it has enabled those words to point to the "things" that Pound — following his Imagist doctrine — wants to treat directly. By retaining the sound, a homophonically translated proper name creates the sense that a word can have a real relation to its dynamic object; our names, for example, are usually translated homophonically, irrespective of the languages or scripts the names originate from, making sound the most important part of a name. Native American names may be the only exceptions to the rule of homophonic translation. If my name were to be translated semantically, it would be something like "Yellow Special Luck."

Besides personal names, the other proper names that intrigue me are those of currencies, whose meanings are often local and yet whose translations currently constitute a major part of the global flow of meanings, values, and power. Money may be a universal language, but currencies speak vernaculars of their own. Curiously enough, currencies are usually named in their native tongues: dollar, pound, yuan, won, mark, franc, lira, ruble, peso, baht, and so on. We may change their graphic appearances when we transliterate them into English, but their sounds remain. It is as if we must have our own terms, with their sounds as measures, in order to understand, to come to terms with the world and its meaning. Besides being called by their vernacular sounds, monetary terms are often themselves related to sounds in their origin. When a currency is put in circulation, it is technically called "uttered." To utter, according to the *OED,* means "to give currency to; to put in circulation," as well as "to send forth as a sound; to speak, say, or pronounce."

Here I would like to return to Marco Polo, with whom I began this essay. Marco Polo, it turns out, was the first person to mention the use of paper money in China to the West, which caused quite a stir. In this famous part of his narrative, Polo describes the Khan as an alchemist, a conjuror, who causes his voice, his words to be equivalent to all the treasures in the world:

> The Emperor's Mint then is in this city of Cambaluc, and the way it is wrought is such that you might say he hath the Secret of Alchemy in perfection, and you would be right! For he makes his money after this fashion.
>
> He makes them take of the bark of a certain tree, in fact of the Mulberry Tree, the leaves of which are the food of the silkworms, — these trees being so numerous that whole districts are full of them. What they take is a certain fine white bast or skin which lies between the wood of the tree and the thick outer bark, and this they make into something resembling sheets of paper, but black. When these sheets have been prepared they are cut up into pieces of different sizes. The smallest of these sizes is worth a half tornesel; the next, a little larger, one tornesel; one, a little larger still, is worth half a silver groat of Venice; another a whole groat; others yet two groats, five groats, and ten groats. There is also a kind worth one Bezant of gold, and others of three Bezants, and so up to ten. All these pieces of paper are issued with as much solemnity and authority as if they were of pure gold or silver; and on every piece a variety of officials, whose duty it is, have to write their names, and to put their seals. And when all is prepared duly, the chief officer deputed by the Kaan smears the Seal entrusted to him with vermilion, and impresses it on the paper, so that the form of the Seal remains printed upon it in red; and Money is then authentic. Any one forging it would be punished with death. And the Kaan causes every year to be made such a vast quantity of this money, which costs him nothing, that it must equal in amount all the treasure in the world.[13]

The secret of the Khan's alchemy lies in the "as if" effect: "as if they [the pieces of paper] were of pure gold or silver." And the key to the success of the poetic conflation is to get rid of the "iffiness" and turn "as if" into "as."

The Khan becomes King Midas; his words, as deputed by his officials, change into gold when they fall onto sheets of paper. His voice is not just golden; it is as good as gold, or is gold.

What the Polo passage demonstrates is not only the sound origin of currency, a feature that would become increasingly important when we move into the twenty-first-century economy of the intangible, in which the economic landscape is shaped no longer by physical flows of material goods and products but by ethereal streams of data, images, and symbols. The passage also shows the localness of monetary imagination. It seems that unless Polo renders everything in Venetian terms, such as tornesels and groats, his European contemporaries would have no way of imagining what he has seen. Throughout his travelogue, Polo constantly asks his reader/listener to look at, or rather hear, things in terms of Venetian currency:

> First there is the salt, which brings in a great revenue. For it produces every year, in round numbers, fourscore tomans of gold; and the toman is worth 70,000 saggi of gold, so that the total value of the fourscore tomans will be five millions and six hundred thousand saggi of gold, each saggio being worth more than a gold florin or ducat.[14]

Or,

> In the mountains belonging to this city, rhubarb and ginger grow in great abundance; insomuch that you may get some 40 pounds of excellent fresh ginger for a Venice groat.[15]

Here we can almost hear the jingling of the moneyed mind of a cosmopolite, whispering in the ears of his listeners and enticing the locals to imagine a world of wonder in their own terms.

Here, we can also hear the sounding of the monetary origin of Pound's Confucian notion of "correct naming," we can understand that his dream of becoming "lord of his work and master of utterance" is also about the "utterance" of money, and finally we see the necessity of retaining the original foreign words in his poetry rather than "converting" them into English. As Pound insists, he has never used a foreign word where an English counterpart would do. Most likely it won't do because poetry may otherwise become a "Chinese whisper" translated from Persian or other languages.

TRANSLATING THE SOUND IN POETRY: SIX PROPOSITIONS / ROSMARIE WALDROP

1. Sound in poetry is not a simple phonetic matter. It cannot be separated from the semantic dimension. Even in everyday speech, the linguists tell us, the "same" sound is changed by the sense. For example, the onomatopoeia in "the little birds cheep" does not sound like the same phoneme in a pet store owner's statement that "the little birds are cheap." The famous parodies bring this home. It takes very little to turn Tennyson's euphonious "murmuring of innumerable bees" into the far from beautiful "murdering of innumerable beeves."

If different semantic contexts make us hear the same phonemes differently, poetry compounds this effect by poetic devices. We hear the word *splice* differently in a statement like "the splice after frame 39" and in the pun "the splice of life." And this holds also for rhythm: when A. E. Housman admired the "furies and the surges" of William Blake's rhythm in "Tyger, Tyger, burning bright / In the forests of the night," Pound countered with: "Tiger, Tiger, catch 'em quick! / All the little lambs are sick."[1] But in poetry it also works the other way round. A new cadence means a new idea, as Ezra Pound said. A string of words related by sound may make an argument stronger than logic. I will come back to this.

2. This means it is impossible to translate the sound in poetry because the union of sound/sense will not be the same in any other language.

3. From this it follows that translators are forced to separate what cannot be separated. Translators are forced to kill the original — and then to try to resurrect, to reproduce, recreate it.

It is possible to stay at this stage of separation — not totally, of course, but in terms of emphasis. If emphasis is put on the semantic dimension at the expense of sound and other formal features, we get a trot or the kind of version that Walter Benjamin has dismissed as "inaccurate transmission of an inessential content," for "what does a literary work 'say'?"[2]

The opposite possibility, privileging the sound over the meaning, can be delightful. Consider or better read out loud Ernst Jandl's "surface translation" of Wordsworth's "My heart leaps up when I behold":

> mai hart lieb zapfen eibe hold
> er renn bohr in sees kai
> so was sieht wenn mai läuft begehn
> so es sieht nahe emma mähn
> so bie wenn ärschel grollt
> ohr leck mit ei!
> seht steil dies fader rosse mähn
> in teig kurt wisch mai desto bier
> baum deutsche deutsch bajonett schur alp eiertier[3]

for:

> My heart leaps up when I behold
> A rainbow in the sky:
> So was it when my life began;
> So is it now I am a man;
> So be it when I shall grow old,
> Or let me die!
> The Child is father of the Man;
> And I could wish my days to be
> Bound each to each by natural piety.

It is not so delightful when the translator has a mechanical understanding of sound and form. We've all read translations of poems that boast of keeping rhyme and meter — and make it hard to believe the poem was worthwhile to start with.

4. But of course we want both sound and sense. And we have the example of Zukofsky's monumental *Catullus,* a grandiose experiment in trying to bring both sound and sense across at the same time, in exactly the same sequence. With some stunning successes ("miss her, Catullus" for *miser Catulle* . . . since that is what the poem is about) and much that misses another aspect of the sound/sense compound, namely, the tone of the original. I consider it a monument to be admired rather than an example to follow.

5. So, in practice, what's the poor translator to do? I would say the first step is to analyze what elements are dominant in a poem. If the sound is as primary as in Verlaine's "Il pleure dans mon coeur," you might as well despair. I have not found any version that can even approximate what Verlaine tellingly places under the title of "Romances sans paroles":

Il pleure dans mon coeur
Comme il pleut sur la ville
Quelle est cette langueur
Qui pénètre mon coeur?

O bruit doux de la pluie
Par terre et sur les toits!
Pour un coeur qui s'ennuie,
O le chant de la pluie!

Il pleure sans raison
Dans ce coeur qui s'écoeure.
Quoi! nulle trahison?
Ce deuil est sans raison.

C'est bien la pire peine
De ne savoir pourquoi,
Sans amour et sans haine,
Mon coeur a tant de peine.

The poem is almost sheer melody woven out of very few notes. It works by constant repetition, of the opening "statement" (with small variations), of whole words (especially the key word *heart*), and of sounds. It is the latter that is a problem for the translator.

In the first stanza one sound (rhyme plus half-rhyme) *pleure-coeur-pleut-langueur* knots together the rainy day with weeping, a heavy heart, a state of listlessness. *Coeur* recurs in every stanza. In stanza 3, it comes doubled (with grammatical variation: *ce coeur qui s'écoeure)* and intensifies the listlessness to disgust, dejection, discouragement. The repetition of the same sound makes for a monotonous, melancholy music that perfectly embodies the situation. In English, the key words have little sound in common, so their connection is less convincing. Moreover, the lines are very short. There are barely more words than the ones with the *eu*-sound. (Among those few, alliteration links *comme, quelle, qui* and, more importantly, links *pénètre* with *pleure* and *pleut.*) There is no leeway for the translator. It is not surprising that versions tend not to diverge wildly:

> Tears flow in my heart
> As rain falls on the town;
> What langor is this
> That creeps into my heart?[4]

> Tears in my heart
> Like rain on roofs.
> What pining is this
> That razes my heart?[5]

Both translators choose tears over weeping and play up the consonant *r* as the shared sound element of the key words. The second version has a better rhythm and also approaches the tightness of the French lines. But neither can approach the effect of the original.

But most poems are not as extreme. So it helps to analyze how sound is used and, more generally, what goes on in the poem and how this relates to its language and tradition. What Benjamin called its "mode of intention" and what I have called its genetic code.

Then, as a second step, try to do similar things — not necessarily in the same places but wherever you can. In other words: take as the unit of translation not the single word, not even the line, but the whole poem. This will make for a different poem because sound correspondences do establish semantic threads, but at least the overall effect is going to be somewhat similar to that of the original.

I am at the moment struggling with the German poet Ulf Stolterfoht, who often heaps up rhyming words in quick succession as a send-up of the convention of rhyme, just as he gets a regular beat going only to juxtapose it with very prosy lines. But he will also use rhyme differently, in a more traditional manner, to tie together sequences of words. For instance in *Fachsprachen* II, 6, he shows the expressionist painter and poet Otto Nebel painting in obedience to inner voices that also tell him to hang himself. The homophony *horchen gehorchen* (listen obey) in the third stanza is crucial for the poem. But, in addition, there is the sequence *zwang — drang — befehlsergang–hanf schlang,* where the rhyme gives extraordinary power to the connection of compulsion, urge, and eventual suicide by hanging. I could not establish these same connections but tried to heap up as many rhymes and half-rhymes as I could in this area:

ganz ohr zumal sie wohlverstanden
nie einer aussenwelt entstammten doch
das ist nachprüfbar erfolgten: "hier muss
ein gelb beschwichtigt werden" — hört er

und wird man später sagen: tuts. um got-
tes willen dann (bildblinden auges wegen
zwang) ein hellrot zu ermuntern kann
man in sachen schwarz auf weiss der

zugerauntheit sicher sein: er wird das grau
schon locken. horchen gehorchen drang
(— in worten: warten auf befehlsergang)
den hanf um die laternen schlang dem

es vergönnt war zu entöden . . . [6]

[all ears especially as they of course
never came from outside but still were
definitely heard as can be checked: "we
here need to appease a yellow" he hears

and later they say does it. for heaven's
sake then to encourage (with image-
blind compulsion) a bright red you may
in matters of black on white be sure of

inspiration: he'll lure the gray OK. to
listen to obey the urge (in words:
wait for commands to surge) to loop
the rope around the lantern and be

granted to unmope . . .]

    6. Last: there is no recipe. Each poem requires its own approach. No translation is definitive. Compare the versions by Paul Blackburn and W. D. Snodgrass of the first stanza of Guillaume IX's "Farai un vers de dreyt nien":

Farai un vers de dreyt nien
Non er de mi ni d'autre gen,
Non er d'amor ni de joven,
Ni de ren au,
Qu'en fo trobatz en durmen
Sobre chevau.
    (Guillaume de Poitou)

I shall make a vers about
nothing,
downright nothing, not
about myself or youth or love
or anyone.
I wrote it horseback dead asleep
while riding in the sun.[7]
    (Paul Blackburn)

Sheer nothing's all I'm singing of:
Not me and no one else, of course;
There's not one word of youth and love
Nor anything;
I thought this up, once, on my horse
While slumbering.[8]
    (W. D. Snodgrass)

Snodgrass decided the most important factor is that the poem is a song — a song whose original tune is actually preserved. Hence he paid careful attention to the rhythm and the structure so that his version could be sung to that original tune. Blackburn, on the contrary, pays little attention to the sound except for one rhyme. He does not even pay attention to the anaphoric "not — not — nor." Yet his version is lively and has its own charm. You may prefer one or the other. It is good to have both.

"ENSEMBLE DISCORDS": TRANSLATING THE MUSIC OF MAURICE SCÈVE'S *DÉLIE* / RICHARD SIEBURTH

As John Hollander observes in his classic study, *The Untuning of the Sky: Ideas of Music in English Poetry, 1500–1700,* for nearly a millennium Boethius's *De institutione musica* set the terms for the Western imagination of music. This sixth-century treatise influentially divided music into three parts: *musica mundana, musica humana,* and *musica instrumentalis.* By *musica mundana* Boethius intended the overall harmony of the universe, ultimately grounded in the Pythagorean music of the spheres but also perceptible (or rather, intelligible) in the cosmological order of elements, astral bodies, and seasons. Boethius in turn described *musica humana* as "that which unites the incorporeal activity of the reason with the body ... a certain mutual adaptation and as it were a tempering of high and low sounds into a single consonance" — with the crucial notion of "temperament," as Hollander points out, here referring not only to the tuning of strings but to the proportionate tempering of the various parts of the human whole (body and soul, thought and feeling, etc.). Boethius's third category, *musica instrumentalis,* refers to what Hollander terms "practical" (as opposed to "speculative") music, that is, the actual singing or playing of music (flute, lyre, harp, or, as we move into the Renaissance, viol or lute).[1] In the following pages, I would like to briefly address the music of Maurice Scève's *Délie* (and the possibilities of its translation) in terms of this tripartite Boethian model, still very influential in mid-sixteenth-century Lyon through its more recent reformulation by Ficino.[2]

Composed of 449 *dizains* interspersed with fifty emblematic woodcuts, the *Délie* is commonly acknowledged to be the first illustrated *canzoniere* of its kind. Unlike Petrarch's *Rime sparse* whose "vario stile" included sonnets, ballads, and sestinas, Scève's lyric sequence of 1544 is devoted to the manic (depressive) hammering home of a single chord 449 times in succession, each of its *dizains* composed of ten lines of ten syllables and each observing the identical claustrophobic rhyme scheme: *ababbccdcd*. A first challenge to the translator: how to maintain what John Ashbery has called the "fruitful monotony" of this kind of grid composition while at the same time allowing for all its minute variations and overtones?[3] Or: how, within the compact ambit of each of these ten-by-ten matrices, produce a *harmonia* that would be faithful both to the original Greek meaning of the term (that is, the ratios of scales or horizontal melodic schemata taking place in time) and to its more modern polyphonic developments (that is, the blending of simultaneously sounding musical tones in a vertical all-at-onceness)?[4] Given the importance of the visual emblems to the overall rhythm of the *Délie*, these two kinds of harmonies — the temporal and the spatial — also inform the ways in which the text speaks both to the reader's (or lover's) eye and to his ear, for Délie, the obscure object of desire, is experienced throughout the sequence both melodically and chordally, that is, both as a gradual disclosure of fetishized partial objects and as a kind of sudden and overwhelming *jouissance* that strikes her lover blind or dumb.

True to Boethius's tripartite schema, the microcosm of the lover's *musica humana* in the *Délie* (i.e., the whole agon of inarticulate sobs, sighs, cries, and "silentes clameurs" that constitutes the ground tone of Scèvian song) is frequently situated vis-à-vis the *musica mundana* of the macrocosm. Délie, "Object de plus haulte vertu" (as she is described in the subtitle), may be an anagrammatic embodiment of the Platonic *Idée* (like Samuel Daniel's *Delia*), but she is also, as the following *dizain* rather programmatically declares, a mythical sky goddess and cosmic instance of the interdependence of eros and thanatos, day and night. Bearing within her name the solar radiance of the Delian Apollo, she is also his sister Diana, goddess of the moon and — in her more archaic Greek guises — Artemis the virgin huntress, Hecate the witch, and Persephone, queen of the underworld:

Comme Hecaté tu me feras errer
Et vif, & mort cent ans parmy les Vmbres:
Comme Diane au Ciel me resserer,
D'ou descendis en ces mortelz encombres:
Comme regnante aux infernalles vmbres
Amoindriras, ou accroitiras mes peines.
　　Mais comme Lune infuse dans mes veines

Celle tu fus, es, & seras DELIE,
Qu'Amour à ioinct a mes pensées vaines
Si fort, que Mort iamais ne l'en deslie.

[As Hecate, you will doom me to wander
Among the Shades, alive & dead a hundred years:
As Diana, you will confine me to the Sky
Whence you descended to this vale of tears:
As Queen of Hell in your dark domain,
You will increase or diminish my pains.
   But as Moon infused into my veins,
You were, & are, & shall be DELIE,
So knotted by Love to my idle thoughts
That Death itself could never untie us.]
      (D 22)⁵

How translate the overtones of proper names? In the original, lines 8 and
10 wittily exploit the homophony of the name DELIE and the verb *deslie*
(here rhymed as "untie"). *Lier* in turn derives from the Latin *ligare* (to bind
or gather, as in *religio,* the bond between man and gods) — which provides
one of the most crucial vocables in the entire work, namely, the word *lien*
(not unrelated to the city of *Lyon,* another metonym of Délie), at once the
bitter bondage that sadomasochistically links master to slave and the musical legato that provides the sweetest ligature of love. Given the paranomas-
tic poetics of the *Délie* — where letters, words, and semes continuously tie
and untie themselves into different knots — the verb *délier* can occasion a
veritable anagrammatic *délire,* a hermeneutic delirium in which reading, like
dreamwork, forever unravels into a mis- or dis-reading (*dé-lire*) that is never
far from . . . translation.⁶

The masculine subject in the above-quoted dizain plays a rather passive
role vis-à-vis the all-powerful cosmic object of his desires. As the unquiet
shade of an unburied body, he is condemned by Hecate to wander — still
"alive," not yet fully "dead" — through the underworld for a Platonic century
before he can reach the place of eternal rest. Or, like the hunter Orion who
offended Artemis/Diana, he has been "confined" or "restrained" to the sky
in the shape of a constellation, condemned to revolve endlessly through the
heavens. And finally, like the sick man under the influence of the moon, his

fevers merely increase or decrease according to her waxings or wanings. The medical metaphor is made even more explicit in D 383:[7]

> Plus croit la Lune, & ses cornes r'enforce,
> Plus allegeante est le febricitant:
> Plus s'amoindrit diminuant sa force,
> Plus l'affoiblit, son mal luy suscitant.
> [The more the Moon waxes, & extends her horns,
> The more she soothes the sick man's ague:
> The more she wanes, & loses force,
> The more he ails, & wastes away.]

As one can hear, the anaphoric "plus ... plus" ("the more ... the more," with the caesura falling after the fourth syllable in both the French and the English) serves to establish the rhythmic and causal link (or *lien*) between the *musica mundana* of the phases of the moon and the *musica humana* of unruly temperatures. The period between the recurrences of this kind of intermittent fever was called an "interval" during the Renaissance. This space in between, this respite from pain, this caesura, provides a duration of time — ranging from the shortest of moments to the longest of years — in which the sufferer is promised (erroneously it turns out) some sort of solace:

> O ans, ô moys, sepmaines, iours, & heures
> O *interualle,* ô minute, ô moment,
> Qui consumez les durtez, voire seures ...
>
> [O years, O months, weeks, days & hours,
> O *intervals,* O minutes, O moments
> Who swallow up the pain, however sour ...]
>   (D 114)

This conception of time as made up of series of salvific gaps (or feast days, as in the *intervalle* defined by Cotgrave's dictionary as "the flesh-daies between Christmas and Ashwednesday") in turn prepares for the more musical definition of the term *interval* — the distance separating two sounds in harmony or in melody — that is beginning to make its way into French via the Italian around the time that Scève publishes the *Délie.*[8] This new usage makes it possible to read the "interval" of the dizain below as referring not only to the measurement of geographical features but to the more traditional figure of the *musica mundana*. Here the challenge to the translator was how rhythmically to convey Scève's condensation of the whirling *energeia* of an entire Renaissance *mappemonde* into the microcosm of a mere hundred syllables — even if the artful ligature of the *e muet* across the comma gap following the fourth syllable of line 5 ("intervalle, ô") proved impossible to reproduce:

> De toute Mer tout long, & large espace,
> De terre aussi tout tournoyant circuit
> Des Montz tout terme en forme haulte, & basse,
> Tout lieu distant, du iour et de la nuict,
> Tout *interualle,* ô qui par trop me nuyt,
> Sera rempliz de doulce rigueur.
> > Ainsi passant des Siecles la longeur,
> Surmonteras la haulteur des Estoilles
> Par ton sainct nom, qui vif en ma langueur
> Pourra par tout nager a plaines voiles.

> [Every long, & wide expanse of Sea,
> Every whirling tract of solid land,
> Every Mountain ridge both low, & high,
> Every distant site of day, & night,
> Every *interval,* O you who unsettle me,
> Will be filled by your sweet severity.
> > Thus surpassing the spans of Time,
> You will climb beyond the spheres of Stars,
> Your sacred name, sped by my misery,
> Traversing all creation at full sail.]
> > (D 259)

These are but a few examples of how Scève attunes the music of the spheres to the private tempers of the scorned lover's febrile body and soul. Boethius's third category of music, *musica instrumentalis,* makes itself felt less through the occasional references to lyre or lute (in D 158, D 316, D 344) than through the traditional wordplay (which Hollander informs us goes back to Cassidorus) on the possible homophonic confusion between the Latin *chorda* (string or catgut*)* and *cor, cordis* (heart) — which gives us the expression "heartstrings."[9] As the concordance to the *Délie* reveals, Scève's *canzoniere* contains a relatively high incidence of the terms *accordes* (2), *accordz* (5), *discord* (1), *discords* (1), *discordz* (3), *concordes* (1) and *cordes* (2), all resonating within (and against) the sounds of two of the most frequent words in the book, *Coeur/coeurs* (114) and *corps* (59).[10] In D 376, the dizain moves from an initial "Corps" to a terminal "discords" (or "dis-corps"?) as the lover, no longer an infernal shade doomed to errancy by Hecate, now becomes the "shadow" of the body of the beloved, a male moon reflective of the dark light of his female sun. The suggestion of celestial bodies, in any event, encouraged me to (liberally) translate "En me mouant au doulx contournement / De tous tes faictz" as "As you move me to assume my orbit / Around all you do or say" — with the rotations of this *musica munda* in turn leading me to register the final "discords" not simply as "discordant" (etymologically from *dis + cor,* apart + heart) but rather as the more explicitly musical "out of tune" (*dis + chorda*):

Tu es le Corps, Dame, & ie suis ton vmbre,
Qui en ce mien continuel silence
Me fais mouuoir, non comme Hecate l'Vmbre,
Par ennuieuse, & grande violence,
Mais par pouoir de ta haulte excellence,
En me mouant au doulx contournement
De tous tes faictz, & plus soubdainement,
Que lon ne veoit l'vmbre suyure le corps,
Fors que ie sens trop inhumainement
Noz sainctz vouloirs estre ensemble discords.

[You are the Body, & I your shadow, lady,
In my abiding silence, you govern
My motion, not as Hecate holds sway
Over the Shades by violence, & disarray,
But by the attraction of your excellence,
As you move me to assume my orbit
Around all you do or say, far swifter
Than a shadow chasing after its body,
Were it not for something inhuman
When our two wills fall out of tune.]
        (D 376)

Behind the oxymoronic "ensemble discords" of the last line of this poem lies the rich tradition of *concordia discors* — the term Horace used to describe Empedocles' vision of a world shaped by the perpetual strife between the four elements, yet ordered by love into a higher "discordant harmony." The *concordia discors* trope, as many scholars have argued, is fundamental to Scève's poetics; it is most succinctly stated in book 2 of his *Microcosme:* "Musique, accent des cieux, plaisante symfonie / Par contraires aspects formant son harmonie."[11] Scève's deployment of the topos in the above dizain is far more bitter, however, for the beloved's indifference or willfulness produces not the ultimate harmony or "symfonie" of *musica humana,* but a note "trop inhumainement" jarring to the poet's well-being — "something inhuman / When our two wills fall out of tune."

D 344, "Leuth resonnant, & le doulx son des cordes," the sole dizain in the collection that actually mentions a lute — even though seven poems of the *Délie* were set to music during Scève's lifetime — provides one of the most achieved examples of Scève's wryly ironic music of discordance.[12] This lyric has often been compared to Louise Labé's celebrated sonnet 12, "Lut, compagnon de ma calamité" — the authenticity of which, however, has been recently cast into doubt by Mireille Huchon, who argues that the work of La Belle Cordière was mostly written by Scève and his circle of male poet friends.[13] In Labé's sonnet (so its witty conceit runs), the lute has been not only her faithful "companion" in calamity but also the "témoin irreprochable" (irreproachable witness) of all of her sighs and the "controlleur véritable" (accurate accountant or secretary) of all her sorrows. But the problem is: so often has the lute accompanied her in her complaints, so deeply has it been touched by her piteous tears that even should she try to make some sort of more pleasing noise ("quelque son delectable"), the instrument, grown so accustomed to her sad songs, simply renders back all her joys as laments: "Et si te veus efforcer au contraire, / Tu te destens & si me contreins taire." Or to paraphrase: no matter how I try to force you to play otherwise (i.e., to respond to my joy), you come unstrung and reduce me to silence. Here is Labé's sonnet 12, followed by my English accounting of it:

> Lut, compagnon de ma calamité
> De mes soupirs témoin irreprochable,
> De mes ennuis controlleur veritable,
> Tu as souvent avec moi lamenté:
>
> Et tant le pleur piteus t'a molesté,
> Que commençant quelque son delectable,

Tu le rendois tout soudein lamentable,
Feingnant le ton que plein avoit chanté.[14]

Et si te veus efforcer au contraire,
Tu te destens et si me contreins taire:
Mais me voyant tendrement soupirer,

Donnant faveur a ma tant triste pleinte:
En mes ennuis me plaire suis contreinte,
Et d'un dous mal douce fin esperer.

[Lute, my companion in calamity,
Irreproachable witness of my sighs,
Faithful accountant of all my cries,
How often have you grieved with me:

My piteous tears have left you so undone
That should some sweet sound be meant
You quickly turn it back into a lament,
As if the same old song had again begun.

And if I want you to sing a different tune,
You come unstrung and strike me dumb:
But seeing all the tender sighs that I expend,

You indulge me in my sad complaint:
To pleasure in pain am I thus constrained,
Hoping grief this sweet shall meet a sweet end.]

This discordance between performer and instrument, between the lyric
"I" and the conventions of the poetry of complaint to which it must submit — a theme also treated by Wyatt's nearly contemporaneous "Blame not
my lute" — is brilliantly explored in Scève's D 344, a brief companion piece
to Labé's sonnet that again turns on the crucial wordplay of *cordes, accordes,*
and *accordz:*[15]

Leuth resonnant, & le doulx son des cordes,
Et le concent de mon affection,
Comment ensemble vnyment tu accordes
Ton harmonie auec ma passion!

The initial apostrophe to the lute delicately attunes the vibrating sibilance of the *s*'s to the more guttural pluckings of the hard *c*'s, both of which resonate across the nasalized sequence of vowelings. The caesurae within each line establish a slight pause, allowing for internal rhyme (resonant / concent / Comment / vniment) to play itself off against the alternating masculine and feminine endings of the lines. The diereses, which extend the Latinate rhyme words by a syllable (*affec-ti-on, pass-i-on, occupa-ti-on*), add a further vibratory duration to these plucked strings.[16] As in Labé's sonnet, however, this initial statement of harmony, wherein the lute seems to act in unanimous concert with the poet's own passion, swiftly gives way (by a transitional "lors" that echoes "cordes" and "accordes") to its opposite:

> Lors que ie suis sans occupation
> Si viuement l'esprit tu m'exercites,
> Qu'ores a ioye, ore a dueil tu m'incites
> Par tes accorz, non aux miens ressemblantz.

The symmetrical syntax of line 7 ("ores a ioye, ore a dueil") underscores a typically Scèvian moment of cyclothimia (now joy, now grief) — here incited, paradoxically, by the chords/strings of the lute that leave him no respite in his "unoccupied" state of even-temperedness or equanimity and instead "excite" his spirits into discord. One more turn (via a crucial "car"), and the end of the poem screws down like a vise: "Car plus, que moy, mes maulx tu luy recites, / Correspondant a mes souspirs tremblantz." The soft *s*'s and hard *c*'s of the opening lines here return, but they voice a significant reversal of the initial situation. If at the outset of the poem the lute's "harmony" was in unanimous "accord" with the speaker's "passion," here the instrument (or again, the poetic genre of complaint itself) seems to betray the poet — precisely because of its articulateness (that is, its capacity to "recite" his pains to his lady) and its mellifluousness, to which the deep, sincere *alogos* of his own "souspirs tremblantz" (trembling sighs) proves capable only of a distant "correspondance."[17]

Of the following English translation of this dizain I can only say that like the lute (or lover) in both Labé's and Scève's poems, it tries to provide companionship to the original, aware that its acts of faithful witnessing or accurate observation will inevitably -cause it to waver between harmonious accord and outright dissonance. Like the unresembling "accorz" of Scève's D 344, the "discord" of a translation vis-à-vis its original almost always lies in the various ways in which it is forced to become more explicit, more articulate, more "clear" (and more disincarnate) than the trembling sighs it tries to body forth in another language — even if it manages (as here below) to provide a "sympathic vibration" in response to the original's rhyme scheme, the patterns of its caesurae, and the swift skitter of its tetrameters:[18]

> Resounding lute, & sweet pluck of strings,
> And the concert of my affection,
> How you accord into a single song
> Your harmony and my passion!
>   Yet when I am without occupation,
> You put my mind through so many paces
> That from joy to sorrow it now races
> In your chords, so unresembling mine.
>   For you speak to her with such graces
> Of the pain I only tremble forth in sighs.

D 17, the final dizain I would like to address in this quick survey of Scèvian musics — be they *mundana, humana,* or *instrumentalis* — is a lyric that ecstatically celebrates the *harmonia* that obtains between the poet and his beloved. Although the precise term *harmonie* (used on several occasions in the *Délie)* does not occur here, it is nonetheless present through the double negative of line 4, "Qu'auec nous aulcun discord s'assemble" (literally, "than no discord assemble itself among [or between] the two of us") — which, seeking to foreground the theme of "sympathic vibration" that runs throughout the *canzoniere,* I have translated as "Than any discord throw us out of tune." Like the anaphoric "plus . . . plus" of D 383 previously discussed, this dizain is governed by a similar trope based in the mathematical (or musical) notion of proportion, here expressed through the temporal figure (repeated three times) of "plus tost . . . que" — an adynaton that expresses the counter-factual condition of *impossibilia* (e.g., before our love could change, the unthinkable would have to happen). Whereas in the previous poems we have examined, the *musica humana* composed by the two lovers was often related "sym-phonically" to the *musica mundana* (or what Scève sometimes calls "l'Angelique harmonie") made by the turnings of celestial bodies (earth, sun, moon, constellations), here he fuses an implicit allegory of cosmic harmony with the literal features of the landscape around Lyons — the river Rhône roiling down from the Alps and flowing into the more placid waters of the

Saône while the two large hills Mont Fourvière and Mont de la Croix-Rousse overlook this convergence from on high:

> Plus tost seront Rhosne, & Saone desoinctz
>
> Que d'auec toy mon Coeur se desassemble:
>
> Plus tost serons l'vn, & l'aultre Mont ionctz,
>
> Qu'auecques nous aulcun discord s'assemble:
>
> Plus tost verrons & toy, & moy ensemble
>
> Le Rhosne aller contremont lentement,
>
> Saone monter tresuiolentement,
>
> Que ce mien feu, tant soit peu, diminue,
>
> Ny que ma foy descroisse aulcunement.
>
> Car ferme amour sans eulx est plus, que nue.

This is a poem of conjunctions and disjunctions, of gatherings and dispersals, as played out in the rich rhymes of the first five lines: "desoinctz," "ionctz," "desassemble," "s'assemble" "ensemble." As Gérard Defaux points out in his recent edition of the *Délie,* Scève lifts all these rhymes directly from a poem by his master, Clément Marot, who here, at the concrete level of *sound,* plays the Rhône that flows into Scève's Saône just as much as does Petrarch — whose *Rime,* 208 popularized the *figura etymologica* of *Rhodanus rodens,* "Rapido fiume, che d'alpestra vena / rodendo intorno (onde 'l tuo nome prendi)" (Swift river, from your Alpine spring gnawing a way for yourself, whence you take your name), which Scève in turn translates in D 417, "Fleuve rongeant pour t'attiltrer le nom / De la roideur en ton cours dangereuse."[19] The dramatic confluence of the Rhône (male, violently "gnawing" its course down from the Alps) and the Saône (peacefully female) at Lyons does not merely provide Scève with a metaphor for erotic harmony but also, given the explicit intertextual echoes that resound through this poem, allows him to locate his own Lyonese *Délie* as the intersection where his great precursors, Petrarch and Marot, receive their most achieved *translatio.*

Translation, like love (or music) — as I have been trying to suggest with Scève — involves being apart together, mutually ingathered by an interval or caesura that, as he puts it in D 376, renders us "ensemble discords." One of the particular typographical features of the original 1544 printing of the *Délie* that I was anxious to maintain in my edition was the productive dissonance of its spelling and its pronunciation — that is, the disjunction between how Scève's words *look* on the page and how they *sound* (even though, like so much poetry from the distant past, it may be well-nigh impossible to ac-

curately reconstruct its actual music — veni, vidi, vici or weni, widi, wiki?).
In D 17 and elsewhere, the rivers Rhosne and Saone (as Scève spells them,
though I use the modern French spellings Rhône and Saône in my translation) indeed chime perfectly to the ear, even if they do not exactly rhyme
to the eye. This disparity — this *différance?* — between pronunciation and
orthography opens a gap, an aporia, in which the temporality of the proper
name — its history, its etymology — makes itself felt. Thus the *s* in Scève's
"Rhosne" becomes a placeholder for the river's evolution from its Latin Rhodanus into Renaissance French, just as the circumflex on the modern Saône
roofs over its Latin onomastic origins as the river Segona or Saucona — all
these consonants and syllables that have been lost in the course of the etymological riverrun now contracted into the rich vowely O's of RhOWne and
SOWne, so clearly audible when the two enter into rhyme at Lyons and then
flow south together where they eventually spill into the Mediterranean Sea
in a final *Liebestod:*

> N'apperçoy tu de l'occident le Rhosne
> Se destourner, & vers Midy courir,
> Pour seulement se conioindre a sa Saone
> Iusqu'a leur Mer, ou tous deux vont mourir?
> (D 346)

In my English version, I have tried to capture the *concordia discors* of Rhosne/
Saone by avoiding the obvious end rhymes and instead displacing them to the
inside of the line ("Don't you *see*," "From the *east*," "And die in their *sea*").
I then close the dizain with a purely anagrammatical eye rhyme (Saône /
as one):

> Don't you see the Rhône turn
> From the East, & rush South,
> To conjoin with its Saône
> And die in their Sea as one?

To conclude, I would like to call attention to a further typographical feature of the original printing of Scève's *Délie,* a feature that only I. D. Mac-
Farlane's 1966 edition of the poem retains but that every single subsequent
French edition (including Defaux's) omits — namely, Scève's eloquent use of
the ampersand (which is "normalized" into an *et* by all of his French editors).
To return to D 7, here is how the harmony between the Rhône and Saône is
typographically expressed: "Plus tost seront Rhosne, & Saone desioinctz."

This pattern of disjunctive conjugation, which involves two terms at once linked by an ampersand yet separated by a comma, is repeated two more times in the poem (with the same interplay of a metrical caesura after the fourth syllable and an optical blink of the eye after the fifth or sixth): "Plus tost seront | l'vn, & l'aultre Mont ionctz. . . . Plus tost verrons | & toy, & moy ensemble." In adopting this rather idiosyncratic form of punctuation — "*x* comma and *y*," or "both *x* comma and *y*" — Scève (or his printer in Sulpice Sabon's shop) was following the rules laid down by yet another of his mentors, the humanist, publisher, and translator Etienne Dolet. Dolet published his treatise on punctuation, *De la ponctuation de la langue Francoyse,* as part of his *La maniere de bien traduire d'une langue en aultre* in Lyons in 1540, four years before Scève's *Délie.*[20] It is perhaps no accident that it took a *traducteur* of Dolet's eminence to understand that the minute visual and rhythmic interval defined by the tmetic comma preceding an ampersand provides a perfect *punctum* for the music of Scève's poetry and . . . its translation:

> Rhône, & Saône shall sooner be disjoined
> Than my heart tear itself away from you:
> The two Mounts shall sooner be conjoined
> Than any discord throw us out of tune:
> Together, we shall sooner see, I, & you,
> The Rhône tarry, & reverse its course,
> The Saône roil, & return to source
> Than this my fire ever die down
> Or my fidelity ever lose its force.
> True love, without these, is but a cloud.

THE POETRY OF PROSE, THE UNYIELDING OF SOUND / GORDANA P. CRNKOVIĆ

I can still remember the first time I read Emily Dickinson's "Because I could not stop for Death" in the original English.[1] Until that time, I knew it only in translation into my native Croatian — a translation that curiously transforms the original. To mention only a few variants in the first few lines: the word "death" (*smrt*) is a feminine noun in Croatian, so a translation could not preserve the masculine gender of Death in the original and the relationship between I (a woman wearing a gossamer gown) and He (the gentlemanly Death).[2] Consequently Death became a "moment of Death," "moment" (*trenutak*) being a masculine noun, and "I could not stop" became "I did not have time to stop," thus transforming the relationship between "I" and "he" of the original. The brisk iambic meter of Dickinson's verse, hard to imitate in the language of translation, got replaced with a dactyl-based rhythm, resulting in a much slower pace. Possibly in order to reduce the prolixity of the Croatian version, the translators chose one-word past tenses (aorist and imperfect) over two-word ones (perfect) and also dropped the personal pronoun "I" from the first verse, because the verbal form itself indicates the first person. But then the aorist and imperfect cause a slower rhythm themselves on account of their being archaic, and the erasure of "I" leads to the loss of emphasis stating that it is only I in this relationship with Death, not anyone else ("The Carriage held but just Ourselves — // And Immortality"). And so on.

In the case of poetry, we accept such challenges: no translation, we know, can approximate the texture and substance of a Dickinson lyric. In the case of prose, however, specifically contemporary prose fiction, it is generally assumed that the translation is the novel. Indeed, Eastern European fiction is known in the anglophone world almost exclusively in translation. Readers of such writers as Danilo Kiš, for example, rarely question the adequacy of the translations themselves. In this essay, accordingly, I want to put before my anglophone readers the difficulties that occur when the poetic prose of the modern Yugoslav novel is rendered in English. My example is Meša Selimović's celebrated novel *Derviš i smrt,* first translated for Northwestern University Press by Bogdan Rakić and Stephen M. Dickey, under the title *Death and the Dervish,* exactly thirty years after its original appearance in 1966.

The novel was published in Sarajevo, Yugoslavia, in the language that was then officially called *srpsko-hrvatski* and *hrvatsko-srpski* (Serbo-Croatian and Croato-Serbian).[3] Set in premodern Bosnia, then part of the Ottoman Empire, and written in first-person narrative, the novel is a chronicle of events intimately related to the narrator, a dervish named Ahmed Nuruddin of the Islamic Mevlevi order, and of his subjective and material responses to these events. The politically motivated murder of his brother causes the dervish to act — reluctantly, without knowing how, and in different ways — starting a chain of events that will lead to the deaths of those responsible for his brother's death and also, ultimately, to his own.

The novel engages in a complex dialogue with, among other things, the contemporary moment of Yugoslav socialism and with the Koran. Self-identified as a direct speech from God, the Koran is famed for the beauty of its language. *Dervish and Death*'s own lasting popularity, despite the narrative and temporal complexity and the pervasiveness of subjective states over any externalized action, may itself be largely attributed to the specific intensity and force of the novel's language. It is as if *Dervish and Death* takes up the implicit challenge of the Koran and creates a language of a human, mortal individual that is both the language of prose and the language of poetry, with such presence of sound that it makes the reader return to parts of the text over and over again.

Brought about by intense sound patterning, the "incomprehensibility" of language (as only referential, literal) works in different ways. I want here to look more closely into the translation of the two ways in which sound and meaning relate; first, into the "says more" dynamic, and second, into the "goes against" dynamic, where the sound seems to go squarely against the semantic meaning of the text. I am taking the 1996 Rakić-Dickey translation as a springboard for this discussion.[4] This translation is to be commended for its willingness to engage with an extremely difficult text in order to bring this text to English-language readers for the first time. I will attempt to show, however, the ways in which this translation of prose as mostly "only prose" — rather than as (also) poetry — may miss the sound-related aspects of text. Critics have pointed out the "poetic" aspects of *Dervish and Death*, and Henry R. Cooper Jr.'s introduction to this translation notes "the prose's rhythmicity, its repetitions, its similes becoming metaphors" and also brings up Thomas Butler, who has elaborated on this issue.[5] The poetic aspect of the novel is thus mentioned in the critical text accompanying this translation, but the awareness of what all this entails is often not sufficiently present in the translation itself.[6]

The "More" of Poetry

Dervish and Death opens with this stanza:

> Bismilâhir — rahmanir — rahim!
> I call to witness the ink, the quill, and the script,
> which flows from the quill;
> I call to witness the faltering shadows of the sinking evening,
> the night and all she enlivens;
> I call to witness the moon when she waxes, and the sunrise
> when it dawns.
> I call to witness the Resurrection Day and the soul
> that accuses itself;
> I call to witness time, the beginning and end
> of all things — to witness that every man always suffers loss.[7]

Although the original has an author's footnote that states that these verses are "from the Koran," this passage is actually a montage of sometimes substantially altered verses from various chapters of the Koran. The alteration of the Koran and the forceful assertion of a human, poetic "I" within and with a divine text at the very outset of the novel send a potent and complex signal to the reader. Among other things: by starting the novel with the "Basmala" phrase (meaning "in the name of God, the Merciful, the Compassionate"), which starts all but one chapter (*sura*) of the Koran, the text calls for the reader's undivided supreme attention, the attention that is given to a sacred text.[8] Second, this beginning stanza invokes the sound of a gathering in a collective prayer, of the oral (sounds of the Koran) as communal. Through the invocation of the Koran, a reader is transported to a place where words are more heard than seen, and the stage is set for a reading that is oral as much as or more than visual, and — as oral — social, foundational, and archaic.[9] The writing — or the speech — of an individual challenges the authoritative communal text and speech, by itself claiming the space of orality as the space of the social. Third, the whole "citation" also announces a text that may be related to this citation not only through its semantics but also through its form and above all its sound, a text that itself may in some ways be poetic.

With this tuning up of the ear, the prose of the novel opens with this sentence, given first in its original language and then in translation:

> Počinjem ovu svoju priču, nizašto, bez koristi za sebe i za druge, iz potrebe koja je jača od koristi i razuma, da ostane zapis moj o meni, zapisana muka razgovora sa sobom, s dalekom nadom da će se naći neko rješenje kad bude račun sveden, ako bude, kad ostavim trag mastila na ovoj hartiji što čeka kao izazov. (9)

The above is translated as:

> I begin my story for nothing, without benefit for myself or anyone else, from a need stronger than benefit or reason. I must leave a record of myself, the chronicled anguish of my inner conversations, in the vague hope that a solution will be found when all accounts have been settled (if they may ever be), when I have left my trail of ink on this paper, which lies in front of me like a challenge. (3)

One long original sentence is broken into two in the translation, setting the pattern for the translation of the whole opening paragraph of the novel: the original five sentences are translated into nine, or almost double the original number. In addition, the patterns of sound that create a strong rhythm, and could warrant writing this sentence in verse rather than prose, are only partially preserved (as shown below). The sound of the original sentence, and the main impact of this sound, is compromised and diminished, affecting, in turn, the whole pragmatic function or "practice" of this sentence.

The original sentence is broken down with commas or else with short prepositions (e.g., *bez* [without], *iz* [from]), with the resulting units that can be seen as verses. Here is again the original formatted as verse.

1   Počinjem ovu svoju priču,
2   nizašto,
3   bez koristi za sebe i za druge,
4   iz potrebe koja je jača
5   od koristi i razuma,
6   da ostane zapis moj o meni,
7   zapisana muka razgovora

8   sa sobom,
9   s dalekom nadom
10   da će se naći neko rješenje
11   kad bude račun sveden,
12   ako bude,
13   kad ostavim trag mastila
14   na ovoj hartiji
15   što čeka kao izazov.

The sentence starts with the word *počinjem* (I begin), which repeats the first syllable (*po*) of the five-times-repeated refrain of the preceding Koran-based stanza (*pozivam* [I call]), the *o-i* pattern (*pozivam, počinjem*), the ending *m*, and the metric foot of that word (*pozivam* and *počinjem* are both dactyls <macron breve breve>). This echoing of the two words functions as a sub-conscious signal to the reader: following the Koran-based verses that all start with *pozivam*, one would tend to read and hear the beginning prose sentence of the novel, opening with a very similar *počinjem*, in a like manner, carrying on the poetic reading from the preceding stanza into this prose and noticing the sound with increased attention.

The original sentence can be heard as a stanza with verses of loosely similar length, with most of them having seven to ten syllables, punctuated with a few shorter ones (*nizašto, sa sobom, ako bude,* with three or four syllables) that give more surrounding silence and thus more emphasis to the words spoken through them: *nizašto* (for nothing), *sa sobom* ("with oneself," here meaning "with myself"), *ako bude* (if it will have been [that way]). The sentence is full of not only repetitions of whole words (*koristi — koristi, za — za, zapis — zapis[ana], bude — bude, kad — kad*), but also al-literations based on replications of beginning consonants or whole syllables (*počinjem — priču — potrebe, razuma — razgovora — račun, da — dalekom — da, nadom — naći — neko, moj — meni — muka*), coupled with the almost constant repetition of stress on these mutually echoing first syllables. All these reiterations create a clear sound pattern that progresses from looser to denser, picking up the speed of the stanza: the repetitions in verses 1 and 4 (*počinjem, potrebe*) and alternate verses 3 and 5 (*koristi, koristi*) and 5 and 7 (*razuma, razgovora*) are complemented — and the rhythm made faster — with repeti-tions in successive verses, which start in verses 6 and 7 (*zapis — zapisana, moj — meni — muka*) and appear again in 9 and 10 (*dalekom — da, nadom — naći — neko*), with verses 11, 12, and 13 having reiterations in both alternating and successive verses (*kad — kad* in 11 and 13, *bude — bude* in 11 and 12). The movement of the sound gets faster toward the end, the sound denser, and then the last two lines, suddenly much more "unhinged" and different from the sounds that preceded them, enact an abrupt stop to this flow, with the final consonant *v* of *izazov* (challenge) curtly cutting off the flow of the vowels that end all but three of the preceding verses. There is a *na* (on) in this couplet, which echoes the previous ones, and *kao* (like) that sounds similar to the two close instances of *kad* (when), but "on this paper // that waits like a challenge" altogether opposes rather than continues the previous flow of the sounds, with "na ovoj hartiji // što čeka kao izazov" really sounding like a challenge, not just saying it.

It may be impossible to recreate in English translation "that intended effect upon the language," as Walter Benjamin puts it in his seminal essay "The Task of the Translator," echoing the one made by sound in the original, but it seems to me that, in this particular case, the preservation of the original structure of this passage and its maintenance as one sentence could have helped.[10] In the same vein, this particular translation may have benefited from an attempt to preserve the repetition of the same or derived words (without replacing them with synonyms) and the occurrence of mutually echoing words, to maintain the original punctuation (only commas, there are no brackets in the original and of course no periods), and to achieve some of the alliterative effects of the original.[11]

With a more forceful recreation of the original sound, sound could come across as a much more dominant presence, the way it does in the original. One should not be able to read this sentence as fast as one usually reads longer narrative prose, or in the way one can read the existent translation of this sentence, made easier by a changed syntax and the "combing out" of the sound pattern. The poetic sound of the original makes this sentence much more independent — it could be read as a stanza, or even as a poem itself — and the separateness of this "poem," which is a part of a narrative flow but which also stands by itself because of its sound, works against its being understandable as solely a building block of a much longer text; it makes it, to an extent, incomprehensible as being (only) that.

This sentence's specific dynamic between the intensity of its sound and the "incomprehensibility" of its words is not the same as in conventionally acknowledged poetry, which usually combines graphic verse and rhythmic speech with some measure of nonliteral ("nonprosaic") language. Yet this dynamic is also not of the kind that is customarily found or expected in a "more prosaic" prose. This sentence works in the terrain between the two poles on account of its strong poetic sound that makes its meaning less prosaic, less comprehensible, and less one-dimensional.[12] The European Middle Ages seem to have had a rather useful view of the relationship between prose and poetry, viewing them not as two but rather as both one and many, with, as Ernst Curtius puts it, a "variety of linguistic art-forms" made by their various crossings, in which "the terminologies of poetry and prose easily interchange."[13] The sound of *Dervish and Death* echoes such a premodern era of language practice with its gravity and its resonant overlapping of poetry and prose.

Not Only Part of a Narrative

The dynamic between the emphasized presence and effect of a sound on the one hand, and the ensuing incomprehensibility of a certain prose passage as only a part of a longer narrative on the other, has to be sensed in order to be translated properly. Many sections of *Dervish and Death* are written in this space between "prose" and "poetry," where the force and organization of sound produce a situation where "clear" words become not so clear after all, or where what is clear about them is not the only thing there is. The prominence of the sound takes these sections out of their narrative contexts and makes them more independent, giving them additional layers of potential meaning and the more universal resonance commonly associated with poetry rather than with bits of a particular narrative.

I shall briefly sketch two additional simple examples of this dynamic. The moment the dervish hears about his brother's death, for example, is rendered thus in the original:

> Upitao sam, žureći da se utopim u crnu vodu:
> — Za brata?
> — Jest, za brata.
> — Je li živ?
> — Ubijen. Prije tri dana. (200)

This short dialogue is translated as:

> I asked him, rushing to immerse myself in the black waters:
> "About my brother?"
> "Yes."
> "Is he alive?"
> "Dead. They killed him three days ago." (192)

The clear sonic characteristics of the original include a two-measure rhythm (three-syllable question, two-part answer), with a shorter question twice "trumped" by a longer answer, making a regular pattern of alternating short and long lines, closing with the longest line (eight syllables long).[14] The replication of the words *za brata* (about the brother) in close proximity in the original is not for semantic purpose but rather for rhetorical effect; the repeated sound of the word *brata* cradles the brother now that he is gone. The recurrence of the syllable *je* (in *jest, je, ubijen, prije*) also makes a poignant echoing of this *je* — meaning "is" — within the lines telling of the brother's death. Also, in the original, it is as if the two words, a one-syllable *živ* (alive) and the three-syllable *ubijen* (killed), contend in a moment over the word whose length is exactly in the middle between them, the two-syllable word *brata* (brother). The longer and heavier *ubijen* wins and closes with finality, quite like a gravestone, the ascending hope of the questioning *živ?* (alive?). This sound clash should be preserved in the translation; it would thus be better to use the longer word "murdered" than the shorter one "killed."

The existing translation does not recreate the impact of the sound of the original, but it adds nonexisting semantic specificity: "I asked him" rather than only "I asked," "about my brother" instead of "about the brother," "Dead. They killed him three days ago" rather than merely "Murdered. Three days ago." As a result, the translation creates a more "prosaic" text about here and now, about a specific person in a specific moment with a specific question about his specific brother. The original, on the contrary, both with its word choice and even more with its simple and efficient poetic sound, may again appear as a simple stanza or a poem, the most basic dialogue with two unidentified voices — the first one asking questions, the second one responding — about the only thing that matters: "Is he alive?" To preserve a sense of the original sound characteristics, an alternative translation could be:

I asked, rushing to drown myself in the black water:
About the brother?
Aye, about the brother.
Is he alive?
Murdered. Three days ago.[15]

Another example of this loss of poetic sound occurs in the removal of the sound contrast between the language of the gradual dying and the language of the sudden awakening of life, appearing at the point of the narrative when the dervish is imprisoned deep in the lightless dungeon where he gradually loses the sense of time, himself, reason, life, and language. The beginning of this slow descent into nothingness is foreshadowed in the prison guard's initial words, "Jelo dijelimo jednom. Samo. Ujutro" (229), translated as: "We give out food once a day. Only once. In the morning" (221). The translation does not preserve the original's reduction of language and its sound into one-word-long, awkwardly amputated sentences a short step away from complete silence. The prison guard's speech is torn, unused to being used, barely moving. The word that alone makes the second sentence, *samo* (only), is a qualifier that is almost never used alone; one says, for example, *samo tako* (only in this way), or *samo malo* (only a little bit), or, indeed, *samo jednom* (only once). But the guard says only *samo* (only), and that is his whole sentence. The original phrase could be translated as, for instance, "We give food once. Only. Mornings." The existent translation ("We give food once a day. Only once. In the morning"), on the other hand, transforms a minimally referential language (one has to read the last word, "in the morning," to understand that the food is given once a day, and not, say, once a week), barely articulate, into redundant and overexplaining language, conventionally formed (the second sentence as a rounded "only once," instead of the abruptly cut-off and awkward "only"), and eager to explain and communicate. And the effect of the decrease of the sound of the original utterance is lost too.

One should attempt to preserve this silencing in the translation, because a reader should still hear it some time later, when, after an immeasurable time of imprisonment, a dervish's account of how he received a gift of gentle summer cherries from unnamed "friends" (tangible proof that he is not forgotten) enacts a clear strengthening of language and the assertion of increasingly victorious sound. This part of the sentence could easily be written out in verse:

> ruke su mi šuplje,
> ruke su mi radosne,
> ruke su mi lude i nemoćne,
> pritisnule su . . . (233)

The above could be translated as, for example, "my hands are hollow, my hands are joyous, my hands are crazy and powerless, they pressed . . . "; or perhaps better, with the less semantically accurate "my hands are full of joy" (in the second clause) instead of the more literal "joyous," in order to preserve the increase of the sheer body of language in each subsequent clause.[16] But the phrase is in fact translated as "[m]y hands were unsteady, joyous, crazy and weak; they pressed . . . " (225). In this sentence, the enlargement of language is the enlargement of life; the increasing abundance and loudness of the sound of language could and should be recreated more forcefully in the translation so that it enacts this increase of language as life, and so that it makes a strong aural contrast to the curtness and dissolution of the prison guard's speech.[17] The sound of the translation would also benefit from preserving the jarring switch of the tenses in mid-sentence, as well as the original punctuation and the original adjectives.[18] The resulting poetic sound would then, in a way, take this sentence out of its narrative context and make it into a poetic utterance that says what it says but also "says more," articulating with its sound the shapes of a sudden revival against the still sounding past of a gradual dying.

Incomprehensible Sound and Comprehensible Meanings

From the example of this translation, one may perhaps conclude that not recognizing the poetry of prose leads to translations of prose that make the following two groups of mistakes: first, such translations fail to recreate the original presence and impact of sound by avoiding a number of basic repetitions of sounds and words necessary for the articulation of the sound patterns (e.g., by the omission of reiterated whole words or by the replacement of the replicated word with synonyms). They also change the original syntax and punctuation, not just to suit the language into which they are translating, but also in order to make the text more "clearly" organized or, as it were, more conventionally prose-like. And they pay little attention to the sound of the individual words and their groupings and to what these sounds may do in the original. Second, the translations then add words that are not in the original, words that explain and specify things. Words that were originally used because of their sound disappear and are replaced by words that are injected into the translation because of their meaning. Incomprehensible sound is replaced with comprehensible meanings. Lost are the texts (and the rhetorical impact or practice of the texts) that are parts of the novel but that should, at the same time, be heard as a certain kind of poetry as well.

Sound versus Meaning

Some parts of *Derviš i smrt* are orchestrated in such a way that sounds do not just "say more" but instead seem to work against the alleged meaning to such an extent that this meaning is subverted. In these places, the dynamic that the sounds create among themselves is clearly at odds with the semantic meaning of the passage. If one does not see such independent motion of sound, one translates by subsuming the sound under meaning and by flattening the "nonsensical" poetry into understandable prose.

At one point early on in the narrative, the desperate dervish experiences a sudden desire for the material world to cease existing; the part of this paragraph is translated as follows:

> [T]hey [the flowers] should have been torn out and trampled down, so that only thistle and barren ground would remain, a graveyard without any markers, which would not remind anyone of anything, so that an abstract human thought would be all that was left, lacking images and scents, lacking any connection to the things around us. Even the river should have been stopped so that its scornful gurgling would cease, and the birds in the treetops and under the eaves should have had their necks wrung, so that their senseless twittering would end. All the water mills where the naked girls bathed should have been torn down, all the streets closed, and the gates nailed shut, all life silenced by force, to prevent evil from sprouting. (34)

While the translation captures some of the rhythm of this passage, the original text has much more prominent sound features, so that it again feels more "natural" to write this passage out in a free verse stanza:

1   počupati bi ga trebalo,
2   pogaziti nogama,
3   da ostane samo čkalj i pusta ledina,
4   da ostane mezarje, bez oznaka,
5   da ne podsjeća ninašto,
6   da ostane gola ljudska misao,
7   bez slika,
8   bez mirisa,
9   bez veze sa stvarima oko nas,
10 i rijeku bi trebalo zaustaviti
11 da ne žubori podsmješljivo,
12 i ptice podaviti po krošnjama
13 i pod strehama
14 da ne ćućore besmisleno,
15 i porušiti sve vodenice
16 pod kojima se

17 kupaju gole djevojke,
18 zagraditi sokake,
19 zakovati kapije,
20 silom utišati život,
21 da ne buja zlo. (39)

The readily heard elements of sound are recurring anaphoras (based on the repetition of words *da, da ostane, bez, i, za* [of *zagraditi, zakovati*]), joined with the repeated echoing of the vowels *o* and *a* ending all but two of the verses in the first part (verses 1 through 14), and additionally tying the words ending with *a-a* (*nogama, oznaka, krošnjama, strehama*), *a-o* (*trebalo, ninašto, misao*), or *i-a* (*ledina, slika, mirisa*). The second part of the stanza (verse 15 on) changes the ending vowel pattern, switching into the five times repeated final *e* (*vodenice, se, djevojke, sokake, kapije*), and ending with two lines of which the first closes with the consonant (*t* in *život*) that abruptly "shuts" this verse down in opposition to the previous ending vowels, which sound away for a longer time (sounding more like *djevojkee, sokakee, kapijee*), and the second one — also the last line of the whole "stanza" — ends with the very prominent stress on the last syllable, the only such stress in the whole "stanza," falling on the one-syllable word *zlo* (evil).

In addition to echoing each other through shared anaphoras, some of the lines have syllabic equality as well: lines 11 and 14, "da ne žubori podsmješljivo" and "da ne ćućore besmisleno," with nine syllables, and lines 18 and 19, "zagraditi sokake" and "zakovati kapije," with seven syllables. The end-of-line rhyme, which can be faintly heard already in the first part (*oznaka — slika* and the similarity of *nogama* and *ledina*), appears clearly in the second part of the stanza, with *krošnjama — strehama* (in 12 and 13), and *djevojke — sokake* (in 17 and 18). And there is a very prominent internal rhyming created by eight infinitives ending in *ti* (*počupati, pogaziti, zaustaviti, podaviti, porušiti, zagraditi, zakovati, utišati*), placed in all positions within the verses (beginning, middle, end), and creating their own sound pattern, not only with their rhyming, but also with the repetition of their length (all but one four syllables long, and all together being consistently the longest words in the stanza, with only three other words having four syllables).[19] The pattern of infinitives resounding their final *ti* also creates a pace that quickens toward the end, with five infinitives spread in the first fifteen verses, and three given in dense succession in the short lines 18, 19, and 20 (*zagraditi, zakovati, utišati*).

The translation loses much of the strong poetic sound of the original and "flattens" the language. The forward movement of one sentence is broken by translating it (starting before the cited part) into no less than five English sentences. The strong anaphoric sound effect based on the four-times-repeated *da* (so that), starting four lines, is destroyed: "so that" appears only twice in the translation, and not successively but rather in clauses that are quite far apart from each other. The original's assertive repetition of *da ostane* (so that remains [this or that thing]) is also destroyed by having the equivalent semantic cluster appear in two different versions in the translation, where the second version replaces with a synonym the original's threefold repetition of the same word.

Here is again this part of the original, written out in verse:

da ostane samo čkalj i pusta ledina,
da ostane mezarje, bez oznaka,
da ne podsjeća ninašto,
da ostane gola ljudska misao . . .

And here is the translation of this part, also written out in verse for easier comparison:

so that only thistle and barren ground would remain,
a graveyard without any markers,
which would not remind anyone of anything,
so that an abstract human thought would be all that was left . . .

The same avoidance of anaphoras and destruction of the sound and rhythm of the original language appear in the translation of the cluster "bez slika, bez mirisa, bez veze sa" into "lacking images and scents, lacking any connection." The staccato movement of the original short words, the quick tempo of the short units punctuated with commas, is replaced with a more pedestrian phrase with longer units, muted repetition, and more "cerebral" words. *Bez* means "lacking," but it can also be translated as a simpler "without" or "with no," the latter of which options allows the better rendering of the original quick succession of short words; *veza* is "connection," but it could also be translated as a "tie," a shorter word more instantly heard and processed. A translation more appreciative of the original sound may want to replace the original plurals ([with no] "images," "scents," etc.) with the singular; something like "with no image, with no scent, with no tie with . . . " would altogether better recreate the original sound and its impact.

The four-time repetition of *i* (and) is also taken out in the translation:

ORIGINAL	LITERAL TRANSLATION	RAKIĆ-DICKEY TRANSLATION
i rijeku	and the river	even the river
i ptice	and birds	and birds
i pod strehama	and under eaves	and under eaves
i porušiti	and tear down	all the water mills
		[should have been torn down]

The translation does not heed a poetic structure and its emphasis on sound; instead, following the pattern of previous examples, the translation enforces a more "logical" (prose, explanatory) structure, adding words that create explanations and connections not present in the original.[20] This addition of specifications not present in the original contributes to the creation of a text that works much more with explanations and much less with the sound than the original text. A poetic passage is transformed into a "flatter" prose.

The sound of this entire passage, with its quick and quickening rhythm and its ineluctability, creates strong forward motion and constitutes such a powerful realization of the potentials of the sound of the Bosnian/Croatian/Serbian language that it could well be heard as the proverbial rush of victorious life itself. But this effect of sound is in stark contrast to the meaning of the passage, which is a "wish for everything not to be" (*želja da ničega ne bude*), or for everything material, corporeal, or natural (flowers, images, scents, sounds) to cease existing, leaving only a "naked human thought." The meaning of all eight prominent infinitives is a cessation or destruction of something: to tear out and trample down (the flowers), to stop (the river), to strangle (the birds), to tear down (water mills), to wall in (streets), to nail shut (gates), to silence (life). Yet the sound created by these same infinitives in the original text, with their identical length and their eight-time rhyming of the ending *ti,* creates a very different effect, that of a language dance, music, and abundance that are the opposite of any cessation and any silent "naked human thought."

The meaning of the passage singles out sound as the main thing that needs to be destroyed if all is to be destroyed: "[one should] stop the river so that it does not gurgle scornfully," "[one should] strangle the birds so that they do not twitter senselessly," metaphorically leading to a "negative" crescendo of the final "[one should] silence life." Yet the sound of the passage works against this meaning and asserts itself so strongly that it subverts and changes the meaning of the passage to something much less understandable. Even the penultimate couplet, with its straightforward meaning of "[one should] wall in the streets, nail shut the gates," "zagraditi sokake, zakovati kapije," makes the reader who really hears these words so taken with the playful exhibition of the possibilities of the short (seven-syllable-long) verse, with a pyrrhic foot, dactyl, and amphibrach in the first verse (*zagraditi sokake,* <breve macron breve breve breve macron breve>), and paeon and dactyl in the second (*zakovati kapije,* <macron breve breve breve macron breve breve>) — as if the verses are taking on a life on their own, improvising variations on a given theme, showing off and in a way saying "hear what we can do!" — that the meaning of these same words (closing, shutting, stopping, silencing) is subverted and shifted away onto some other plane of much less easy overall comprehensibility. The assertion of the sound of this passage goes against its meaning, a wish for everything not to be and for the sound of life to be silenced. And the translation that aims to do justice to the text should try, however hard it may be, to preserve this clash between the meaning and the sound.

Addendum: On the Virtues of Remaining Ignorant in the Face of Art

I had the notion when I was asked to write ... to write a text against the "march of understanding," and to make clear the virtues of remaining ignorant in the face of art ... I work at ... keeping it mysterious. Instead of understanding it, I would like, if I can, to help keep the work of Joyce mysterious.

JOHN CAGE

The increased assumption of knowledge and understanding of what the text is about, and the decreased "not-knowledge," can be detrimental when it comes to translations of sound. The translation of that which one knows, of the presumably understood aspects of the text, destroys that which one does not know, or that which cannot be known because it is a physical impact that affects the senses directly and cannot be translated into thoughts and meanings. The translation of prose as a translation of meaningful language does not hear its "nonmeaningful" language, the seemingly senseless words and sentences in which their own foregrounded sound plays with the supposed meanings.

The supremacy of knowledge over nonknowledge, or of "understanding" (concepts) over "mystery" (sounds) in matters of translation can be seen as a part of a much older and broader struggle between philosophy and art, or conceptual cognition and sensual apprehension. Art apprehends the world and we apprehend the art though our humanized senses — our ears, eyes, touch. This sensual apprehension profoundly affects us and changes our minds, but in ways different from those caused by clear concepts. From Plato on down, however, European and Western philosophy has commonly deemed such aesthetic apprehension to be inferior to conceptual cognition that deals with immaterial and disembodied ideas and that employs words that are, above all, comprehensible, working with their meanings rather than with their incomprehensible vocal bodies. The superiority of philosophy over poetry reappears in modern philosophy as well, even though some thinkers write differently of the relationship between philosophy and art.[21] But when the translations of poetic prose subsume the unknowable sounds under knowable meanings, they put themselves, as it were, on the side of philosophy rather than poetry and enact the supremacy of the "march of understanding" over (sensitive) ignorance, and the victory of presumed meanings over sounds.

In the longstanding "quarrel between philosophy and poetry . . . philosophy will always have the last word," says Curtius. But he cautions:

> Plato's criticism of Homer is the culmination of the quarrel between philosophy and poetry, which was already "ancient" in Plato's time. . . . This conflict is grounded in the structure of the intellectual world. Hence it can always flare up again . . . and philosophy will always have the last word — because poetry does not answer her. Poetry has her own wisdom.[22]

"Poetry has her own wisdom," and her wisdom lies greatly in her specific incomprehensibility, the incomprehensibility connected to the poetry's bewitching sound that keeps us, the listeners, "charmed" and spellbound in a way similar to that in which the Homeric bard kept his listeners "'spellbound,'" a characterization perhaps echoing "the original kinship of poetry and magic."[23] And if poetry and prose are not so separate after all, if it is actually not the case that, in prose, a word merely "means what it says," then the awareness of as well as sensitivity and allegiance to this incomprehensible enchantment of the sound of poetry — which plays tricks with the meaning of words — has to be a more assertive part of every prose translator's box of tools.

PART II / PERFORMING SOUND

SOUND POETRY AND THE MUSICAL AVANT-GARDE: A MUSICOLOGIST'S PERSPECTIVE / NANCY PERLOFF

Critical writing on sound poetry has been the domain of poets and literary scholars, who study its semantic, syntactic, and linguistic attributes and the ways in which it redefines the function of language. This seems entirely appropriate, since the composition of sound poetry generally begins with a text. A handful of sound poets have had musical training (Jackson Mac Low, Greta Monach, Henri Chopin), but from its beginnings in the early Russian and Italian avant-gardes, sound poetry has been a hybrid form created by poets. Yet an effective analysis of a sound poem's text must consider its realization in live performance and hence the very nature of its *sounds* — their intelligibility, their relation to other sounds in the poem, their use of the pronunciation of a particular spoken language, their role in articulating a structure. Since sound poetry, while not constituting music, is a poetic form that works between media, the perspective of musicology and of avant-garde and experimental music can help us interpret its aural dimension. Moreover, avant-garde music and sound poetry emerged out of a common interest in incorporating sounds produced by new kinds of musical instruments and by virtuosic vocal techniques. This more inclusive content expanded the scope of each to encompass all sounds and challenged traditional distinctions between sound and speech, sound and music, sound and noise, music and noise.[1] In this essay, I will argue that sound poetry and music developed from similar origins and that, in the twentieth century, poets and composers followed parallel trajectories by exploring a radically new conception of poetic and musical sound. I will posit that live performance brings these issues to the fore. Avant-garde music discards lyricism, just as sound poetry rejects meaning, and in performance we hear their probing of the limits of intelligibility and referentiality.[2]

If we assume, as Steve McCaffery does, that sound poetry has been present throughout the history of Western literature, then the origins of sound poetry and music can be traced to the ancient and medieval practices of chant. McCaffery charts three phases in the history of sound poetry and calls the first the "paleotechnic era." This era, he explains, comprises the "vast, intractable territory of archaic and primitive poetries, the many instances of chant structures and incantation, of syllabic mouthings and deliberate lexical distortions still alive among many North American, African, Asian, and Oceanic peoples."[3] McCaffery cites folk and children's rituals, such as language games, nursery rhymes, skipping chants, and folk-song refrains, as primitive forms of sound poetry.

Music likewise originated in chant. The earliest manuscripts of medieval plainchant (monophonic unaccompanied sacred song) contained only the liturgical texts. Singers learned the melodies by heart and performed them from memory. Early neumatic notation, introduced in the eleventh century, consisted of signs developed from grammatical accents and placed above the text. It provided information about the number of pitches and whether they moved up or down, thus serving as a memory aid for singers already familiar with the melody, who circulated it as part of an oral tradition. With the introduction of heightened neumes, positioned higher or lower on the page to indicate a note's relative pitch, singers could begin to read and perform a melody they didn't know.[4] In the late medieval, Renaissance, and Baroque periods, as composers experimented with counterpoint, harmony, rhythm, meter, and texture, they introduced notation that specified these different musical parameters. They moved past music's origins in voice and language.

McCaffery's "second phase" (1875–1928) marks a period in which poets and artists of the European avant-garde sparked small revolutions through their experiments with the acoustic, nonsemantic properties of language. Composers, like poets, began to draw upon what John Cage has called "the entire field of sound."[5] They introduced non-Western scales, popular tunes, syncopated rhythms, and an expanded role for percussion. The inventions of the phonograph (1877), radio (1891), and tape recorder (1934–35) accelerated these developments by broadening the repertoire of sounds and, in the case of magnetic tape, enabling poets and composers to manipulate recorded sound through splicing, speed modification, and the superimposition of sound layers.[6] In 1921, with its popularity soaring in Europe, Velimir

Khlebnikov wrote an essay entitled "The Radio of the Future," in which he marveled at the use of the radio to "[inundate] the whole country in supernatural singing, in the sound of beating wings":

> The Mussorgsky of the future is giving a coast-to-coast concert of his work, using the Radio apparatus to create a vast concert hall stretching from Vladivostok to the Baltic, beneath the blue dome of the heavens.
>
> On this evening he bewitches the people, sharing with them the communion of his soul, and on the following day he is only an ordinary mortal again. The artist has cast a spell over his land; he has given his country the singing of the sea and the whistling of the wind. The poorest house in the smallest town is filled with divine whistlings and all the sweet delights of sound.[7]

In 1937, a little over a decade later, John Cage anticipated the importance of electrical instruments for musical composition when he spoke of the need to establish centers of experimental music, where composers could use "the new materials, oscillators, generators, means for amplifying small sounds, film phonographs" to make sounds.[8]

The poetry of the Russian avant-garde, the Italian futurists, and German Dada belongs to McCaffery's second phase, while his third phase encompasses the 1950s and beyond, when sound poetry, shaped by the invention of the tape recorder, abandoned the word altogether. I take my cue from his discussion, with the proviso that many of the revolutionary developments that McCaffery attributes to the third phase had already taken place in the second. I begin with the Russians, whose poems marked the "first concerted attempts to isolate the concrete, phonic aspect of language as an autonomous focus of interest."[9] Their poetry, which they wrote in the language of *zaum*, or "beyonsense," (*za* [beyond]; *um* [the mind]), can be traced to an eclectic range of sources, including the incantations of Russian Orthodox priests and village shamans, the nonsense syllables of nursery rhymes, and the cacophony of the modern city. In his essay "On Poetry," from 1919, Khlebnikov relates the suggestive, nonsemantic language of *zaum* to paganism and magic, as a way of explaining why a poem, unlike a street sign, is not meant to be understandable:

> What about spells and incantations, what we call magic words, the sacred language of paganism, words like "shagadam, magadam, vigadam, pitz, putz, patzu" — they are rows of mere syllables that the intellect can make no sense of, and they form a kind of beyonsense [*zaum*] language in folk speech. Neverthe-

О, рассмейтесь, смехачи!
О, засмейтесь, смехачи!
Что смеются смехами, что смеянстуют смеяльно,
О, засмейтесь усмеяльно!
О, рассмешищ надсмеяльных - смех усмейных смехачей!
О, иссмейся рассмеяльно, смех надсмейных смеячей!
Смейево, смейево!
Усмей, осмей, смешики, смешики!
Смеюнчики, смеюнчики.
О, рассмейтесь, смехачи!
О, засмейтесь, смехачи!

Figure 1. Velimir Khlebnikov, *Zakliatie smekhom* (Incantation by Laughter), 1908–9.

less an enormous power over mankind is attributed to these incomprehensible words and magic spells.[10]

In the *zaum'* poetry of Khlebnikov and Alexei Kruchenykh, the word remains the linguistic unit, but each poet approaches it differently. In his early *zaum'*, Khlebnikov develops a Russian word etymologically by creating neologisms that extend the meaning of the root of this word. He also identifies the semantic connection between the sound of a word and its referent. In *Zakliatie smekhom* (Incantation by Laughter), for example, Khlebnikov selects the word *smekh* (laugh) and develops its root *sme-* (сме) by adding suffixes that normally do not go with it (see fig. 1).

O, rassmeites', smekhachi!
O, zasmeites', smekhachi!
Chto smeiutsia smekhami, chto smeianstvuiut smeial'no.
O, zasmeites' usmeial'no!
O, rassmeshishch nadsmeial'nykh — smekh usmeinykh smekhachei!
O, issmeisia rassmeial'no, smekh nadsmeinykh smeiachei!
Smeivo, smeievo,
Usmei, osmei, smeshiki, smeshiki,
Smeiunchiki, smeiunchiki,
O, rassmeites', smekhachi!
O zasmeites', smekhachi!

[O laugh it out, you laughsters!
O laugh it up, you laughsters!
So they laugh with laughsters, so they laugherize delaughly.
O laugh it up belaughably!
O the laughingstock of the laughed upon — the laugh of Belaughed laughsters!
O laugh it out roundlaughingly, the laugh of laughed-at Laughians!
Laugherino, laugherino,
Laughify, laughicate, laugholets, laugholets,
Laughikins, laughkins,
O laugh it out, you laughsters!
O laugh it out, you laughsters!][11]

The resulting neologisms become parts of speech, producing plural nouns (*smekhachi* [laughlings, laughsters]), verbs *(smeianstvuiut* [laugherize]), and adverbs (*smeial'no* [delaughly]).[12] Khlebnikov frequently adds prefixes as well as suffixes, thus embedding his root *sme-* within the neologism (*rass-meites', nadsmeinykh, usmei*). The repetition of the sounds *smekh, smei,* and *smesh* in different neologisms and of the phonemes *kh, i, sh, ch, k* mimics the repetitive, sometimes abrasive sound of laughter. Far from creating nonsense, the overabundant contexts for the core referent overdetermine its meaning. Moreover, by connecting the meaning of *smekh-* with the verbal mimicry of laughter, Khlebnikov creates a language that is universal. *Zakliatie smekhom* lends itself to performance, as well as to reading. The poem's rapid repetitions of a single sound in different permutations require technical virtuosity on the part of the vocalist. The development of a Russian root to produce sounds previously unknown is an avant-garde gesture that parallels the work of composers of the early 1920s, who extended performance techniques and modified instruments in order to discover new sound worlds.

In contrast with Khlebnikov's practice of overdetermining meaning, Kruchenykh's *zaum'* aims to create a "language which does not have any definite meaning, a transrational language."[13] Kruchenykh accomplishes this, explains Craig Dworkin, by "[attempting] to increase the play of reference and achieve an ever greater indeterminacy."[14] In his manifesto "New Ways of the Word," published in *Troe* (Threesome) in 1913, Kruchenykh speaks about neologism and the loosening of syntax:

We were the first to say that in order to depict the new — the future — one needs totally new words and a new way of combining them.

This absolutely new way will be the combination of words according to their

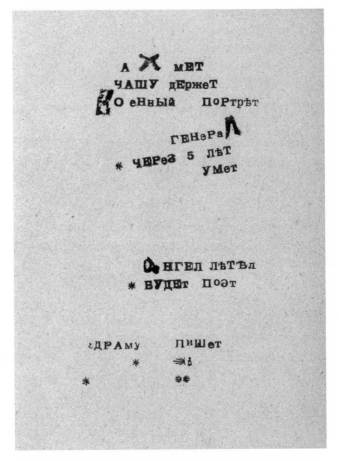

Figure 2. Alexei Kruchenykh, "Akhmet." Rubber-stamping. In
Kruchenykh and Velimir Khlebnikov, *Mirskontsa* (Worldbackwards)
(Moscow, 1912), 10. Research Library, The Getty Research Institute,
Los Angeles, California.

inner laws . . . and not according to the rules of logic or grammar as was the case
before us.[15]

In a later manifesto, Kruchenykh identifies the "transrational" as one form
of "word-creation" and introduces another that he calls the "random (alogical, accidental, creative breakthrough, mechanical word combination: slips
of the tongue, misprints, blunders . . .)."[16] Such alogism permeates the aural
structure of Kruchenykh's rubber-stamped poem "Akhmet," in *Mirskontsa*
(Worldbackwards; fig. 2).

Akhmet
Chashu derzhet
Voennyi portret
General
Cherez 5 [piat'] let
Umet
Angel letel
Budet poet
Dramu pishet

[Akhmet
Holds a cup
Military portrait
General
In 5 years
Poop
An angel flew
Will be a poet
Is writing a play]¹⁷

A lithographic portrait of the fictional Eastern character Akhmet by Mikhail Larionov directly precedes the poem (see fig. 3), indicating that the two are companion pieces. In his drawing, Larionov divides Akhmet's hand-written name into two syllables on one side of the head, but curiously omits the final *t*. This *t* becomes the aural focus of the poem, which follows a sequence of full and partial rhymes on the stressed and unstressed *et* (*AKHMET, portrET, lET, umET, letEL, BUDet, poET*). In the two lines that frame the poem, however — *chashu derzhet* and *dramu pishet* — Kruchenykh subverts the aural structure by using *et* words in which the stress falls on the first, rather than the second, syllable, namely *DERzhet* and *PISHet*. According to Russian pronunciation, when the first syllable receives the stress, the *e* in the second syllable is pronounced as a short *I* (*DERzhit, PISHit*). Kruchenykh's verse thus follows a pattern of repeated sounds and stresses, only to unexpectedly disrupt this pattern. The source for the poem's alogical sound structure is the name "Akhmet" which, if pronounced as a Russian name, contains a stressed first syllable followed by a short *i*. Since it is a foreign name, however, both syllables of "Akhmet" receive stress and the *e* sound is retained, thus highlighting the difference between written and spoken Russian that characterizes *derzhet* and *pishet*.¹⁸ The importance of sound in Kruchenykh's

Figure 3. Mikhail Larionov, *Portrait of Akhmet.* Lithograph. In Alexei Kruchenykh and Velimir Khlebnikov, *Mirskontsa* (Worldbackwards) (Moscow, 1912), 8. © 2009 Artists Rights Society (ARS), New York/ ADAGP, Paris. Research Library, The Getty Research Institute, Los Angeles, California.

poem begins to explain the mystery of the missing *t* in the lithographic portrait. Above Akhmet's ear, Larionov has placed a lyre as a symbol of poetry and poetic sound. The resemblance of the lyre's curves and its three parallel strings to the Cyrillic uppercase *T* suggests that it serves as a stand-in for the missing letter.

In his miscellany *Vzorval* (Explodity), Kruchenykh likewise discards conventional typesetting for hand-lithography and rubber-stamping. He arranges the letters and words of his *zaum'* poetry with seeming randomness and irregularity across the page to suggest an "explodity" (a transrational word) of sound and language. In the poem "Tyanutkonej" (They haulhorsies), sound, rather than semantics, drives word choice and imparts unity.

Tyanutkonej
Zametil ty
Kak zlykh koney
Nosili kopyty
I ty
Vskrichal zazhatyy
Dobro
Vezut . . . rogatyi
Kidayte khaty
Ne bedny ne bogaty
Konets vezut
Staro

[They haulhorsies
You noticed
how angry nonies
carried hooves
And you
squeezed cried out
Good
They transport . . . the horned one
Throw huts
Not poor not rich
The end they transport
oldly][19]

Kruchenykh's selection of words that end with the sound *ty* encourages the listener to anticipate the rhymed endings, as in "Akhmet." In a gesture of alogism, however, he abruptly detours from the rhyme by inserting the words *dobRO* (goods) and *vezUT* (they are transporting) in the middle of the poem and *STAro* (oldly) after *vezUT* at the end. Seen on the page, *STAro* appears to rhyme with *dobRO,* yet the difference in stress patterns, which is audible when the words are spoken, undermines the rhyme. Moreover, although all three words have meaning, their verbal sequence follows no logical sense, nor does their context provide a rationale. Instead, they function as "words as such," that is, as sound materials Kruchenykh intended to be *heard* and *performed,* rather than read.

Both the Russian avant-garde poets and the Italian futurists explored the potential of language to produce nonreferential sounds. Both ventured beyond reading into the world of live declamation and performance. Rather than constructing neologisms, however, the Italians made elaborate use of onomatopoeia and treated typography as "a design-equivalent for speech."[20] According to the poet F. T. Marinetti, founder of the Italian futurist movement, deep changes in technology and science and in concepts of time and space called for the reinvention of all the arts, including music and literature. In his futurist literary genre, the *parole in libertà* (words-in-freedom), Marinetti sought to convey the speed of technology and urban life and to free words from the straitjacket of the sentence by abolishing syntax, punctuation, adjectives, adverbs, and conjunctions and by retaining verbs as action words. The futurists' use of three or four colors of ink on one page, varying densities of ink for emphasis, up to twenty different typefaces, vertical, horizontal, and diagonal placements of letters and words, and boldface or italics for onomatopoeia marked a revolution in printing as well as in sound. Marinetti explained that this typography enabled him to "to treat words like torpedoes and to hurl them forth at all speeds: at the velocity of stars, clouds, aeroplanes, trains, waves, explosives, molecules, atoms."[21]

In contrast with *zaum'* poetry, the *parole in libertà* convey meaning more conventionally by narrating a story through typographic design. Marinetti's "Après la Marne, Joffre visita le front en auto" (After the Marne, Joffre visited the front by car) (1915) uses the form of a military map to recount General Joffre's victorious tour of the troops after the Allies saved France by halting the German advance toward Paris in 1914 (see fig. 4). Black serpentines suggest the winding roads that the general's car follows, as well as the movement of the river Marne. This sense of geography continues with the use of the letter *M* to indicate the outline of mountains, although Marinetti gives the letter multiple associations by linking it as well with the first letter of Marne and with the first letter of the words the general speaks: "Mon ami" and "Ma petite." The onomatopoeic "traac craac" with its machine-like evocations (lower left), "ta ta ta ta" suggestive of machine guns (middle), and "toumb toumb" (lower left) which recalls the echo of gunfire appear in tiny fonts and light ink, indicating their role both as sounds from the past and as distant, ever fainter sounds of the present. The curious mélange of indecipherable

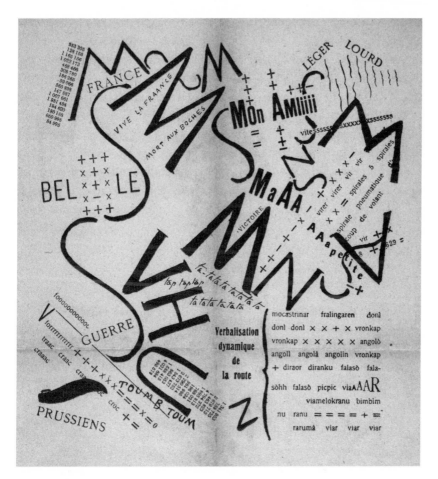

Figure 4. Filippo Tommaso Marinetti, "Après la Marne, Joffre visita le front en auto" (After the Marne, Joffre Visited the Marne by Car). In *Les mots en liberté futuristes* (Milan, 1919), 99. © 2009 Artists Rights Society (ARS), New York / SIAE, Rome. Research Library, The Getty Research Institute, Los Angeles, California.

foreign words (upper and lower right) could allude to the merging of foreign languages in the crowd that follows Joffre.

The design of "Après la Marne" may be the first instance of visual notation in poetry. It speeds a bewildering array of letters, words, numbers, plus and minus signs, and serpentines in different directions to convey what Marinetti calls a "dynamic verbalization of the route." He also uses typography as an expressive marking, so that changes in letter size indicate an increase or decrease in volume, onomatopoeic repetitions of letters and words dramatize wartime sounds, and heavily or lightly inked letters indicate verbal emphasis. Words like "léger" (light) and "lourd" (heavy) (upper right) may be stage directions for the general's speech. The sonic and theatrical implications of Marinetti's typographic "score" can be realized only in live performance.

German Dadaists working with sound poetry in the 1920s dispensed altogether with semantic units.[22] Kurt Schwitters presents an especially compelling case for Dadaist verbo-vocal innovation in his sound poem the *Ursonate* (1922–32). This thirty-five-minute performance piece follows the structure of a classical four-movement sonata, with a first movement that contains an opening rondo with four themes, a largo (modeled on the characteristic slow movement), a scherzo-trio (the dance movement), and a presto finale that includes a lively cadenza. In the program note for the *Ursonate,* Schwitters's personification of his themes parodies the descriptive language used in eighteenth- and nineteenth-century art music: the "military severity of the rhythm of the quite masculine third theme" in the opening movement, the "tremulous and mild as a lamb" character of the fourth theme, and the "accusing finale, with the question 'tää?'"[23] In both the first and the last movements, Schwitters applies the techniques of a classical development, so that the themes' different characters are heard in combination. Recapitulations may occur in each of these movements, but development is most audible.

The recorded performance of the *Ursonate,* made on May 5, 1932, begins with Schwitters's introduction of the piece as the "Sonate in Urlauten" (Sonata in Primitive and Original Sounds). His suggestive verbal themes consist of repeated consonants (nnzkrrmüü) and vowels (beeeee), repetitions of similar phonemes with a change in one letter (Grimm glimm gnimm bimbimm), and vocables extended by additive writing, as in "böwö böwörö böwöböpö." Unlike the onomatopoeia of Marinetti, these strings of letters are not pictorial or semantic, although their pure vowel sounds and umlauts have connotative meaning and convey the distinctive inflections of modern German. By repeating and slightly varying his minimal combinations of letters, Schwitters makes the structure of his piece audible.

Schwitters composed the *Ursonate* over a ten-year period (1922–32), giving improvised readings, designing and publishing provisional scores, and expanding the piece. When he published the full score in his magazine *Merz* 24 (1932), he used a phonetic notation of his own invention. Figure 5 shows this notation in a rare booklet version of the score published on different colored paper by W. Jöhl and a group of students in Zürich in 1953.[24]

EINLEITUNG   1

Fümms bö wö tää zää Uu,
                    pögiff,
                        kwii Ee.

Oooooooooooooooooooooooooooooooooooooo,   6

dll rrrrrr beeeee bö,   (A)   5
dll rrrrrr beeeee bö fümms bö,
    rrrrrr beeeee bö fümms bö wö,
            beeeee bö fümms bö wö tää,
                bö fümms bö wö tää zää,
                fümms bö wö tää zää Uu:

ERSTER TEIL

thema 1:
Fümms bö wö tää zää Uu,   1
                    pögiff,
                        kwii Ee.

thema 2:
Dedesnn nn rrrrrr,   2
            Ii Ee,
                mpiff tillff too,
                            tillll,
                                Jüü Kaa?
                                (gesungen)

thema 3:
Rinnzekete bee bee nnz krr müü?   3
                    ziiuu ennze, ziiuu rinnzkrrmüü,

rakete bee bee.   3a

thema 4:
Rrummpff tillff toooo?   4

ÜBERLEITUNG

Ziiuu ennze ziiuu nnzkrrmüü,   ü3
Ziiuu ennze ziiuu rinnzkrrmüü,

    rakete bee bee? rakete bee zee.   ü3a

DURCHARBEITUNG

Fümms bö wö tää zää Uu,   ü1
Uu zee tee wee bee fümms.

        rakete rinnzekete   (B)   ü3+
        rakete rinnzekete   3a
        rakete rinnzekete
        rakete rinnzekete
        rakete rinnzekete
        rakete rinnzekete
        Beeeee
        bö.

Figure 5. Kurt Schwitters, *Ursonate* (Ursonata). Mimeograph version of the original score of 1932 by W. Jöhl and students in Zurich. Letterpress. © 2009 Artists Rights Society (ARS), VG Bild-Kunst, Bonn. Research Library, The Getty Research Institute, Los Angeles, California.

The notation served both to document the piece and to enable poets, artists, and musicians to perform it. For instance, Schwitters made intermittent but abundant use of umlauts in order to accentuate the importance of German pronunciation. As he explained in his program note, "The letters applied are to be pronounced as in German. A single vowel sound is short." Schwitters's notation identified the sections of his poem (Einleitung) and the themes (Thema 1) and occasionally provided tempo, meter, and expressive and dynamic markings. He also inserted performance instructions, such as those in the largo, which specified pitch changes: "Each successive line is spoken a quarter tone lower than the previous, thus must one begin at a commensurately high pitch."[25] Schwitters's phonetic notation and his recorded performance create an impression of astonishing vocal dexterity. Moreover, Schwitters's difficult-to-pronounce letter clusters blur the distinction between speech, pitched speech or song, and pure vocalized sound. If speech conveys meaning, then Schwitters's *Ursonate* occupies a different realm. His program note concludes: "Listening to the sonata is better than reading it. This is why I like to perform my sonata in public."

Whereas the modern sound poets I've discussed are considered the avant-garde of their time, their counterparts in music followed a path that diverged from the harmonic and formal innovations of Debussy, Stravinsky, Schoenberg, Berg, Webern, Bartók, composers whom most music historians deem the great twentieth-century modernists. The mission of the musical avant-garde, like that of the sound poets, was to invent a radically new conception of musical sound. The French composer Erik Satie crafted irreverent stories and essays and iconoclastic compositions in which he slyly provoked his fellow composers to break with German romanticism and French impressionism. Satie mocked what he considered to be the pedantry, academic seriousness, and artistic sublimity of this repertoire and advocated a pared-down music that fused art with everyday sounds and styles.[26] He spent the decade of the 1890s working as an accompanist and composing songs at the Chat Noir and other prominent Parisian cabarets. From the cabaret and *café-concert,* he developed an interest in tuneful melodies, varied repetitions of minimal material, dance rhythms, and bitonality, all of which became central stylistic features of his *Trois morceaux en forme de poire, Pièces froides,* and other pieces from this decade. In his 1917 ballet *Parade,* a collaboration with Picasso, Cocteau, and Diaghilev, Satie accompanied Cocteau's bittersweet scenario — a story of a fairground sideshow, in which the Chinese Magician, the Little American Girl, and the Acrobats fail to lure the audience inside the tent — with a rapid, disjunct succession of popular styles, including ragtime, that mirrored the speed, the swift changes, and the diversity of the Parisian music hall.[27] Satie and Cocteau drew inspiration from Parisian popular venues and from Marinetti's manifesto on the variety theater, with its embrace of speed, surprise, practicality, and all other aspects of modern life.[28] It was Cocteau's idea, moreover, to shock Parisian audiences with noises of a typewriter, sirens, a pistol shot, whistles, a *bouteille-ophone,* and a lottery wheel, which he purposefully clashed with Satie's simple, unobtrusive score. These noises bore no narrative relationship to the ballet's scenario.

Cocteau's insertion of noise in *Parade* had its precedent in the daring experiments of the Italian futurists, especially those of the painter Luigi Russolo, whose manifesto, *L'arte dei rumori* (The Art of Noises), appeared four years earlier, in 1913. Challenging the "musical sounds" of modern music, just as Khlebnikov and Kruchenykh rejected symbolist lyricism, Russolo declared:

> We must break out of this narrow circle of pure musical sounds, and conquer the infinite variety of noise-sounds. . . . Let us wander through a great modern city with our ears more alert than our eyes, and enjoy distinguishing between the sounds of water, air, or gas in metal pipes, the purring of motors . . . , the throbbing of valves, the pounding of pistons, the screeching of gears, the clatter of streetcars on their rails, the cracking of whips, the flapping of awnings and flags. We shall enjoy fabricating mental orchestrations of the banging of store shutters, the slamming of doors, the hustle and bustle of crowds, the din of railway stations, foundries, spinning mills, printing presses, electric power stations, and underground railways.[29]

Russolo disavowed any claims to be a musician and found himself motivated by the same determination to "renew everything" that propelled Marinetti. With his noise machines, which he labeled *Intonarumori* (Noise Intoners), Russolo demonstrated his theories. He divided the machines into six main categories, modeled on the four divisions of the symphony orchestra (strings, winds, brass, percussion). Each category contained its own template of sounds (see fig. 6). Of particular relevance to sound poetry were Russolo's categories 2, 3, and especially 6, which comprised "Voices of animals and men: Shouts Screams Groans Shrieks Howls Laughs Wheezes Sobs." This spectrum of high-volume vocal sounds uncannily anticipated the nonsemantic vocalizations of postwar and contemporary sound poetry. The sounds of urbanism and technology suggested by categories 1 and 4 call to mind the

1	2	3	4	5	6
Rumbles	Whistles	Whispers	Screeches	Noises	Voices of
Roars	Hisses	Murmurs	Creaks	obtained	animals
Explosions	Snorts	Mumbles	Rustles	by percus-	and men:
Crashes		Grumbles	Buzzes	ion on	Shouts
Splashes		Gurgles	Crackles	metal	Screams
Booms			Scrapes	wood	Groans
				skin	Shrieks
				stone	Howls
				terracotta,	Laughs
				etc.	Wheezes
					Sob

Figure 6. Luigi Russolo, chart of sound categories for *Intonarumori,* c. 1913.

sound effects of the pilot and airplane in Kruchenykh's opera *Victory over the Sun,* while category 5 anticipates John Cage.

Russolo first demonstrated his *Intonarumori* at a concert in Milan in April 1914. Also in April, three of his noise pieces — *The Awakening of a City, Luncheon on the Kursaal Terrace,* and *Meeting of Automobiles and Aeroplanes* — received performances. For the first of these, Russolo introduced a notation that replaced traditional music writing with a number system and a network of solid lines. It is interesting that just as Russolo devised a notation uniquely suitable for performance by his Noise Intoners, so Schwitters was to create a phonetic notation designed specifically for performances of the *Ursonate.* The link between futurist "musical" notation and futurist typography, each designed for performance or declamation, also dramatizes the importance that the score began to assume both in sound poetry and in avantgarde music, especially as noise, electronic sound, and extended performance techniques became prevalent.

Experiments like Satie's with popular entertainment and Russolo's with new musical instruments prompted European and American composers to venture further in extending the resources of sound. The Californian Henry Cowell introduced new performance techniques on the piano, such as pitch clusters played by the hand and entire forearm, as early as 1912 in his *The Tides of the Manaunaun.* In 1916, Cowell devised unique notations to prescribe performance of the clusters and the rhythmic complexities he had in mind. By the mid 1920s, his piano techniques included harmonics, and plucking and scraping of the strings, both of which figure prominently in his *Aeolian Harp* (1923) and in his most famous piece, *The Banshee* (1925). For the notation of the latter, which is played on the open strings of the piano, Cowell assigned symbols with letter names to each piano technique and provided performance instructions below the staves of the score, as in "A": "indicates a sweep with the flesh of the finger from the lowest string up to the note given." Like Marinetti's typographic notation and Schwitters's phonetic score, Cowell's notation was generated specifically for the performance of this piece. Also in the 1920s, the French composer Edgar Varèse, enamored of the sounds of percussion and noisemakers, composed his *Ionisation* (1929–31), scored for thirty-seven percussion instruments and celesta and piano and thirteen players. The repertoire of Cowell and Varèse demanded virtuosic performers, who had supreme mastery of their instruments and the flexibility to adjust their techniques to the requirements of the composition. In the case of Russolo and Cowell, the interpretation of special forms of notation posed an additional technical challenge.

Cage acknowledged the inventions of Satie, Russolo, Cowell, and Varèse and lauded them as experimentalists in articles he wrote in *Silence* in 1939. His article on Satie, which juxtaposes his own commentary with excerpts from Satie's writings, indicates that his lifelong admiration for the French composer began when he discovered Satie's irreverent mockery of Beethoven and studied his radical approach to rhythmic structures. Cage's "History of Experimental Music in the United States" praises the extended performance techniques and new methods of sound production in the early piano music of Cowell and observes that the use of tone clusters and playing on the open strings "pointed towards noise and a continuum of timbre."[30] Cage's writings on Varèse were sometimes critical, as when he called him "an artist of the past," who did not "deal with sounds as sounds, but with sounds as Varèse." Yet Cage followed this statement with praise:

> However, more clearly and actively than anyone else of his generation, he [Varèse] established the present nature of music. This nature does not arise from pitch relations . . . or from twelve tones nor seven plus five . . . , but arises from an acceptance of all audible phenomena as material proper to music.[31]

By choosing to write on Satie, Russolo, Cowell, and Varèse, Cage revealed his interest in claiming a particular musical past and divorcing himself from canonical modernism. The past represented by these figures was both European and American. They were, in Cage's view of music history, the first "experimentalists," because they probed what musical sound might be. In his proclamation "The Future of Music: Credo," which originated as a lecture for the Seattle Artists' League in 1940 and was strongly influenced by Russolo's *L'arte dei rumori,* Cage assumed the position of spokesman for experimentalism and offered a new definition of music: the "organization of sound."[32] In a statement on noise as the primary material for experimental music, he explained:

> I believe that the use of noise to make music will continue and increase until we reach a music produced through the aid of electrical instruments which will make available for musical purposes any and all sounds that can be heard. . . . Whereas, in the past, the point of disagreement has been between dissonance and consonance, it will be, in the immediate future, between noise and so-called musical sounds.[33]

Cage wrote his early compositions for percussion, which he considered a "contemporary transition from keyboard-influenced music to the all-sound music of the future."[34] His methods of writing percussion music had as their goal the *rhythmic structure* of a composition (considered by Western composers to be less important than harmony) and the use of sounds of indefinite pitch.[35] He built his *First Construction (in Metal)* (1939–41), for example, around a structure of sixteen units, each with a duration of sixteen measures. Six players had the option of producing sixteen different types of sounds, some of which were unpitched. Cage scored the piece for an array of gongs (including Balinese button gongs, Japanese temple gongs, suspended gong), bells, cymbals, suspended thundersheet (a sheet of bronze that the performer strikes with a mallet), tam-tam, and string piano. The term "string piano" originated with Cowell, who first used it to describe a grand piano in which the strings are played upon with a metal rod.[36] This percussive treatment led, in 1940, to Cage's invention of the prepared piano. He inserted screws, felt weather stripping, and rubber inside the strings, then played at the keyboard, transforming the piano into an orchestra of gongs and delicate percussive sounds.

The musical avant-garde's expansion of the "field of sound" through extended techniques, modifications of traditional instruments, and inventions of new sound resources had important precedents in the poetry of the Russian and European avant-gardes, in which the use of onomatopoeia, neologism, and repeated morphemes entailed a new virtuosic use of the human voice. Cage's interest in sound as a phenomenon that encompasses music and noise and his introduction of chance systems have, in turn, influenced the work of contemporary sound poets. The American poet Jackson Mac Low, who trained as a composer, began using chance procedures in the 1950s to create unique, visually striking graphic scores, which he accompanied with instructions explaining the notation and the various methods for realizing it. Live performance consisted of improvised, nonsemantic vocalizations by Mac Low and fellow poets and musicians. The German poet Bernard Heidsieck creates tape compositions that combine recordings of his voice and of everyday street sounds with live performance. The French sound poet and visual artist François Dufrêne writes phonetic poems that have no written score and are disseminated by means of the tape recorder. Dufrêne's atomization of words by means of individual letters or phonemes "exploded language in order to unleash the possibility of a different language," thus harkening back to the invention of *zaum*.[37]

The sound texts of Heidsieck, Mac Low, and Dufrêne place unusual demands on the performer, who is also the poet and therefore uniquely equipped to master the elaborate vocal techniques. In their scores of the 1950s, Cage and his New York colleagues Morton Feldman, Earle Brown, and Christian Wolff confronted the performer with analogous challenges but invented unique notations and performance requirements not for themselves but for another musician — the virtuosic American pianist David Tudor. Since the graphic notations of these composers left some musical parameters (whether rhythm, pitch, meter, or texture) unspecified, Tudor had to study the symbols and instructions and sometimes make preparatory charts of measurements and timings, in order to meet the specifications and invent performance techniques that would enable him to play the piece. Feldman's *Intersection III,* for example, composed for Tudor in 1953, directs the pianist to select pitches within specified ranges. Feldman's notation indicates the number of pitches to be played in each range on a given beat, which sometimes requires the pianist to play as many as ten pitches at a time. Tudor solved this hurdle by playing the dense ten-note clusters with his forearm, a feat of remarkable virtuosity especially when performed at Feldman's breakneck tempo. Aware that Cage, Feldman, Brown, and Wolff intended their "indeterminate" compositions to be interpreted and performed in many different ways, Tudor preferred nonetheless to arrive at fixed realizations, which he transcribed using traditional notation.

Cage's *Solo for Piano* (1957–58), written for Tudor (see fig. 7), consists of

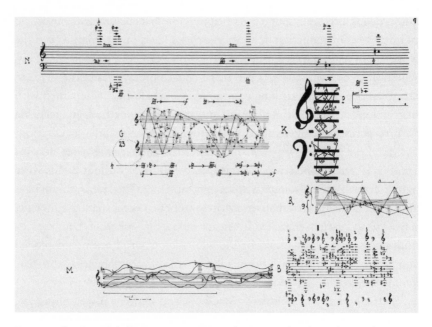

Figure 7. John Cage, *Solo for Piano.* From *Concert for Piano and Orchestra* (1957–58), 9. Copyright © 1960, renewed in 1988, by Henmar Press Inc., C. F. Peters Corporation, Sole Selling Agent. Used by permission. All rights reserved.

eighty-four different types of graphic notation, each with its own instructions for realization and sound production. In addition to documenting an indeterminate composition, this score, like Feldman's, can be interpreted as an abstract work of art. Graphs and graph paper (Cage and Feldman), white spaces to indicate silence (Feldman), lines, circles, and waves overlaid on the musical staff (Cage), and a seemingly random and nonlinear arrangement of graphic notations (Cage) represent the harnessing of conventional notation to visual ends that suggest chance and the indeterminate, chaos, or the purity of mathematical forms. Kruchenykh, Marinetti, Schwitters, and Mac Low similarly expressed their transformation of the voice and the word through an array of visual devices that served as their notation, including uneven letter spacing, text misalignment, the use of handwriting and rubber-stamping, phonetic writing, and typographical design.

This essay has placed sound poetry and avant-garde music within a shared history of sound and live performance. In tracing this history, I have selected American and European composers whose interest in noise, popular melody and rhythm, and extended performance techniques sets them apart from the avant-garde of harmonic and formal innovation, even as it finds intriguing parallels in modern and contemporary sound poetry. Indeed the context of sound poetry offers a new perspective on the musical avant-garde by illuminating its radical expansion of the range of possible sounds, blurring of the line between sound and noise, and invention of new forms of notation. Conversely, the analysis of sound poetry in the context of avant-garde music propels live performance to the forefront, since whether it be Khlebnikov and Kruchenykh, Marinetti, Schwitters, Mac Low, or Dufrêne, the complex interplay of sound and sense, the virtuosic vocal techniques, and the extent to which unintelligible sounds retain the inflections of the poet's spoken language can be appreciated only when the poem is performed. Differences as well as similarities enrich our understanding of the two art forms. For instance, whereas avant-garde music is not generally performed by the composer, sound poetry is performed by the poet. This practice raises provocative questions about the criteria for evaluating a performance of sound poetry if a different poet steps in. Other forms of critique can also be affected by live performance. Such questions should provide fertile ground for future studies of sound poetry in relation to the musical avant-garde.

CACOPHONY, ABSTRACTION, AND POTENTIALITY: THE FATE OF THE DADA SOUND POEM

STEVE MCCAFFERY

No sound is dissonant that tells of Life

SAMUEL TAYLOR COLERIDGE

SAMPLE

ELEFANTEN KARAWANE

jolifanto bambla ô falli bambla

grossiga m'pfa habla horem

égiga goramen

higo bloiko russual huju

hollaka hollala

anlago bung

blago bung

blago bung

bosso fataka

ü üü ü

schampa wulla wussa ólobo

hej tatta gôrem

eschige zunbada

wulubu ssubudu uluw ssubudu

tumba ba- umf

kusagauma

ba — umf

HUGO BALL, *"Elefanten Karawane"*

Prelude

The sound poem is the last of three rapid developments within the performative poetics of Zurich Dada that appeared between late March and June 1916. Marcel Janco, Richard Huelsenbeck, and Tristan Tzara introduced the simultaneous poem (a genre invented by Henri Barzun and Fernand Divoire), at the same time as Huelsenbeck inaugurated his quasi-ethnographic "negro songs."[1] Both types were first presented at Hugo Ball's new Cabaret Voltaire on March 30, 1916, along with Ball's own contribution (a poetry without words) on June 23, 1916. In the simultaneities, such as Tzara's inaugural "The Admiral Is Looking for a House to Rent," sound, text, discrepant noises, whistles, cries, and drums interweave in a sonic version of collage. Interlocution collapses into a texture of parlance and polylogue at the same time as linguistic fragments, in French, German, and English, intersect and combine into efficacious new phrases (it is surely no coincidence that the three languages utilized are respectively those of the three main combatants in the Great War). Although as a collective manifestation the simultaneity attains the status of a *Gesamtkunstwerk* only as parody, it nonetheless brings about that desired confluence and borderblur of song, bruitism, music, and dance that Dick Higgins in the 1960s christened intermedia.[2] Ball has left a succinct definition of the simultaneous poem:

> a contrapuntal recitative in which three or more voices speak, sing, whistle, etc., at the same time in such a way that the elegiac, humorous, or bizarre content of the piece is brought out by these combinations.[3]

Ball too shows sensitivity to the more somber, existential implications of this cacophonous, combinatorial genre; it represents "the background — the inarticulate, the disastrous, the decisive," expressing "the conflict in the *vox humana* with a world that threatens, ensnares, and destroys."[4]

Huelsenbeck's *chants nègres* were conceived as whimsical abstractions designed to evoke the rhythms and "semantics" of African songs. As stereotypical and racist as Vachel Lindsay's 1914 poem "The Congo" (Huelsenbeck's versions mix phrases of calculated nonsense, each refrain ending with the phrase "umba umba"), they nonetheless gained limited authenticity when Huelsenbeck substituted an authentic African song for happy senselessness (retaining, however, his beloved end-refrain). The *chant nègre* took on a genuinely ethnopoetic dimension when Tzara incorporated fragments of authentic African songs culled from anthropology magazines that he read in Zurich.[5]

From its very inception the twentieth-century sound poem has been shrouded in contradiction and uncertainty. There are at least two antecedents to Ball's "invention:" Christian Morgenstern's "Das Grosse Lalulà" (1905) and an untitled piece by Paul Scheerbart (1900). Indeed, a German or Swiss audience would have been familiar with the basic form of Ball's "poetry without words." Scheerbart's begins:

> Kikakoku!
> Ekoralaps!
> Wiao kollipanda opolasa

While Morgenstern's poem, which appeared in the immensely popular *Galgenlieder* (Gallows Songs) and which the author referred to as a "phonetic rhapsody," opens:

> Kroklokwafzi? Semememi!
> Seiokronto-prafriplo;
> Bifzi, bafzi; hulalemi:
> Quati basti bo . . .
> Lalu lalu lalu lalu la![6]

The sound poem's "historical" origin and definition, however, are generally attributed to the German poet émigré Hugo Ball, who first performed his own samples on June 23, 1916, the same date as his diary entry recording his definition of the new genre:

> I have invented a new genre of poems, "Verse ohne Worte" [poems without words] or Lautgedichte [sound poems], in which the balance of the vowels is weighed and distributed solely according to the values of the beginning sequence.[7]

It is tempting to theorize the *Lautgedicht* as Ball's voluntary abnegation of meaning, a splendid and festive nihilism designed to discover a self outside the limitations of reason and semantics. Yet neither the logic of the phoneme (Ball's chosen unit of composition) nor the poet's own recorded reflections support such a judgment. Ball's sound poem is thoroughly grounded in historical sense and awareness; it is formulated as a response not to symbolism or to any other rival avant-garde (such as cubism or futurism), but to the contemporary state of discourse under early twentieth-century capitalism. Moreover, to understand Ball's invention beyond a merely formal synopsis requires investigating his motives, activities, and state of mind both on and prior to June 23, 1916.

Ball's exodus from semantic verse was certainly influenced by his own involvement in the emerging German expressionist theater and by his pre-Zurich studies of Chinese theater. Demoralized and traumatized by the horrors of actual combat, Ball came to realize the catalytic possibilities of theater to effect revolutionary change by way of expressionistic exaggeration. Directed to the subconscious, this new theater developed a code of the festive, with archetypes and loudspeakers used to bypass realism.[8] Less atavistic than transcultural in its propensities, the new theater drew heavily on Chinese and Japanese sources. Ball believed that especially Chinese theater preserved a mantic character — a character carried over into his own sound poetry.

A diary entry for April 2, 1915, is of especial interest precisely because of its implicit comparison of actual war to the theatrical representation of battle:

> When a general receives orders for a campaign into distant provinces, he marches three or four times around the stage, accompanied by a terrible noise of gongs, drums, and trumpets and then stops to let the audience know he has arrived. . . . the holy man sings and grabs the leader of the Tartars by the throat and strangles him with dramatic crescendos. The words of the song do not matter; the laws of rhythm are more important.[9]

Ball is clearly intrigued by the inflection of singing into the representation of violent physical conflict and the concomitant downplay of semantic value within the song in favor of rhythmic law; it is a patent blueprint for the *Lautgedicht*.[10]

There is clearly a forcefully political dimension to Ball's sound poem, and to understand some of its ramifications we need to bear in mind the current climate of a Europe at war. Zurich at that time was a city in a neutral nation surrounded by the carnage of a mad war of attrition. In March 1915 Ball's friend and future Dadaist Walter Serner joined the staff of *Der Mistral,* a self-styled "literary newspaper" whose editors, Hugo Kersten and Emil Szittya, launched a prescient attack not on the current military conflict per se but on the linguistic structures of the bourgeois institutions — religion, law, politics, the current culture industry — that collectively composed a "grammar of war." To supplement this editorial policy (so anticipatory of Foucault's work on discourse and the critique of language launched by Language poetry), poems were included and chosen on the basis of their deliberate undermining of grammatical and syntactic norms (hence the appearance of Apollinaire's *calligrammes* and F. T. Marinetti's *parole in libertà*).[11]

Ball was unquestionably sympathetic to this agenda — he had hopes on his arrival in Zurich from Berlin in May 1915 of collaborating with Serner on *Der Mistral,* but those aspirations did not come to fruition — and he considered his own sound poem a frontal attack on the contemporary condition of instrumental language.[12] However, the origin of Ball's existential unrest dates to well before the war. As early as 1913 he reflected on a life "completely confined and shackled" by an unremittingly compartmentalized world in which serialized existence binds human beings to a monstrously specific and repetitive functionality. The antidote he offers is resolutely nonfuturistic and a surprising anticipation of Georges Bataille's theories of heterology and general economy:

> What is necessary is a league of all men who want to escape from the mechanical world, a way of life opposed to mere utility. Orgiastic devotion to the opposite of everything that is serviceable and useful.[13]

I find it significant that at this time Ball directs his ire at the dehumanizing rhythms of the machine (it is this target of invective that marks Ball's radical dissent from futurist valorizations). Whereas in a few years Ball will inveigh against the language of journalism, in 1913 he offers a savage analysis of the material implications of the printing press itself:

> The machine gives a kind of sham life to dead matter. It moves matter. It is a specter. It joins matter together, and in so doing reveals some kind of rationalism. Thus it is death, working systematically, counterfeiting life. It tells more flagrant lies than any newspaper that it prints. And what is more, in its continuous subconscious influence it destroys human rhythm. . . . A walk through a prison cannot be so horrifying as a walk through the noisy workroom of a modern printing shop.[14]

It is sobering to compare Ball's account of the state of the work of art in an age of mechanical reproduction with Benjamin's more famous document.

Before the horror of war and its incomprehensibility, Ball reacts to the horrors of the machinic imaginary, and this reaction is carried over into wartime. Indeed, Ball emerges as the paramount Dada Luddite writing in late 1914, after returning from a visit to the Belgian front: "it is the total mass of machinery and the devil himself that has broken loose now." And he later adumbrates on this comment in a letter on June 26, 1915, attributing the war to an ontological and tactical confusion: "the war is based on a crass error. Men have been mistaken for machines. Machines, not men, should be decimated."[15]

June 1916 and After

Ball's diary entry for June 24, 1916 (previously incorporated into the program notes for the June 23 performance), proclaims, in manifesto-like fashion, the theory of his sound poem:

> In these phonetic [*sic*] poems we totally renounce the language that journalism has abused and corrupted. We must return to the innermost alchemy of the word, we must even give up the word too, to keep for poetry its last and holiest refuge. We must give up writing second-hand: that is, accepting words (to say nothing of sentences) that are not newly invented for our own use.[16]

This passage is remarkable for its synthesis of clarity and enigma. It carries a lucid call to praxis, yet at the same time it petitions a vague mystery and pro- phylaxis. To neologize in order to innovate? Most certainly, and not without precedent, for Ball follows in the footsteps of the Russian futurist poets Ve- limir Khlebnikov and Alexei Kruchenykh, whose practice of *zaum'* (transra- tional language) produced texts and phrases of deliberate incomprehension, to which Ball was introduced by Kandinsky.[17] As well as marking a stark re- versal of his earlier beliefs in the dangers of neologism (Ball had recorded on November 25, 1915, that "each word is a wish or a curse. One must be care- ful not to make words once one has acknowledged the power of the living word"),[18] it advances a poetic ontology of bold individualism, one conse- quence of which is an indirect critique of German ideology.[19] For by revert- ing to the phoneme and to the force of haptic, pathic affect, Ball removes the very possibility for the propositional constructions and narratives on which any national language can be constructed. If Tzara's simultaneous poetry dis- members national language, Ball's *Lautgedicht* effectively destroys it.

So far so good, but major questions now arise: what is "the innermost alchemy of the word"? Where is, let alone *what* is, poetry's "last and holiest refuge"? Ball's critical vector slides at this point from social disgust into a vague spiritual poetics, a veritable poetical theology. Indeed, the *Lautgedicht* surpasses any sociolinguistic critique of the contemporary, ambient condi- tions in the warring, secular world to encapsulate the very spiritualization of politics, sounding the redemption of the word via the power of abstract phonematicity. Ball offers an alchemical poetics of alembication by which the word, in being pulverized, is preserved as a higher distillate through re- finement from its semantic dross. He summarizes his achievements five days prior to the first performance of the *Lautgedicht*:

We have loaded the word with strengths and energies that helped us to rediscover the evangelical concept of the "word" (logos) as a magical complex image.[20]

It is clear that by June 18 Ball had worked out not only a new genre of acoustic poetry but a new theory of the image, one carried not by words but by phonemic rhythm and called by him a "grammalogue." (It is difficult not to think of Pound's own modification of the poetic image. Where Pound uncouples image from a pictorial paradigm. redefining it as an emotional and intellectual complex in an instant of time, Ball converts image into gramma-logue, a sonic shorthand for a mnemonically charged acoustic force.)

Jeffrey Schnapp speculates (somewhat unsuccessfully in my judgment) on the precise nature of the *Lautgedicht*'s alchemical potential, seeing in it a "generative mode of expression that, tapping the innermost alchemical pow-ers of the word, renders unfamiliar worlds familiar by means of semantic [*sic*] units that are simultaneously words, pictures and incantations."[21] A less esoteric explanation lends itself via the logic of phonemic articulation itself. The abstract, vocabolic string registers a confluence of negation and potenti-ality, transforming denotation into an unpredictable, indeterminate vertigo of connotational possibilities — and Ball himself seems aware of this:

> We tried to give the isolated vocables the fullness of an oath, the glow of a star
> And curiously enough, the magically inspired vocables conceived and gave birth
> to a *new* sentence that was not limited and confined by any conventional meaning.
> Touching lightly on a hundred ideas at the same time without naming them, this
> sentence made it possible to hear the innately playful, but hidden, irrational char-
> acter of the listener, it weakened and strengthened the lowest strata of memory.[22]

Here, as elsewhere, Ball shows himself susceptible to the same intoxication by analogy that patinated Marinetti's futurist poetics, yet the gist of his claim is clear: the sound poem is a departure not from semantics per se but rather from the doxa of conventional meaning. Indeed, the mantic power within the *Lautgedicht* creates a semantic condition in which meaning is *potential-ized* and that way *unconventionalized*. This is not a commitment to Cratylism (that ancient belief that a word possesses a natural relation to the thing it des-ignates), but it certainly represents a significant move toward a radical cona-tive poetics grounded in irrational, infantile, and primary forces. Ball strives for that magical center Auden speaks of in his "Homage to Clio," but where Auden's great poem is testimony to the failure of visual paradigms, Ball's *Lautgedicht* registers as a beacon to sound's capacity to transcend the visual and situate the phenomenal and imaginary in a mantic space of indeterminate intellectual and mnemonic eruptions. By introducing difference into continuity, the phoneme inflects the sonic with the haunting potential of meaning. The quotidian issue raised by any phonetic, nonsemantic poetry is, precisely what happens to meaning? And the answer is quite clear: phonetic poetry has a repositional rather than negative effect upon meaning; it situates the semantic order elsewhere — meaning becomes potential in its marginality.

Indeed, how to discern an abstract, senseless sound poem from authentic xenoglossia when both are interchangeable with respect to realizing the desired "cabaret" is a central question arising in both the *chant nègre* and the phonetic *Lautgedicht*.[23]

Further complicating the sound poem's status is the fact that Ball's alembication of the word continues Mallarmé's 1886 proposal in *The Crisis of Poetry* that separates two distinct verbal orders: the one of immediate and unrefined words and the other of the "essential" word. The *Lautgedicht* enjoys the identical connotative powers that Mallarmé aimed for: the ideal suggestion of an object. One is thus left questioning whether Ball broke away from the tenets of symbolist poetics or enriched those poetics by adding an abstract method onto a poetics already geared to suggestion. The constitutional paradox at the heart of the *Lautgedicht* is readily apparent: when precise denotation is eliminated, the connotational potential of the phoneme and phonemic string — as well as its susceptibility to stirring the irrational and mnemonic strata in the addressee — is maximized.[24] Lacking the abstract acoustic constructions so evident in Raoul Hausmann's untitled "kp'erioUM lp'er" and the *letterklankbeelden* poems by Theo van Doesburg, Ball's poems — like Paul Scheerbart's and Christian Morgenstern's — read and sound like extreme attempts at creating the effect of "another" language; they carry a strong propensity to ignite mental associations and sensory stimulations.[25] Moreover, in some of his six *Lautgedichten,* the title frames the poem within a mimetic project; "Elefanten Karawane" (Elephants Caravan) is a clear example, and Ball himself acknowledges the onomatopoetic intention in that poem to evoke "the plodding rhythm of the elephants."[26] The appeal, however, to instigated depths of primordial memory adds a genuine complexity to the sound poem — and this is the significant aspect in Ball's poetics.

Significant but not egregious, for the psycho-anthropological thinking Ball inherits marks his grammology as more typical of the times than exceptional. His theory of regression and deep memory finds support in the work of Cesare Lombroso (1835–1909), whose own theories on the relation of creativity to dementia shifted mental illness from a disease of the brain to a disorder of the mind.[27] In his 1864 *Genius and Madness* (a book that Ball did not read until August 1916 and that hence could not have been a direct influence on his poetics), Lombroso records his examination of the creative output of 107 patients, concluding that creativity in dementia produces work bearing a striking resemblance to artworks from earlier evolutionary times — what Lombroso refers to as "primitive cultures." Lombroso's atavistic theory is in broad concurrence with Wilhelm Worringer's 1908 study *Abstraction and Empathy,* a book that influenced Kandinsky's thinking on the parallelism of modern and tribal and that still remains a basic tenet of contemporary ethnopoetics.[28] This dual influence helps explain the common fascination among several Dadaists with the creative possibilities of irrationality and insanity, together with the masks and songs of tribal cultures that informed the *chants nègres* and pervaded Dada.[29]

In retrospect Ball shows a close affinity to this nascent ethnopoetics of the irrational, as the following passage makes clear:

> The new theories we have been advancing [the *Lautgedicht* or Dada at large?] have serious consequences for this field. The childlike quality I mean borders on the infantile, on dementia, on paranoia. It comes from the belief in a primeval memory, in a world that has been supplanted and buried beyond recognition, a world that is liberated in art by unrestrained enthusiasm, but in the lunatic asylum is freed by a disease.[30]

The Swoon and the Aftermath

Ball left a vivid record of his famous first (and last) presentation of the *Lautgedicht* in which he recalls his mental and emotional transmogrification during the performance. After describing his dramatic entrance onto the cabaret stage in darkness, dressed quasi-ecclesiastically in a cardboard cubist costume, with claw hands and blue and white striped "witch doctor's hat," immobile (because of the costume) and therefore carried onto the stage, he recalls:

> I do not know what gave me the idea of this music, but I began to chant my vowel sequences in a church style like a recitative and tried not only to look serious but to force myself to be serious. For a moment it seemed as if there was the pale, bewildered face in my cubist mask, that half-frightened, half-curious face of a ten-year-old boy, trembling and hanging avidly on the priest's words in the requi-

ems and high masses in his own parish. The lights went out, as I had ordered, and bathed in sweat, I was carried off the stage like a magical bishop.[31]

I find it hard not to be skeptical of this image of the forty-year-old Ball's regressive epiphany on that Zurich night in June, and the dubious may rightly place the Magical Bishop scenario on a par with Coleridge's strategic fiction of the Person from Porlock.[32] Notwithstanding the factual uncertainty of his psychosomatically induced state, the condition described attunes accurately with Ball's general theories of primordial memory and the complex imbrications of the child and the irrational. Renouncing one type of institutional codification, Ball returns involuntarily to another: the Catholic church. Ball predicts that in the conditions experienced in the world around him art "will be irrational, primitive, and complex; it will speak a secret language and leave behind documents not of edification but of paradox."[33] This adds an acromatic dimension to the *Lautgedicht,* and Ball's grammology reveals itself to be also a cryptology. There is yet another dimension that further convolves the intentions of Ball's sound poetry and is implicit in his final pre-Zurich diary entry: "if language really makes us kings of our nation, then without doubt it is we, the poets and thinkers, who are to blame for this blood bath and who have to atone for it."[34] The *Lautgedicht* does not offer a soteriological solution to humanity but rather gestures toward an alliance of penitence and creativity. Ball's poetic mission is atonement, the assumption (not the renunciation) of the burden of guilt for a senseless war, and the *Lautgedicht* is Ball's method of atonement.

I conclude with a brief consideration of a couple of passages from Ball's now famous "First Dada Manifesto" of July 14, 1916, which simultaneously introduce and close the brief history of the *Lautgedicht* and mark I believe Ball's final break with Dada:

> How does one achieve eternal bliss? By saying dada. . . . With a noble gesture and delicate propriety. Till one goes crazy. Till one loses consciousness. . . . Dada m'dada. Dada mhm'dada da[35]

Of all Zurich Dadaists Ball alone elevates the playful name of Dada to the level of a mind-altering mantra. Jonathan Hammer insists that Ball constructs the repeated phoneme as a password in order to gain "access to the ineffable meditation."[36] If so, then Ball's Dada was not a movement but a shibboleth appropriated as the tetragrammaton of a new century.

I will serve to show how articulated language comes into being. I let the vowels fool around. I let the vowels quite simply occur, as a cat miaows. . . . Words emerge, shoulders of words, legs, arms, hands of words. Au, oi, uh[37]

I find it hard not to read into this curious dramaturgic equation of words to body parts (surely one of the strangest equations of body to language ever conceived) a reference to the creation of the Golem, a being infused with the illusion of existence, a rabbinical creation from the four elements, a simulacrum destined to serve man in a better way than language. Ball's *Lautgedicht* with its grammological power finally turns out to be a language homunculus.

I believe this passage marks the end of Ball's belief in the *Lautgedicht;* in 1917 he will continue his fascination with magic and will meditate on the relationship of the mantic to ascetic individualism. Magic will become for him "the last refuge of individual self-assertion, and maybe individualism in general" and "the final result of individualism will be magic" — a far cry from the collective jubilation that signifies the spontaneous community of the simultaneous poem.[38]

Perhaps no other Dadaist wrote himself into the history of the avant-garde in such a brief space of time and with such a meager contribution. Ball's career remains testimony to how a conative poetics of the self, linked fundamentally to collective memory and made manifest in the form of incantatory phonemes, can find an end in solipsism and enigmatic soliloquy. The *Lautgedicht,* Ball's creation and gift to Dada, proved to be an ephemeral moment in an equally transient movement, and he left both behind. Two *Lautgedichten* found their way into his fantasy novel *Tenderenda the Fantast,* and his total legacy to the new genre is a mere six poems plus a handful of equally short statements (most of which this essay supplies).

On June 18, 1921, long after his departure from Dada, Ball recalls an almost Pauline experience, a Christian abduction-through-interpellation that parallels his swoon as the Magical Bishop: "When I came across the word dada, I was called upon twice by Dionysius. D.A. — D.A."[39] It may be coincidental that *D.A.* are the first two letters on the way to spelling out *DAMASCUS,* the locus of Paul's conversion, but it is not coincidental that these are the initials of that most famous of Neoplatonists, the sixth-century Dionysius the Areopagite on whom Ball was subsequently to write in great detail in his *Byzantine Christianity.* Ball's theologization of the avant-garde is complete, poetry is atonement not critique, articulate language is a homunculus, and for the poet of the *Lautgedicht* "DADA" becomes "BYE-BYE."[40]

WHEN CYBORGS VERSIFY / CHRISTIAN BÖK

Writing is pre-eminently the technology of cyborgs.

DONNA J. HARRAWAY

My composition *The Cyborg Opera* is a long poem in progress — a linguistic soundscape that responds to the ambient chatter of technology by arranging words, not according to their semantic meanings, but according to their phonetic valences. While the title of the poem might suggest that the work is a kind of libretto, the word *opera* in this case does not refer to a genre of musical drama so much as the term abbreviates a technical "operation" — a procedure by which to imagine a hitherto undreamt poetics of electronica. Even though critics, like Harraway, might imply that cyborgs have almost become the updated subject in our humanist theories of History, poets do not yet seem ready to write poems that might address a whole class of beasts, robots, and clones, all of which await their own unique brands of "liberation." We are perhaps the first generation of poets who can reasonably expect in our lifetime to write poems for a machinic audience — but despite the foretold approach of this artificial readership, poets continue to address only each other in the lyric voice of our human drama. I suggest that even though we have become ever more detached from our voices (owing to the advent of such technologies as vocal recording, vocal telephony, and vocal synthesis), poets continue to argue that, nevertheless, we must find ways to access the unique music in our inborn styles of speech. I might also suggest that even among the avant-garde, poets have yet to begin a thoroughgoing investigation of computer-assisted composition (like the kind seen, for example, in recent trends of popular, digital music). I have, therefore, begun to wonder how a poetic cyborg of the future might grow to find its own voice amid the welter of our cacophonic technology.

The Cyborg Opera is in part a critical reaction to some of the more "theurgical" traditions of modernism — traditions that have striven to reclaim the magic of words from the mechanical utterances of everyday dialogue. Varied poets of the avant-garde (including, among others, such writers as Alexei Kruchenykh and Kurt Schwitters) have often argued that in order to resuscitate an atrophied language, one asphyxiated by the utilitarian constraints of bourgeois discourse, poetry must revert to a more primitive, more libidinal, outburst of organic orality (like the kind seen, for example, in the *Lautgedichten* of both *zaum'* and *Merz* — "sound poems" that pulverize the sense of words in order to emphasize the music of their parts). Hugo Ball, the Dada poet, argues, for example, that "we must return to the innermost alchemy of the word," recreating the ancient cadence of liturgical ceremonies so that we may all become magical bishops. Such poets insist that if poetry hopes to go "beyond reason," then it must disintegrate meaning, perhaps through primal shouts or ritual chants, so that words may recapture a "primordial feeling" (as is the case for Kruchenykh) or a "primordial concept" (as is the case for Schwitters).[1] Such acts of either glossolalia or thaumaturgy can supposedly transform language into a universal, originary discourse — an *Ursprache,* capable of returning the performer to a much more "integrated" experience of the self. Even though this "phono-philic," if not "quasi-mystic," sensibility has spawned an august oeuvre of sound poems, such a sensibility seems all but untenable in the face of our technological augmentations, which already threaten to overwhelm the organic coherence of any unified performer.

The Cyborg Opera responds directly to these issues of primordial experience, insofar as my work reacts to the precedent set by Schwitters in his poem *Die Ursonate* (one of the most beautiful, but most difficult, *Lautgedichten* in the world to perform). *Die Ursonate* consists of four movements, inspired in part by the classical structure of a sonata (complete with a rondo and a largo, a scherzo and a cadenza) — and each movement enacts a series of variations upon a theme, riffing off the phonetic phrasing in several Dadaist poems by Raoul Hausmann.[2] Schwitters requires about forty minutes to perform his poem in its entirety, and to my ear his rendition almost calls to mind the melodies of birdsong; however, I have garnered some notoriety over the years for reciting an updated version of this poem in as little as ten minutes, performing a kind of "speed-metal" variation intended to emphasize the machinic intensity of the original.[3] While my peers have admitted that I might demonstrate estimable skill in the performance of such a vocal score, they always wonder aloud whether or not I might demonstrate an equivalent skill in the composition of my own sonic verse — and consequently, they have dared me to upstage this challenging masterpiece, extending its poetic usage of primal sounds into a verbal arena of modern noises. I am hoping that my newer "operetta" might eventually constitute such a potential contender, one that can capitalize upon the kind of mechanical elocutions learned through my accelerated performance of the older "sonatina." I know that my own research into electronica has stemmed largely from this initial impetus to improve upon a euphonious masterwork by one of the geniuses of the avant-garde.

The Cyborg Opera strives not only to extend, but also to exceed, this poetic legacy — a legacy that has sought to document the most primitive, most intuitive, utterance at the sudden moment when it emerges, both authentically and spontaneously, from the body of the ecstatic organism itself. Rather than rehearse, however, the unargued liberties afforded us so far by such celebrated traditions (including *zaum'* and *Merz*), my own poem perhaps strives to revisit, with critical wariness, the more disputed liberties promised us by Marinetti in his concurrent aesthetics of futurism, with its unique genre of *parole in libertà:* phonic poetry, whose onomatopoeia gives voice not to the ecstatic impulses of an organic anatomy but to the electric impulses of an operant machine. Rather than reassert the absolute humanity of the performer, *parole in libertà* strives "to make literature out of the life of a motor," doing so in order to redefine the performer as either a species of mechanic or a species of engineer — a "multiplied man," whose rapport with industrial mechanisms might provide a model for authorship in a cyborg future of automatic scription.[4] When Marinetti goes on to aver that within such a future "men can write in books of nickel no thicker than three centimeters, costing no more than eight francs, and still containing one hundred thousand pages," he almost seems to presage the modern advent of the laptop, itself a kind of metal codex, akin to an artificial, detachable organ, capable of amplifying the will of its user to a planetary influence.[5] He argues, moreover, that within such a future "panels bristling with dials, keyboards, and shining commutators ... are our only models for the writing of poetry."[6]

The Cyborg Opera takes for granted that we have already started to inhabit such a world of superhuman machinists; however, my poem goes on to take issue with the bombastic militancy of such a mechanized aesthetics. Even though Marinetti might beseech the poets of the future "to listen to motors and to reproduce their conversations," the dubious, aesthetic merits (if not the dubious, political themes) implicit in his protofascist *Lautgedichten* have, no doubt, caused subsequent versifiers to balk at the artificial enhancement, if not the prosthetic replacement, of their own vocalizations.[7] Even though a vanguard novelist like William S. Burroughs might later argue that "a tape recorder is an externalized section of the human nervous system," only a spartan coterie of sound poets have ever committed themselves to the use of such technology — among them, Henri Chopin (the inventor of the *audio-poème*).[8] When, in his *poésie sonore,* Chopin modulates an audiotape of his own buccal output — excising, then splicing, the smallest vocables of his voice, attenuating them and overdubbing them — he frees his utterances from any anatomical constraint, doing so by using the microphone as a kind of probe, ready to extract an unexamined repertoire of sounds from all the resonant chambers in his organs of speech. Even though Chopin might celebrate the invention of such a magnetophone, saying that "without this machine, *sound poetry* ... would not exist, as no human diction, however ... skillful, could produce it," other poets have, nevertheless, rebuffed these technocratic opportunities for innovation, often doing so in order to preserve the performative authenticity of the human voice itself.[9]

The Cyborg Opera has, likewise, refrained from deploying any electronic prosthesis in its own composition. This is not because I harbor any Luddite reaction toward the use of either vocoders or remixers; on the contrary, I do hope to experiment with such machines as part of my artistic research. However, I have preferred in the meantime to rethink what Marinetti might call the "passéism" of a reliable, but outdated, style in order to imagine the "futurity" of a foreseen, but untested, trope. Unlike *Die Ursonate,* which uses as its model the classic formats of chamber music, my opera refuses to replicate a passé music, preferring instead to portray the contemporary labor of poetry under technocratic duress. When subsequent performers of *Lautgedichten* have resorted to a musical metaphor in order to explain their compositions after 1950, they often look back and cite jazz as a prime model for their use of improvised methods and syncopated rhythms: for example, Paul Dutton (a former member of the Four Horsemen and the author of a vocal suite entitled "Jazz") expresses such a typical poetics of freestyle jazziness: "I pursue the sounds that suggest themselves, discovering the form within the material rather than imposing form on it" — doing so because "that instrument is happiest not knowing what [is] coming next."[10] Even though jazz has had an important influence upon the literary cadences of poetry (particularly among Americans of the Beat generation, including, among others, Allen Ginsberg and Bob Kaufman), jazz for me has nevertheless become a nostalgic, if not an antiquarian, paradigm. We have already created a poetic version of this older, improv form, but we cannot readily imagine a poetic cognate for a newer, techno beat.

The Cyborg Opera, therefore, does not deign to reiterate any of the jazzified theatrics that have gone on to characterize the current troupes of either "spokenword" performers or "neobeatnik" bohemians, many of whom vocalize "def rap" from memory at slams. Even though such poets often exploit updated, musical styles of speech (like dub, rap, or ska), all of which emanate from the technocratic environments of urban youth, the practitioners of these varied poetic genres still value the performative authenticity of a sincere speaker, whose literary charisma can establish an organic rapport with an intimate audience. Even though the musical regimes that inspire these "spokenword movements" might exploit all the gadgetry of mobile discos, literati who perform such oral work often eschew any audiophonic enhancement more high-tech than a microphone. They do not recite sound poems so much as retell rhyming stories, riffing off hip-hop phrases, for example, in a manner that still calls to mind the average, beatnik raconteur at a jazz club. When Bob Holman (the impresario of poetic slams and the ringmaster of verbal duels) remarks that for competitors at such venues, "performance is another step of editing," he signals the degree to which such acts of reading extend acts of writing into a public domain, where audiences can then evaluate a performer in the expedient but authentic throes of improv action.[11] Such poetry strives to return the poet to the theurgical conditions of an oral rite. I argue, however, that in order to explain avant-garde sound poems through the trope of music, poets of today may have to adopt a genre better suited to express our millennial anxieties in an era now driven by the hectic tempos of our technology.

The Cyborg Opera disavows the apparent humanity of the voices that might recite it; instead, the poem uses words to compose a kind of "spoken techno" — a vocal genre whose music emulates the mechanical rhythms and cacophonic melodies heard in the throb of our machines. When asked about my preferences in music, I always confess, with hints of irony, that I like "music by machines for machines" — which is to say that, for whatever reasons of aesthetic judgment, I have grown to prefer music without any lyrics, unless of course such a vocal track has already been sampled and remixed from a precedent recording. When asked to justify such an eccentric prejudice,

I respond by saying that nowadays the weak link in any performance of lyric verse is probably the human agent. Of all the art forms at our disposal, music has evolved to become not only the most dominant, and most abstract but also the one whose progress has begun to outstrip our capacity both to compose it and to consume it without the aid of ever more advanced devices. To a greater degree than other art forms (like painting and writing), which often solicit a contemplative, if not a philosophical, response from their audiences, music induces in its listeners a whole spate of autonomic reflexes and emotional twitches, any of which can transform the audience into an unthinking prosthesis of the medium itself. Is it not fair to say that beats of music (rather than daubs of paint or words in verse) can more readily convert a quiescent person into a turbulent rioter? I argue that whenever we enter the dance floor, we do so in order to become the robotic puppets of deejays, who use music to command our nervous systems via remote control.

The Cyborg Opera anticipates a future poetry that, when performed by a human being, transforms the versifier into a kind of athletic, musical engine — one able to spit out each word with the accuracy, if not the velocity, of a rivet. Modern genres of electronica (like techno or trance) have already supplied a paradigm for this literary activity. Such genres of contemporary, computerized music use turntables and synthdrums to fabricate tracks in 4/4 time at a tempo in excess of 120 beats per minute (well beyond the athletic capacity of any average drummer). Such music typically features assertive bass lines made amenable for dancing, and because the work almost always remains instrumental without any accompanying vocalization, such compositions often avoid any overtly melodic structure, relying instead upon synched rhythms, modified by reverbs and filters. When deejays use sequencers to automate the crossfading and overdubbing of these effects, they outsource a portion of their creativity to an alien brain, and I guess that my use of the word *cyborg* refers in part to such an assemblage — the "symbiosis," if you like, between the musical instrument and the musical technician, both interlocked inside the feedback circuits of their own interlocution. When Paul D. Miller (the artist better known as DJ Spooky) remarks that "DJ-ing is writing, writing is DJ-ing," he signals the degree to which literature and musicology have already begun to exploit the same repertoire of techniques — be it through the repeated fragmentation of prior works (via sampling) or through the collaged juxtaposition of cited parts (via remixing).[12] I am hoping that the "arias" in my opera might yet provide the vocal grist for similar acts of deejaying.

The Cyborg Opera includes, among its varied tracks, a "faux aria" entitled "Mushroom Clouds" — a sequence of nonsense, inspired by the acoustic ambience of the videogame *Super Mario Bros.* by Nintendo. While Japan has so far remained the only country on the planet to suffer atomic attack, the nation has, eerily enough, chosen to counterstrike, not with its own military weapons of mass destruction, but with its own cultural symbols of cute disposition: Hello Kitties and manga girlies. The poem responds to this modern milieu of global terror by combining, purely for phonic effect, silly words from the popular culture of globalized capitalism, doing so in order to suggest that, under atomic threat, life itself has taken on the cartoonish atmosphere of our pinball arcades. The bloops and bleeps of the originary videogame sound humorous, of course, and my work merely imitates some of this goofiness for comic usage. The "aria" serves as a kind of videogame that I play through the activity of speaking aloud — and if my performance induces laughter in the audience, I suspect that such listeners might be responding in part to an experience of the "uncanny" while watching a funny human behave like an artsy robot. Moreover, the silliness of the poem does indeed contrast with its overtones of atomic horror, and the audience may find itself laughing at the mordant ironies of a poet saying "oops" in response to the potential accidents of nuclear détente. If "mankind . . . can," as Benjamin argues, "experience its own destruction as an aesthetic pleasure of the first order," then undoubtedly my opera must find a way to compete with such unthinkable apocalypses for the sustained attention of its foredoomed readership.[13]

The Cyborg Opera also features a "bonus track" entitled "Synth Loops" — an operatic addendum that has grown out of my search for a kind of "robotic lexicon," a usable palette of words that might evoke, through onomatopoeic connotations, the noises of various devices, be they engines or buzzers, dynamos or beepers. Such research has resulted in a sidelong interest in the work of beatboxing performers, who use their voices to simulate the toolkit of deejays, mimicking the riffs of turntables and the loops of synthdrums. Even though avant-garde sound poets, like Dutton, have studiously avoided the use of musical mimicry in their own performances of *Lautgedichten,* preferring to do verbal improv based at times upon libidinal outbursts of emotion, beatboxers like Razael or Dokaka have demonstrated so marvelous a technical expertise in their own vocal works that their activity in popular culture (such as their appearance on the album *Medulla* by Björk) has begun to put to shame some of the achievements by more classical producers of phonic poetry. The beatboxer must learn an alphabet of resonant plosives and sonorant vibratos, all of which combine, like letters, to form a fund of alien words that, when spoken at a fast pace, generate the acoustic illusion of multiple machines operated at the same time. My opera may come to include such overtures of verbalized percussion — but so far these tracks constitute an amateurish experiment, documenting some of my initial efforts to master some of the elementary vocabulary for a few of the drum kits most often used by beatboxers. I am hoping that, with advanced practice, I can soon integrate some linguistic variations of these effects into the structure of my poem.

The Cyborg Opera does promise to be a lengthy project, evolving in response to my ongoing research, but so far I am hoping that this essay might illuminate some of my rambling thoughts about the role of avant-garde sound poems in a growing, digital culture — a culture where poetry falters in its attempt to retain even a dedicated, but dwindling, readership. Poets in such a command economy of information make almost no money from their work — and in fact they can barely give their poetry away for free. Such a plight represents an extreme version of the conditions already faced by other artists, particularly musicians, whose work gets copied and given away online with almost no hope of enforceable restitution; however, such artists do gain a potential audience that might in turn demand other commodified experiences, such as lectures, seminars, or readings. Poets now probably make more money from selling such "services" (in the form of talks) than from selling their "products" (in the form of books). Under these conditions, poets must at least offer some demonstrable, performative competence in order to justify the expense of their appearance in person at a venue — and thus I have done my best to live up to such standards by emulating the acrobatic technique of performers like Chopin and Dutton (or better yet, Razael and Dokaka), all of whom have perfected a glorious delivery free from error and ennui, despite the superhuman virtuosity needed to voice their works. I suspect that in the social milieu of our cyborg future the very idea of a "fine performance" by a writer has already started to take on the technical overtones that competent mechanics might hear in the "high performance" of an engine.

Poetic Appendices[14]

EXCERPT FROM "MUSHROOM CLOUDS" IN *THE CYBORG OPERA*

Hong Kong
King Kong hop-along ping-pong

dingbat ding-a-ling
wingding sing-along

deafening
ding-dong diphthong of a gong

my tongue muttering
an unsung lettering

guys sing
something from some folk song

hillbilly billabong
boom bang boomerang

you bring
a dang kangaroo to a gangbang

ongoing boing boing
of a long bedspring

your gang
ogling the oblong bling bling

ingots of lingering
doom in a mood ring

whiz-bang
lightning striking the Viking

king of us Niebelung
die Götterdammerung

yo-yo Tokyo peyote
okay
opium Pinocchio

go-go dance akimbo
baby
bebop obliggato

pop a pill to play
Day-Glo pinball

pogo-jump
a ping-pong ball

judo-kick
a ding-dong bell

lob a bomb to bomb
Pop-Art gewgaws

Ubu buys Enola Gay

pygmy lollapalooza

zoo
kazoo bazooka

big
igloo palooka

kooky gobbledygook

eureka kabuki

yucky
blue buckaroo

kinky
pink pachinko

cuckoo kaboom

bikini kahuna

burka
play peekaboo

karma
boom babushka

voodoo vavoom

RONDOS FROM "SYNTH LOOPS" IN *THE CYBORG OPERA*

Bhm — T — Nsh — tpt'Bhm — T — Nsh [thsss] —
BhoBho-TT-**pfH**-TT — BhoBho-TT-Nsh [thsss]
Bhm — T — Nsh — tpt'Bhm — T — Nsh [thsss] —
BhoBho-TT-**pfH**-TT — BhoBho-TT-Nsh [thsss]
Bhm — T — Nsh — tpt'Bhm — T — Nsh [thsss] —
BhoBho-TT-**pfH**-TT — BhoBho-TT-Nsh [thsss]
Bhm — T — Nsh — tpt'Bhm — T — Nsh [thsss] —
BhoBho-TT-**pfH**-TT — BhoBho-TT-Nsh [thsss] — Bhm!

BhoBho-TT-**pfH**-TT — BhoBho-TT-Pff-TT —
BhoBho-TT-**pfH**-TT — BhoBho-TT-Nsh [thsss]
BhoBho-TT-**pfH**-TT — BhoBho-TT-Pff-TT —

BhoBho-TT-**pfH**-TT — BhoBho-TT-Nsh [thsss]
BhoBho-TT-**pfH**-TT — BhoBho-TT-Pff-TT —
BhoBho-TT-**pfH**-TT — BhoBho-TT-Nsh [thsss]
BhoBho-TT-**pfH**-TT — BhoBho-TT-Pff-TT —
BhoBho-TT-**pfH**-TT — BhoBho-TT-Nsh [thsss]

BhoBho-TT-**pfH**-TT — BhoBho-TT-BhoBho-TT
BhoBho-TT-**pfH**-TT — BhoBho-TT-BhoBho-TT
BhoBho-TT-**pfH**-TT — BhoBho-TT-BhoBho-TT
BhoBho-TT-**pfH**-TT — BhoBho-TT-BhoBho-TT

BhmThm-Pff-TT — BhoBho-TT-**pfH**-T
BhmThm-Pff-TT — BhoBho-TT-**pfH**-T
BhmThm-Pff-TT — BhoBho-TT-**pfH**-T
BhmThm-Pff-TT — BhoBho-TT-**pfH**-T

BhmThm-BhmThm
BhmThm-BhmThm
BhmThm-BhmThm
BhmThm-BhmThm

Bhō-T-[K] — tpt'Bho-[K]-T — Bhō-T-[K] — tpt'Bho-[K]
Bhō-T-[K] — tpt'Bho-[K]-T — Bhō-T-[K] — tpt'Bho-[K]
Bhō-T-[K] — tpt'Bho-[K]-T — Bhō-T-[K] — tpt'Bho-[K]
Bhō-T-[K] — tpt'Bho-[K]-T — Bhō-T-[K] — tpt'Bho-[K]

BhōBhō — [vvvhb]-BhmPff
Bho-p'ThmBhm-Pff-[K] — MmmBhm-Pff —
Bho-p'ThmBhm-Pff-[K] — MmmBhm-Pff —
Bho-p'ThmBhm-Pff-[K] — MmmBhm-Pff —
Bho-p'ThmBhm-Pff-[K] — MmmBhm-Pff —
b'Bhm — p'ThmBhm-Pff

Ung-TT-Ung-TT
Ung-TT-Ung-TT
Ung-TT-Ung-TT
Ung-TT-Ung-TT

Ung-T-Nsh-T — Ung-T-Nsh
Ung-T-Nsh-T — Ung-T-Nsh
Ung-T-Nsh-T — Ung-T-Nsh
Ung-T-Nsh-T — Ung-T-Nsh

Ung-T [thsss] Ung-k'TT-Nsh
Ung-T [thsss] Ung-k'TT-Nsh
Ung-T [thsss] Ung-k'TT-Nsh
Ung-T [thsss] Ung-k'TT-Nsh

Nsh-T'k — Ung-T [thsss] Ung
Nsh-T'k — Ung-T [thsss] Ung
Nsh-T'k — Ung-T [thsss] Ung
Nsh-T'k — Ung-T [thsss] Ung

Ung-T [thsss] Ung-k'TT-NshNsh
Ung-T [thsss] Ung-k'TT-NshNsh
Ung-T [thsss] Ung-k'TT-NshNsh
Ung-T [thsss] Ung-k'TT-NshNsh
Ush-NshNshshsh. . . .

KEY TO NOTATION

Bhm	Kick Drum (Classic)	T	High Hat (Closed)
Bho	Kick Drum (Classic)	TT	High Hat (Double)
Bhō	Synth Drum	tpt	High Hat (Combo)
[K]	606 Snare Drum	Ung	Techno Bass
Mmm	Reverb Effect	Ush	Techno Bass
Nsh	909 Snare Drum	b	Kick Drum (Quick)
		k	Rimshot (Quick)
Pff	Snare Drum (Classic)	p	Kick Drum (Quick)
pfH	Snare Drum (Reverse)	[thsss]	808 Snare Roll
Thm	Brushed Snare	[vvvhb]	Reverse Kick

HEARING VOICES / CHARLES BERNSTEIN

What's the difference between the alphabetic text of a poem and its performance? So much depends upon whether one imagines the poet's performance as an extension of an authorized and stable written work or as a discrete work in its own right. While the first view might allow the performance as a variation of the original, the second implies that textual and vocal instances of the poem offer discrepant versions of the work.

Any reader can perform the written text of a poem, and indeed many poems need to be read out loud in order to make tangible the rhythm and sound patterning. But a poet's reading of her or his own work has an entirely different authority. The poet's performance, both live and recorded, poses an arresting issue for poetry, for the differences among the alphabetic, grammaphonic, and live are not so much ones of textual variance as of ontological condition.

But why this focus on the poet's performance? Isn't this just another way of fetishizing the author and the author's voice? The facts on the ground are these: the archive of recordings, as well as the live performance, of contemporary poems is almost exclusively composed of poets giving voice to their own work; in the first instance, the claim for the significance of poetry performance is less theoretical than an acknowledgment of actually existing poetic practice. Nonetheless, I would welcome an outpouring of cover versions of contemporary poems, let's say William Shatner reciting Leslie Scalapino's *Considering how exaggerated music is* or Harold Bloom declaiming John Ashbery's *Girls on the Run*.[1] The closest thing we have to this in contemporary poetry might be Kenneth Goldsmith's highly rhythmical and markedly accented recitations of signature moments of Western aesthetic thought.[2]

In a voice that sometimes sounds a bit like Danny Kaye, Goldsmith reads Wittgenstein with Stravinsky in the background, performs Adorno over a sonic bed of Satie, and does Barthes layered with the Allman Brothers. *He Do the Theorists in Voices*:[3] Goldsmith's New York accent gives a local, not to say ethnic, flavor to what might otherwise sound like deracinated ideas, reminding us that poetry's all about accent while theory has a tendency to sound the impersonal.

Striking an altogether different note, Caroline Bergvall, in a 2006 performance, samples, warps, and not so much rearticulates as reaccents Geoffrey Chaucer, bringing the putative godfather of English poetry into a multilectical and ideolectical sound spectrum that includes Middle and contemporary English, French, and Latin. Bergvall's "Shorter Chaucer Tales" is Jack Spicer's "low ghost" in the flesh: a glossolalic ghost looking for a medium.[4]

For the contemporary poet, though not necessarily for her or his reader, performance is the ultimate test of the poem, both stress test, in which the rhythms are worked out in real time, and trial of the poet's ability to engage listeners. At least this is true for those poets for whom performance is a central part of their practice. For poets so engaged, there are as many modalities of poetry performance as there are styles of poems. While most of the performances archived at PennSound involve poets reading scripts, some poets, as different as David Antin and Tracie Morris, work without prior texts, while other poets, usually associated with "Spoken Word," present memorized versions of written poems.[5]

Today's memorized recitations should not be conflated with the non-scripted poetry of analphabetic cultures or with the use of memory as part of the poetic process. The poetry of analphabetic cultures used prosodic formulas both to aid meaning and to goad composition. Since there were no scripts, literal memorization was inconceivable. Memory, as a poetic practice, involves an active exploration of the unknowable in ways that impart an evanescent presence. Memorization is post-script technique that requires precise, literal reproduction of a prescribed source. In contrast, the oral poetry of analphabetic cultures is a technology for the storage and retrieval of cultural memory that involves variance, repetition, improvisation, elaboration. In this sense, memorization in poetry is a theatricalization of orality rather than an instance of it. So it's not surprising that, currently, memorized spoken word is the most marked "performative" style of poetry presentation, which often resembles an actor's performance (motivated character and all). "Spoken word's" opposite number — the chamber music performance of the words in more antitheatrical styles of poetry reading — is no less a performance. Moreover, the performance of virtually unmemorizable, nonformulaic scripts is one of the signal features of a postalphabetic poetry in an age of photo/phono/digital reproduction. And when such scripts are performed from memory, and by actors, as in Mac Wellman's *Terminal Hip,* Fiona Templeton's *You — the City,* or Olivier Cadiot's *Colonel Zoo,* it is uncanny and exhilarating.

If live performance of poetry can be, as Antin once titled a talk, "a private occasion in a public space," then recorded poetry might be thought of as a public occasion in a private space.[6] Indeed, one of the fundamental conditions of the grammaphonic voice of the poet is its ghostly presence. Listening to such recordings, we hear a voice, if not of the dead, then one that sounds present but is absent, a voice that we can hear but that cannot hear us. Perhaps this touches on the reason poets read the work of their contemporaries almost only at memorial gatherings, as a space of mourning in which we keep the poet among the living for one last time.

And so yes, I do fetishize the acoustic inscription of the poet's voice, or at least I take it as aesthetically significant — partly because doing so returns voice from sometimes idealized projections of self in the style of a poem to its social materiality, to voicing and voices. In that sense, though, any performance of a poem is an exemplary interpretation, that is, one that imagines itself as rehearsal rather than as a finalization.

The alphabet, with its thirty or so marks, offers a remarkably agile technology for noting speech sounds, which, in our digital environment, makes it remarkably easy to cut, paste, and transmit. In contrast to alphabetic writing, the grammaphonic inscription offers an immensely thicker description of the voice, making explicit many vocal features that need to be interpolated when a poem is read from an alphabetic script.

There are four features, or vocal gestures, that are available on tape but not page that are of special significance for poetry: the cluster of *rhythm* and *tempo* (including *word duration*), the cluster of *pitch* and *intonation* (including *amplitude*), *timbre,* and *accent.* The first two of these features can be visually plotted with waveforms; the gestalt of these features contributes to *tone.*

The performed rhythm and tempo of a poem are not identical to its meter, and as Reuven Tsur has suggested, dynamic performances of metrical poetry may work against the implied metric of the text. For Tsur's perception-oriented cognitive poetics, performance comes after and rearticulates prosody. If performed rhythm trumps idealized meter, tempo can be used to telescope or attenuate articulated rhythmic patterns.

Nonmetrical and polymetrical poems will have rhythms and shifts of pitch that are not necessarily apprehendable on the page even while they are foregrounded in performance and visible in waveform graphs. Rhythm and pitch/intonation are not something inherent in the alphabetic script of the poem but extended, modified, improvised, invented, or enacted in performance.

In his recent, far-ranging discussion of the sounds and senses of Coleridge's "Kubla Khan," Tsur contrasts two cognitive modes of literary criticism, Negative Capability and Quest for Certainty.[7] For Tsur, critics who tend toward a Quest for Certainty display an intolerance of ambiguity, uncertainty, and multiple interpretative possibilities; a resistance to symbolism in favor of allegory; a perceptual dependence on the concrete and an inability to process multiple abstractions; a tendency to reduce a poem's meaning to a single level (a form of what I call frame lock); a propensity for "extreme" and "polarized evaluations, namely, good-bad, right-wrong, black-white"; "a greater insensitivity to subtle and minimal cues and hence a greater susceptibility to false but obtrusive clues."[8] Ambiguity intolerance is also associated with a desensitization to the nonthematized emotional dynamics of a poem, the very kinds of dynamics that are intensified in performance. Tsur notes that his categories are related to psychological studies of dogmatism and the authoritarian personality. I would add that they resonate with Wittgenstein's analysis of "aspect blindness" and George Lakoff's distinction between the cognitive framework of the "strict father" and that of the "nurturing parent."[9] What distinguishes Tsur's study is its detailed critique of examples of literary criticism and his stress on the sound of poetry and poetic performance as a prod to interpretive uncertainty and emotional intensification.

Performance allows the poet to refocus attention to dynamics hidden within the scripted poem, refocusing emphasis and overlaying immanent rhythms. The performance opens up the potential for shifting frames, and the shift of frame is itself perceived as a performative gesture. The experienced poetry performer can't help but loop this experience back onto the compositional process. The implied or possible performance becomes a ghost of the textual composition, even if the transcriptive pull is averted, just as a reader can't help but hear an overlay of a previously sampled voice of the poet, a ghostly presence steaming up out of the visual script.

No consideration of the poetry reading can leave out the significance of the timbre of the poet's voice, yet the subject tends to elicit little more than a blank, if knowing, nod. Like the face of the poet, timbre is both out of the immediate control of an author and the best picture we have of the poet's aesthetic signature or acoustic mark. Camus is said to have remarked that after a certain age each person is responsible for her or his face. After a certain age, each poet is responsible for his or her voice.

If timbre is a given dimension of a poet's performance, accent is a technical feature that can be used to perform and deform social distinctions and variations. For the modernist poetics of the Americas, the artifice of accent is the New Wilderness of poetry performance, that which marks our poetries with the inflection of our particular trajectories within our spoken language.

While script permits the poet to elide, if not to say disguise, accent, performance is an open wound of accentual difference from which no poet escapes. This is not the accent of stress but accents of distressed language, words scarred by their social origins and aspirations. The tension of iambic stress against the accents of the vernacular is one of the hallmarks of Claude MacKay's Jamaican dialect poems and a legacy of Paul Laurence Dunbar. In those cases, orthography was bent in service of the sound of the spoken language; but words spelled according to the standard can be pronounced slant.

Accent is a matter of technical investigation for poetry performance, fully as much as rhythm. For modernist American poetry, the performance of accent needs to be read within the context of the emergence of mass literacy, the prevalence of second-language speakers of English, the new presence of sound reproduction technologies, and generations of poets for whom poetry was as much an arena to resist cultural and linguistic assimilation as a place that marked such assimilation. In a sense the modernist period represents a reaccentuation of English, but not by the English. Indeed, the new ways of alphabetically representing or refusing accentuated speech is a primary area for technical innovation in poetry during the modernist period.

In "Poem Beginning 'The,'" a very young Louis Zukofsky writes of the temptation to assimilate into the English literary tradition. "Assimilation is not hard," he tells his mother; but the burden of the poem is to register both the difficulty of resisting assimilation and the unexpected and irreparable costs of not resisting.[10] The "The" of Zukofsky's poem is "The Waste

Land." Zukofsky's critique provides a very early and profound recognition of that poem as establishing a fault line for high culture that is self-defeating in its exclusion of the minor keys of accent and inflection that Zukofsky's poem ludicly enumerates. Zukofsky recognized that Eliot's poem, great as he undoubtedly thought it was, created an impasse for poetry in its wake, at least for those on the outside of Eliot's brand of the major literary tradition. Eliot's own performance of his poem, originally called "He Do the Police in different Voices," can be described as having as its baseline a deaccentuated, not to say impersonal, voice that is haunted by the often sudden intrusion of accented voices:[11] "April is the cruellest month"; "*Marie, Marie, hold on tight*"; "*When Lil's husband got demobbed, I said —*"; "'Speak to me. Why do you never speak?'" One answer is that when poetry does speak, those too enmeshed in the literary tradition either refuse to listen or are just unable to hear, partly because it's not the speech they are accustomed to hearing; indeed it may not sound like voice or speech at all. Accented voices are easily dismissed as unrefined, crude, even ignorant, just as accented or deformed syntax may register as just noise.

Zukofsky understood that radical modernism, like racial modernism, inevitably connected to the multiplicities of spoken sounds. The burden of modernist composition was to articulate the range of sounds in complex patterns, not purify the language. In his 1940 study for "A"-9, Zukofsky creates one of the wittiest and most trenchant dialect poems of Second-Wave Modernism. "A foin lass bodders," is his translation of Guido Cavalcanti's thirteenth-century poem "Donna mi prega" into Brooklynese (itself a foil for Yiddish dialect). With this work Zukofsky is responding to Ezra Pound's 1928 "traduction" (as he called it) of "Donna mi prega":

> Because a lady asks me, I would tell
> Of an affect that comes often and is fell
> And is so overweening: Love by name.
> E'en its deniers can now hear the truth,
> I for the nonce to them that know it call,
> Having no hope at all
> that man who is base in heart
> Can bear his part of wit . . . .[12]

While Pound's traduction makes Cavalcanti come alive in quasi-idiomatic English rhythms that play to, while transforming, historically mediated standards of high lyric sonorousness, "A foin lass bodders" is obtrusively anti-

assimilationist, not to say dissident, anti-absorptive both cultural and poetically. The poem begs performance as we read it:

> A foin lass bodders me I gotta tell her
> Of a fact surely, so unrurly, often'
> 'r 't comes 'tcan't soften its proud neck's called love mm ...
> Even me brudders dead drunk in dare cellar
> Feel it dough poorly 'n yrs. trurly rough 'n
> His way ain't so tough 'n he can't speak form above mm ...
> 'n' wid proper rational understandin'. . . . [13]

Zukofsky's dialect, one might even say shtick, translation of Cavalcanti is
noisy, disruptive, brilliant, and unacceptable all rolled into one.

Performance always exceeds script, just as text always outperforms audibility. The relation of script to performance, or performance to script, is necessarily discrepant, hovering around an original center in a complex of versions
that is inherently unstable. Poetry readings proliferate versions of the poem,
each version displacing but not replacing every other. As such, close listening
presents an ongoing challenge to readings that, in their intolerance of ambiguity, associative thinking, and abstraction, reduce the poem to a single level
of meaning, banishing from significance — as stray marks or noises — all but
the literal or concrete.

Recognizing that a poem is not one but many, that sound and sense are as
much at odds as ends, makes the study of poetry's sound a test case for mi-
drashic antinomianism, a new approach to critical studies that I am launch-
ing here, and one that I am sure will take a prominent place in the general
field of Bent Studies.

> Which is to say, to come to some conclusions
> A work of art always exceeds its material constructions
> As well as its idealizations Physical or digital instantiations
> Anterior codes or algorithmic permutations
> Experiences while reading or viewing are no more than weigh stations
> And any number of interpretations, contexts of publications, historical
>   connections —
> All these have a charmed affinity
> Clustering around a center that is empty.

That empty center or blank space is the possibility of freedom.

IMPOSSIBLE REVERSIBILITIES: JACKSON MAC LOW / HÉLÈNE AJI

In her discussion of performance art, Kristine Stiles argues that we are deal-ing with aesthetic as well as ethical decisions that reshape art experience into a "transpersonal" experience and construct the work "as an *interstitial con-tinuum* linking subjects to subjects through mutual identification."[1] The loci of author and reader (or artist and spectator) lose their specificities, not to become interchangeable but to refer constantly to one another and allow for the transfer of some functions from one to the other. Such an assessment implies a shift of focus from the poem or art work as autonomous object, to be experienced in relative passivity, to the process of its production: sharing the realization of the work and inscribing plurality within the procedures of its creation place an emphasis on the very nature of these procedures. Un-derpinning this process lies the unstated and often unacknowledged fantasy of reversibility that the exchange implies. This dream of reversibility or os-cillation between sounding the visual in performance and visualizing sound either as a script for performance or in a transcript from performance is at the core of a number of contemporary works in American poetry, especially works by the late Jackson Mac Low (1922–2004).

"Simultaneities": Integrated Works of Awareness

From the beginning, Mac Low's works have transgressed the basic distinc-tion between genres and media: their aim, in part, is to integrate the po-tentialities of other literary forms or of other art forms into the domain of poetry, a project inscribed in the modernist agenda at least since Ezra Pound and Gertrude Stein. But Mac Low's performative works go further, occupying a domain between visual and sound work. There is a dynamic in the idea of sounding a visual work, or of visualizing a sound work, which on some occasions can evolve into a dialectic so that the work itself consists of the problematic relations between its various actualizations: many of Mac Low's texts, because of their layout, call into question the very passage from written to sound text. The interaction between visual and audible versions constitutes one type of possibility, but one might also think of the interaction between the visual as stabilized on the page and the visual as enacted on a stage or on video. In the same vein, one might take sound as either voice or instrumental sound (or both): the whole gamut is available in Jackson Mac Low's work as early as the 1940s. Placing these various and heterogeneous versions on an equal footing, so that they are not inadvertently organized along an assumed chronological line, making them stand, at least in the mind, together at once and at the same place is one of the challenges posed by Jackson Mac Low's own definition of his work in terms of "simultaneities." Of course, the very method of our conservation and investigation of these works may thwart, or even prevent, the recognition and evaluation of simultaneity, leading the work to be experienced negatively in terms of irreversibility — the impossibility of going back or returning from one version of the work to previous ones, because there is no return, only concomitance. What generates the idea of "simultaneities" in Mac Low's poetics is the potential for iteration that his work entails. Iteration, but not without structural variations — in a sense very akin to Gertrude Stein's practice of repetition. The specificity of Mac Low's practice lies in the way he bases his work on the conception and execution of installations and processes that are not confined to their textual, visual, or musical dimensions but rather aim to redefine the poem as the integrated coexistence of all three dimensions to form the complete work. Again, in the same way as our methods of apprehending the work of art challenge the apprehension of these works, the conventional modes of "publication" — which these works must of course adopt to be known at all — challenge their plural dimensionality and marginalize them. Their publication not only proves problematic but at times hinders their analysis.

In an interview with Barry Alpert in 1974, Jackson Mac Low outlines the various influences that shaped his poetic experiments, stressing their double aspect: the preoccupation with the forms of the poem, and the underlying political awareness that generates these forms.[2] Poetry in Mac Low's poetics can be understood in both these senses, as the persistence of the poetic work under all circumstances (and not just in so-called poetic contexts, be it the quietness of solitary reading or the higher visibility of staged poetic events), and its significance in the existence of all the agents involved with the work, from its inception to its multiple actualizations. The impulse to share authorship is an impulse to share responsibility for the poem, which leads Mac Low to devise works whose unfolding involves interventions from others. The focus on complex visual organization, which entails intense activities of deciphering, and on sound production, the result of performance in most cases, is a direct consequence of this intention. In all this, the interaction with and mediation of John Cage is central: both Cage and Mac Low were students of the Zen master Daisetz Suzuki at Columbia University between 1954 and 1957; Mac Low joined Cage and Merce Cunningham at Black Mountain College in experimenting with aleatory methods of composition, in the elaboration of multimedia works, and in the increased awareness that readers can be empowered at the same time as they are made to experience being controlled through the poem. As Eric Mottram points out, "Jackson Mac Low is above all concerned with non-matrixed performance," the way agents are turned into "repetiteurs" of a set of actions: in life, the dehumanization this entails is not necessarily perceived; in the poem, it is experienced and acknowledged simultaneously; potentially it is also questioned.[3]

These works' intensity of existence comes from the fact that they reverberate from the moment of their inception onto other times and places. Yet the modes of their reverberation vary: where a given printed text is reprinted, for example, duplication does not produce an identical text; it is always slightly altered. Inscribing the uniqueness of the work of art, in typography or on canvas, finds alternatives in the reenactments or reactualizations of scenarios in time and space. This impels the audience toward a comparison with music, but that parallel can also prove limiting: we are not dealing with the plurality of interpretations for a single score, an equivalent for a master text since plurality can affect many levels. Artists play on an increasing number of variants, constantly working on the different parameters of the work so as to obtain ever changing results. This appears most clearly in Mac Low's procedural poetry, when the parameters are fixed once and for all at least for one piece of work. The resulting pieces stand out as provisional and ephemeral organizations meant to persist mainly in their subsequent reenactments, works that amount to temporary aesthetic formations of social space.

The Theater of Sound

In "The Pronouns: 40 Dances for the Dancers" (1964; fig. 1), Jackson Mac Low elaborates a theater in which the genesis of the poem is to be staged: each of the poems and each of the micro-plays in the sequences of "The Pronouns" are made of a series of instructions that agents or actors have successively drawn from a collection of cards.[4] The card system was first elaborated in a homage to Simone Forti in which the cards were called "nuclei," the atomic cores from which the poetic events could radiate (fig. 2). The cards ordered by the selection process can produce different types of work: pantomimes in which the actors play out the instructions on the cards (or their interpretation of them); sound events in which they read aloud the instructions or utter spontaneous associations triggered by the instructions; texts shaped like poems and forming a poetic sequence (as on the manuscript pages of "The Pronouns"). As a matter of fact, one could continue to enumerate possibilities for the finalization of the process initiated by the "nuclei," and the primary suggestion by Mac Low himself that the poems can be seen both as dances and as texts is an opener onto these multiple possibilities. Basically, the work questions the nature of poetry, the nature of the poetic gesture, its modes of composition as well as its modes of reception. But because "The Pronouns" can still be read as a conventional poetic sequence, they retain their explicit questioning of one of Jackson Mac Low's central thematic preoccupations: democracy and freedom; the complex network of modern society; the ideological pressures over individuals; the effects of authority, imperialism, dogmatism. Worked into the variations on pronouns, these relations become unsettled and problematic. How to figure an ideal of freedom of action, without renouncing authorship altogether? Because they are scenarios, the sections of "The Pronouns" imply that the work remains ever at work or in play, without fixing itself into one single version. If one focuses back on the dialectics between the visual organizations (the card collection or the page of the manuscript) and their sound versions (reading aloud or freely associating), one realizes that the different aspects of the work function in a system whose consequences cannot be grasped unless the system is seen as the heterogeneous whole that it is, and not as the linear unfolding of a creation whose horizon would be performance. The repetitiousness of the process (Mac Low incites us to repeat his experiments, to create our own sets of cards, etc.) triggers the possibility — maybe the necessity — of keeping it simultaneously present at least in the mind.[5] A consequence of this attempt page 12 of THE PRONOUNS--A COLLECTION OF 40 DANCES--FOR THE DANCERS--J. Mac Low--page 12

18TH DANCE -- PLANTING -- 1 March 1964

Anyone begins by penning anything or anyone,
cleaning something,
blackening something,
doing waiting,
& then planting.

A little later, anyone may be reacting to orange hair.

Then, anyone is printing.

At the end, anyone is sponging.

19TH DANCE -- GOING UNDER -- 1 March 1964

First, anybody gives gold cushions or seems to do so,
while doing something under the conditions of competition,
after which anybody boils delicate things,
being in flight,
doing something consciously,
& keeping up a process.

Next, anybody gets an orange from a hat, takes it, & keeps it;
then anybody goes under,
while doing something under the conditions of competition, STET COM
& ends ~~up xxxxxxxx~~ (by) putting in languages other than English.

Figure 1. Jackson Mac Low, "The Pronouns." From the Jackson Mac Low Papers (MSS 180, box 58, folder 58), New Poetry Archive, Mandeville Special Collections, Geisel Library, University of California, San Diego. Reprinted with kind permission of the Estate of Jackson Mac Low.

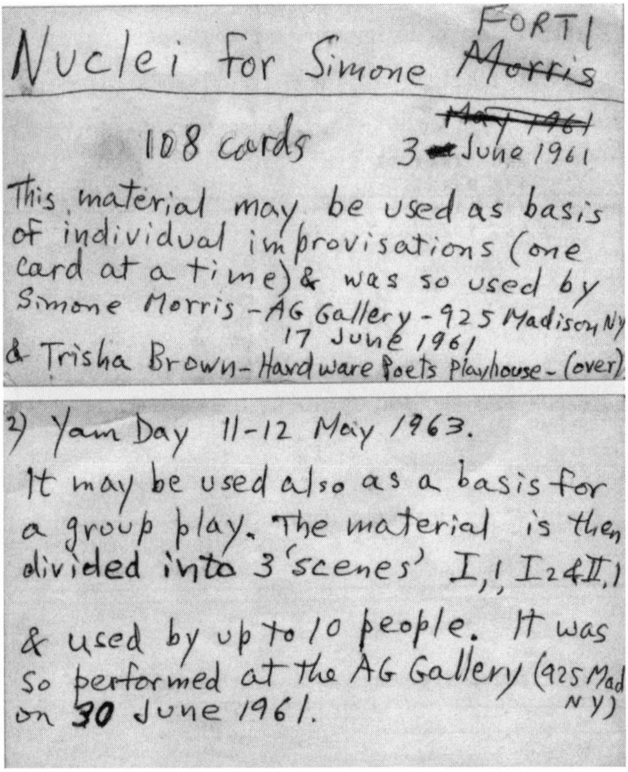

Figure 2. Jackson Mac Low, title cards for "Nuclei for Simone Forti."
From *Doings: Assorted Performance Pieces, 1955–2002* (New York:
Granary Books, 2005), 59. Reprinted with kind permission of the
Estate of Jackson Mac Low.

to achieve simultaneities gives rise to a series of experiments that have major consequences for the typographical organization of text on the page and for the conditions of sounding itself.

From this perspective, Mac Low's *Is That Wool Hat My Hat?* (1980; fig. 3) can be seen to create unstable conditions for reading, since the organization of the text on the page is ambiguous. Since Mac Low understands his work both as a poet and as a musical composer, the material on the page can be taken as verbal text or as musical score. One can elaborate an entire series of possible readings. First, there is a prescribed reading, which one finds in the instructions for performance and in the actualizations that follow them. We are dealing with a score for four voices numbered one to four. The first voice, for instance, iterates the eponymous question without change until its fourth line, when the repetition of "wool" introduces a discrepancy. "Wool wool wool" replaces "Is that wool"; "hat" is refracted; syntactic coherence dissolves; the interrogation mark disappears, introducing the possibility that questions could be assertions in disguise, and indeed the question about the

"Is That Wool Hat My Hat?"

for two, three, or four voices

Four voices is optimum, but two or three can perform this. All four *words in each column* (or the top two or three), are to be spoken simultaneously, following an even beat. One performer (or a separate conductor) should beat time throughout. Do *not* use a metronome.

1.	Is	that	wool	hat	my	hat?	Is	that	wool	hat
2.	Is	that	wool	hat	my	Is	that	wool	hat	my
3.	Is	that	wool	hat	my	hat?	Is	that	wool	hat
4.	Is	that	wool	hat	my	hat?	Is	that	wool	hat

1.	my	hat?	Is	that	wool	hat	my	hat?	Is	that
2.	Is	that	wool	hat	my	Is	that	Is	that	Is
3.	my	hat?	Is	that	wool	hat	my	hat?	my	hat?
4.	my	hat?	Is	that	wool	hat	my	hat?	Is	that

1.	wool	hat	my	hat?	Is	that	wool	hat	my	hat?
2.	that	Is	that	Is	that	Is	that	wool	hat	my
3.	is	that	my	hat?	Is	that	my	hat?	Is	that
4.	wool	hat	my	hat?	Is	that	wool	hat	my	hat?

1.	Is	that	wool	hat	my	hat?	wool	wool	wool	hat
2.	hat?	Is	hat	hat	hat	wool	hat	my	hat?	wool
3.	my	hat?	Is	that	my	hat?	Is	that	my	hat?
4.	wool	hat	wool	hat	wool	hat	wool	hat	wool	hat

1.	hat	hat	hat	hat	Is	that	wool	hat	my	Is
2.	hat	my	wool	hat	my	wool	hat	my	wool	hat
3.	Is	that	that	wool	hat	my	hat?	Is	that	wool
4.	my	hat?	Is	wool	hat	my	hat?	Is	wool	hat

Figure 3. Jackson Mac Low, "Is That Wool Hat My Hat?" From *Representative Works: 1938–1985* (New York: Roof, 1986), 307. Reprinted with kind permission of the Estate of Jackson Mac Low.

hat implies the denial of recognition ("this wool hat is not my hat"). The first voice keeps the basic elements that it shares with the others but does not coincide with them any longer. The variation in the simultaneous rapports between the voices underscores the general instability of language paradigms, the divergence of identical paradigms that initially deluded one into meaning and into the sharing of meaning.

A second reading strategy would recognize that we are dealing with a linear text, made up of blocks of four lines each (stanzas, maybe, whose lineation would be emphasized by numbering), so that one would read line 1, then line 2, then line 3, etc. In such a configuration of reading, the initial utterance is rapidly dismantled, to be reformed and again decomposed in a vertiginous succession of interrogations. The question is constantly shifting or oscillating; now it bears on identification, now on possession, now on the status of the subject and of the object, then on the referential capabilities of language. The mind's attempts at ordering what is after all a fairly simple set of events suddenly seem desperate: what are actually the conditions of recognition, and consequently, how can one rely on recognition, what with the effects of defamiliarization that the very effort at recognizing can trigger?

Finally, yet another possibility would be to remember the page organization of Asian poetry, printed into vertical columns, columns that would go down the whole length of the page or only down four lines, so that this option decomposes into two. The original question, formulated in the title of the piece, is then immediately shattered into the shards of its elements, and meaning emerges only from the heart of total disturbance, when one reads for instance in columns 5 and 6, "my hat is hat." Itemized and iterated in paranoid series, words lose their intrinsic, concrete meaning: "wool" and "hat" become the structural symptoms of a disturbance in language. Meaning becomes incidental when the chances of combination flittingly coincide with the accepted architectures of language. In the case of "Is That Wool Hat My Hat?" the disorientation of reading and voicing that the visual layout on the page entails leads to the simultaneous canceling and restating of meaning.

In the performance given by children and available online, the initial instructions for reading are followed so that the text unfolds with overlapping voices (feminine and masculine, including the voice of an adult) at times coinciding and stressing some parts of the question: when the "is that" comes out, the text takes on the value of an existential questioning, whereas when the "wool hat" is predominant, the opacity of the object increases to the level of an effect of estrangement and defamiliarization.[6] The performance is made to the rhythm of the metronome, an addition of the performers, since Mac Low did not plan the use of external, partly instrumental, elements: the failure to strictly maintain the rhythm is thus emphasized, conveying the idea of the artificiality of collective order and the possibility of undoing that threatens any common action. At times, the performance reaches the playfulness of singing in canon (most probably the primary motivation of this children's performance), but it also runs the gamut of choral sounding and acquires the mystical dimension of mantra chanting. The passage from one status of the chanted text to another blurs the limits between modes of performance otherwise distinguished and sometimes opposed, at the same time as it alters the meaning of the text according to the modes of its sounding. The use of a most common sentence allows Mac Low to transfer the meaning-inducing properties of reading from silence to sound, a practice that he aptly calls "translation."[7] The idea that translation can happen not only in a transfer from one language to another but also in the transfer from one medium to another, or one mode to another, is central to his poetics.

The plurality of voices and the proliferations of meanings inside and outside the text also lead to a reassessment of the rules presiding over communication in language and of the hierarchies at work in the enforcement of these rules. The plastic qualities of text reforms the page into the map of a territory to be explored both within and without the conventions of reading. In Marjorie Perloff's words, poetry would literally be happening "on and off the page."[8] Because of the variety and multiplicity of what is taking place, it is tempting to read these works under the sign of disorder and chaos: taking into account the way they seem to cancel our customary modes of hierarchic organization, one could be stranded in the maze of potentialities. But this impression of an overall checkmating of method is the mere result of a temporary crazing of reading, of a poetic wager that suspends the activities of deciphering, not to suppress them but to enforce the actuality of plural and coexistent modes of deciphering, all of them systematic but according to varying systems.

Out of the Labyrinth and into the Maze

Whereas labyrinths are structures of radical disorientation and loss of control that only luck or cunning can defeat, the maze is man-made and possesses a rationale: it is a place that is designed to convey meanings, that can be centered on powerlessness, but that can also induce epiphanic moments of understanding through the discovery of a previously hidden scene. The maze is thus a locus not of disorder but of apparent disorder, where the conditions of loss are recreated with a horizon of recovery. The generation of apparently chaotic structures that coalesce into ordered configurations is not new when Jackson Mac Low starts practicing it: ciphering and deciphering as concomitant movements is the dialectic presiding over the experiments around page organization, and one could go back to Stéphane Mallarmé's "Coups de dés," to Guillaume Apollinaire's calligrammes—or even further back to the micrographics of medieval Jewish scribes.

However, recent experiments in this field have integrated a thematization of reading as part and parcel of the creation process and as a demanding physical participation from the reader. This aspect of the work is explored at length by Craig Dworkin in his reflection on Charles Bernstein's "Veil" and the ways this "illegible" work in fact involves modes of legibility that thematize the conditions of reading.[9] Similarly, in "Om in a Landscape" (1961) (fig. 4), the reader has to follow the trajectory of the text: not only does one have to move one's eyes along the lines of the text, but one has to turn the page so as to keep reading, and at times one simply has to come to terms with the impossibility of keeping on reading.[10] The line is disrupted, meets an obstacle, becomes a line in the strictest sense of the term, loses itself in a swirl. The itinerary of the text, whose mantra-like repetitiveness induces a numbing of the quest for meaning, places the word in a landscape, as suggested by the title. Yet one is also forced to see that the word itself creates this landscape. Sounding "Om in a Landscape" creates a linearity that is endangered by the text on the page: the repetition of the phoneme, if divorced from Mac Low's visual layout, stresses the repetition of the same, its hypnotic power, and is infused with boredom. One of the ways out of this boredom is "translation" in its pragmatic sense. If one comes to think that in French *om* and *homme* (man) are homonyms, the repetition of "homme" turns into a humanistic statement, the obstinate assertion of humanity over the silence of dehumanization. If "homme" is put back into the context of a reading of "Om in a Landscape," another relationship establishes itself between the visual projection of the text and its sounding: once one has heard "homme" repeated over and over, the work takes on a new dimension according to which man comes to inhabit and construct the landscape of the page, a form of invasion and intervention that refers to the impact of an author on his text. Charles Bernstein rightly refers to such Mac Low texts as "architectures" meant for man to "inhabit," in this case through sounding:

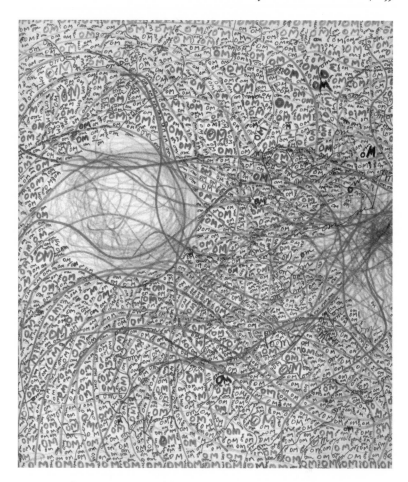

Figure 4. Jackson Mac Low, detail from "Om in a Landscape." From *Doings: Assorted Performance Pieces, 1955–2002* (New York: Granary Books, 2005), 65–66. Reprinted with kind permission of the Estate of Jackson Mac Low.

[Mac Low] has generally been more interested in his written texts in building structures than in inhabiting them (leaving, that is, the inhabitation to performance — his or yours). Yet it is the consistency and relentlessness of this position that makes Mac Low's work so fundamental a contribution to the poetry of our language. His work is a great testament to the possibility for structures in and of themselves, and for the sufficiency of possibility. That it is architectures that shape the world, but *we* who must fill them up.[11]

One would be tempted to add that both constructing and inhabiting are man's work and that the ambivalence of a sounding of "om" brings about a plurality of visual projections ("om" and "homme") that put into question the status of the text as score. There might be voicings of "Om" using several voices, adding to the meaning of the poem distinctions of gender (man repeating "homme," as contrasted with woman repeating "homme") or age (young boy dreaming of "homme"), etc.

This architectural polyvalence of the poem is more obvious still in Mac Low's "gathas," in which the projection of a grid onto the page gives it structure, turns the letters composing the words into landmarks so that each of the words emerges as the consequence of so many authorized or preprogrammed moves on a chessboard. Thus, as we read, or look at, Mac Low's "1st Vocabulary Gatha in Memoriam Armand Schwerner" (1999, the year Armand Schwerner died; fig. 5), the grid maps out the page, but as the words indeed outline

		R		A	É	R	E	R			A			A		R
			A				C		E		D		M		D	A
		A	W	E	S			R			A		A	E		
					E		A	A		M	R	N	A	D	E	R
					W				N		A	E				E
			D		A		E				M	N				S
			A			R			A	E	A					E
			C				N	C			N					A
	A	C	H				M			A	D					R
	A				A	M	A	D	A	M	E					C
	R	E	N	N	E	S	D	E	E			N				H
	D			E			R		H	M	E					
		A		A	A	C	A	D	E	M	E		A		A	M
		R		M			E			D	M	S		A		
				E						E	E				S	
	M	E	A	N		S		W	E	R		R	D			
	E		E		E	A			A	W	E	S				
	N		M	A	E	N	A	D			E		H			
	É	A				A			A			R				
	D		C		D		R	R	R			E				
	E		H		E			E		H	A	S		D	D	S
		A	E			E	A		A		A		A			
	M			R	A	S	E	R	D		D			R		
	A		W		A		A		È						A	
	N		E		N		S	R		C		A	A			H
		D	E	R		A	E	E		H		D				
	N			E	N	N	E	A		E	A		A		M	
	E	A		S		E		H	A	S	E	N	R		R	
		M			H		S				A	A				
		R			E			A				H		N		
	A	C	H	A	R	N	E	R								

Figure 5. Jackson Mac Low and Anne Tardos, "1st Vocabulary Gatha in Memoriam Armand Schwerner." From *Doings: Assorted Performance Pieces, 1955–2002* (New York: Granary Books, 2005), 249. Reprinted with kind permission of the Estate of Jackson Mac Low.

a number of authorized moves, they also function negatively, making us see the large number of unauthorized moves that we can do but perhaps will be reluctant to achieve since they do not immediately make sense. Such visual organization, introduced as it is by the key to the choice of words and letters (all are derived from the name of poet and friend Armand Schwerner), summons a controlled exercise of freedom, caught between the effort to reconstruct the name of Armand Schwerner in a personal reenactment of the homage (an effort to decrypt the encrypted name) and the temptation to try out new combinations with each new approach to the text. Actually, this temptation soon becomes the reality of the reading experience, since the sound text produced by reading is never the same, depending on the moves on the grid, be they directed by improvisation or through predefined procedures. The "gatha" summons plural and variant readings, imposing on the reader a vision of the poem as a place of many inhabitants. A single visual text generates an acute awareness of the poem as the locus where plurality is exercised, synchronically (as a "simultaneity") through the variety of readings from different individuals, and diachronically through the iterated and ever changing reading attempts of one individual.

In the 2000 performance of the Armand Schwerner gatha by Jackson Mac Low and Anne Tardos, the two voices, and the decisions they make in their performance, show the diversity induced by the presentation in a grid and the permission given by the author to the reader to follow instructions and improvise on them.[12] The communication of meaning occurs on several levels: linearity is given by voice lines that articulate what can occasionally be construed as a fragmented discourse, an imitative commentary on the poetry of Schwerner; the feminine voice privileges sudden variations in pitch and the reading of letters or phonemes instead of complete words, drawing attention to the very makeup of language but also bringing forth the musical dimension of the work, when letters and notes collapse onto one another; the monochord of the masculine voice recalls the possibility of neutral reading and underlines the emotional dimension brought about by variations in pitch, thus foregrounding the inner, secret, and outer, strident, expressions of mourning. The use of words from other languages than English (French, German, etc.) produces a threefold effect: unrecognized, these words become pure sound and point to the musicality of language and the musical dimension of language in poetry; recognized, they force an attempt to translate, most often countered by the rapid succession of words and the jumps from one language to another; recognized but untranslated, then, they evidence impossibilities in the circulation of meaning. A return to the grid might yield these words, but it would first and foremost yield a new and different reading, and consequently a new and different performance of the gatha. In this sense, going back and forth from text to sound never allows for a return to the same (original) place: on the contrary, it makes us experience the impossibility of return, the condition of irreversibility that is ours.

The Texts and Sounds of Irreversibility

Irreversibility is further stressed when the visual layout of the gatha becomes not just one source for several sound performances but also one possibility among several visualizations for a single sound event. The suggestion or invitation to create visual actualizations of a sound text prevents us from falling prey to the simplification according to which this grid would just be a form of maze in language, for us to get lost in or desperately try, again and again, to find new ways in or out. Consequently, with "1st Sharon Belle Mattlin Vocabulary Crossword Gatha" (1976), we do find our readings limited through the imposition of selected words, complete or partial anagrams of Sharon Belle Mattlin's name, as was the case with "1st Vocabulary Gatha in Memoriam Armand Schwerner."[13] In the declared process of actualization of the work, we are indeed invited to sound the visual as we travel from one square to the next, following mutable itineraries. The sound performance of the grid helps us simultaneously understand that what is on the page is a transitory state of the work and that what we hear is but one among many possible resulting texts.[14] Up to a certain point, then, poetry would somehow reach the condition of music . . . Up to a certain point only because we discover that we never actually have a master score or master text on the page from which actualizations are to be derived according to a one-way trajectory. Plurality affects each and every level. First, the constitution of a vocabulary or word repository, insofar as it is the list of the words that come to the poet's mind using the same letters as the name (in a work entitled *Daily Life* Mac Low thus suggests the possibility for the reader to create his or her own "daily life" stock of sentences).[15] Second, the visual projection of the vocabulary on the page (the gatha projection is one possibility for inscription; the grid pattern proves optional as another page fills up with curves made of the words in the Mattlin vocabulary). And third, the sound actualizations, which coexist with a variety of visual projections: the grid or the maze, in this instance.

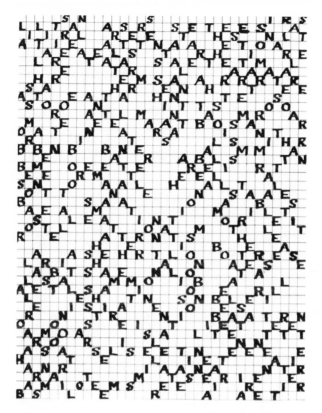

Figure 6. Jackson Mac Low, "1st Sharon Belle Mattlin Vocabulary Crossword Gatha." From *Representative Works: 1938–1985* (New York: Roof, 1986), 244. Reprinted with kind permission of the Estate of Jackson Mac Low.

If one wants to revert to a unique source, one is stumped — reversibility is evidenced as mystification.

This insistence on delusions of reversibility that can be found in Jackson Mac Low's experiments prompts us to reconsider the vectorization of a number of works involving events (sound and otherwise) as well as raising production issues. What if this very impulse to reversibility that gives its oscillating momentum to Mac Low's work were to be played with or radically questioned by the works themselves? What is also at stake is not so much the potential for reversibility or the reader/spectator's freedom to travel along paths of reversibility as he or she strives for reversibility and its systematic thwarting. Indeed, what reversibility implies is the persistence of poles, de-

Figure 7. Jackson Mac Low, detail from "A Vocabulary for Sharon Belle Mattlin." From *Doings: Assorted Performance Pieces, 1955–2002* (New York: Granary Books, 2005), 93–94. Reprinted with kind permission of the Estate of Jackson Mac Low.

parture points and arrival points, a departure text or audiovisual document and a resulting work that might in its turn be thought of as the departure piece. Plurality intervenes as the poles turn out to be more than two (a text score giving rise to a verbal event or to a musical performance when word letters are read as musical notes, to a sequence of actions, these actions or scores sending back to several text organizations). Strangely enough, the text of the poem, given its uniqueness, becomes central again, by default, as reversibility is compromised by proliferating pluralities. It becomes interstitial in the strongest etymological sense of the term: something that obstinately stands in between, a screen or an obstacle rather than a passage or a link, something to be overcome through appropriation. What is staged, in

Jackson Mac Low's poems, is thus the contingency of the work against its fetishization, the plurality of its forms, and the delusion lying in assigning a point of origin and a fixity to any work. What remains of the work, to pick up Giorgio Agamben's formulation in the original title of his reflection on the Holocaust ("quel che resta di Auschwitz"), is a form inscribed in time against loss and in space against absence, in the fragile temporalities and spatializations of a provisional page.[16] With Jackson Mac Low, this form is neither visual text nor musical score nor script, it is not even a poem in itself, it is a method for multimedia polysemic creation: "the method is the first thing. The method is what comes by inspiration, calculation."[17] A method to do again and again, with the persistent awareness that what is done cannot be redone or undone.

THE STUTTER OF FORM / CRAIG DWORKIN

Beginning again and again is a natural thing even when there is a series.

GERTRUDE STEIN

Often my writing is nothing but "stuttering."

LUDWIG WITTGENSTEIN

Everyone stutters. Statistically, between 7 and 10 percent of all speech is dysfluent, with phonemes repeated, prolonged, distorted, suspended — or even, at times, not audibly produced at all. The ideology of transparent and referentially communicative language is so strong, however, that we tend to automatically overlook those dysfluencies or not consciously register them in the first place. Indeed, communicative transparency has such symbolic force that we tend to forget the extent to which a range of corporeal opacities are in fact a perfectly normal part of speech production. The intake and exhalation of air, the pool and swallow of saliva, disadhesions of moist flesh within the mouth, all the small percussive taps and clicks from the articulatory structures of the glottis, tongue, teeth, and lips: such sounds are all necessary accompaniments to the normal operation of the gross physiological components of speech production (pulmonary, tracheal, laryngeal, pharyngeal, nasal, buccal). In the same way, instances of stuttering accompany the psychological and neurological coordination of all speech. The stutter, as Herman Melville wrote of it, is a thoroughly "organic hesitancy."[1]

Stuttering, in other words, is less a condition that does or does not exist than a rate at which one aspect of the normal mechanism of speech can no longer be overlooked or ignored. Language, in this way, operates like a machine. As Ludwig Wittgenstein recognized, the symbolic force of the machine — the machine as idea and ideal — abets an ideology in which the machine becomes the exemplary model of smooth, efficient, perfectly regular operation. For that idea of the machine to function smoothly and efficiently in turn it must distract our attention from the friction and entropy of real machines. When we talk about machines in the symbolic sense, Wittgenstein observes,

> we talk as if these parts could only move in this [perfectly smooth] way, as if they could not do anything else. How is this — do we forget the possibility of their bending, breaking off, melting, and so on? Yes; in many cases we don't think of that at all.[2]

Wittgenstein is primarily concerned in this passage with questions of rule following and the problems of private language, but we might push his insight even further in the direction of his example itself and recognize that what is conventionally understood as "malfunction" is not an exception to the operation of machines but one of their fundamental aspects.

Keeping this perspective of the necessary malfunction in mind, one can begin to recognize moments at which the stutter does not merely register itself in language, as the palpable end result of a physiological process but at which language itself stutters. Merely registered *in* language, the literary stutter has tended to be either a qualification of characters' speech ("'Listen,' she stuttered") or a graphically approximated marker of idiolect ("L-l-l-listen"). Registered *as* language, the stutter becomes a structural principle, so that, in Gilles Deleuze's terms, "it is no longer the character who stutters in speech; it is the writer who becomes *a stutterer in language.*"[3] In this essay, accordingly, I want to listen carefully to the mechanics of the stutter in order to recognize moments at which the stutter moves from being merely descriptive to becoming an integral part of the formal structure of a text. In some sense, this essay will thus focus on the sound of the text in order to apprehend its silence. As Deleuze goes on to explain: "*When a language is so strained* that it starts to stutter, or to murmur or stammer . . . *then language in its entirety* reaches the limit that marks its outside and makes it confront silence."[4] Strained to its limits, the communicative sounds of any particular speech (*la parole*) are silenced, but even at that inaudible limit language (*la langue*) continues to tell us something. All language is referential, but it need not reflect concepts; when language instead refers back to the material circumstances of its own production, we can hear the murmur of its materials. When speech continues without communicating anything, when speech intransitively reaches the limit at which its communication becomes silent, we can hear the body speak. This essay will try to listen to what the body says, over and over, again and again.

The audible silencing of language, the move from the interior to the exterior of language in Deleuze's terms, from a stutter in language to the stutter of language, can be clearly heard in the work of Alvin Lucier. One of the key figures in late twentieth-century experimental music, and a member of the Sonic Arts Union (along with Robert Ashley, Gordon Mumma, and David Behrman), Lucier pioneered a wide range of musical activities. Part of that groundbreaking work investigated the physics of acoustics: patterns of wave motion; ionospheric disturbances; the inframince harmonics of near pitches; and the resonant or propagatory properties of various media. Lucier's now-classic *Music on a Long Thin Wire* (1977 / rec. 1980), for instance, reimagines the college acoustics laboratory as a concert hall. To conduct the piece (in all senses of the word), Lucier passed a fixed fifty-foot wire through a magnetic field; the wire was then driven by a sine-wave oscillator while contact microphones registered its amplified vibrations and converted changes in the frequency and magnitude of its oscillations into an audible quiver of chords in sheer spherelike oneiric celestiations. Lucier's other primary contribution to post-Cagean experimental music comes from his focus on phenomenology and the body's potential to both produce and perceive periodic patterns. In *Music for Solo Performer* (1965 / rec. 1982), for example, electrodes from an electroencephalogram register the brain's alpha waves, which are then amplified and routed to drive a series of percussion instruments in a performance that is both literally and figuratively cerebral in its origins and at the same time quite viscerally physical in its percussive results. Although entirely controlled by the performer's concentration, the specific effects of the music are all unpredictably beyond the performer's intention. With a similar use of physiological data to generate music, *Clocker* (1978 / rec. 1994) measures the body's electrical resistance with a galvanic skin response sensor. But rather than using the electrodermal data for a polygraph test or New Age psychotherapy, Lucier routs the output voltage through a delay that regulates the rate of tocks from an amplified clock. The music of time — the steady familiar beat we associate with the regular counting of each second — is thus warped, a chronographic percussion sped and distended with the uncanny illusion that the performer's body has contracted and expanded time itself.

Lucier's 1970 composition *I Am Sitting in a Room* combines his investigations into the physics of acoustic waves with his interest in how the everyday activities of the body — its idiosyncratic and uncontrollable fluctuations — can be transformed into music. Lucier describes the piece in a text that also serves as its score:

> I am sitting in a room different from the one you are in now. I am recording the sound of my speaking voice and I am going to play it back into the room again and again until the resonant frequencies of the room reinforce themselves so that any semblance of my speech, with perhaps the exception of rhythm, is destroyed. What you will hear, then, are the natural resonant frequencies of the room articulated by speech. I regard this activity not so much as a demonstration of a physical fact, but more as a way to smooth out any irregularities my speech might have.[5]

To perform the piece, Lucier's "speaking voice" — the sound source for his musical composition — reads the paragraph above with evidence of its noticeable "irregularities," his marked stutter, on display. Lucier's recording of his voice is then simultaneously played back and rerecorded "again and again," with the astonishing result that one can hear his body's resonant cavities projected onto the architectural space of the room in which he first spoke. This prosthetic transfer occurs because the procedure of repeated recording and playback ensures that some aspects of Lucier's original reading are incrementally diminished as the recording device fails to register in full fidelity and, moreover, as the echoic interference of the room causes certain frequencies to be damped, faded, and ultimately eliminated. At the same time, the procedure correspondingly emphasizes other aspects of his reading, as the particular dimensions of the room and the physical properties of its space happen to reinforce certain of the source sound's wave patterns. So while some frequencies in Lucier's speech cancel, others amplify, interfering with one another in a series of resonant harmonies until — in their exchange of sympathetic vibrations — the mouth implies the room, and the room mimics the mouth. Faced with its own reflection, "language itself will begin to vibrate and stutter."[6]

First performed at the Guggenheim Museum (New York) in 1970, and recorded for the audio supplement to the magazine *Source: Music of the Avant-Garde, I Am Sitting in a Room* also exists in a more recent recording that cycles Lucier's speech through thirty-two generations over forty-five minutes, a full half hour longer than the *Source* recording.[7] *I Am Sitting in a Room* begins as documentation, with the unmarked and unmanipulated recording of Lucier reading his source text. The timbre of the second reading changes almost imperceptibly, though already by the third iteration the increased depth of echo is immediately noticeable. With further repetitions that echo gives way to a metallic distortion around the dynamics of the higher pitches and sibilants, the very phonemes emphasized by Lucier's slight lisp and one of the triggers of his stutter ("semblance," "smooth").[8] As the voice recedes and abstracts, it suggests a public address system heard through a subway tunnel, a hypnotist's instructions as one slips from consciousness, the alien speech of science fiction robots. After about a quarter of an hour, the articulation has been blurred beyond the point of recognition, the markers of human speech receding as the electronic aspect of the rerecorded sound moves to the fore. Although the work is performed with electromagnetic tape, its tones begin to evoke the relay of samplers and delay effects. By this point, even without knowledge of Lucier's source speech, the work gives the sense of sound heard at the wrong scale. Not just out of sync, but unequalized, too loud, too slow, simultaneously too much and not enough — the listener is left with waves washing beyond the capacity of the electronic meshes meant to capture them.

By the recording's midpoint, the chambered spaces of Lucier's room and mouth have traded places, sounding the nodes of standing waves oscillating within a resonant cavity. Replaced by the surge and shudder of sound without any sense of etiology, speech passes into music, its words and phonemes drowned in a resounding cathedral of echoes and harmonics. The recursive feedback loop of one chamber within another, from mouth to room to microphone to tape to speaker to tape to room and back again, transforms that inscriptive relay — what Friedrich Kittler would call an *Aufschreibesystem* — into an instrument capable of timbres somewhere between a sophisticated glass harmonica and a primitive synthesizer.[9] In another ten minutes the spacemusic pulses have smoothed to organ tones played against a constant low thrum, and they then flatten further toward the drones of long wires, evoking electrical lines stretched across deserts into the invisible alkali distance, humming in a miraculous mix of electricity and solar wind. At some point toward the end of the recording those drones narrow to whines, their pitches rising and peaking with the pierce of feedback, which then in turn again begin to stretch and mellow into more melodic and tonal passages. Sympathy, the work insists, leads to harmony. With a final witty turn the last movements of the piece suggest the repetitive pulses of minimalist music — something like Steve Reich doing the soundtrack for *A Space Odyssey* — reminding the listener that the whole piece was built from the elaborations of discrepancy and margin measured over thirty-two repetitions of the same paragraph.

Those repetitions, of course, are all to the point; played back "again and again," as Lucier's description underscores, the work's procedure provides a formal analogue to the stutter evident in his reading. With its predetermined permutational logic, the composition replaces the idiosyncratic and unpredictable repetitions of speech, which Lucier characterizes as "extremely personal," with the impersonal and mathematically predictable space of classical Newtonian physics. Similarly, the cyclic patterns that result from the repetitive process of the work — the tremulous vibrato of the wave interference that comes to replace the voice — extend the local instances of Lucier's stutter to the entire sonic field, making the stutter into the most salient characteristic of the music as a whole. Despite Lucier's claim to "regard this activity not so much as a demonstration of a physical fact, but more as a way to smooth out any irregularities my speech might have," the activity in fact reduplicates and amplifies the "irregular" reduplications of his stutter. Moreover, the tremolo of Lucier's stuttered syllables are one of the very last characteristics of his speech to survive the degradation of the tape recording; they remain rhythmically recognizable even after the syllables themselves can no longer be discerned. So, as Christof Migone points out, "Lucier's intent to smooth out his stutter provides the impetus for the piece but what results is a heightened stutter."[10]

Like Lucier, Pierre Guyotat has also attempted to smooth out the stutter, and with similar results: radically deforming the comprehensibility of language and transferring the logic of the stutter to the text itself. In many ways, the two could not be further apart; Lucier's hygienic, barely intrusive minimalism and flatly descriptive prose stand in stark contrast to Guyotat's aggressively maximalist excess. The comparison is instructive, however, because Lucier's clear model of how content extends into form — how conventionally discursive and referentially communicative speech can be systematically transformed in order to draw out its musical properties — helps to highlight the same process at work in Guyotat's later prose, where the deformations are just as systematic but less immediately apparent because the formal logic of his sound experiments is masked by the distractingly lurid content.

Recognized as one of the "indisputably major literary talents of his generation" — the generation of the 1960s who followed the *nouveaux ro-*

manciers and were associated with the marriage of Joycean experimentation and leftist politics, including writers such as Philippe Sollers, Julia Kristeva, Jacqueline Risset, and Marcelin Pleynet — Guyotat came to prominence in the mid-1960s with work that fused literary experimentation with hardcore pornography and a postcolonial sensibility dramatically opposed to the French occupation of Algeria.[11] Pursuing the dream of an experimental fiction that aspired to be as radical in form as in content, Guyotat became a mythic figure of the *arrière-garde:* keeping the faith of verbal violence valorized by the historical avant-gardes and writing novels that can still manage to elicit a genuine shock. Guyotat's 1975 novel *Prostitution* opens:

[debout, la bouch' !, j'a b'soin ! »] [. ., te m'veux, m'sieur l'homm' ? » — « j'vas t'trequer au bourrier ! » — « j't'déslip', m'sieur l'homm' ? » — « oua. ., tir'-moi l'zob du jeans a j'vas t'triquer ! » — « te peux m'trequer en sall', m'sieur l'homm' ! » — « oua. ., put' !, te veux m'piéger la pin' ! » — « me, j'veux qu'te m'l'encul' chef, m'sieur l'homm', a qu'ton gros poil de couill' m'étrangl' l'bouquet !. ., mets !. ., mets ! » — « mlih !. ., mlih !, porq'qu't'se hâtée qu'j'te matt' l'chaloup' » — « cheï !, l'homm' !, ma ia des bourr' qu'viann't sonder les bourriers ![12]

([yeah, on yer' feet, dat' mout', gonna gim' me it!"] [. ., yuh want muh, mis'er guy?" — "gonna poun'ya out atda dumpster!" — "c'n I get dos' shorts off, mis'er guy?" — "uh-huh. .,yank dat pork out dos' levi's an ahl start poun'in!" — "yuh c'n poun' me in da room, mis'er guy!" — "uh-huh. ., slut, ya gonna booby-trap ma tree!" — "bu' I wanch'ya as'fuc' me,suh, mis'er guy, so dos' big nu' hairs strangle mah 'rroids!. ., work!. ., "work!" — bueno!. ., bueno! bu' why da hurry me givin' ya a mas' for dat sloop!" — "nada!, guy!, bu' some pigs jus' finished stakin' th' dumpsters!)[13]

The book continues, and intensifies, for another 365 pages. Writing in the particularly French tradition of avant-garde pornography that took its cue from Donatien A. F. de Sade and Isidore Ducasse, peaking in the twentieth century with Georges Bataille, Antonin Artaud, and Jean Genet, Guyotat sets a relentless litany of sexually violent acts within a colonial military mise-en-scène. That combination initially provoked a correspondingly extreme response: Guyotat's third novel, *Tombeau pour cinq cent mille soldats* (1967), was forbidden to French troops and threatened with the kind of suppression that in fact met his next novel, *Eden, Eden, Eden* (1970); in an uncharacteristic act of post-Vichy censorship upheld throughout the 1970s, the French government ruled that *Eden, Eden, Eden* could not be displayed, advertised, or sold to minors.[14] The difference between the two novels is less one of content, however, than of form. At their most horrific, the two works share equally repellent scenes of abject abuse. Stylistically, however, the scenes of corporeal indiscretions and intersections in *Eden, Eden, Eden* — the myriad permutations of possible bodily penetrations and the bestial coupling of different human and nonhuman species — find a parallel in the text's linguistic promiscuity. Guyotat mixes argot and patois with phonetic spellings, Kabyle vocabulary and Algerian pronunciation with contemporary urban slang, and colloquial idioms with archaisms of recherché etymological precision. Moreover, *Eden* dispenses with the romantic rhetoric, linear narrative, and familiar novelistic structure in which *Tombeau* couches its hallucinatory depictions of violent copulation. Starting with *Eden,* and intensifying in the novels that have followed, Guyotat simultaneously disassembles and distends language into what Roland Barthes termed a "sovereign metonymy": distilling the telegraphic style of Louis-Ferdinand Céline into an even more finely fragmented parataxis and extending the concatenation of those atomic fragments to the length of the book itself, eliminating those conventional fictional devices — chapters, paragraphs, dialogue, discursive markers — that might have organized or contained the rapid precession of brief, broken phrases.

In response to the government's ruling, a number of writers associated with the journal *Tel Quel,* including Roland Barthes, Marguerite Duras, Phillipe Sollers, Michel Leiris, Claude Simon, Jacques Derrida, and Michel Foucault, publicly defended Guyotat, focusing not so much on the graphic pornographic content of *Eden, Eden, Eden* as on the formal character of its prose. Indeed, contrary to what any reader of the English translations of Guyotat's work might expect, his defenders typically characterized *Eden* as if it were a pure play of the signifier with negligible referential content, as if it were more Stéphane Mallarmé than Denis Roche. As Roland Barthes writes, in a text used as a preface to Guyotat's novel, "*Eden, Eden, Eden* est un texte libre: libre de tout sujet, de tout object, de tout symbole" (*Eden, Eden, Eden* is a free text: free of any subject, any object, any symbol).[15] For Barthes, the remarkable aspect of Guyotat's writing is not the transgression of the narrative ("c'est sans doute la même chose," he dismisses), but a new textual unit:

[une] phrase unique qui ne finit pas, dont la beauté ne vient pas de son "report" (le réel à quoi elle est supposée renvoyer), mais de son souffle, coupé, répété, comme s'il s'agissait pour l'auteur de nous représenter non des scènes imaginées, mais la scène du langage, en sorte que le modèle de cette nouvelle *mimèsis* n'est plus l'aventure d'un héros, mais l'aventure même du signifiant.

[a single, endless sentence whose beauty arises not from its "message" (the reality to which it is supposed to correspond), but from its breath — cut, repeated — as if it were the entire task of the author to show us not imagined scenes but the scene of language, so that the model of this new mimesis is no longer the adventure of a hero, but the adventure of the signifier itself.][16]

Those adventures include a number of 'patalinguistic pursuits akin to Velimir Khlebnikov's experiments with "internal declensions": the application of the Latin ablative absolute to French (in order, as Guyotat explains, "to efface anthropomorphism and make different processes take place simultaneously"); outrageous anthimeria (novel gerunds and nouns conscripted as verbs); and a severely restricted grammatical palette that further shifts suggestions of agency and narrative time onto those words that remain ("Totally suppress adverbs in order to relieve the action of temporal and psychological burdens," as Guyotat writes in his composition notebook). Most striking, perhaps, is Guyotat's orthographic tendency to eliminate silent vowels, particularly the final *e,* writing French as if it were a Semitic language.[17] By deforming French in these ways, as if it were subject to the laws of another language, Guyotat undertakes something akin to what Walter Benjamin theorizes as "the task of the translator."[18] In Benjamin's well-known argument, that task "consists in finding the particular intention toward the target language which produces in that language the echo of the original."[19] Pursuing a kind of linguistic (rather than semantic) literalism, in which the details of one language are preserved within the structure of another, such translations are unnatural and unidiomatic, but they open a space — not unlike the space of Lucier's room — in which the fundamental characters of the two languages can resound and interfere. "Instead of imitating the sense of the original," such a translation "must lovingly and in detail incorporate the original's way of meaning."[20]

One might apply Benjamin's distinction between meaning and the "way of meaning" to the other translations Guyotat's texts effect. To begin with, he translates between literary genres, writing novels as if they were verse. Where *Tombeau* imitated some of the *sense* of surrealist verse — abrupt non sequiturs, a fantasy dream logic, the libidinous drives of the unconscious — *Eden* incorporates poetry's *way* of meaning. Guyotat proclaims: "c'est par le rythme, par la poésie, donc, qu'on peut renouveler la fiction aujourd'hui" (it is through rhythm, through poetry, that is, that we could revitalize contemporary fiction).[21] Accordingly, as Stuart Kendall notes, "Guyotat does not write novels; he writes epic poems that must masquerade, however ineffectually, as novels in today's marketplace. *Tombeau pour cinq cent mille soldats* is subtitled 'Sept chants,' *Progénitures* is set in versets, strophic records of breath."[22] The distinction, however, is more than nominative or merely metaphoric, more than the blasphemous *épater* gesture of using "versets" ("verses" in the sense most often used with the holy scripture of the Bible or Koran), and far more than a matter of marketing; in Guyotat's most recent writing his descriptions of sexual activity *sans mesure* are written in a carefully measured prose. As Guyotat explains:

> c'est ce chemin vocal qu'il faut entendre dans *Progénitures*. Ce que je sais, c'est que mes versets sont calculés, syllabiquement calculés comme on le faisait pour les vers encore au siècle dernier. Mais ils sont deux, trois, quatre fois plus longs que ces vers calculés d'autrefois; et ils intègrent des libertés, des licences — élisions, contractions, etc. — qui n'avaient plus cours alors. La mesure de ce rhythm syllabique rigoureux, le calcul des pieds, est un des actes principaux du travail sur Progénitures: les nécessités de la métrique, souvent, engagent le sens, voire la direction de la fiction; dans ces moments de grande activité rythmique, je crois l'avoir dit ailleurs, déjà, c'est le monde environnant qui est touché; les panneaux publicitaires, les titres des journaux, les menus de restaurant, le courrier qu'on reçoit, les panneaux horaires des trains dans les gares, les annonces de départ et d'arrivée d'avion dans les aéroports, tout ce qui se voit et s'entend hors de la pièce de travail est re-rythmé selon la mesure du moment dans le travail.
> [One must comprehend the vocal path in *Progénitures*. That is, my versets are calculated, syllabically calculated in the way poetry was composed in the last century. But they are two, three, four times longer than that old metrical poetry; and they incorporate some liberties, some licenses — elisions, contractions, etc. — to which they did not formerly have recourse. The measure of that rigorous syllabic rhythm, the calculation of metrical feet, is one of the main tasks of the work on *Progénitures:* the metrical necessities often take on the meaning of the fiction, even engaging the trajectory of the plot; in these moments of great rhythmic activity, as I believe I have already said elsewhere, the real-world environment is touched: billboards; headlines; menus; junk mail; train schedules; airport flight announcements — everything one sees or hears beyond the work is re-rhythmed according to the measure of the moment in the work.][23]

Creating "un drame du sens et du son" (a drama of meaning and sound) — or, indeed, a drama of sound *as* meaning, where "le rythme invente de nouveau sens" (rhythm invents a new meaning) and "the stutter *is* the plot" — Guyotat grafts the essential logic of poetry onto fiction, returning the counting to account, all with the hope of further translating that new hybrid to the quotidian nonliterary genres of advertising and mass transit schedules.[24]

At the same time, Guyotat is also translating between body and text. In general, he locates the formal properties of his metrical prose in the irreducible physiologic formations of his own individual body: idiosyncrasies of lung capacity; cardiac rhythms; the architecture of the throat.[25] The measured rhythms of his *versets* are based on a body that they in turn regulate, recording a corporeal capacity that subsequent silent readings subconsciously register and that oral readings — like Guyotat's infamous, periodic, marathon recitations at the Centre Pompidou — must attempt to approximate. Rhythm, for Guyotat, brings the sound of poetry to fiction, and by incorporating the respiratory measure of the breath that literary rhythm in turn carries with it the sound of the body:

> cela pose la question du souffle, *le souffle,* il faut le répéter, *sous-tend continûment le travail textuel,* d'autant qu'il porte la voix ; je travaille avec un *paquet de voix* dans la gorge (bouillie de voyelles, de consonnes, de syllabes, de mots entiers même, qui demandent à sortir, à gicler sur la page).
>
> [that raises the question of the breath, *the breath,* it must be repeated, *continually underlies the textual work,* all the more so because it carries the voice; I work with a *vocal package* in my throat (pulp of vowels, of consonants, of syllables, of whole words even, which need to get out, to squirt onto the page.][26]

"Dans la gorge" (in the throat) or "à l'intérieur de ma gorge" (inside my throat) is the site of the vocal packages that underlie not only Guyotat's text but also those that threaten to provoke his stutter:

> Je dois alors dans les boutiques, aux caisses, préparer, à l'intérieur de ma gorge, la phrase de demande que je vais faire, prévoir le petit commentaire, et quoi, et comment y répondre, choisir les mots d'appui du début, du milieu et de la fin de la phrase, répéter ces paroles à plusieurs reprises, placer de telle façon ma main sur le comptoir pour appuyer l'émission de la phrase ; placer mon pied sur le sol pour exister, apparaître comme autre chose qu'un fantôme.
>
> [In shops, therefore, I must, at the counter, prepare, inside my throat, the inquiry that I am going to make, envisage the little comment, and what, and how to answer there, choose my supporting words from the beginning, the middle, and the end of the sentence, repeat the words several times over, place my hand on the counter in such a way as to support the utterance of the sentence, my feet on the ground in order to exist, to appear as something other than a ghost.]

The commercial backdrop against which Guyotat dramatizes the social terror of stuttered speech is not coincidental.[27] The scene at "le comptoir" (the counter) further underscores the parallel between the numerically calculated syllables of his poetic "vocal packages" and the patterns of everyday patter he hopes they rerhythm. With this sense of rhythm, "répéter ces paroles à plusieurs reprises" might be the hallmark of either literary language or stuttered language. Moreover, Guyotat again describes handling and delivering those vocal packages, first chokingly trapped in the throat and then blurted out, as the essence of both his literary compositions and his stuttered speech. Simultaneously a condition of blockage and of flow, of phonemes prolonged and postponed, a linguistic production at once excessive and insufficient, the stutter — like the concatenated units of his sentence-long novel — is both too much and not enough. As Guyotat recalls:

> Ce qui marque principalement ma petite enfance . . . c'est mon bégaiement (je ne puis "lancer" les phrases qui débutent par une voyelle, etc.), qui contraint mes premiers maîtres à me faire écrire toutes les "interrogations" orales, bégaiement en même temps que, si la parole était déclenchée sur ma propre initiative, une grande faconde pour raconter à des adultes, femmes le plus souvent, les romans et récits d'exploration que je lisais à ce moment.
>
> [What chiefly marks my childhood . . . is my stutter (I cannot get out sentences that begin with a vowel, and so on), which required my first teachers to have me write all the "oral" examination, a stutter at the same time as, if the word were started on my own initiative, a great fecundity for recounting to adults, most often women, the novels and adventure stories that I happened to be reading at the time.][28]

Language, for Guyotat, is either frozen and immobile (he cannot launch [*lancer*] his sentences) or else — when taking the form of stories or when squirted on the page ("à gicler sur la page") — unusually fertile (*un grande faconde*), with the hint of being spermatozoically motile. That fecundity, significantly, is both explicitly literary, assuming the outlines of novels (*romans*), and once again associated with counting. Guyotat can free language from the throat when it is recounted (*raconter*), or at the counter [*comptoir*], or metrically counted (*calculé*).

Across his critical and autobiographical writings, Guyotat's stutter thus comes to be rhetorically associated with his literary composition. Moreover, as in Lucier's composition, Guyotat's compositional techniques actually project and amplify the poetics of the stutter onto the structure of the texts themselves. The attendant contradictions, furthermore, work much as they did in *I Am Sitting in a Room*. On first reading, one might hear Guyotat's distinctive style as an attempt to "smooth out" the irregularities of his stutter, or even to counter and thwart it outright; his neologistic contractions not only suggest a Semitic orthography but also tend to remove vowels: precisely the type of phonemes that most provoked his stammering as a child and prevented him from speaking. Indeed, Guyotat's radical syncope, at both the syllabic and the grammatical level, clips and slurs elements rather than multiplying them, as if he were intent on moving language in the opposite direction of the stutter's reduplications and away from the kind of repetitions suggested by the insistently stuttered title with which *Eden, Eden, Eden* opens. At the same time, however, Guyotat's texts emphasize the fundamental logic of the stutter in other ways: working at the submorphemic level of phonemic particles, regulating the consonantal tattoo of his syncopic language into rhythmic patterns, and creating a grammar at once broken (those "vocal packages" that erupt in the short bursts and blurts that often typify the speech of stutterers) and simultaneously prolonged — suspended without grammatical or narrative resolution.

Moreover, this is the point at which Guyotat's themes extend to meet up with his form. An excessive, spasmodic, convulsive lack of bodily control describes not only the stutter but also the anarchy of Guyotat's characters, with their general abandonment of social constraints and all the local bodily events of visceral reflex that cause so much blood and semen and excrement "to splatter on the page" (à gicler sur la page).[29] In short, Guyotat's later prose presents a series of ejaculations, in both formal and thematic terms. Similarly, the pervasive prostitution and sexual slavery in Guyotat's fiction, from the ubiquitous bordello settings to the eponymous title of his 1975 novel, relate economically to the metrical accounting of the text that describes them. But slavery, moreover, has also long been linked in the popular imagination, at least since Aesop, with stuttering.[30] In an inflected projection of the author's dysphemia, form and content thus double back on one another in Guyotat's work, where the "form of content" reiterates the "form of expression" (to adopt Deleuze's terms). Form, when recognized *as such,* is always the stutter of content.

To triangulate the broad literary field mapped by the poetics of stutter I want to turn to a third work, Jordan Scott's poetry collection *blert*. In most respects, Scott's project stands quite far from either *I Am Sitting in a Room* or *Progénitures,* instead resembling the family of post-language-poetry lyrics published since the 1990s. Indeed, the publication and reception history of Scott's work associates it with poetry from the Calgary small press community (Ryan Fitzpatrick, Derek Beaulieu, Christian Bök) and other Canadian writers (Peter Culley, Mark Truscott, and Jill Hartman among many others) using lyric disjunction as a primary compositional mode.[31] A typical page from *blert* reads:

> Coca-Cola tonic krill
> gill baleen
> dream wrenched
> Kleenex smack
> Baltic Pyrex
> megahertz humpback
> kickback: flex
> nukes flub
> blubber sexy
> plankton number

The agrammatical frisson and microphonic sound play of these lines immediately recall the pioneering work of Bruce Andrews, and one can hear echoes, in Scott's verse, of Andrews's signature alliteration, internal assonance, and syntactic collisions, as well as his habit of pairing technical scientific vocabulary with colloquial phrases. Compare Scott's stanza above, for instance, to lines from almost any of Andrews's poetry: "selectary slam simplomatic dinge dinabee coca-colonization cubbyhole shack"; "drawer natural wrench annex allure"; "putty pups / trick or treat . . . plankton catcall / Placebo addiction."[32] Poets such as Andrews no doubt gave a necessary license to Scott's experiments, but the phonemic density and radically disjunctive couplings in *blert* arise not so much from the facture and fracture of language poetry as from the details of Scott's own lifelong stutter.[33] In Scott's particular case, his stutter seems to be tripped by initial stressed syllables beginning with nasal stops or plosive occlusives (whether aspirated, partially voiced, or voiced nasals) and exacerbated by terminal fricatives and the repetition of internal vowels across words. *Blert,* in short, is a text written to be as difficult as possible for its own author to read. The work is thus a formal analogue to Scott's dysphemia, transferring the etiology of his stammer onto the structure of poetic language. While some aspects of Scott's poems, like some aspects of Guyotat's prose, might be read as reflecting the speech habits of a typical stammerer — short phrasal bursts (the "blurts" signaled by the poem's title), a sophisticated vocabulary developed by the need to substitute for certain difficult-to-pronounce words, a similarly high degree of apposition — *blert* is not primarily a mimetic representation of stuttering, or the reproduction of a stutter's symptomatic results, but rather a statistical mapping of the interior logic of the stutter's neurolinguistic structure and its initial lexical triggers. Enacted rather than named, the stutter here is not an affect registered *in* language but rather an effect *of* language.

Blert, however, also stutters in other significant ways. By basing his text on particular types of phonemes placed in particular syllabic sequences within words, Scott has essentially created a system of rhyme that is formal, motivated, and palpable to the ear, but in which the recurrence of any particular sound is never quite predictable. The densely packed patterns of unexpectedly repeated sounds in *blert* weave a thicket that even the most fluent reader will find hard to navigate without some stumbling. At the same time, the nimble reader who actually does manage to succeed in a fluent pronunciation *necessarily stutters* when reading the poem; the many intentionally paired syllables in words such as "cuckoo," "coco," "cocoons," "coca-cola," "Zsa Zsa," "tam tam," "cucumber," "bubble," "bumblebee" require that the perfectly proper and fluid pronunciation of *blert* is the stuttered pronunciation. *Blert* thus offers a strange combination of inducement and evasion, concealment and display: foregrounding the stutter at its most fundamental level and encouraging readerly dysfluency while simultaneously camouflaging its sounds behind the proper reduplications of the alliteratively repeated syllables of legitimate words. Accordingly, one might say of Scott what Deleuze says of Charles Péguy: his "stuttering embraces the language so well that it leaves the words intact, complete, and normal, but it uses them as if they were themselves the disjointed and decomposed members of a superhuman [that is, structurally linguistic] stuttering."[34]

"Poetry," in one of Roman Jakobson's definitions, "is a province where the internal nexus between sound and meaning changes from latent to patent and manifests itself most palpably and intensely."[35] The poetry of *blert* is precisely such a nexus (though perhaps not quite in the way that Jakobson envisioned), and Scott's poems perform the same kind of formal stutter registered in Guyotat's fiction. The formal, material, sonic aspects of his poems, that is, not only re-embody his stutter but also, in turn, explain the otherwise frankly inexplicable thematic content of the book, which disjunctively returns, again and again, to a very specific constellation of interwoven themes: glaciers, neurotoxins, marine mammals, the geology of small rocky debris,

THE STUTTER OF FORM / 181

and human skeletal anatomy. In fact, part of the initially restive estrangement of the book — the asemantic frisson that suggests the work of a writer like Andrews — is that these themes seem at first to be entirely unrelated, a vocabulary "unhinged from a narrative construction," as Derek Beaulieu describes it.[36] On closer inspection, however, the reader finds that these themes in fact hinge at very precise points on single key words. The line "Chorus clast," for just one example, recalls Scott's use of "osteoclast" in another poem and enacts a self-reflexively broken version of the word *clastic,* from the Greek *klasos* (broken), which denotes broken pieces of older rock as well as small, segmented, anatomical structures such as the carpal bones of the hand. *Carpal,* not coincidentally, is a word that in fact repeats often in Scott's poetry and rhymes with another repeated word, *scarp,* as in the phrase "Limestone talus scarp."[37] *Scarp* is the geological term for a steep hill or cliff, precisely the kind of geological structure at the base of which clastic talus accumulates, and *talus* is both a kind of *scree* ("a pile of small broken rocks at the base of a cliff or incline," as the *Oxford English Dictionary* has it) as well as the name for the ankle bone — and so back, again, to *clastic,* in both senses of the word.

Such instances could be multiplied, but although the seemingly disconnected themes of Scott's poetry are in fact concatenated in these local ways, the logic of the themes themselves — the single category that can encompass them all at a more abstract level — is explained only by the dialectic pull of the stutter, its paradox of suspension and falter. In a line that Jakobson cites just before giving the definition of poetry quoted above, Paul Valéry defines the poem in terms that might equally describe the stutter: "le poème, hésitation prolongée entre le son et le sens" (the poem: a prolonged hesitation between sound and meaning).[38] In the dysfluent space that opens between the two possible referents of Valéry's phrase, between the poem and the stammer, we can glimpse the key to Scott's poetics of stutter. The standard clinical description of the two corresponding categories of typical stuttering — either "freezing" a syllable or "breaking" syllables — offers the ready explanation for Scott's themes of freezing (the arctic, obviously, but also the neurotoxins, which turn out, on inspection, to all be paralysants) and breaking (bones and rocks and glacial debris). Small broken rocks, moreover, are famously associated with the history of stuttering through the great orator Demosthenes. In Plutarch's frequently reiterated documentation:

> Demetrius, the Phalerian, tells us that he was informed by Demosthenes himself, now grown old, that the ways he made use of to remedy his natural bodily

infirmities and defects were such as these; his inarticulate and stammering pronunciation he overcame and rendered more distinct by speaking with pebbles in his mouth.[39]

Similarly, the emphasis on the clastic bones enumerated in *blert* points not only to their frequent "breaking" but also — in the context of vocabulary naming tendons and ligaments and connective tissue — to their idiomatic link with "articulation."

Fluency and stutter, the articulate and the broken: the same dynamic explains the deep sea whales that recur through Scott's poem, which are known for both their mellifluous *singing* (singing, interestingly, seems to obviate stuttering even among those for whom speech is a problem) and their *blubber* in the obvious sense of cetacean lipids but also always suggesting an inarticulate voicing — a *wailing* as the homophone would have it. Moreover, the first entry for *blubber* in the *Oxford English Dictionary* defines the word as "the foaming or boiling of the sea," so when Scott entitles one of the poems in *blert* "jokulhlaup," the Icelandic word for the kind of "boiling of the sea" that the U.S. Geological Survey defines as a "glacial outburst flood," he captures — in a word made almost unpronounceable for the non-Icelandic speaker by its stuttered *l*'s — both the technical sense of *blubber* and the blubbering logic of the stuttered blurt: an excessive, flooding outburst that is at the same time paradoxically glacial, prolonged and hesitating, fast and slow, frozen and boiling, fluid with water and viscous with rocky debris.

That same paradoxical logic defines "the poetics of stutter," as I have been using the phrase. The stutter structures language in two opposing directions, both blocking certain speech and impeding the facile consumption of language, while at the very same time permitting or producing literary compositions based on its formal characteristics. Under the sign of that poetics, "the poem is free to be inarticulate," as Peter Quartermain writes, "even to stutter."[40] Those working within the poetics of stutter, like the three writers under consideration here, demonstrate a way of addressing the formal rather than the mimetically thematic or representational aspects of a "disability aesthetic."[41] Indeed, when heard in the context of disability studies, the stutter — understood as a critical category flexible enough to negotiate between the impeding and the productive, between the embodied individual and the social abstract — offers one way to understand the full range of inarticulate effects on display in the writings of the avant-garde and its broad challenge to the ideologies of normalcy, fluency, transparently communicative expository eloquence, and any notion of a dematerialized or disembodied language. Moreover, the poetics of stutter calls into question what Michael Davidson has recognized as "the larger implications of corporeality in the arts."[42] "Which," as Davidson has written elsewhere, "is why a poetics — as much as a politics — of disability is important: because it theorizes the ways that poetry defamiliarizes not only language but the body normalized *within* language."[43]

Bodies, like poems, always mean what they ceaselessly say: that even if they could speak — and they can — we would not understand them.

THE ART OF
BEING NONSYNCHRONOUS

YOKO TAWADA

Translated by Susan Bernofsky

1

I first encountered the term "native speaker" in a junior high school English class in Japan. Our teacher said: "Now let's listen to the pronunciation of a native speaker" and switched on a sturdy black cassette recorder that resembled a family altar. At first all we heard from the machine was a crackling noise, but soon it was followed by a voice reading the text from our book.

The sound of this language had a surprisingly powerful effect on me: The *a* of *cat* opened its jaws like a furious tomcat. The *m* of *mother* held a sip of whiskey in its mouth without a word, while the *p* of *pen* exploded with impatience.

Imitating these sounds was difficult. The cassette recorder had no mouth, so you couldn't see how it was producing the one or the other sound.

Even today the term "native speaker" makes me think not of a person but of a cassette recorder.

Many years later I had the opportunity to observe a person speaking English more closely. I then realized that to speak English it was necessary to open one's mouth not just vertically, but horizontally as well. Up to this point I had been unable, for example, to distinguish between *ear* and *year,* but once I saw the speaker's lips, I started to hear two different sounds. In other words, hearing isn't done by the ear alone; the eye hears as well.

When I first arrived in Germany as a twenty-two-year-old, I was surprised to find that in every major city nearly every evening there was a poet willing to read his poems to an audience. In Japan, poetry readings are rare. I found it just as surprising that on German television the samurais in a Kurosawa movie spoke German fluently, as did the figures in anime films. Even Lieutenant Columbo, who on Japanese television had spoken only Japanese, now spoke German as if he'd done so all his life.

Although the lieutenant's face remained the same as ever, I had the impression he'd now become another person. I was just as surprised to hear a friend of mine suddenly speaking a different language. Usually my image of people was based on their voices, their choice of words, and the little pauses between words that made up the rhythm of their speech.

But when you speak a different language, both your voice and your speech rhythms differ as well. I wondered whether I really knew this woman or just a cassette recording inside her. Can the body be compared to a cassette player in which you can keep changing the tape?

When I was little, one of my playmates showed me a doll that could talk. When the doll was undressed, you could see two little doors in its back. One of them concealed a battery and the other a tiny cassette containing a recording of the doll's voice.

The word "to dub" is *fukikae* in Japanese. *Fuki* means "to blow" and *kae* "to exchange." A different voice is blown into a body and replaces the old one. Dubbing is a shamanic activity. If for example a person wishes to speak with his dead mother, he goes to a shaman who summons the souls of the dead. The soul of the dead woman enters into the shaman's body and speaks through his mouth. Like a film actor, he lets himself be dubbed.

Poetry readings always make me think about dubbing and shamanism. To begin with, we have the body of the poet. We have his voice, through which we are hearing the poem, and then there's this poem as written text. But what do these three things have to do with one another?

When you watch a dubbed movie, you should theoretically be able to notice a discrepancy between the lip movements and the voice if you look closely enough. This thought has troubled me for some time. Like a woman possessed, I stare at the actors' lips, waiting to discover moments where the synchronization doesn't work. Sometimes I find myself so preoccupied I miss the plot of the movie.

What I am hoping to see is a pair of lips standing still while I am hearing a word, or lips broadly, lustily in motion, producing inaudible sentences. But dubbing techniques nowadays are so sophisticated, it's practically impossible to find an error. Film and television actors express themselves fluently in languages they don't speak, as if there were no such thing as a language barrier, no division between their voices and bodies.

One day I saw an installation that once more drew my attention to the dubbing process. Unfortunately I've forgotten the artist's name and have been unable to find him on the internet. This was in 2001, at Art Basel, the international art show held in Basel once a year. A drive-in theater had been set up outside the exhibition center, and on the large screen I saw two cowboys dismounting from their horses and chatting with the reins in their hands. "A typical scene from some Western, what's the point," I thought. You couldn't hear the sound, but even a person like me who has never seen a Western from beginning to end could easily imagine the sorts of things they were saying. An empty car was parked in front of the screen, and when you got inside and put on headphones, you could hear the cowboys' voices. And what a surprise! The film had been dubbed with philosophical texts. A writer who was there with me shouted in delight: "It's Heidegger!" The work was perfect: There was no apparent discrepancy between the text and the movements of the cowboys' lips.

It's quite possible, in other words, to take a voice from some far-off location and arbitrarily place it in the body of a film actor.

To whom does the voice belong? The voice erases the question of whom. On the other hand, the voice is often used in democratic society as a metaphor for a person's authentic opinion. We speak of people being given a voice when they are able to assert their political will, and in some languages, such as German, a vote is literally called a "voice."

Hearing a poet read his work only strengthens my impression that the voice is coming from far away or from a person not literally present. You stare at the poet's lips to reassure yourself that you really do have before your eyes the authentic source of the poem. But the more closely you watch his lips, the more difficult it is to say where the sound of a poem comes from.

2

Ever since the invention of sound recording technology, it's been just as easy to preserve the human voice as a manuscript. Not only can a voice be recorded and played back again as often as desired, it can be copied, cut, and edited as well. The voice is no longer something that must be produced on the spot from a living body. It's now become commonplace, one can say, for the owner of a voice not to be physically present when the voice is heard. When we sit in a movie theater, for example, the actors who appear in the film are usually, with very few exceptions, elsewhere and not in the theater itself. And how fortunate it is that the people we see on television are not actually sitting in our living rooms! In our day-to-day lives, we devote a great deal of time to the telephone and internet.

At night, the intimacy of a voice has a stronger effect than during the daytime. The people whispering in my ear from the radio are not sitting beside me. Some of them are even dead. But the ghostly immateriality of a voice is not generally seen as cause for alarm. It's only on rare occasions that you'll find yourself suddenly struck by the uncanniness of a disembodied voice. In my case, this happened with an onboard navigation system in someone's car. The voice, which I couldn't even assign to any particular body, responded to the driver's presence and told him where to go. This voice was sitting quite close beside the driver, closer than would be possible in reality. It was like an imaginary character speaking in a lonely person's head.

Before digital technologies became a part of everyday life, the letter was considered one of the most important instruments for the transport of words. Even the telephone was unable to destroy the culture of letter writing. People who before had frequently written letters continued to do so to communicate things they preferred not to say on the telephone. The letter has developed its own form of distance that allows people to express things it might be difficult to say in person. This has less to do with inhibitions or politeness than with style. Writing a letter, you can borrow this or that turn of phrase from literary tradition to apply to your own life much more easily than on the phone. It wasn't until the advent of electronic communication that the culture of letter writing began to lose some of its dominance. There are many differences between an email and a letter on paper, but one in particular stands out, namely, the consciousness on the part of both sender and recipient of the distance between them. Even in the case of an overseas email, people tend to expect a response in the next few hours, as if the recipient's desk were in the same room. Mentioning the time difference or weather in an international email can already be interpreted as a personal, even romantic gesture. A handwritten letter, however, almost automatically announces the writer's absence to its recipient.

Yasushi Inoue's story "The Hunting Gun" (1949) consists for the most part of three letters written by three women to a man. The first letter is written by the daughter of the man's lover. The young woman is making an assumption about distance when she writes that he surely isn't here in the city but rather in his country house. And she demands an even greater distance: She writes that she never wants to see him again. The second letter is from his wife, who writes it sitting at her husband's desk in his absence. It is a farewell letter in which she calmly but quite clearly proposes a divorce. The third letter is the last will and testament of the man's lover. By the time he receives this letter, she is no longer alive. Her absence is then complete.

A person who's lost his hearing feels the isolation more acutely than one who's lost his vision. Hearing someone's voice can make you feel a certain closeness to that person. Even an electronic reproduction of a voice is capable of simulating proximity. Where is the voice coming from? Where is the voice at the moment we are hearing it? The invisible waves touch our eardrums, which are stretched taut deep within our ears. Every voice from outside resonates within our head, not before our eyes. Many commercial films take advantage of this property of the voice and attempt to use the synchronization of image and sound to eliminate our distance from the characters. This seduces the viewer into identifying with the characters.

The sort of art I value doesn't try to make its medium invisible but rather thematizes it in the work itself. A poem ought to contain its own theory of poetics and speak not only of its visible "contents" but of writing itself. A play should always reflect the formal properties of the theatrical arts. Thus I am particularly interested in films that emphasize certain forms of synchronization, for example, dubbing. There are classic examples, such as Wim Wenders's film *Lisbon Story,* in which the sound engineer with his large recording apparatus plays a major role. In this essay, however, I would like to discuss a few more recent examples I have experienced in person.

In the summer of 2002 I attended an international theater festival in Hamburg and saw a performance entitled *Memory* put on by the Theater am Neumarkt from Zurich. On the screen, a filmed interview with three old women was projected without sound. An actor and two actresses stood on stage dubbing the film. There was something surprising and touching about the juxtaposition of these young voices with the old faces. The discrepancy was not only of age but of gender: one of the speakers on the stage was male, while all three faces on the screen were female. The face of the woman being dubbed by the male actor looked so beautiful and multifaceted, as though it had already received into itself many male and female faces. Thus it was fitting that her voice was being dubbed by a male actor and not an actress.

I was instantly reminded of an old female shaman who spoke through the mouth of a dead man. This shaman was possessed by the man, and thus she turned her body into a medium. The dead man no longer had a body; he needed a medium in order to speak.

This was a form of dubbing. But unlike dubbing of the usual sort, which attempts to simulate the identity of voice and body, the theater piece *Memory* intentionally showed us that the voices were coming not from the projected faces on the screen but rather from a medium, in this case the body of another person.

After the show I happened to overhear a critical question being posed by an audience member as we were filing out: Why had they robbed the old women of their voices? Why hadn't they been allowed to use their own voices to tell their stories? There are particularly high expectations of "authenticity" when it is a question of autobiographical narrative. And yet all too often one forgets that even in a documentary film, the material is subjected to a number of manipulations, even when the voices appear to be presented in their original form.

Where does a voice come into being? Perhaps a vibration is first created in the vocal chords, the palate, on a person's tongue. But this is not yet a voice. Only in the listener's head is it constructed as the voice of a person. We hear selectively, we correct, add to, and adulterate what we are hearing. Otherwise it would be impossible to understand the person speaking to us. We contribute to this process by bringing in our own knowledge, preconceptions, imagination, and repressed thoughts. Thus every act of listening is already a dialogue, even before we open our mouths to reply.

Little children dub books when they read them aloud. The storytelling voice, which at first was the voice of the author, the voice of one of the characters or of the mother, is thus transformed into the voice of the reader. This reader takes in a story by first placing the words on his tongue and only afterward enjoying them with his ear. I can still remember the glorious feeling I sometimes had as a child when I read my books aloud: It was as if I myself were creating the stories.

Even big kids — by which I mean all of us — take pleasure in reading literary texts aloud. When this is a text written by someone else, it becomes mine when I read it aloud. When it is my own text, reading it aloud turns it into something separate from me.

In 2004, at the same festival in Hamburg two years later, I saw a performance by the Lebanese artist Rabih Mroué that bore the title *Biokhraphia*. An actress stood onstage performing a scene in which a journalist was interviewing an artist. The actress was playing the roles of both the one being questioned and the questioner. The effect was completely natural, perhaps even more natural than in the usual sorts of interviews you see on television. We were seeing the face of the actress through a thick wall of glass, hollow on the inside, that was slowly beginning to fill up with water. But our view of her was scarcely distorted since the water was clear. But soon a second liquid was injected into the water, and all at once a chemical reaction made all the liquid turn milky. You could no longer see the actress's face until a face was projected onto the white surface. It was the same face, but now it appeared to be coming from a projector. This video must have been recorded beforehand, but the lip movements corresponded exactly to the voice we had been hearing without interruption since the beginning of the performance.

At the end of the show, the actress divided the liquid into little bottles and placed them on a table like schnapps. They were for sale. What was in these little bottles? The voice that had come to us through the wall of glass or the face that had been projected on it? Unfortunately I don't know since I didn't have any money on me that day and thus was unable to buy a bottle.

In February 2007 during the Berlin Film Festival I saw Guy Maddin's *Brand upon the Brain* at the Deutsche Oper. It was a silent film, and black and white as well, though it had been produced not during the 1920s but in 2006, in Canada. The actress Isabella Rossellini accompanied the film with onstage narration. The sounds in the film were produced live by three musicians working with musical instruments, water, pieces of wood, vegetables, and other objects. When you stared at the screen, the images and sounds fit together well, as in an ordinary film. But every time you glanced at the stage, it was a surprise. On the screen, for example, you might be seeing a person whose bones were being broken, while onstage one of the musicians was crushing a fennel bulb with his bare hands.

Adulterated sounds have become part of everyday life. There are now sound designers for electrical products. A vacuum cleaner, for example, makes an appropriate noise when you turn it on. And we often forget that this sound, too, has been composed and is not "authentic." For when a vacuum cleaner is too quiet, it's difficult for its owner to believe it is truly effective in eliminating dirt. The actual sound has been dampened and then dubbed with an artificial sound to make it appear more "real."

I like to think back on an old-fashioned studio I once visited where at one time radio plays were produced. In the studio one saw a tub of water, a flat aluminum box filled with dried peas, and a squeaky wooden door in a frame. I often picture this studio when I am listening to a radio play, though nowadays most of the sounds are produced digitally. The German word *O-Ton* (original sound) tends to be enunciated respectfully, with the *O* an exclamation of surprise, as it is unusual for a *Ton* to be original. But what does it mean for a sound to be original? So-called original sound is sound that has been recorded and then processed before being broadcast on the radio. The sounds aren't necessarily coming from the thing we're looking at. The voices aren't coming from the persons whose lips are moving in an appropriate fashion. Has the entire optically perceptible world that surrounds us been dubbed? This suspicion is nothing new; we repress it day after day.

In 2005, a unique opera project was put on in Graz, Austria, by the composer Peter Ablinger. The goal was to turn the entire city into an opera. How can a musician think up a city? What sort of singing voice might a city's mouth emit? I was the so-called librettist for this project, but my libretto was not to be put to music and sung as in ordinary circumstances. Rather I attempted to make a book out of the city's song. I began my work by carefully listening several times to the tape recordings Ablinger had made in the city. There were more than four hundred recordings he had made on the street, in factories and schools, on various bridges, in private homes, restaurants, bars, streetcars, and other locations in the city. The visitors to the audio-space, which was housed in a building in the city, could put on headphones to listen to this collection of sounds. Several fragments from the collection appeared in the symphony Ablinger composed. The sounds of the city struck me as refreshing and strangely organic in the context of this symphony. Because of the huge number of tapes he had made, I could listen to only an embarrassingly small subset of them. Therefore I made a point of not informing myself beforehand as to the locations where they'd been recorded. But soon I realized that what I'd be able to write down was not what I was hearing but rather just my "guesses." I wrote, for example, that someone was opening a door. But how was I supposed to know it was a person? Perhaps it was only the wind opening this door and not a person at all. And how could I be sure it was a door? Perhaps it was an oar scraping the side of a boat. Suddenly I saw a lake at night, a boat swaying upon its waters. The door was no longer a door, it was a boat, and the person was wind. And the moon in the sky? The voice of a coot? In place of the bird's voice I heard a sound that might have come from a zipper. My thoughts quickly returned to the room I'd visualized at the beginning. It had to be a suitcase with a zipper like that. Or did the nocturnal landscape itself have a zipper you could open to see the sunrise? It's a hotel room, not a room in a private home, I thought. Otherwise the person wouldn't have opened the door so slowly and carefully. I didn't want to subordinate the sound to an image to render it explicable. But I was no longer able to slow down the images that kept popping up one after the other, ever more of them.

My writing process took several more detours and seemed to go on forever. I didn't want to just write down the images the sounds evoked in me but rather take the sounds themselves into my hand like concrete objects and then set them down on the paper. How can something we've heard be translated into language? Is an onomatopoeic expression a solution? Should I write, "crackling, scraping, tinkling"? But these onomatopoeic expressions are also culturally encoded, they aren't pure sound. When I write *shitoshito* in Japanese, only Japanese speakers can hear the sound of a gentle rain. A strong rain, on the other hand, is *zaazaa,* but this too works only in Japanese. The German verb *plätschern* (to patter) sounds similar to the Japanese *pichapicha* and is also quite similar in meaning, but such coincidences are rare.

An onomatopoeic expression automatically entails the specification of what is being described. A pattering sound cannot come from a block of wood. But when I was listening to the recordings, I sometimes couldn't tell whether a sound was coming from thunder or a sheet of metal. I wanted to represent the sound, not the person who was producing it, nor its metaphorical significance. It took me quite some time to come up with a solution: My solution was not to find a solution, but rather to enter into the crevice between sound and language and make countless little notes. This dark crevice was a treasure trove of possibilities for what language can be: Language can produce an image from a sound or juxtapose several images. It can clumsily imitate various sounds and invent new words precisely because of its clumsiness. Language can link a sound to a color, or think up an adjective to go along with it while at the same time questioning its legitimacy. Language can compare what we hear with other things. Then the images invoked only by way of comparison begin to assert their independence. Language can offer up its own hollow interior for use as a concert hall or sing songs of its own upon the stage. And all the while it keeps secretly repeating: "I am not music, even though music is part of what I am. That music is the other sort." There are so many possibilities in the dark treasure trove between language and the audible. It is so difficult to keep the door to this chamber ajar that holding it open can be seen as an achievement in its own right.

The desire to hear an authentic voice becomes stronger in particular contexts, for example, in the art of ethnic minorities and immigrants. There is always a lack of simultaneity between the character being described and the one doing the describing, even in the case of a first-person narrator who appears to be telling an autobiographical story. Added to this is an indigenous voice that intervenes in the narration, participating in the storytelling process. To this extent, every autobiographical narrative is also a dialogue. The 2003 film *WOZUHAUS* (WHEREISHOME) made by Hyun-Sook Song in collaboration with Jochen Hiltmann consciously plays on this problematic circumstance. The first scene of the film shows a woman pounding a pole into the earth in a rural landscape. You can see the slow, regular motions of her enormous wooden hammer, but the image and the sound arrive separately. Later in the film we hear the following words: "One is never synchronous. One is never simultaneous with the object one is painting or filming, about which one is thinking or writing. And the appeal of such activities lies not in eventually becoming synchronous but in increasing the paradoxes to attain a feeling for slowness and fastness in, for example, painting. As you will see, one can hurry or hesitate. Speech detaches itself from the mouth, the sound detaches itself from the object, the skin detaches itself from the body, posing the question: What is it that at the speed of light reaches us from strange worlds?"

What is appealing about art is not achieving good synchronizations. It is precisely through visible discrepancies that the voice gains its poetic independence.

Before the invention of recording technology, the conventional forms of dramatic representation coexisted with other performing arts in which body and voice asserted their mutual independence. In the Japanese puppet theater bunraku (*ningyoojooruri*), for instance, a form of theater developed in the seventeenth century that is still practiced today, the puppeteers are joined by a narrator who sits to one side of the stage along with a few musicians and speaks all the different roles. The puppeteers move the puppets without making a sound. In kabuki theater, which got started around the same time and is still popular today, the live actors speak their lines themselves, but in part they are imitating the typical movements of the puppets in bunraku theater. The secret link between the bunraku puppets and the kabuki actors was brought to my attention in a surprising way in 1999 when I was collaborating on an international theater project in Graz directed by Ulrike Ottinger. She was putting on *Das Verlobungsfest im Feenreiche* (Betrothal in the Fairy Realm) by Johann Nestroy (1801–62) with an international cast. While the Japanese actors, two of whom came from the kabuki tradition, were performing, the Austrian actress Libgart Schwarz stood onstage speaking all the parts in German. Sometimes the Japanese actors spoke as well: either sentences that were then repeated in German or lines that were clear from context without translation. One might say that a sort of dubbing was taking place here, but this synchronizing of the lines was not being used to make the foreign elements of the production easier to understand; rather, it underscored this marvelous juxtaposition of bodies and voice on the stage without eliminating their differences. Various voices and the rhythms of various languages joined together with various movements to create a sort of music.

I prepared a Japanese translation of the play and during rehearsals whispered it into the ears of the Japanese actors who didn't know any German. I tried to speak my translation in the same tempo in which the Austrian actress was speaking German. I even corrected my translation so that the Japanese sentences would have the same length and, whenever possible, the same structure as the German ones. This, then, was my personal work experience with dubbing. At some point during a rehearsal one of the kabuki actors said that he no longer needed a translation, as he was, in any case, able to orient himself only by the rhythm of the German language, not its meaning. This was one of the moments in which I learned something important about the theater.

It should probably be added that Ulrike Ottinger, who is even more famous as a filmmaker than as a theater director, doesn't have her films dubbed. In *Johanna in Mongolia,* for example, German, French, and Mongolian are all spoken without dubbing. Sometimes a subtitle appears, sometimes what is said is made comprehensible by other means. The foreign languages are never treated as an unavoidable inconvenience but rather are used as important aesthetic elements in the composition of the work as a whole.

I would like to conclude my thoughts on the subject of synchronization by describing an opera. On the evening in question, Berlin's Komische Oper was bringing back a production of Mozart's *Entführung aus dem Serail* (Abduction from the Seraglio) that had premiered in 2004. There are various things that can be said about this controversial production by Calixto Bieito, but I will limit myself to recounting what took place on this particular evening. The singer who was to play the role of Konstanze had fallen ill. And her understudy was not quite well either, so that she could be present onstage but was unable to sing. And so a third singer stood to the right of the stage, singing the role of Konstanze without moving. She had on a simple dark green dress, whereas all the other women onstage were playing up the eroticism of the work with their costumes and the way they wore them. The singer who was singing reminded me of the narrator in bunraku theater. I was surprised and delighted at the coincidence that an opera was being dubbed on the very evening when I was intending to finish writing this essay. This was a turn of events that involved not one but several chance occurrences. The production was outstanding. The soprano voice sounded so colorful, plastic, and dynamic that I even thought to myself: A singer should always lose her voice and turn into a body so that another singer whose body is not present can sing in her place. For the separation of body and voice must remain visible to make us appreciate the miracle that occurs whenever the two come together on the stage.

PART III / SOUNDING THE VISUAL

WRITING *ARTICULATION OF SOUND FORMS IN TIME* / SUSAN HOWE

On May 17, 1676, the Reverend Hope Atherton and Steven Williams, along with 160 members of a local militia, marched out into nature from Hatfield, Massachusetts, on a botched expedition against neighboring Sqakeag, Nipmunk, Pokumtuck, and Mahican tribes before the land was subdued. I found their narratives in George Sheldon's *A History of Deerfield, Massachusetts,* published in 1895 by the Pocumtuck Valley Memorial Association.

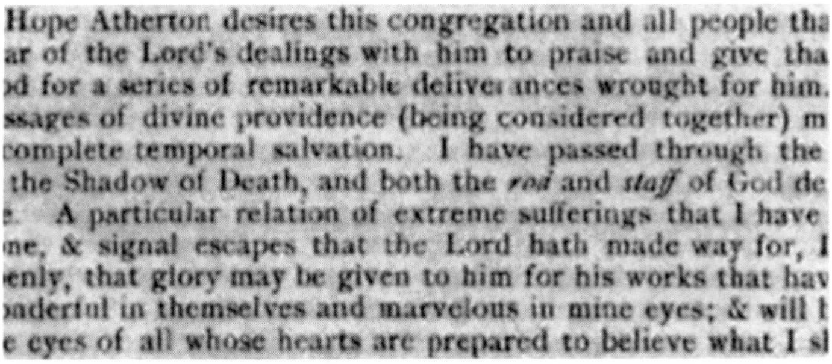

Hope Atherton desires this congregation and all people tha
ar of the Lord's dealings with him to praise and give tha
od for a series of remarkable deliverances wrought for him.
ssages of divine providence (being considered together) m
complete temporal salvation. I have passed through the
the Shadow of Death, and both the *rod* and *staff* of God de
. A particular relation of extreme sufferings that I have
ne, & signal escapes that the Lord hath made way for, I
enly, that glory may be given to him for his works that hav
nderful in themselves and marvelous in mine eyes; & will I
e eyes of all whose hearts are prepared to believe what I sl

Figure 1. "Hope Atherton desires . . . " From George Sheldon, *A History of Deerfield, Massachusetts* (1895).

A sonic grid of homely minutiae fallen away into posterity carries trace filaments. Tumbled syllables are bolts and bullets from the blue.

I vividly remember the sense of energy and change that came over me one midwinter morning when, as the book lay open in sunshine on my work table, I discovered in Hope Atherton's wandering story the authority of a prior life for my own writing voice.

During the 1970s and early '80s I was a poet with no academic affiliation. We moved to Connecticut from Manhattan because my husband's job required that we live in the general area of New Haven. We found a house in Guilford only a five-minute walk from Long Island Sound. This particular Connecticut landscape, with its granite outcroppings, abandoned quarries, marshes, salt hay meadows, and paths through woods to the center of town put me in touch with my agrarian ancestors.

David's position provided certain benefits to his family, most importantly, access to Yale's Sterling Library. It was the first time I experienced the joy of possessing a green card that allowed me to enter the stacks of a major collection of books. In the dim light of narrowly spaced overshadowing shelves I felt the spiritual and solitary freedom of an inexorable order only chance creates. Quiet articulates poetry. These Lethean tributaries of lost sentiments and found philosophies had a life-giving effect on the *process* of my writing.

scow aback din

flicker skaeg ne

barge quagg peat

~~sieve catacomb~~

stint chisel sect

In Sterling's sleeping wilderness I felt the telepathic solicitation of innumerable phantoms. The future seemed to lie in this forest of letters, theories, and forgotten actualities. I had a sense of the parallel between our always fragmentary knowledge and the continual progress toward perfect understanding that never withers away. I felt a harmony beyond the confinement of our being merely dross or tin; something chemical, almost mystical, that, thanks to architectural artifice, these gray and tan steel shelves in their neo-Gothic tower commemorate in semidarkness, according to Library of Congress classification.

tub epoch too fum alter rude recess emblem sixty key

Font-voices summon a reader into visible earshot. Struggles of conscience are taken up as if they are going to be destroyed by previous states of fancy and imagination. Former facts swell into new convictions. Never the warning of ends, only the means. More and more I wished to express the critical spirit in its restlessness.

severity whey crayon so distant grain scalp gnat carol

A number of shelved volumes that are tougher have so compressed their conjested neighbors that these thinner, often spineless pamphlets and serial publications have come to resemble smaller extremeties of smallest twigs along Guilford's West Wood Trails during a dry season. Often a damaged edition's semi-decay is the soil in which I thrive. Armed with call numbers, I find my way among scriptural exegeses, ethical homiletics, antiquarian researches, tropes and allegories, totemic animal parents, prophets, and poets. My restrospective excursions follow the principle that ghosts wrapped in appreciative obituaries by committee members, or dedications presented at vanished community field meetings, can be reanimated by appropriation. Always remembering while roving through centuries that, apart from call number coincidence, there is no inherent reason a particular scant relic and curiosity should be in position to be accidentally grasped by a quick-eyed reader in reference to clapping.

The problem is that libraries are hushed places, and this essay is for a book called *The Sound of Poetry / The Poetry of Sound.*

Hook intelligence quick dactyl.

Bats glance through a wood
bond between mad and maid

anonymous communities bond and free

Perception crumbles under character
Present past of imminent future

I believed in an American aesthetic of uncertainty that could represent beauty in syllables so scarce and rushed they would appear to expand though they lay half smothered in local history.

During the 1980s I wanted to transplant words onto paper with soil sticking to their roots — to go to meet a narrative's fate by immediate access to its concrete totality of singular interjections, crucified spellings, abbreviations, irrational apprehensions, collective identities, palavers, kicks, cordials, comforts. I wanted jerky and tedious details to oratorically bloom and bear fruit as if they had been set at liberty or ransomed by angels.

In 1862 Thoreau begins his retrospective essay called "Walking" by declaring: "I wish to speak a word for Nature, for absolute freedom and wildness." He tells us that when he walks or rather saunters out into nature from Concord, Massachusetts, "Hope and the future. . . . [are] not in lawns and cultivated fields, not in towns and cities, but in the impervious and shaking swamps." He enters each swamp as a sacred place, a *sanctum sanctorum*.

> Muffled discord from distance
> mummy thread undertow slough

I wished to speak a word for libraries as places of freedom and wildness. Often walking alone in the stacks, surrounded by raw material paper afterlife, my spirits were shaken by the great ingathering of titles and languages. This may suggest vampirism because while I like to think I write for the dead, I also take my life as a poet from their lips, their vocalisms, their breath. So many fruits, though some that looked firm in the spring and seemed to be promising, now amassed according to an impervious classification system. One approach to indeterminism might be to risk crossing into rigmarole as fully stated *ars poetica*. Sauntering toward the holy land of poetry, I compared the trial of choosing a text to the sifting of wheat, half wild, half saved.

> In Deerfield Meadows he found some horses' bones, from which h got away some small matter; found two rotted beans in yᵉ meadow where yᵉ indians had thrashed yᵗ beans, & two blew birds' eggs, wᵗ was all yᵉ provision he had till he got home. He got up to Dfᵈ tow plat before dark, Saturday, but yᵉ town was burned before & no ir habitants, so he kept along. His method of travelling was to go little ways & then lye down to rest, & was wont to fall asleep, but i yᵉ nᵗ twice he mistook himself when he awoke, & went back agai till coming to some remarkable places, he was convinced of his mis take & so turned abᵗ again, & at length he took this method, to la yᵉ muzzell of his gun towards his course, but losing so much, he wa discouraged & laid himself down once & again, expecting to dye; bu after some recruit was encouraged to set forward again, but meetin wᵗʰ these difficulties he spent yᵉ whole nᵗ in getting to muddy broo (or, as some call it, bloody brook); here he buried a man's head i yᵉ path, yᵗ was drawn out of yᵉ grave by some vermin, wᵗʰ clefts (wood, &c., and upon yᵉ road to H'f'd was (like Samson after th slaughter of yᵉ Philistines) distressd for want of drink, & many time ready to faint, yet got no water till he came to Clay Gully, but dive

Figure 2. "In Deerfield Meadows he found . . ." From George Sheldon, *A History of Deerfield, Massachusetts* (1895).

Hope Atherton is lost in the great world of nature. No steady progress of saints into grace saying Peace Peace when there is no peace. Walking is hard labor. Match any twenty-six letters to sounds of birds and squirrels in his mouth. Whatsoever God has provided to clothe him with represents Christ in cross-cultural clash conscious phonemic Cacophony. Because the providence of God is a wheel within wheels, he cannot afford to dishonor any typological item with stark vernacular. Here is print border warfare *in situ.*

> rest chondriacal lunacy
>
> velc cello viable toil
>
> quench conch uncannunc
>
> drumm amonoosuck ythian

Each page is both picture and nonsense soliloquy replete with transgressive nudges. It's a vocalized wilderness format of slippage and misshapen dream projection. Lots of blank space is essential to acoustically locate each dead center phoneme and allophone tangle somewhere between low comedy and lyric sanctity.

> P r e s t try to set after grandmother
> revived by and laid down left ly
> little distant each other and fro
> Saw digression hobbling driftwood
> forage two rotted beans &etc.
> Redy to faint slaughter story so
> Gone and signal through deep water
> Mr. Atherton's story Hope Atherton

"Prest" — gives the effect of rushing forward into a syntactic chain of associative logic under pressure of arrest. Ready for action in a mind disposed to try but being upset in advance of itself by process of surrender. In our culture Hope is a name we give women.

> Philology heaped in thin
> hearing

— only a windswept alphabet monument.

> Cries open to the words inside them
> Cries hurled through the woods

If I were to read aloud a passage from a poem of your choice, to an audience of judges in sympathy with surrounding library nature, and they were to experience its lexical inscape as an offshoot of Anglo-American modernism in typographical format, it might be possible to release our great-great-grandparents, beginning at the greatest distance from a common mouth, eternally belated, some coming home through dark ages, others nearer to early modern, multitudes of them meeting first to constitute certain main branches of etymologies, so all along there are new sources, some running directly contrary to others, and yet all meet at last, clothed in robes of glory, offering maps of languages, some with shining tones.

> *from seaweed said nor repossess rest*
> *scape esaid*

True wildness is like true gold; it will bear the trial of Dewey Decimal.

> Kneel to intellect in our work
> Chaos cast cold intellect back

JEAN COCTEAU'S RADIO POETRY

RUBÉN GALLO

"Radio and avant-garde poetry are the Siamese twins of modernity," wrote in 1926 a literary critic who perceived the many affinities between broadcasting and experimental writing.[1] Many of the early twentieth century's most radical poets were also interested in radio and in exploring the parallels between broadcasting and experimental writing: F. T. Marinetti modeled his poetic theory of "the wireless imagination" on wireless broadcasting; Apollinaire celebrated the Eiffel Tower's status as Europe's most famous antenna in his calligrammes; Velimir Khlebnikov composed "The Radio of the Future"; and the Mexican futurist Kyn Taniya published a book called *Radio: Wireless Poem in Thirteen Messages*.

This fascination with radio introduced a new twist to the complex relationship between sound and poetry that had preoccupied every writer since Homer. The new medium of wireless broadcast that gained popularity in the same decades — the 1920s and 1930s — that saw the rise of the historical avant-gardes was used to transmit both words and music. In some countries, radio became the preferred medium for the transmission of both poetry and music: the Estridentistas, for instance, inaugurated radio broadcast in Mexico City by reading a poem about the radiophonic experience, a recitation that was immediately followed by a concert.[2]

The possibilities of the new radiophonic medium inspired a new form of sound poetry: one that incorporated elements from the soundscape created by the new technology. Along with the possibility of broadcasting words and music across countries and continents, the wireless introduced a series of new sounds: the buzzing and crackling of receivers, the high-pitched screeches of interference, as well as the short-and-long beeps of Morse code that dominated the first generation of "wireless telegraphs," as the earliest of radios were known.

Conservative critics dismissed these new sounds of modernity as noise — the German word for radio interference is Störung, a "disturbance" of listening — but many avant-garde poets saw in them the source for a new music. In *Parade* Erik Satie used typewriters to make "music" with the noises of the modern world, and the infamous *Ballet mécanique* went as far as to incorporate sirens, whistles, and even airplane propellers into the realm of melody. Radio noises were one more element that avant-garde figures from Marinetti to John Cage heard as the new music of the modern era. As Christian Bök and Craig Dworkin stress in this volume, the meaning of "music" has to be expanded to encompass the realities of the twentieth and twenty-first centuries: a noisy reality that includes trains, cars, motors, typewriters as well as radio. In this essay, I will explore one of the most original attempts to compose a sound poetry inspired by radio–, a radio-poetic experiment that was neither a poem nor a piece of music but a film: Jean Cocteau's *Orpheus*.

Like his contemporaries, Jean Cocteau was fascinated by radio, and he created what is perhaps the most elaborate, sustained, and mysterious homage to the medium: the 1950 film *Orphée* (Orpheus), starring Jean Marais and Maria Casarès. But unlike the experimental writings of Apollinaire or Marinetti, Cocteau's film has never been studied as a radiophonic work. In the pages that follow, I propose reading *Orpheus* as a work inspired by early twentieth-century debates on the artistic possibilities of wireless broadcast and as one of the most radical experiments in creating a new kind of sound poetry.

Cocteau actually produced two *Orphées:* a play, written in 1926, and a film, released in 1950, which departs from the original theatrical script in a number of ways. Both works stage the classical myth in modern France, presenting Orpheus as a poet who overcomes his writer's block by transcribing cryptic messages sent from the realm of the dead, a netherworld called "the zone" in Cocteau's film. After his wife Eurydice dies, he manages to bring her back from the realm of the dead, but the condition for her return to the world of the living — that Orpheus never look at her — proves too much for the poet, who sneaks a peek at her and thereby sends her back to the underworld. Unlike the myth, Cocteau's tale — in both its stage and screen version — has a happy ending: Orpheus manages to resurrect Eurydice a second time, and the story closes with a scene of domestic bliss, with both spouses sitting down for dinner in a bourgeois house.

When Cocteau reworked the original script for the screen in the late 1940s, he introduced new roles, added new subplots, and altered some scenes. The film, for instance, introduces a new character named Cégeste, an extremely popular poet whose avant-garde texts displace Orpheus's more conventional composition in the Paris literary scene. The film actually opens with a very funny scene shot in the "Café des Poètes," a locale Cocteau imagined as a parody of the Café de Flore on the Boulevard Saint Germain, where Jean-Paul Sartre and Simone de Beauvoir held court in the postwar years. In the opening scene of *Orpheus,* a table of young intellectuals open a book called "Nudisme" to find a collection of blank pages, a "nude" text. The hip habitués of the café worship Cégeste's conceptual literary experiments and violently dismiss Orpheus as an outdated writer.

But the most significant change in the film has to do with the otherworldly messages that so captivate Orpheus: in the play these come from a white horse who taps letters with his leg—one tap represents an *A,* two a *B*—as if he were a living Ouija board, while in the film they emerge from a wireless radio receiver. Curiously, Orpheus can tune into these broadcasts only from one rather eccentric post: the car radio inside a black Rolls Royce driven by Death. To Eurydice's dismay, her husband begins to spend every waking moment inside the car, listening obsessively to the radio and transcribing its cryptic messages. "Je ne trouve ce poste nulle part ailleurs" (I can't find this station anywhere else), Orpheus tells Eurydice after she begs him to emerge from the car, to which she retorts, with obvious annoyance: "Alors, si je veux profiter de toi il faudra vivre dans une voiture ?!" (So will I be forced to live in a car if I want to enjoy your company?).[3]

The transmissions are cryptic and seemingly nonsensical: they often begin with a long series of telegraphic beeps and blips, continue with a series of numbers, and repeat a sequence of obscure phrases. Among the broadcasts transcribed by Orpheus are the following:

> Le silence va plus vite à reculons. Trois fois... Un seul verre d'eau éclaire le monde ... Deux fois... Attention, écoute. Un seul verre d'eau éclaire le monde... Deux fois... Un seul verre d'eau éclaire le monde. Deux fois
> [Silence goes faster backward. Three times. A single glass of water illuminates the world. Twice. Attention, listen. A single glass of water illuminates the world. Twice. A single glass of water illuminates the world.]

And also:

L'oiseau chante avec ses doigts. Deux fois. L'oiseau chante avec ses doigts. Deux fois. Je répète. L'oiseau chante avec ses doigts

[The bird sings with its fingers. Twice. The bird sings with its fingers. Twice. I repeat. The bird sings with its fingers.]

In other instances, the transmissions sound more like a mathematical table: "39 . . . 40 . . . Deux fois [Twice] . . . 38 . . . 39 . . . 40 . . . Deux fois."

At first sight these broadcasts seem as cryptic as much of the avant-garde literature written at the time — Joyce's *Finnegans Wake*, Pound's *Cantos*, Artaud's poems, and Gertrude Stein's compositions. But like all avant-garde texts, they can be read, interpreted, and analyzed — like dreams in psychoanalysis. When read correctly, these messages represent a new kind of radiophonic avant-garde poetry, one that plays with the tension between sound and meaning. But how are we to interpret these cryptic messages?

Cocteau himself gave readers some hints about the nature of the radio broadcasts. In *Orphée film,* he explained that the telegraphic beeping, the numerical sequences, and the seemingly nonsensical phrases were meant to evoke the coded broadcasts of Radio Londres, a station set up by the French resistance in England, under the auspices of the BBC, during World War II.[4] In another text, Cocteau declared that the broadcasts were meant to introduce an element of everyday life, to make the classical myth more familiar to twentieth-century viewers: "Radios in cars, coded messages, shortwave signals and power cuts are all familiar to everybody and allow me [the director] to keep my feet on the ground."[5]

The broadcasts are deeply ambivalent: on the one hand, they are meant to make familiar a story that might seem remote to many modern viewers. On the other, the radio transmissions bring messages from the netherworld, putting Orpheus — and the film's viewers — in touch with a realm that is unfamiliar, uncanny, and — like Freud's concept of the *Unheimlich* — far removed from ordinary, everyday life. Orpheus tunes into phantasmatic broadcasts, eerie messages that, as we soon discover, are broadcast by the dead poet Cégeste from the underworld — a radio station of the living dead. Paradoxically, radio in *Orpheus* is both dead and alive, familiar and unfamiliar, *heimlich* and *unheimlich,* earthly and otherworldly, technological and spectral.

But what do the messages received from "the zone" mean, and why does Orpheus become obsessed with them to the point of neglecting his wife and his friends? Phrases like "Un seul verre d'eau éclaire le monde" or "L'oiseau chante avec ses doigts" are puzzling constructions that seem to defy logic: a glass of water does not emit light, and even if it did, how could such a small, ordinary object illuminate the entire world? Birds sing, but they don't have fingers, and even if they did these appendages would be of little use for their chirping.

The last phrase is especially mysterious: it is a striking image, and one that despite its apparent senselessness would seem to contain a secret meaning, a hidden message. Birds sing with their fingers: could this be a creative metonymical displacement? Fingers can be used to play an instrument — a violin, a flute — and thus, metaphorically, they can be said to sing. And though birds don't play instruments, the verse assimilates their singing to the music of flutes, clarinets, oboes, and other finger instruments.

But illuminating vessels and chirping fingers can also be read otherwise: as Surrealist images, as verses that could have been written by André Breton, Louis Aragon, or any of the other authors that had been concocting similar phrases for several decades before *Orpheus*. In the first "Manifesto of Surrealism" Breton defined the Surrealist image as a construction designed to generate a "poetic spark" by juxtaposing two radically disjointed elements, as in Lautréamont's "chance encounter of an umbrella and a sewing machine on a dissecting table." As Breton explains, "from the fortuitous juxtaposition of the two terms, a particular light [springs], the light of the image, to which we are infinitely sensitive. The value of the image depends upon the beauty of the spark obtained; it is, consequently, a function of the difference of potential between the two conductors."[6]

Could Cocteau have been thinking of Surrealist images when he composed the messages broadcast from the zone? The phrases jotted by Orpheus certainly create poetic sparks by amalgamating elements as dissimilar as glasses of water and light, birds and singing fingers. "The glass of water that illuminates the world" could be Cocteau's jocular *clin d'œil* to Breton and his theory of poetic sparks.

Some of Cocteau's critics have read the radiotelegraphic messages as parodies of Surrealist poetry. Walter A. Strauss argues that the broadcasts from the zone are a variant of automatic writing. Orpheus tunes his radio for the same purpose that Breton and Philippe Soupault attended séances: to receive texts emitted from an otherworldly source.[7] In his "Manifesto of Surrealism" Breton wrote that the Surrealist poet must transform himself into a "modest recording instrument" of poetic images generated by someone else, and this is precisely what Orpheus does in Cocteau's film.[8] In contrast to the

Surrealists, who were fond of typing messages received from beyond, rendering their writing not only automatic but also mechanical (the French word for typewriter is *machine à écrire* or "writing machine"), Orpheus opts for a wireless automatism: one that brings him ready-made verses through the technological mediation of wireless broadcasting.

But does Orpheus's obsession with radio messages represent a parody of Surrealist poetics, as Walter Strauss suggests? Though Cocteau's rapport with Breton and the Surrealists was certainly a complicated one, *Orpheus* casts the poetic images received from "the zone" in a positive light: these verses have the virtue of bringing Orpheus out of his writer's block and rekindling his passion for literature. These automatic-radiophonic texts are his salvation: without them he would have renounced poetry.

Perhaps *Orpheus*'s radiophonic messages are inspired by Surrealist poetics, but not necessarily by Breton's. In *Orphée film,* Cocteau reveals the source of one of the zone's most striking broadcasts. "The bird sings with its finger," he explains, was a verse Apollinaire had once written him in a letter. Could it be that the radio transmissions are Cocteau's coded homage to Apollinaire, the poet who coined the term "surrealist" long before Breton's manifesto?

The image of the dactyloid bird had an important place in the French avant-garde: *Birds sing with their fingers,* in the plural, was the title of a watercolor Apollinaire sketched and gave to Picasso around 1906 (fig. 1). The work shows a colorful harlequin dancing around empty space, his oversize hands framing a phrase written in yellow and blue block letters: "Les oiseaux chantent avec les doigts." According to Peter Read, the work was a homage to Picasso, who had painted a number of harlequins, including the self-portraits in *Au Lapin agile* and *Famille de saltimbanques.* And in *Le Poète assassiné,* Apollinaire transformed the artist into "l'oiseau du Bénin," the bird from Benin. Picasso was thus both harlequin and bird — but why does he "sing with its fingers"? Read suggests that the cryptic title is actually a poetic evocation of cubist painting: "The phrase 'Birds sing with their fingers,'" he explains, "evokes the song emanating from the fingers of the Harlequin-painter."[9] Picasso painted with his hands, but in Apollinaire's synesthetic transposition his fingers produce not visual images but musical tunes.

Willard Bohn, another critic who has studied the drawing, argues that the harlequin is actually juggling with words: the phrase "Les oiseaux chantent avec leurs doigts" appears suspended in midair between the figure's hands, its colorful block letters serving the function of textual juggling pins. And juggling with words was an apt metaphor for the avant-garde poetics that led

Figure 1. Guillaume Apollinaire, *Les oiseaux chantent avec les doigts* (Birds Sing with Their Fingers) (1906). Musée Picasso, Paris. Photograph by Jean-Gilles Berizzi. Photograph: © Réunion des Musées Nationaux / Art Resource, New York.

authors like Apollinaire to make music with their pens and thus "sing with their fingers." "This must be a portrait of the poet," Bohn writes. "Is it not the poet's task to establish a magical equilibrium among words?"[10]

These are perceptive readings of Apollinaire's image of the singing bird, but they leave a crucial question unanswered: why does this phrase play such an important role in *Orpheus?* What could be the link between the 1906 watercolor and the eerie radio broadcasts in Cocteau's film?

To answer this question, we need to take a brief detour and consider the role of radio in twentieth-century literary and artistic debates. Broadcasting flourished in the years separating *Orpheus* the play and *Orpheus* the film: between 1926 and 1950 radio went from being the hobby of a handful of eccentric amateurs to one of the most important technologies of the modern world. Radio became a crucial — and ubiquitous — medium for transmitting news and other important information. In the prelude to World War II German broadcasting was seized by the Nazis, and even after the peace treaties were signed the medium retained the power to terrify the masses, as Orson Welles proved in *The War of the Worlds.*

The rise of radio attracted the attention of intellectuals around the world, who debated the virtues and shortcomings of the new medium. Some, like Rudolf Arnheim, had a utopian conception of radio as a medium that would bring the world together, encouraging listeners to learn foreign languages, understand their neighbors, and tolerate cultural differences. In his 1936 essay *Radio,* the first theoretical analysis of its kind, Arnheim celebrates broadcasting as a symbol of freedom. "Wireless," he writes, "passes all customs officers, needs no cable, penetrates all walls and even in house raids it is very difficult to catch."[11] Arnheim penned these words in the 1930s, at a time when house raids had become an everyday phenomenon for German leftists. He considered wireless broadcasting, free and uninhibited, as the antithesis of Nazi intolerance.

Other thinkers were less enthusiastic about radio's impact on the world. Georges Duhamel, one of the most conservative critics of his time — and a figure whose antitechnological views inspired Walter Benjamin to write "The Work of Art in the Age of Mechanical Reproduction" — believed radio would eventually kill European high culture, replacing serious literature with advertising jingles and philosophical reflection with sound bites. In a 1932 book called *Defense of Letters* — letters were being defended against the pernicious influence of radio, film, and other modern technologies — Duhamel lamented that broadcasting was effectively lobotomizing its listeners and pointed the finger at the loud sounds broadcast by the medium. Speaking of "the real radio lovers," he argued:

> those simple people who really need education, are beginning to prefer noise to books . . . they absorb everything pell-mell: Wagner, jazz, politics, advertising, the time signal, music hall, and the howling of secondary waves. . . . We are in

utter confusion . . . today the man in the street is fed, morally as well as physically, on a mass of debris which has no resemblance to a nourishing diet. There is no method in this madness, which is the very negation of culture.[12]

Unlike Duhamel, Cocteau found "the howling of secondary waves" — a new, technological sound — interesting enough to give it an important place in his film. The radio messages in *Orpheus* are so intriguing, in part, because we are not sure how to interpret them: do these belong to the serious realm of political discussion? To the frivolous world of advertising? In any case, they are certainly radio sounds that Orpheus finds fascinating.

Arnheim saw radio as a symbol of liberty while Duhamel attacked it as a threat to high culture. Between these two extremes, other thinkers had more nuanced positions: Bertolt Brecht celebrated the potential inherent in radio broadcasting but disliked the fact that listeners were unable to respond to the broadcaster: he suggested the ideal would be a two-way radio, a system that allowed listeners to play an active role in broadcasting.[13] Kurt Tucholsky worried that freedom of expression was virtually nonexistent in radio, since every broadcast had to be palatable to "a host of uncontrollable, irresponsible and nearly superstitious bureaucrats and independent reactionaries, average citizens, and obedient little shopkeepers."[14]

Cocteau had a more nuanced position: he was neither as optimistic as Arnheim, nor as pessimistic as Duhamel. In his most elaborate meditation on the subject — a passage included in *The Art of Cinema* — he writes an unusually levelheaded appreciation of broadcasting:

> Radio is pernicious if it flows into every home like a stream of lukewarm water. It is very important if it brings culture to people who had no conception of culture. All this seems patently obvious to me, but some people say radio is essential, and others that it is harmful. Radio is neither essential nor harmful. It is an invention of genius and consequently a dangerous one.[15]

Cocteau was interested in radio as a medium of expression, and he mused on the possibility of writing a radio play. And though he never undertook this adventure, he did have strong ideas of what would make a successful radio play. Like Arnheim, he criticized those authors who simply read a theatrical piece on the air, and he argued that radio actors and announcers had to find a truly innovative way of communicating with listeners: "It would be difficult," Cocteau wrote in the same passage in *The Art of Cinema,* to create a living radio as long as it requires written scripts. Reading gives the radio a tedious banality, even with an expert reader. It is above all a medium of improvisation. On the other hand, I know that it is impossible to base a programme on chance. These are the reasons why I have never seriously thought about radio.[16]

Like Orson Welles, Cocteau believed the most interesting use of the medium would be to jolt listeners out of complacency:

> radio is so widespread and extensive that it tends to obey: to obey its listeners, when it would be better if the listeners were to obey it. In other words, if one could reach a high level of creation through sound apparatus, this would be an excellent achievement.[17]

Cocteau was in fact arguing for what other critics called "radiogenic experiments" — works, like *The War of the Worlds,* conceived specifically to exploit the possibilities offered by the broadcasting medium:

> Radio is terrifyingly intimate. The whole problem is that it has to enter a room and impose itself in such a way that those who listen to it set aside whatever was on their minds, and let themselves be captivated by whatever is on ours. An off button is easy to turn. On the other hand, if the radio is just a background accompaniment to people's own private concerns, it loses all interest and becomes just another tap in the house.[18]

Cocteau thought of broadcasting as a struggle between broadcasters and listeners: programs and radio plays had to be designed to give announcers and actors the upper hand. Innovation and surprise would whet the listeners' interest and keep them from pressing the off button.

Despite having very specific ideas about the medium, Cocteau never wrote a radio play, though he did participate in several radio programs, including a famous broadcast in which he described in detail his visit to an ailing Marcel Proust.[19] But though Cocteau never became a radio author, he did create a work featuring his ideal use of wireless broadcasting and radio sounds: *Orpheus,* the film.

Radio transmissions in *Orpheus* correspond to the ideal use of the medium Cocteau theorized in *The Art of Cinema.* Far from being "another tap in the house," radio becomes the center of Orpheus's life, leading the poet to abandon all other interests and activities so he can devote every single minute of his life to receiving messages from the zone. "La moindre de ces phrases," he tells Eurydice, "est plus étonnante que mes poèmes. Je donnerais ma vie entière pour une seule de ces petites phrases!" (The simplest of these phrases is more astonishing than any of my poems. I would give my entire life for a single one of these little phrases). As Cocteau had fantasized, in his film radio enters a room and "impose[s] itself in such a way that those who listen to it set aside whatever was on their minds, and let themselves be captivated."

Interestingly, Cocteau opted for making a film about the ideal broadcast instead of writing a piece to be transmitted over the airwaves. Perhaps he feared that even the most intensely engaging radio play could fall on deaf ears and fall victim to the bored listener's resort to the off button. Nothing of this sort ever happens in his film, where every word sent through the airwaves mesmerizes Orpheus, an ideal radio listener. Creative spirits like Orpheus and Cégeste abandon themselves to the radio, while ordinary mortals like Eurydice fail to appreciate its magic ("Tu ne peux pas passer ta vie dans une voiture qui parle . . . Ce n'est pas sérieux!" [You can't spend your entire life inside a talking car . . . it is not serious], she scolds a wired Orpheus). Perhaps Cocteau believed that only an otherworldly message — a poetic voice from the realm of the spirits received by a literary soul — would fulfill his ambition for an eternally titillating radio broadcast.

But let's return to our investigation of the singing bird. Does Cocteau's theory of radio shed light on the mystery of the "bird [that] sings with its fingers"? The relation between Cocteau's views on radio and his use of Apollinaire's text becomes clear when we consider the origin of the radio broadcasts in *Orpheus*. As viewers soon discover, the messages that so captivate Orpheus come from "the zone," where the dead poet Cégeste is in charge of broadcasting. One of the film's most mesmerizing scenes, shot inside Death's villa, shows us a blond Cégeste seated in front of an early radio transmitter — equipped with both a telegraph and a microphone — transmitting his verses into the air. Ironically, Orpheus never finds out that Cégeste, his archrival, is the author of the radio message.

Cégeste transmits using both a telegraph and a microphone, and thus many of his messages begin with the series of short and long beeps so characteristic of early telegraphic transmissions. In the nineteenth century the first transmitters could broadcast only Morse code, and radio was first known as a "wireless telegraph," or *télégraphe sans fil* in French. In the early years of the twentieth century, new technologies were developed to transmit voice — and not merely Morse code — over the airwaves, and this new invention became the "wireless telephone" (or *téléphone sans fil* in French). Until the 1950s, the

French used the acronym TSF — which could refer to either wireless telegraphs or telephones — as shorthand for radio.

Cégeste's radio is both a wireless telephone and a wireless telegraph, a TSF that is both a *télégraphe sans fil* and a *téléphone sans fil*. His apparatus brings together nineteenth- and twentieth-century radio technologies, allowing him to send both Morse code and voice messages on the airwaves. In one scene, we see a close-up of Cégeste and his radio: a portrait of the artist as a young broadcaster. Donning a pair of headphones and facing a bulky microphone, the poet taps a telegraphic key resting on the desk, sending short and long beeps, followed by words, into the air. As he taps the keypad, the lights in the room flicker — a synesthetic moment during which intermittent sounds are represented as flickering lights.

This scene also explains Cocteau's use of Apollinaire's verse "The birds sing with their fingers." As he taps the keypad, Cégeste is in fact singing with his fingers, sending radiotelegraphic songs into the airwaves. And he becomes a technological bird of sorts, since he is at home on the air, and his messages, transformed into Hertzian waves, crisscross the skies to reach Orpheus. Cégeste is thus the bird who sings with its fingers, a poet tapping telegraphic keypads to send radio music to an ideal listener.

It is significant that Cocteau appropriated a verse by Apollinaire as the perfect metaphor of radio broadcasting. Apollinaire was one of the first avant-garde figures to write enthusiastically about the TSF (Françoise Haffner calls him "le premier poète des ondes télégraphiques" [the first poet of the telegraphic waves]),[20] and "Lettre-Océan," one of his most famous calligrammes, is a literary homage to the effects of radio broadcasting on modern poetry.[21] Apollinaire was another bird who sang with its fingers: though he never took part in radio broadcasts, he handwrote calligrammes featuring graphic representations of airwaves and telegraphic transmissions.

Now that we have cracked the enigma of "the bird that sings with its fingers," I'd like to consider one final question relating to Orpheus's radio transmissions. What is the moral of the story? How are we to interpret Orpheus's obsession with the radio, with the messages broadcast from the zone, and with Cégeste's poetry? According to Peter Read, Cocteau wanted to represent "the danger faced by every poet whenever, having lost confidence in his own creativity, he renounces the authentic voice of a personal poetry for the contaminating influence of an external source."[22] Read thus takes *Orpheus* as a moral tale warning poets to remain true to their inner voice lest, like Orpheus, they end up becoming plagiarists *malgré eux*.

Read's interpretation is compelling, but I would beg to differ. Cocteau, the eternal *enfant terrible,* was not fond of moral tales, and he did not care much about originality. In fact he once declared: "I detest originality. I avoid it as much as possible. One has to take an original idea with the greatest of care in order to avoid looking as if one is wearing a new suit."[23]

Taking into account Cocteau's dislike of originality, *Orpheus* can be interpreted as a playful attack against the myth of the original creative genius. In the beginning of the film Orpheus appears as a poet past his prime, tormented by both a creative block and a midlife crisis. Though he has enjoyed glory and fame for most of his life, a new generation of avant-garde poets — the patrons of the Café des Poètes — have now stolen the spotlight. Orpheus cannot compete with the younger poets' conceptual experiments, symbolized by *Nudisme* (a sexy parody of blank verse) and the technologically inflected automatic writing favored by Cégeste.

In the end, Orpheus finds a way out of his creative impasse by copying the radio messages and presenting them as his own poetry. Though he ignores the origin of these broadcasts, he imagines that they come from far away, from another realm, from the skies or from the underworld. In his mind, he is following the example of nineteenth-century romantic poets — and twentieth-century ones like W. B. Yeats and James Merrill — who turned to the world of the spirits as a source of poetic inspiration.

But what Orpheus does not know is that the radio messages are broadcast by Cégeste, his avant-garde rival, and thus his new poetry has less to do with romantic spiritualism than with avant-garde appropriation. Like Apollinaire, like Marcel Duchamp, like Marinetti, Orpheus ends up copying other people's writing and incorporating it into his poetry. But unlike these avant-garde figures, Orpheus is not aware of what he is doing: he is an avant-garde poet *malgré lui.*

Cocteau makes Orpheus into a practitioner of what Craig Dworkin and Kenneth Goldsmith have called "uncreative writing," a form of appropriation that subverts the romantic ideal of the creative genius, of an inspired poet composing unique and original creations.[24] Orpheus, who is first introduced as a creative writer in crisis, evolves into an uncreative writer by the end of the film: he becomes a mere "recording instrument" — to use Breton's term — of other writers' words. And only this avant-garde gesture of appropriation, mediated by radio, saves him from the creative anxiety that torments him at the beginning of the film.

There is a crucial difference between Cégeste's radio messages and Orpheus's transcriptions: Orpheus jots down the words he hears on the radio, but he does not transcribe the radio noises — short and long beeps, the howlings of interference, and other technological cracklings — framing Cégeste's words. Perhaps this is why Orpheus seems frustrated and unhappy even as he is copying the enigmatic messages: he has understood that Cégeste is a sound poet, an avant-garde and technologically literate sound poet who has exploited the complete acoustic potential of the new radiophonic medium. His poetry mixes words and music, albeit the loud music of twentieth-century modernity. Orphée, on the other hand, has lost his lyre: his poetry has words but no music. Even as he copies Cégeste's verses, he remains a mute poet, one who cannot hear the vibrant sounds of the radiophonic era.

If we wanted to read *Orpheus* as a fable, the moral of the story would be the following: in the century of ready-mades and avant-gardes, originality has become a quaint myth. A poet can be original only by becoming unoriginal and embracing the practice of uncreative writing. Apollinaire inserted advertising copy into his calligrammes; Marinetti transcribed war dispatches in *Zang Tumb Tumb;* and Orpheus copies messages from the radio, the modern medium of pastiche and heterogeneity.

Orpheus's appropriation of Cégeste's words mirrors Cocteau's own use of Apollinaire's "Les oiseaux chantent avec les doigts." But unlike Orpheus, who acted unawares, Cocteau avowed his unoriginal use of his fellow poet's verses. Peter Read reads this gesture as an expression of an ambivalent attitude toward Apollinaire, but I believe Cocteau is actually paying homage to his fellow avant-gardist.[25] By appropriating Apollinaire's verse, Cocteau paid homage to his friend, whose calligrammes took textual appropriation to poetic heights.

It is significant that such an appropriation is mediated through radio. Radio, as Marinetti, Apollinaire, and Cocteau concluded, was the ideal medium for pastiche, the twentieth-century harbinger of that practice the twenty-first century avant-garde would call uncreative writing. And as *Orpheus* shows, uncreative writing can become addictive: it can lead even old fogies to drop everything and tune in to someone else's sound poetry.

SOUND AS SUBJECT: AUGUSTO DE CAMPOS'S *POETAMENOS* / ANTONIO SERGIO BESSA

Meine Zunge ist ungelenk:
ich kann denken,
aber nicht reden.
(My tongue is not supple:
I can think,
but not speak.)

ARNOLD SCHOENBERG, *Moses und Aron*

O olhouvido ouvê
(The eyear hearsees)

DÉCIO PIGNATARI

With a poetic program that strongly emphasized the "visuality of language," it would seem that the Noigandres poets embraced design to the detriment of sound. Their effort to render language iconic, one might think, would push concrete poetry to the brink of aphasia. Indeed, the poems from the so-called heroic phase of concretism display a heightened sense of design that seems to overwhelm other aspects of the text. Some of those poems appear on the page like highly modernistic architecture, while others strike the reader rather like graphic riddles that need to be decoded in order to be read: an operation for the eye only, with the ear playing a very small role in the reading process. But it would be a mistake to affirm that sound was altogether out of the Noigandres picture. I suggest that in the work of these poets, sound was submitted to as rigorous a program as the written text.

Nevertheless, this rigor, as I hope to make clear in this essay, did not imply the loss of a sense of humor or the negation of pleasure.

In several texts written in the early 1950s by the Noigandres poets, collectively and individually, one finds repeated references to sound, particularly the emerging new music of composers like Pierre Boulez, Guido Alberto Fano, and Karlheinz Stockhausen. These references are telegraphed throughout the cryptic text of "Pilot Plan for Concrete Poetry," the concretist period's culminating manifesto, but other texts explored some of the same themes to a greater extent, and these lay out Noigandres's understanding of the role sound ought to play in poetry. Among these early writings, Décio Pignatari's seem mostly concerned with form and design. But even in the midst of an argument about structure or organizing principles, we find references such as this:

> Mário de Andrade, in "Prefácio interessantíssimo" [Most Interesting Preface], after commenting on the common melodic verse, approaches what he calls the harmonic verse, formed by words without any immediate connection among themselves: "These words, by the very fact of not forming a coherent sequence, superpose over themselves and form, to our senses, not melodies, but harmonies. ... Harmony, combination of simultaneous sounds."[1]

Taking off from Andrade's proposition of a "harmonic verse," Pignatari traces a formidable microcompendium of the last century's great synthesizers, including Lewis Carroll, Stéphane Mallarmé, Ezra Pound, James Joyce, and the filmmaker Sergei Eisenstein. His idea of poetic "organization" is a composite that might include portmanteau words (Carroll and Joyce) arranged according to ideogrammatic principles (Pound, Ernest Fenollosa) spliced together, as in a film (Eisenstein). Eisenstein via Pignatari: "(sonorous!) representations objectively expressed gathering together to create a unified image, other than the perception of its isolated elements."[2]

Haroldo de Campos seems to agree with Pignatari's equation of visual organization and musical harmony. Compare Pignatari's argument with the following quote from "Olho por olho a olho nu" (Eye for an Eye in Daylight), a text by de Campos from 1956:

> THE CONCRETE POEM aspires to be: composition of basic elements of language, optical-acoustically organized in the graphic space by factors of proximity and similitude, like a kind of ideogram for a given emotion, aiming at the direct presentation — in the present — of the object.[3]

One senses in these writings a certain hesitancy with regard to addressing sound (or music, or melody) head on. Note how "acoustics" is appended to "optical," and how the word "composition" remains ambiguously undefined: it might equally refer to a musical composition or a piece of writing.[4] But three decades later, in a 1983 interview with Rodrigo Naves, de Campos declared forthrightly that his rapport with the literary tradition was *musical* rather than *museological:*

> Note that both adjectives derive from the same word, *muse* (from the Greek *Mousa*), and that the Muses are the daughters of memory (Mnemosine). I prefer the derivation that ended up in music because I like to read tradition as a transtemporal music sheet, making, at each moment, synchronic-diachronic "harmonies," translating culture's past into a creative present.[5]

Although not entirely without a nod to museum practices, the "translation of culture's past into a creative present" was eventually effected quite literally by both Haroldo and his brother Augusto de Campos in their translation work, a topic I will address later. But also note how de Campos's understanding of the role music plays in his work, as expressed in the two excerpts quoted above, seems to overlap with Ferdinand de Saussure's insight into the structure of the linguistic sign. In his *Course in General Linguistics,* Saussure explains the linguistic sign thus:

> The linguistic sign unites not a thing and a name, but a concept and a sound-image. The latter is not the material sound, a purely physical thing, but the psychological imprint of the sound, the impression that it makes on our senses. The sound-image is sensory, and if I happen to call it "material," it is only in that sense, and by way of opposing it to the other term of the association, the concept, which is generally more abstract.[6]

Saussure's explanation of the "sound-image" in terms of a "psychological imprint" on our senses provides a linguistic basis for Haroldo de Campos's poetic goal of an "ideogram for a given emotion." Although Saussure's name is conspicuously absent from the early manifestos issued by the Noigandres poets, it is worth mentioning that his insight with regard to how language operates is not unlike Mallarmé's "divisions prismatiques de l'idée," a theme often echoed throughout numerous Noigandres texts — language as an operation that makes ideas visible (and/or heard).

Elaborating on Pound's concepts of *melopoeia* and *logopoeia* in yet another interview from around the same period, Haroldo de Campos reveals that his collection of poems *Signantia quase coelum* (Paradisiacal Signifiers) was "conceived in the form of music, as a tripartite composition," and explains the poem's minimalist structure as a visual equivalent of the use of rests in music.[7] And at the end of the interview, de Campos quotes from Severo Sarduy, who wrote that in the texts that compose *Galáxias,* one finds

> la exaltación y el despliegue de una región de la dicción, de un espacio del habla vasto y barroco como el mapa de su país: soplo y articulación, aliento y pronunciación: nacimiento del discurso.
>
> [the exalting and unfolding of a region of diction, of a space of speech as vast and baroque as the map of his country: a puff of air and articulation, breath and pronunciation: the birth of discourse.]

With extraordinary precision, Sarduy sums up the entire concretist approach to sound: the vast legacy of the baroque filtered through breathing, articulation, and pronunciation. The concretist project in Brazil should then be seen as an attempt not only to renew that tradition but also to convey it in an entirely new "voice."

Among the Noigandres poets, Augusto de Campos seems to be the one most overtly interested in sound experimentation. He is the author of two important books on music, *O Balanço da bossa – e outras bossas* (Bossa Nova in Balance — and Other Bossas) and *Música de invenção* (Invention Music), and ever since the 1950s, his poetry has persistently pursued a kind of writing fused with music. His microsequence of sparsely diagrammed poems *Poetamenos* (Minuspoet, 1953) helped launch concretism in Brazil and was admittedly inspired by Anton Webern's concept of *Klangfarbenmelodie* (tone-color-melody). Augusto de Campos's musical ideas, as one might expect, were from the start highly unorthodox — a mix of Viennese dodecaphonic theory and Brazilian bossa nova swing. He prefaced *Poetamenos* with a short text that is still striking in its visionary audacity:

> or aspiring in the hope of a
> KLANGFARBENMELODIE
> with words
> as in Webern:
> a continuous melody dislocating from one instrument to another, constantly changing its color:

instruments: phrase/word/syllable/letter(s), whose timbres
are defined by a graphic-phonetic, or "ideogramic," theme . . .
    reverberation: oral reading — real voices functioning as
timbre (approximately) for the poem, like the instruments in Webern's
Klangfarbenmelodie.[8]

It is worth dwelling for a moment on Webern's concept of *Klangfarbenmelo-die,* because of its deep impact on concrete poetry — a poetics often accused of being too cerebral and devoid of emotion and, on many occasions, of impoverishing language. To the Canadian pianist Glenn Gould, Webern's music was deeply steeped in emotion, and *Klangfarbenmelodie* was the method that heightened its expression:

> The string quartet pieces of Opus 5 are one of [Webern's] first essays in atonal writing. Though nothing could display a less extrovert emotionalism, there is a strikingly sensual quality manifest not only in the treatment of the strings themselves, but also in the manner by which Webern frequently isolates an individual tone or short interval-group, and, by alternating dynamic levels and instrumental timbres, succeeds in immobilizing a particular pitch level around which the oblique shapes of his half-counterpoints seek to fulfill their evolutionary destinies. It seems to me that the expressionistic qualities of this music such as the above mentioned isolated tone procedure — (Klangfarbenmelodie) carries to its zenith the very essence of the romantic ideal of emotional intensity in art.[9]

Like Pound, Webern aimed to "make new" an entire musical tradition, from Bach all the way through the romantics, and the two men would certainly find much to agree upon as far as the issue of *melopoeia* is concerned. In the *Ricercare for Six Voices,* for instance, whereas Bach originally indicated lines for no instrument in particular, Webern disperses the notes among the instruments, transforming the sound of the melody and accentuating its melancholic quality. The rhetorical qualities of baroque music and its doctrine of affects (*Affektenlehre*) are hence recovered by Webern through his method of *Klangfarbenmelodie.*

Freeing music from "themes" and/or "motifs" — his ability to convey "sound clarity" through the pure structuring of musical elements — is generally perceived as Webern's major contribution. According to Boulez, in Webern "the architecture of the work derives directly from the ordering of the series." Composition becomes a system of proportions, of relationships between intervals. This concept can be illustrated by the "Sator Arepo" palindrome found in the ruins of Pompeii, which became a source of great interest to Webern:[10]

SATOR
AREPO
TENET
OPERA
ROTAS

To Webern, this diagram represented the ideal porous structure, as it can be read horizontally or vertically from top left to bottom right and from bottom right to top left. In addition, it uses a minimum of elements (eight letters, five words) to create a greater number of combinations ("Non multa sed multum"). This kind of structure was referred to by Webern as a "Spiegelbild" (mirror-form), a device that enabled him to structure a musical composition around as few as three notes.[11] The "monadic architect of the mirror-form" is what Herbert Eimert, founder of the WDR Studio in Cologne, called Webern.

The idea of mirror-forms had a great, long-lasting impact on Augusto de Campos's development of a concrete poetics. In *Poetamenos,* despite the fact that it's not addressed in the preamble, mirror-form technique is used to different effects, and throughout his career de Campos has refined Webern's practice, quite literally transposing it into poetic terms. In "Vaia Viva" and "Rever," for instance, mirroring is used not only as a method but also as formal solution: in "Vaia Viva" (fig. 1) the font was specifically designed to blur

Figure 1. Augusto de Campos, "VAIA/VIVA." © Augusto de Campos. Reproduced by permission of the artist.

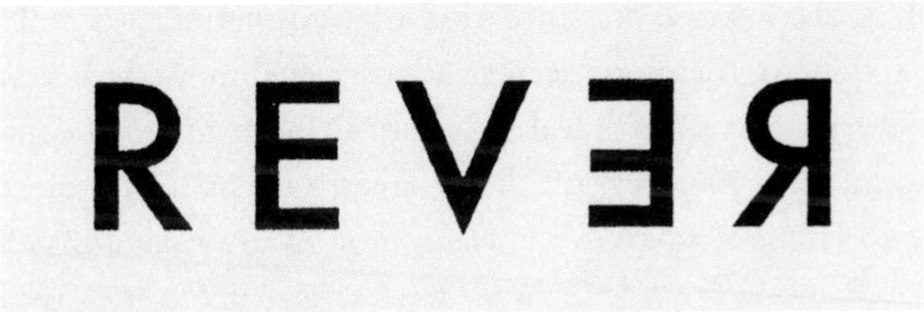

Figure 2. Augusto de Campos, "REVER." © Augusto de Campos.
Reproduced by permission of the artist.

the distinction between the two letters *A* and *V* and accommodate their irreconcilable difference (the same character represents both a vowel and a consonant).

In "Rever" (fig. 2), the suffix *er* is graphically reversed to underline the fact that it mirrors the word's prefix. What is achieved in both cases is the dissipation of meaning, as exultation (*viva*) is turned into its opposite (*vaia* [booing]), and even of the word itself, as the verb *rever* (to review) is reduced to the letter *V,* around which particles (the prefix and the suffix) fluctuate. Despite their extreme economy of means, these poems, like some compositions by Webern, were calculated to exert the greatest possible impact, and, at least in the case of "Vaia Viva," they have resonated deeply in the panorama of Brazilian literature.

In *Música de invenção,* Augusto de Campos writes:

> in Webern we find an unprecedented use of formal concision and of the dialectic between sound and silence (the latter made audible for the first time, and used not merely as pause but as structural element, at the same level as sounds).[12]

Webern's reputation as a difficult, demanding conductor, whose compositions are equally difficult to perform, is a source of great excitement to de Campos, who sees in this difficulty the very sign of genius. When an Uruguayan composer visiting São Paulo in the late 1970s tells de Campos, "To this day, no one has ever listened to Webern! There are no recordings that can reproduce his compositions with fidelity," de Campos seems undaunted and ponders how Webern's work might be even greater than he has already assumed it to be.[13] This incident stresses some of the issues at stake around Webern's work. In the São Paulo of the 1950s, knowledge of dodecaphonic theory was still fragmentary and acquired mostly from rare imported recordings and their liner notes, rather than from live concerts and lectures. Certainly there was the figure of Hans-Joachim Koellreutter championing new musical theories, but the dissemination of information was still minimal. Interest in Webern, therefore, seems to have relied more on his conceptual rigor and his pursuit of an ideal structure than on how his compositions actually sound. On the occasion of a concert of works by Igor Stravinsky, Webern, and Iannis Xenakis in the Festival of Avant-garde Music that took place in São Paulo in 1965, de Campos writes that *Six Pieces for Orchestra,* an early work by Webern, already demonstrates an "extremely concise language, the precise dialectic between sound and non-sound, 'an entire romance in one sigh,' *non multa sed multum,* microcosmusic."[14]

This sketchy background is intended merely as an attempt to situate the poet, who was only twenty-two years old at the time *Poetamenos* was written, vis-à-vis the enormous task he took it upon himself to accomplish, namely, the translation of Webern's musical language into poetic terms, thus creating something close to an acoustic image. This translation was effected not without some violence, as accommodations needed to be made in order to transform Webern's aural concerns into purely visual ones that subsequently would once again be turned into sound.

The Image of Voice[15]

Perhaps it will not be too implausible to argue that *Poetamenos* pushed Webern's *Klangfarbenmelodie* to another dimension, bringing to the forefront issues concerning the interconnectedness of sight and sound.[16] Mirror and echo, the visual and aural means of duplication that hold central roles in both Webern's and de Campos's practice, can here perhaps be used as tropes for the symmetrical relationship between de Campos and Webern, reverse images of each other seen through a metaphorical looking glass that encompasses not only contrasting disciplines but also geographies.

It is also ironic, if we allow ourselves to explore this comparison a little further, that *Poetamenos* has proved to be a work as difficult to perform as any of Webern's pieces. More than half a century after its creation, the series has still not received a fully satisfying performance, with the sole exception of Caetano Veloso's arresting 1979 reading of "Dias, dias, dias." This is by no means a minor deficit, as it suggests that de Campos might have created a work the performance of which eludes him. This difficulty in performing *Poetamenos* brings forth a central issue in Augusto de Campos's oeuvre, namely, his ongoing speculation on the relationship between self and voice, a concern that dates back to his earlier poetry, even before the formulation

Figure 3. Augusto de Campos, "Pessoa." © Augusto de Campos. Reproduced by permission of the artist.

of the concretist paradigm. We see this concern in poems such as "Fábula" (Fable), from 1949, which features a dialogue between a "Powerful Voice" and a "Small Voice," in "Bestiário — para fagote e esôfago" (Bestiary — for bassoon and esophagus), from 1955, and in more recent poems such as "Pessoa" (fig. 3), in which the possibility of attaining individuality is predicated on the ability of the subject ("pessoa") to "sound."[17]

The relationship between sound and subject in the poetry of Augusto de Campos has been approached with great insight by the Brazilian poet Eduardo Sterzi in "Todos os sons, sem som" (All the Sounds, without Sound), one of the essays in *Sobre Augusto de Campos*. Commenting on the complexity of de Campos's trajectory, Sterzi considers the "progressive emptying of the lyrical subject" in de Campos's early poetry, which led to the concretist phase:

> The "I," even if it no longer rules, continues to be the focal point around which the poem is organized, a proposition attested to by the frequency with which it employs the personal pronoun in addition to verbs inflected in the first person singular. And to organize the poem means above all to organize the lyrical subject's private fictions, its interior monologues and dialogues, its *psychomaquias*. Thus, since it's not yet embodied in a definitive form, the main artifice through which the increasing annihilation of the "I" will be achieved, preparing the ground for the appearance of what is known today as "concrete poetry" — I am referring to the fragmentation or the shattering of the voice — is anticipated in embryonic form.[18]

The progressive "shattering of the voice" in the early poetry of Augusto de Campos, a phase Sterzi defines as "ofegante" (breathless), achieved its optimum moment in *Poetamenos*, wherein the poet organized his "private fictions" and "interior monologues and dialogues" during an important moment in his life: the beginning of his relationship with Lygia Azeredo, who later became his wife. This organization took the form not so much of an ideogram, which is what the poet seemed to be aiming at in the series preface, as of a diagram, as Sterzi suggests. As for the poet's use of *Klangfarbenmelodie* as a model, Sterzi notes that "it is significant that the fragmentation of the voice takes the form of choral writing," and adds:

> The initial impression that we are listening to the poet's voice mixed with the voices of his beloved and possibly of her relatives, is replaced by the realization that we are witnessing a dialogue between the poet and his own self, questioning the tools of his writing.[19]

The difficulty of determining whose voice(s) speak(s) in and through *Poetamenos* is one of the series' most complex achievements — one that, beyond its debt to Webern's technique of orchestrating echoes, is intrinsically connected to a major cultural shift taking place in Brazil at the time, which affected the country's speech pattern in a deep way.[20] The reluctance to embrace a voice associated with an outdated model of subjectivity pushed the poet to confront the voice of his own epoch and in the process acquire new tools for his craft. In Brazil, the voice of the epoch was personified by

João Gilberto, who, around the time of the publication of *Poetamenos,* was struggling to get his *canto-falado* style recognized by the mainstream musical establishment. Discussing the first bossa nova recordings in *Bim Bom — A Contradição sem conflitos de João Gilberto,* Walter Garcia notes:

> The kind of singing "that flows in everyday speech" is kept on the threshold between the rhythm of thought, with its chain of ideas, and the rhythm of the body, of feelings and sensations. . . . Sound engineering during record production integrates the voice to the instrumental, while still keeping it in the foreground.[21]

Garcia's observation on the role of sound recording in actually making *canto-falado* possible is a point worth considering, as it relates to core ideas discussed during the formulation of a concrete poetics in the early 1950s.[22] He goes on to elaborate on how technology had made the "big voice" almost pointless:

> One must be reminded that João Gilberto's phonographic oeuvre comprises songs whose structure is defined fundamentally by the voice superimposed onto the beat. Much has been said about how the low voice has been adequate to microphone technology, on the evidence that, around 1958, one does not need a big voice to be able to record.[23]

The new technology opened up the possibility of capturing a kind of speech associated with "natural" rhythms, a voice more in consonance with the realm of ideas and hence able to transmit emotions:

> João Gilberto's spoken-singing, by balancing itself on the line between the origin and the disappearance of the very act of singing, conciliates the rhythm of speech — dictated by the chain of ideas that must be understood intellectually by the listener — and the rhythm of music — created by psychosomatic stimuli to reach the listener's body, and emitted in dissociation combined with its beat.[24]

To corroborate, Garcia quotes from a 1960 interview with João Gilberto:

> I think that singers must feel music as aesthetics, feel it in terms of poetry and naturalness. When one sings one should be as if praying: the essential is sensibility. Music is sound. And sound is voice, instrument. Thus, the singer will need to know when and how to elongate a sharp, a flat, so as to be able to transmit the emotional message.[25]

The discussion about *canto-falado* in *Bim-bom* eventually gets around to considering Augusto de Campos's outspoken defense of a new generation of singers in Brazil in the mid-1960s, known as the "jovem guarda" (youth vanguard):

> Augusto de Campos called attention to the singing of Roberto Carlos, Erasmo Carlos, and Wanderléia for their "clear, unencumbered" style, condemning the "unfortunate technique of *bel canto,* which Bossa Nova was supposed to have freed us from forever" and that, according to him, was being reborn at the moment in the "emphatic, rigid interpretation, full of melodramatic effects (including easy stage lighting tricks)" of Elis Regina. Halfway through his argument Augusto de Campos affirmed that Brazilian pop music belonged to a tradition of "effortless, direct interpretation, almost spoken," whose lineage included Noel Rosa, Mário Reis, and João Gilberto.[26]

A recurring motif throughout Augusto de Campos's work, poetry and essays alike, is his denunciation of "the old," often identified with the figure of the consecrated poet, who becomes an "august bust," his language, no longer living, petrified on a pedestal.[27] At times, this battle against the old assumes oedipal connotations, as in the poem "Ovo novelo." In that poem, as in *Poetamenos,* the bonds between parents and children are rendered as repressive, or even threatening. It comes as no surprise that the "big," operatic voice would be heard as the "voice of the old," and thus associated with an entire network of authoritarian figures. The issue of diction, then, or the establishment of a new speech pattern thus became paramount to Augusto de Campos, from both an individual and a collective perspective. In *Metaphysical Song,* Gary Tomlinson presents a compelling argument for the perception of the "operatic voice" as conveying "an early modern experience of subjectivity," from early Renaissance works by Jacopo Peri and Claudio Monteverdi to the dodecaphonic era of Schoenberg and Webern.[28] In Augusto de Campos's poems, particularly in *Poetamenos,* the voice becomes not only the vehicle through which the poet asserts his individuality but also, as Sterzi maintains, the means whereby the boundaries of this individuality are overcome and "the construction of a possible subjectivity is dramatized."[29]

Vox populi

Augusto de Campos is obviously a refined reader, capable of incorporating into his writing the most avant-garde tendencies available to him. In addition to writing poetry, he has dedicated much of his time to educating the Brazilian public through an extraordinary translation program that includes

authors as diverse as Dante Alighieri, John Donne, Emily Dickinson, Arthur
Rimbaud, Mallarmé, Pound, and Paul Valéry. He is also the author of three
volumes of translations of Provençal poets. It is interesting to note, however,
that despite the great variety of interests evident in his translation work and
writings on music, his own poetry is in essence influenced by specific threads
in Brazilian popular culture. In an essay in *Balanço da bossa,* for instance, he
points out that *Poetamenos* was written under the influence of both Webern
and Lupicínio Rodrigues, a samba composer whose torch songs were popular
in Brazil in the 1950s.[30] In the same essay, he praises Rodrigues's "restrained
expressionism" and notes that Webern "gave classical music the physical dimension of popular music."[31]

De Campos's fascination with Rodrigues motivated him to track down
the singer and composer in his hometown in the Brazilian south, to attend
one of his performances and interview him. He admired Rodrigues's soft
singing, which was the opposite of the big voice current in the 1940s and
'50s. In addition, he was amazed by Rodrigues's lyrics, which make use of
everyday, commonplace language and cliché phrases to the greatest effect.[32]
"Lupicínio," he writes, "attacks them [the lyrics] with naked hands, with all
the clichés of our language, using that which has been discarded to attain
greatness, isolating redundancy from its context to achieve the new." De
Campos marvels at the fact that in popular music, lyric and melody are impossible to dissociate. And in the case of Rodrigues, his very interpretation of
the song must be taken as part of the entire gestalt: "The degree of involvement is complete — one would even say "verbivocovisual" — and cannot be
sectioned off without losses."[33] The interpretation of a song or a poem is an
issue particularly dear to de Campos, one that he regards perhaps as the mark
of a true poet. In this context, the fact that only late in his career was he able
to perform his poems and musical compositions onstage is revealing, and one
is tempted to see in this reluctance to perform a parallel with Schoenberg's
Moses und Aron, as if the poetry envisioned by de Campos would ultimately
elude him in terms of sound. It is also through this complementary optic,
wherein Veloso plays Aron to de Campos's Moses, that Tropicália's rapport
with concretism must be considered.[34]

Ultimately, the bridge between twelve-tone theory and samba proposed
by de Campos is what prevents *Poetamenos* from being a mere illustration
of a thesis. The series is rigorously structured, with three euphoric moments
("paraiso pudendo," "Lygia fingers," and "eis os amantes") and two dysphoric
ones ("nossos dias" and "dias dias dias"); as in Webern, echoes of other works

and styles reverberate throughout: Provençal, baroque, Parnassianism. But from within this rigorous structure, the poet's voice emerges to tell us the story of his love for Lygia, full of longing and youthful yearning.

Translating *Poetamenos*

The six elegiac poems that compose *Poetamenos* were written as homage to the poet's wife-to-be, Lygia, in the tradition of spousal verse, or epithalamium. Throughout the sequence, words are cut into syllables or letters, with their fragments often interspersed among other words. Different colors indicate different timbres, while the spacing between words and lines dictates the rhythm. Words, syllables, and phonemes mirror each other, creating the effect of an echo chamber. Amidst this cacophony other literary works resonate, adding new shades to the poet's erotic reverie.[35]

Poetamenos opens with a lyrical proem, introducing the series' central themes through two felicitous portmanteaux.[36] The first, "rochaedo," suggests the figure of a poet (*aedo,* from the Greek *aoidós*), inert like — or with — the rocks (*rochedo* [cliffs]); the second, "rupestro," suggests that poetic imagination (*estro,* from the Greek *oîstros*) is a force of nature (*rupestre* denotes vegetation that grows on rocks). The voice of the poet seems to be directed to his beloved ("somos um" [we are one]), and at the same time unisonous with hers ("uni/sono" [uni/sonous, or one I am, or I dream I am one]).

The second poem suggests an erotic interlude in a garden, with references to an idyllic setting (first a fig orchard, "figueiral/figueiredo"[37] and later a hanging garden, "jardim suspenso") gradually unfolding into a highly sexualized verbal environment. Nature is first evoked through literature and immediately becomes animated and sexualized. Whether words break ("suspenso" becomes "sus pênis") or unite ("ah braços" [ah, arms] can also be read as "abraços" [embraces]), they seem to refuse definition. For instance, in one line the pairing of "penis" with "flagrante" (flagrant) can be misread as "fragrant penis," and once again "suspenso" is broken, but this time as "sus/penso" (under / I think). Amid this verbal turmoil, the stone-like poet ("petr'eu" [stone I] is brought out of his torpor ("exampl'eu") through the woman's thighs ("fêmoras").[38] The poem features clusters of words highlighted in four different colors — blue, red, green, and yellow — and the overall effect is that of superimposed ideograms. The cluster in red, which starts in the third line and continues up to the last, includes pairings like "pubis/jardim" (pubis/garden) and "paraiso pudendo" (pudendum paradise).

The name of the poet's inamorata, Lygia, is dispersed throughout the third poem, with the letters rearranged in different combinations ("digital," "dedat illa[grypho]," "felyna," "figlia") forming new words until the woman is finally morphed into a "lynx." The poem opens with an apparent grievance: "Lygia finge" (Lygia pretends). But the next line ("er ser") moves meaning in another direction, as "finge" can now be read as "finge-rs." The third and fourth lines confirm this possibility ("digital" and "dedat illa[grypho]").[39] One possible reading, then, is that "Lygia's fingers type" (the poem?), or maybe she "pretends to." The poem's final lines play with family bonds — "mãe" (mother), "figlia" (daughter, in Italian), and "sorella" (sister, also in Italian) — a theme that will appear again in the fifth and antepenultimate poem. There differences are finally balanced: this is visually conveyed by the poem's symmetrical layout, in which, as in a Rorschach blot, and with minor distortions, the right side mirrors the left. Hence we have pairings like "amantes / parentes" (lovers / relatives), "cimaeu / baixoela" (on top me / she below), "estesse/ aquelele" (this it / he that).[40] In this poem, the sexual tension accumulated throughout the series reaches its climax, indicated by another word-valise: "semen(t)emventre," which unfolds in at least two possibilities, "semen inside the womb" and "seed inside womb."

The series closes with a melancholic tone of departure, or absence, conveyed by a concerted series of signs, fragments, and citations: The lovers are apart ("separamante") and out of communication ("sem uma linha" [without a line]); without his muse, the poet becomes a nobody ("expoeta") near his end ("expira"); the beloved becomes enigmatic ("sphinx e/gypt y g"); and, looming over the entire poem, there are hints of family strife, through references in the first lines to a sonnet by Camões and, toward the end, to Lygia's family name.[41]

Poetamenos is a series that is remarkable, paradoxically enough, for both its concision and its opulence, its restrained formalism concealing a torrent of emotions and sexual longing. In it, de Campos's technique comes the closest to uniting in one packet Pound's concepts of *melopoeia* and *phanopoeia*. Each poem is composed as a "lyrical ideogram," to use Jacques Donguy's expression, with express indications for rhythm and tone.[42] Sound — the sound of the voice, that is — is a sign of life, and in *Poetamenos,* the poet seems to be animated by the presence of his lover. Throughout the series, Lygia is the principle that animates, enlivens, and organizes the world around him. Before her arrival the poet is inert, rock-like. Her presence is both a force of nature ("lynx," "felyna") and the possibility of writing ("digital," "dedat illa[grypho]"). She is Echo, or rather Syrinx, channeling the poet's voice onto the page.[43]

This material presents an extraordinary opportunity for translators to immerse themselves in their own languages and meditate on the transformations imparted to them by a process of modernization. Since meter and rhyme are of no immediate concern, there is a great deal of freedom for translators to concentrate on and explore the sonorities, dictions, speech patterns, and colloquialisms of their own languages. The dispersion and reassembling of words, as well as the crafting of portmanteaux, will offer many opportunities for invention. An English translation of the first poem (fig. 4) produced

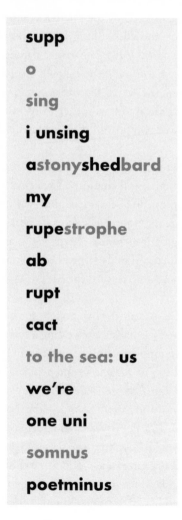

Figure 4. Augusto de Campos, "Poetamenos" ("supp o sing"). © Augusto de Campos. Reproduced by permission of the artist.

surprising new combinations, in addition to successful solutions to original portmanteaux.[44] Note for instance the lines "por/suposto:/'scanto," which has been rendered "supp/o/sing/i unsing"; and also two great finds: "a-stony-shed-bard" (for *rochaedo*), and "rupestrophe" (for *rupestro*).

Literary references throughout the series might present an obstacle, given the obscurity of their sources. The quotes by Camões and Guimarães Junior, for instance, carry a slightly ironic tone; a literal translation wouldn't capture the irony of the juxtaposition of old and new voices in the original. One solution might be to look for cultural equivalents and replace them with quotes by authors in the translator's language who stylistically share a sense of kinship with the authors cited by de Campos. The influence of Lupicínio Rodrigues's singing style is another instance where translators must exert their own judgment and select an equivalent that works for them. Rodrigues's influence is invisible, so to speak, and highly subjective. The equivalent here would be to imagine that a poet like Susan Howe, for example, in addition to her interest in the poetry of Emily Dickinson and the film technique of Chris Marker, was also somehow influenced by the speech patterns of Mississippi Delta blues singers. This very personal choice will not be visible in print but rather will guide the decision-making process in structuring the text.

The greatest challenge in *Poetamenos*, however, has to do with what Marjorie Perloff explored in the poetry of Ezra Pound in terms of nominalism. In her essay "The Search for 'Prime Words': Pound, Duchamp, and the Nominalist Ethos," Perloff asks, "Why this longing to turn words that have specific meanings into proper names — names that designate a particular person or place and hence restrict the possibilities of reference?" The usual answer, she herself responds, "is that the proper name is a form of concrete image." And she continues:

> If as Pound says in "A Retrospect," "the natural object is always the *adequate* symbol" . . . , if, as he puts it later in the *ABC of Reading*, "the Chinese ideogram is the touchstone for poets because, unlike the letter unit of the Western alphabet, the ideogram provides us with the picture of a thing," then the proper name is essential to a poetics of "constatation of fact," of "accuracy of sentiment."[45]

In the case of *Poetamenos*, a series constructed under the aegis of both Webern and Pound, the presence of the beloved animates everything around the poet, in nature and in literature — a presence made felt by the dissemination of her name throughout the series. Hence, a reference to "figueiredo" in the second poem, for instance, bridges the poet's love for Provençal song and for Lygia Azeredo ("filhazeredo" in the last poem). In addition, the word play with *aedo* (*aoidós*), which we first encountered in the portmanteau "rochaedo," also reverberates in "figueiredo" and "filhazeredo" and completes the associative chain that links the possibility of poetry to nature and to the beloved. To translate "figueiredo" as "fig tree" is therefore to lose an entire chain of meanings and references.

Halfway through her text, Perloff moves away from her line of argument to suggest a kinship between Pound's compulsion to name and Marcel Duchamp's idea of a "pictorial nominalism," which, according to Thierry de Duve, "turns back on metaphor and takes things literally."[46] "Pictorial nominalism" seems an apt term for classifying *Poetamenos,* but de Campos seems to complicate things further by turning a noun (Azeredo) into a metaphor (the fig tree), undermining not only Duve's definition but also one of the guiding principles of concretism itself. In the end, this relentless resistance to conforming (to a given principle, to a given form, and even to translation) is precisely what has kept de Campos's protean concrete poem/painting/composition vital for over fifty years.

NOT SOUND / JOHANNA DRUCKER

The origins of poetry may well reside in sound and song. But the transmission history of poetry depends upon visual forms. These two facts do not cancel each other but make for the mobilization of intersecting codes. Some of these duplicate each other, but others operate on independent registers in the process of poetic production (by which I mean both composition and reading). The recognition of the function of the codes of writing and print in the transmission history of poetry and in its perpetuation as an identifiable cultural form does not exclude recognition of the sound structures integral to the same work. But the visual codes of transmission operate on their own terms as instructions during the reading event. Adherence to graphical forms fixed by convention is evident in the organization of poetry on the page, even if such an organization has the ability to be pronounced aloud or "heard" in silent reading. To understand these visual codes, we can draw on cognitive studies in reading, the cultural history of literacy, and the semiotics of graphics.

In the modern period, whether we date this from the beginning of the printing press in the fifteenth century or from the growth of industrialization and its extension of standardizing effects, poetic works based entirely in visual composition take their place in the canon alongside works whose composition derived from song or verse. This independent tradition pushes graphical features to an extreme, and its anomalous character makes it easy to bracket "visual" poetry off as if it were an exclusive domain. But the graphical features of conventional poetic works are not anomalies. Stanza forms, line breaks, even the "spaces between words" analyzed by Paul Saenger, organize a text according to visual rules that sometimes support and sometimes contradict any pattern of sound.[1] One of the great productive tensions in the composition of modern poetry occurs through the use of line breaks to play with the aural/oral expectation. The critical language for analysis of meter, rhyme, stress, and other variants is highly developed in the apparatus of poetic study. But the language of descriptive analysis for visual features barely exists. Perhaps the lightning rod effect by which radical visual innovations claim attention for their dramatic activity takes away the necessary energy for illuminating the more mundane-seeming operations of the encoded spaces of the page, or perhaps the nostalgic attachment to the idea of an "origin" of poetry in song makes us give more significance to sound values over visual ones. The presence of sound is not in dispute. My argument is that whatever the reason, increasing attention to the need for a critical metalanguage for describing visual forms within poetic inscription is evident. Laura Mandell, in an article in *New Literary History,* "What Is the Matter? Or, What Literary Theory Neither Hears nor Sees," makes points that resonate deeply. Her attitudes are familiar to many within the community of poetic studies or work even though one of her motivations is to call digital humanists to attend to precisely these verbal and visual features that are often taken for granted. In a dramatic demonstration of the way one very basic visual code operates — that space between words mentioned above — she subjected William Wordsworth's "Surprized by Joy" to a program that removes them:

surprizedbyjoyimpatientasthewinditurnedtosharethetransportohwithwhom buttheelongburiedinthesilenttombthatspotwhichnovicissitudecanfindlove faithfulloverecalledtheetomymindbuthowcouldIforgettheethroughwhat powerevenfortheleastdivisionofanhourhaveibeensobeguiledastobeblindtomy mostgrievouslossthatthoughtsreturnwastheworstpangthatsorroweverboresave oneoneonlywhenistoodforlornknowingmyheartsbesttreasurewasnomorethat neitherpresenttimenoryearsunborncouldtomysightthatheavenlyfacerestore[2]

The result is of course surprising [*sic*], but hardly joyful, and the difficulties of reintroducing the sound structure into this visual field show immediately how intimately the visual and verbal codes are integrated in transmission on the page — and how dependent on graphical devices our reading habits are. Mandell, drawing on Saenger, comments:

> Different kinds of cognition are mobilized, Saenger argues, when visually distinct blocks of text, "lexical images," operate through visual recognition: readers have stored in their minds thousands of word-pictures that they recognize instantly — and, again, silently. Once there is space between words, Saenger insists,

even readers operating in written languages based upon phonetic alphabets do not have to sound out words phonetically in order to understand them.[3]

I begin this essay on those features of poetic production that are "not sound" with this discussion of Mandell's work because her grounding in eighteenth- and early nineteenth-century romantic poetry is linked to her activities in digital humanities, where the question of what constitutes the "matter" of a work is brought constantly (and urgently) to attention since the tasks of reencoding force question of what "matters" to the fore. Mandell is concerned with major mainstream conventions, not exceptions. Her most vivid example of the work of graphical codes comes in her discussion of Wordsworth's "A Slumber Did My Spirit Seal" (1800), where she recalls a long critical legacy in which attention has been paid to the semantic function of the break between the first stanza's observation of a beloved sleeping and the second describing a woman now dead:

> Visually, as critics from Cleanth Brooks onward have noticed, the space between stanzas of this poem marks the woman's death, whether it be Lucy's death or, as Coleridge would have it, Dorothy's, that Wordsworth imagines.[4]

By beginning with Mandell's discussion of Wordsworth, I am trying to make clear that elaboration of a critical metalanguage to describe the "not sound" elements of poetry describes not features of anomalous works but elements of literary production within any writing space. Some of these features suggest easy analogies with sound — contrasts of scale, or bold and italic for emphasis, are easily *given* voice. But the *codes* in which these contrasts are inscribed are fully, entirely *graphic*. When I put my ear to the page, I hear nothing but the sound of my hair against the surface. If I erase the letters, no "sound" remains. Sound is not *on* the page, even if a graphic transmission allows for its properties to be noted for reproduction in mental or verbal rendering. The argument to be posed here is not one premised on the idea that sound values and graphic values are fully redundant or one in which they are mutually exclusive. Instead, it is meant as a description of the material properties of the graphic codes that instruct and provoke our reading of poetic works, whether they are notations for sound or not.

Even with caveats about anomalies duly noted, we know that graphic poetics is activated most famously in the modern period. Stéphane Mallarmé's *Un coup de dés,* a work that was conceived as a visual form in space, and unfolds through time. Whatever value or sonorous qualities we assign to the sound structure of this piece, we are forced to acknowledge that its visual characteristics have their own effect. Spatialization organizes the semantic field of this work — *Un coup de dés* is made on the page and across the gutter, that most physically material feature of a codex. In Mallarmé's design, the gutter is the literal and virtual spine on which the lines of the work are suspended. Many experimental works that conspicuously explore the potential of graphicality as their initial impulse proliferate within the avant-garde, and the various strains of visual poetics (not just visual poetry but a poetics of material, graphical codes that constitute the work) are well known in twentieth-century literature. Some of these, particularly contemporary poetic works, have no basis in sound. Mary Ellen Solt's now classic "Forsythia," whatever its poetic strengths or merits, is a graphic work almost exclusively.[5] One might argue the same of Steve McCaffery's *Carnival* panels. Jackson Mac Low's many acrostic works are generated by graphic means and patterns. Charles Bernstein's *Veil* embodies its material specificity in print and digital environments through graphical features. In all and each of these works, the realms of sight and sound are neither isomorphic nor redundant nor mutually exclusive, but the specificity of graphical properties exercises an autonomous articulation of features we recognize and cognize.

These autonomous graphic codes sometimes reinforce sound patterns or structures, breaking verse lines so that meter matters or rhyme schemes strike the reader more readily. Sometimes they merely provide the means by which such readings remain available in inscription. But as graphical features they are not pronounced. Some are not even pronounceable. We could quibble about whether or not we enunciate the spaces *between* words, but we do not speak aloud the spaces between letters or within their counters and openings, even though we register and rely on these differences as fundamental clues to text sense. Certainly, the clever reader and insistent critic might "pronounce" or perform a long white space as a silence, but the code in play is graphical. Even a score is not a sound; it is a set of instructions for reading, and reading, as the cognitive studies field acknowledges, is neither a simple translation of visual to verbal signs nor a matter of one operating in the absence of the other.[6] The complicated question of transcription as descriptive vs. prescriptive of sound values allows for much latitude in the interpretation from sound to visual code and back. But the specific operations and features of graphical codes, those specific elements that exist, materially and visually, at the level of inscription as marks on a page, are not sound features.

Such a statement will no doubt divide my readers (not listeners, given this presentation on the page) along a line of faith. My assertion does not negate the obvious — that *any* form of represented text can be used as a *score* for oral performance. We did not need John Cage to show us what the ancients knew in their divinatory readings of signs of the natural world, that any arrangement or configuration of stars, sticks, tracks of birds, and shapes of organs can be *read* — orally — or *sung.* But the fact that an oral analogy can be constructed on the basis of any written provocation and the equally important fact that graphical codes are integral to the transmission of poetic forms are not mutually exclusive. The point of my argument here is to show how these two registers may be distinguished in form and function.

The earliest print artifacts (Bibles and indulgences) extended graphic principles of an earlier manuscript culture into double-columned and hierarchical structures that carried semantic value. Sizes, spaces, divisions of text into larger and smaller, even within the highly constrained resources of first-generation type-casting, are each allocated a role to play in Gutenberg's first efforts that have their origins in visual literacy that tracks into antiquity. The Bible's verses, poetic as they may be, are not scored with line breaks in Gutenberg's presentation; lines run together across the breadth of each column to create the finely textured even page that imitates the best of calligraphic renderings on which the types and layout were based. But even as the codex, once a form associated entirely with secular and classical works (as opposed to scrolls that remained the carrier of biblical and sacred texts), had become the instrument of choice for publication of all textual expressions (except the Jewish holy scriptures), so the characteristics that marked one kind of graphical layout from another had been stabilizing across a period of a thousand years or more of manuscript culture by the time Renaissance print absorbed and further codified its forms.

In early print culture, news ballads such as those announcing the defeat of the Spanish Armada are identifiable as ballads because of the distribution of lines on the sheet — a fact recognizable from a distance. Once approached, the text can be read, but the graphic identity of a ballad is signaled long before its words can be discerned. If rendered orally, the ballad form and rhyme scheme make the sound properties of the verse fully evident of course, but the initial distinction by which the type of text under consideration is determined is visual. This predisposition to read according to categories and types is a cognitive function disciplined by cultural training and historical circumstance. Imagine the surprise of finding, as did readers of André Breton's 1924 *La Révolution Surréaliste,* that what they thought was a scientific journal was in fact an artistic project. Entirely aesthetic, that undertaking was meant to use its masquerade as a device of disorientation. But the claim to authority that Breton's journal made was as genuine as its graphic format, only appropriated to different ends.

The examples of a poster or ballad posted in a public space, or Breton's print masquerade, show that we *see* before we read and that the recognition thus produced predisposes us to reading according to specific graphic codes before we engage with the language of the text. First and foremost, a graphic presentation (and a material one, more on which in a moment) signals to the reader that *this is a poetic text, a poem, or other aesthetic expression.* Then, as we read, features of graphic materiality (such as elements of style and layout) structure our reading. Marks of erasure, censorship, alteration, and annotation encode prior readings and activities in graphical traces as well. These graphical codes simply do not have their origin in sound. They depend on the technologies and materials of writing, the figure/ground distinctions of graphic space, and the conventions that have accrued through use. The difference between "this" and "~~this~~" is a graphical distinction, no matter what oral rendering it may produce. The graphic codes of *USA Today* are rarely put at the service of poetry composition, though they could be adopted, parodied, used, and they would signal an ironic or contradictory situation for the reader with respect to the category of text (poetry or news). The graphic form instructs the eye. These codes provoke a specific, or at least constrained, reading in response. We do not read a poem the way we read a tabloid, though we might, because the graphic presentation has already circumscribed the text of one to indicate it is not the other.

Literalists of materiality suggest that direct description is sufficient to account for the effects of graphic codes — as if an inherent difference between Baskerville and Stymie could be measured on a gradient of absolute values. But graphic codes and other material features are not static, inherent, or self-evident. Description is essential to developing the discriminating capability through which the properties of a modern face can be distinguished from a slab serif. "Egyptian" developed for display can be noted, but "Stymie" doesn't have a "voice" per se. Very few readers are typophiles. Almost none have expert knowledge of fonts and their cuttings, disappearances, and revivals within the complicated history of styles and fashions that have bequeathed their own peculiar legacies of anachronistic use to the current page. We may feel that the difference between setting a scholarly text in Palatino and setting it in Baskerville is trivial, but ask any poet if he wants his work set in **Cracked** or **Chalkboard Bold** and what's at stake in the qualities of graphical style becomes apparent. The lessons of semiotic difference and poststructuralist *différance,* in combination with bibliographical and cultural studies of graphic codes, begin to provide some traction on the complicated reading of forms and styles.

Graphic features are codes of *provocation.* They don't produce direct effect within a signifying system any more than words or images do. All are part of the structured field of possibilities into which a reader intervenes, producing text in reading. Graphic features are part of that system. Their associations and conventions (slab serif, sans serif, display faces, headlines, double-columned pages, initial caps, decorative letters, borders, etc., through the inexhaustible inventory of possibilities) register within the field of perception and probability. The fact that a text is material is not in itself interesting or useful unless *the way* materiality performs within the space of reading comes under discussion. Blunt assertions of literal materialism should be shifted toward analysis of the dynamic, co-dependent condition of reading as performance provoked within associations and possibilities of a text. Graphic features participate in this dynamic reading. Charles Bernstein's virtuoso rendition of *The Yellow Pages* is a striking demonstration of the way a mode of reading — itself materially encoded in terms of expressions, vocalization, timing, emphasis, and other inflections — can transform utilitarian language into poetic work. *The Yellow Pages* are not poetry, and certainly they are not derived from song, but they can be rendered poetical through vocal performance. Neither do its graphical features inscribe meter in an absolute, inherent, essential sense, but meter can be called forth through that same performance. Sound, here, is patterned as interpretation and effect. Making, form giving, attention to *facture,* after all, *is* the poetic act, *poiesis.*

So somewhere between the overlooked (insignificant or considered to be a mere transcription) and the overdetermined (literal materiality) lies a path to attention to graphical codes and the way they work before we read, while we read, and the traces often left after we read. Visual literacy in our era, implicit and unschooled as it is in practice, asserts a massaging effect on the reader through codes and conventions that follow an "understood" consensus about forms. Where is the rule book in which those codes are laid out? Somehow, as with other features of language, we learn how to make well-formed graphic expressions without ever learning "the rules."

What, then, are the graphic properties of poetic texts that are *not* sound, that have their material instantiation in print or writing, white space and its constitutive capabilities, size, scale, fonts, color, proximity, orientation, and other properties whose reading is cognized through visual means? One approach to the study of graphic codes within the space of reading can be structured according to the seven graphic variables identified by Jacques Bertin, the French semiologist of cartography.[7] The variables are (1) size and/or scale, (2) shape, (3) value (gray scale or tonal), (4) color, (5) pattern, (6) orientation (directional orientation with respect to the page or frame), (7) placement (grouping and other relations). Because he was working with print materials, Bertin did not include two other variables that are part of the material codes of digital writing space: timing and movement. All of these variables may be put at the service of creating a score, trying to produce a visual image of sound effects, or otherwise working through analogy to connect visual and verbal dimensions. But the actual codes are graphic ones, which is simply to say, the representational mode in which we receive these is visual.

An example of putting each graphic variable into play shows how at once familiar these are and how infrequently attention is given to these issues in critical analysis. Take size, for instance. The distinction between a title and a poem's body is often marked by a change in size and/or use of capitals in a graphic code that, though renderable, is not primarily a sound pattern. The distinction here is not analogous to a change in volume, or degree of formality of tone, even though the majuscules derive from highly formal roman capitals and the text from a manuscript humanistic roundhand:

JABBERWOCKY
'Twas brillig and the slithy tove

The convention is to read the distinction between title and text simply as a setting apart, a way to note where the body of the poem begins. Such conventions work so strongly that their variants also register as significant.

Changes in font or type are immediately striking to the eye, as this comparison of settings from Byron's *The Giaour* shows:

Fair clime! Where every season smiles
FAIR CLIME! WHERE EVERY SEASON SMILES
Fair clime! Where every season smiles

These style changes might be rendered through changes of voice or accent, but such a rendition would be an approximation, an interpretation, of what the typographic style signals through its graphic qualities. Likewise, a change in grayscale values might be communicated through tone of voice or volume, but we can also see the purpose of a visual effect for its own impact, no matter how readily suited it may be to vocal analogy:

The fog it comes
On little cat feet.

But after all, the point of the effect is to show a correlation with a visual phenomenon, and the softening of tone replicates atmospheric effects, not acoustic ones. To insist on this as a sound effect would push a point rather oddly, as if some absolute principle were at stake in preserving the sound quality of any poetic image. Graphic effects are not in contradiction to the sound one hears in one's head, if one does, or speaks aloud, but they may act independently of it.

Color is rarely used in printing poetry texts, with a few striking exceptions, and it would be a tricky feature to translate into sound if it were, unless one were a synaesthete. Most colored ink printing seems tricky and decorative, though the fabulous Blaise Cendrars and Sonia Delaunay collaboration of 1913, *La Prose du Transsibérien,* is an example that comes to mind as a work whose print colors serve the field of the work on graphic terms without any need for them to translate into vocalization. But what of the many textured, patterned, plaid striped and polka-dotted letterforms? Shadow and drop letters? These cannot be conceived to derive in any way from *sound* patterns, or to serve sound, meter, rhyme, or stress. Imagine Shakespeare's line, "The quality of mercy is not strain'd," rendered in the Flames font or the Holiday motif:

Orientation is another graphic code that does not derive from or lend itself to vocal rendering. What possible vocal analogy maps onto this production that does not simply impose an arbitrary relation of sound to sight:

The quality of mercy is not p,uɪɐɹʇs

Other qualities of placement and grouping also rely on graphic conventions that, when disturbed, register to the eye without necessarily having an impact on the sound pattern or structure, even though, again, such codes can be rendered in sound values:

The quality of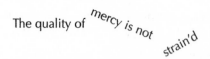

These variations *might* be pronounced by variations in timing and spacing, breathing and phrasing. But in all of these cases, a translation would be performed, not a direct transcription or equivalent. In my examples, the visual or graphic features precede the verbal rendering; they are visual distortions first and foremost and become sound works or patterns only if rerendered.

The exercises through which these variables can be manipulated are inexhaustible, of course, as are the differences in inflection, tone, and timing. But they take place in distinct material systems that play with different associations and channels of communication. The simple combination of

I YOU

can be performed as a poetic, aesthetic text through a set of manipulations that inscribe affect and distance:

I   YOU

I   YOU

I   YOU

Or:

I   GOD

I   GOD

I   GOD

I   god

While we might allow volume or emphasis to increase in speaking this aloud, the final move of distancing the lowercase word from the uppercase letter would have to be rendered by introducing a pause and a diminished voice. But would that exemplify the distinction between capitals and lowercase letters? The visual realm is sufficient in itself. No rendition in sound makes better sense of the visual properties — which are, in fact, perfectly legible, have their own semantic effect, and need not be translated into sound for that to be the case. In fact, the semantic effects are rendered not in sound values at all but through the differences assigned through the graphic means.

Numerous acts of textual editing that involve absent or trace texts are registered graphically: erasure, censorship, and other forms of elimination, annotation, or change. Bars through words, marks and smears, traces of something once present and now gone, marginalia, handwritten or inked notes, folded page corners and smoothed-out creases — all mark the ways in which reading changes and produces a text. What is gone is sometimes still visible in graphical terms. One mode of successful censorship might be that which erases itself entirely so that we never see a trace of its intervention. Graphic marks that inscribe the history of the text under investigation or study provide their own visual richness, sometimes attractive and alluring, as we strain to see what is missing or rubbed out upon the page. Erasure does not immediately suggest verbal analogy, though like all visual scoring effects, it might be given a sound value. Features of erasure trace partially disappeared or no longer present texts. Sound is always a presence, immediate, momentary, ephemeral in our literal perception of it, though it would be simplistic to suggest that any cognitive processing of semiotic systems is isomorphic to the method of its production. The linear sequence of letters on a page does not create a reading along a string of alphabetic beads any more than does the hearing of sound sequences, of course, but the acoustic disappearance of sound does contrast with the duration and persistence of graphical signs. We know from our experience of digital media that materialities have difference degrees of permanence with regard to the specific substrate in which they are encoded, but that all apprehensible signs are materially instantiated. This is part of their identity as signs.

Graphical textuality is a constitutive code of constraints according to which a reading may be provoked and produced. We respond to graphic codes, like other cues to cognitive processing, and then produce a reading. Acculturated as we are, we learn early and well the ways to recognize advertising or poetry and distinguish them, mostly, from each other. The wide world of arts offers plenty of visual sport to our eyes, and we who know how to look see that we read very much according to the modes and decorum of our times — hence our occasional pleasure or dismay at variations from such norms. Communicative codes inscribe habits and attitudes, but the associational values attached are elusive and proliferate daily. The rhetorical force of the visual comes not from its analogy to pronounceable or speakable equivalents but from a distinct and independent realm and register that sometimes parallels and sometimes works independently of sound. But the semantic contributions of graphical codes are also substantive elements of poetic, literary, and textual fields that have acquired their conventions and uses through historical and cultural circumstances. Transmission, like all material practice, is constitutive not vehicular, whether visual, verbal, or part of a dynamic dialogue between these two modes of embodiment.

THE SOUND SHAPE OF THE VISUAL: TOWARD A PHENOMENOLOGY OF AN INTERFACE / MING-QIAN MA

We find certain things about seeing puzzling, because we do not find the whole business of seeing puzzling enough.

LUDWIG WITTGENSTEIN, *Philosophical Investigations*

We are surrounded by noise. And this noise is inextinguishable. It is outside — it is the world itself — and it is inside, produced by our living body. We are in the noises of the world, we cannot close our door to their reception, and we evolve, rolling in this incalculable swell. . . . In the beginning is the noise; the noise never stops. It is our apperception of chaos, our apprehension of disorder, our only link to the scattered distribution of things. Hearing is our heroic opening to trouble and diffusion; other receptors assure us of order or, if they no longer give or receive, close immediately. . . . What remains intelligent in the cursus of the sciences is what is ahead, escaping the law.

MICHEL SERRES, *The Parasite*

In reading contemporary innovative poetry, sounding the visual presents itself as one of the most intriguing tasks of performance. Ranging from paragraphs, sentences, phrases down to words and even letters, typographical visual displays of linguistic units on the page invariably invite, and indeed demand, auditory enactments, which in turn are carried out for various hermeneutic and artistic purposes. However tentative or exploratory, sounding the visual in this verbal context is conditioned, if not dictated, by the psychologically imprinted sound-image coupling on the one hand and, on the other hand, by the acoustic patterns of any given system, be it phonemic,

phonetic, or phonologic.[1] It dramatizes, differently put, an orchestrated chorus in and out of an image amphitheater.

In the very auditory dynamics of sounding the visual as such, there exists, however, a silent space occupied by a peculiar visual phenomenon, a
phenomenon that has hitherto remained acoustically unattended, and to
which existing sound systems, whatever the kind, seem oddly inapplicable.
The textual phenomenon in question is manifested, more specifically, in the
interdisciplinary appropriations and deployments of extralinguistic signs
that assume, in particular, two types of visual configurations. First, there are
geometric figures, scientific schemata, technical charts, mathematical notations, and other similar "non-art images" that, as mute and "affect-less carri-
ers of data," are "geared toward the cold transmission of information" (fig. 1);
and second, there are random drawings, obscure forms, fuzzy shapes, chaotic
aggregates, and the like, which, confusing in representational intention and
seemingly informationless in content, appear to be inarticulate or reticent
(fig. 2).[2] With their respective appearances of a crystal transparency and a

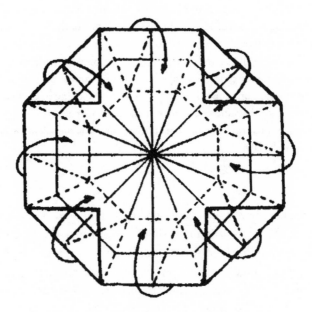

Figure 1. Darren Wershler-Henry, "Folding Pattern." From *Yes-
terday's Tomorrows* (2000–2001), in *Poetry Plastique,* curated
by Jay Sanders and Charles Bernstein (New York: Marianne
Boesky Gallery and Granary Books, 2001), 41. Reproduced by
permission of the artist.

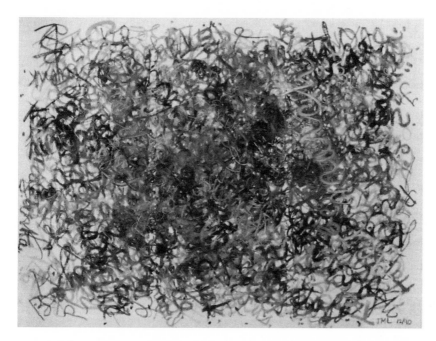

Figure 2. Jackson Mac Low, "Worldpair Poem" (1990). Oil-paint stick on linen. 36 × 48 in.
From *Poetry Plastique,* curated by Jay Sanders and Charles Bernstein (New York: Marianne
Boesky Gallery and Granary Books, 2001), p. 31. Reprinted with kind permission of the
Estate of Jackson Mac Low.

muddy opacity, these two types of visual formations depart radically from
the convention of the sound-image correlation, blatantly defying, each in its
own way, any acoustic appropriations by a frontal visuality at once authori-
tatively distancing and semantically nonnegotiable, demanding an absolute
and unconditional visual absorption. It follows, then, that the reception of
these two types of visual configurations is characterized by two corresponding approaches, both suggestive of a similar understanding of the sound-vision relationship: hermeneutically, they tend to be left alone, elevated onto
the pedestal as silent icons of authority, the signification of which is believed
to be so informatively explicit and self-sufficient as to render their sounding a nonissue; psycho-aesthetically, they tend to be perceived, by virtue of
either a structural transparency or a perceptual unfathomableness, as having reached a "silence," a profound soundlessness that is itself impregnated
simultaneously with a "light" radiating "from within," as Howard Nemerov
would have put it; hence a silence-light, or sound-vision, modality that represents and articulates a transcendent intentionality.[3]

With their express resistance to any acoustic rendering, these two types of visual configurations, though rather limited in their textual appearances, can be read as making a statement. Their explicit foregrounding of seeing over hearing situates and arguments the sound-vision relation in a larger context by evoking a history of metaphysics, one in which the rise of optics is accompanied by the demise of acoustics.[4] Formal and generic complications aside, their textual compositions thus present a critical rethinking more philosophical than simply hermeneutic or psycho-aesthetic; and they posit, more urgently than other issues, a phenomenological inquiry that regrounds, both at a more fundamental level and from a more radical perspective, the problematic of what Roman Jakobson terms "the structural and perceptual relation between visual and auditory signs."[5]

More concretely, the inquiry begins with the obvious. When materialized on the page, these two types of visual configurations beg the question of how their transcendental signification is made possible precisely because their visual lucidity is magnified against a background eerily devoid of sound. They then initiate, in spite of themselves, a self-reflexive re-vision of their own visuality, one that attempts to discern, acoustically, their own auditory contours. Understood from this perspective, visual configurations as such articulate an immanent critique with a twofold objective. On the one hand, they perform a critical-formal parody of ocularcentrism as the hitherto grounding metaphysics of the tradition of epistemology, as the constituting condition for logos.[6] In particular, they call into question, by bringing into visibility, its structure of representation predicated, as Don Ihde has pointed out, on a "double reduction" since "Plato and Democritus": a "reduction *to* vision" and a "reduction *of* vision," culminating in the latter, which "ultimately separates sense from significance."[7] On the other hand, they embark upon an antireductionist exploration of sound dimensions erased in and by the visual as the yet to be heard and acknowledged, as the site of experiential potentials or, in Ihde's terms, of "existential possibilities."[8] In his study of "a *phenomenology* of auditory experience," Ihde's statement provides a useful synthesis of the significance of this twofold objective:

> What is being called visualism here as a symptom is the whole reductionist tendency which in seeking to purify experiences belies its richness at the source. A return to the *auditory dimension* is thus potentially more than a simple changing of variables. It begins as a deliberate de-centering of a dominant tradition in order to discover what may be missing as a result of the traditional double reduction

of vision as the main variable and metaphor. This deliberate change of emphasis from the visual to the auditory dimension . . . symbolizes a hope to find material for a recovery of the richness of primary experience which is now forgotten or covered over in the too tightly interpreted visualist traditions.[9]

That being the case, the question becomes, simply, how to sound these geometric figures, scientific schemata, mathematical notations, random drawings, obscure forms, fuzzy shapes, and chaotic aggregates? What, in other words, is the acoustic valence prior to a perceptual reduction, and what is the initial sound vector accompanying an optical big bang? Central to this twofold objective is, among other issues of course, a fundamentally phenomenological question: What is the sound shape of the visual, as is evoked in graphic configurations as such?

I

Nemerov's silence-light modality, which results from his speculative thinking and psycho-aesthetic understanding of poetry and painting in the context of "the solemnity of the museum," mirrors nonetheless a classical paradigm.[10] Though situated from a poetic-artistic perspective, it amplifies the fact that since the ancient Greeks, the "division of experience itself" into categories is, as Ihde makes it clear, concomitant with the metaphysical privileging of vision over sound and its visually reductive mapping of the world.[11] Once understood negatively, however, Nemerov's modality also presents an anaphoric beckoning, albeit inadvertently, to a before-and-after, a moment of transfiguration whereby experience is processed and metamorphosed into metaphysics. For one thing, his silence-light formation implicitly postulates, as Ihde has explicitly stated, that silence, which belongs to the sound category, is itself also "a 'visual category'"; and before their metaphysical severing from each other, sound and vision are intimately intertwined in "some sort of preexisting harmony," constituting on equal terms one and the same bodily experience.[12] For another, once severed into a category, silence becomes "*relative*," in that, visually, it "adheres to things hidden relatively within present existence," and that, acoustically, it is relegated to a sound-parameter, which is considered redundant and "unnecessary," with its audibility controlled and determined only as an "added value" by the originating intensity of a visual-conceptual luminosity.[13] Silence is relative, in other words, to the degree of its own visibility circumscribed by the decree of a visual supremacy. In this sense, silence is itself what Jakobson calls "visual noise" eliminated to an extent contingent upon the ocularcentric imperatives of visual clarity and accessibility; or, differently put, the visual is itself auditory noise purged in direct proportion to the mandatory level of visual transparency and immediacy.[14]

Sound, in which the world is gestated, is thus veiled by light into oblivion, as Walter Murch puts it ever so poetically, forced to "[withdraw] into the shadows," fated to retreat in face of the ruthless invasion and colonization of "the braggart Sight," into which the world is now born.[15] Worse yet, it has been traditionally derogated as noise, both metaphorically and literally, aesthetically as well as scientifically. In the schemes of things lorded over by the eye, sound as noise is henceforth conceived, since Homeric Greece, as destructive to telos, as is the case with Odysseus, who has to escape from the Sirens' song by tying himself to a mast and by stuffing his sailors' ears with wax in order not to deviate from his homebound voyage. It is subsequently perceived, especially in light of the analogy of Plato's Cave and its shadows, as antithetical to the enlightenment of the universal signified, as is the case with mathematics, which, as Michel Serres argues, represents "an ideal republic," a utopian "city of communication," precisely because it is "maximally purged of noise."[16]

In his study titled *The Domain of Images,* James Elkins brings this prob-

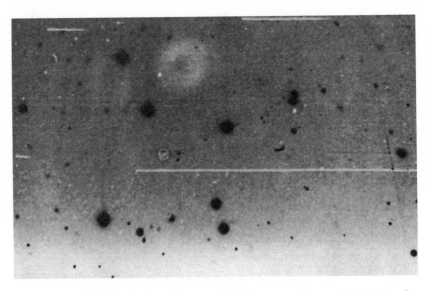

Figure 3. "'Noisy' CCD image." From James Elkins, *The Domain of Images* (Ithaca: Cornell University Press, 1999), 11. Courtesy Harvard-Smithsonian Center for Astrophysics.

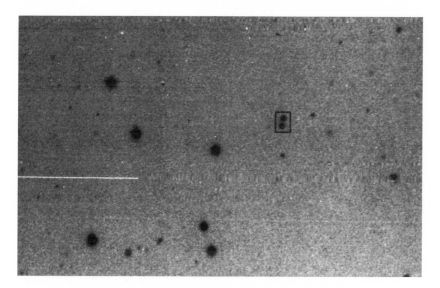

Figure 4. "Processed image, with cursor box drawn around the object QSO 0957+561."
From James Elkins, *The Domain of Images* (Ithaca: Cornell University Press, 1999), 12.
Courtesy Harvard-Smithsonian Center for Astrophysics.

lematic to the forefront, though from a different perspective, and convincingly unveils its symbiotic pervasiveness.[17] Citing as his example a contemporary practice, he points out that astronomers, in their effort to make images "as clear, unambiguous, simple, graphically elegant, and useful as possible," routinely "use a range of image-processing tools to 'clean up' the raw data by the telescopes."[18] Most revealing in Elkins's description of the astronomers' methods of handling the image is an informational-aesthetical value signified by the fact that they identify and characterize the image of the raw data pejoratively by way of an acoustic attribute, dubbing it "the 'noisy' image" (fig. 3), which is subsequently made over and turned into "the 'clean' image" or the silent image (fig. 4).[19] The noises, or more accurately put in Jakobson's terms, the "visual noises" that are removed from the noisy image include, in this particular case, "'electronic bias' (which makes the top of the first [figure] darker than the bottom), a 'donut' caused by out-of-focus dust in the telescope (top center), rows of 'burnt-out pixels' (the bright and dark horizontal lines), a spot of epoxy glue (left of center), and cosmic ray traces (the small dark spots)."[20] Furthermore, what undergirds such practice of visual beautification or silencing of noisy images, Elkins goes on to assert, is "the original, pre-Kantian sense of aesthetics as the 'perfecting of reality'" — an

aesthetics of ocularcentric refashioning of the world whereby denoised images are believed to offer "the most rational version of phenomena."[21]

The same holds true for the visual representation of crystals. In a way
analogous to but on a much different scale from the astronomers' cleanup
of noisy telescopic images, "the history of crystallography can be divided
into two large periods," Elkins observes, "before and after the Abbé Haüy's
Traité de minéralogie (1799) that helped formalize the representation of crystals."[22] Dependent upon a "style of direct and somewhat haphazard drawing"
commonly in use before Haüy, Moritz Anton Cappeller's *Prodromus crystal-*

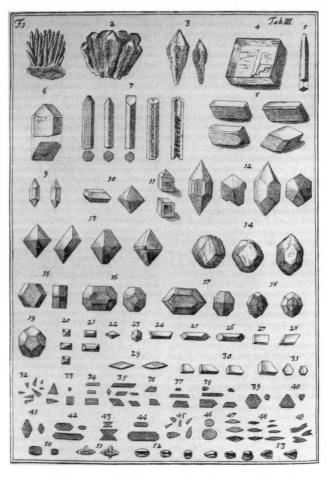

Figure 5. Moritz Anton Cappeller, "Drawing of various crystals" (1723).
From James Elkins, *The Domain of Images* (Ithaca: Cornell University
Press, 1999), 16.

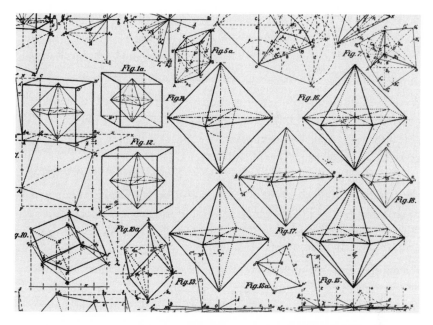

Figure 6. Ludwig Burmester, "Varieties of parallel projection of crystals, detail" (1922–23). From James Elkins, *The Domain of Images* (Ithaca: Cornell University Press, 1999), 17.

lographiæ (1723), Elkins points out, shows some noticeable visual noises as a result (fig. 5).[23] His unawareness of "a standardized light source," for instance, his method of "recording each specimen separately," his "attention paid to texture and shadows," and his episodic "rendering sensitive to the ordinary flaws that crystals always exhibit" are combined to produce noisy images of crystals, as evidenced, among many others, in "the imperfectly formed crystals in the right center, whose facets are curved and irregular."[24] By contrast, the work collated by Ludwig Burmester after Haüy in 1923 showcases processed images of crystals. It cleans up or silences the noises in Cappeller's images of crystals by foregrounding a constructivist visual strategy of representation. The method Burmester resorts to, more specifically, is "parallel projection," which makes it possible for the projected images of crystals to be "fully quantifiable" (fig. 6).[25] Elkins thus summarizes Burmester's graphic method and style and its resultant visual effect:

> Burmester, two hundred years later, has no interest in chiaroscuro, scale, or minor flaws. His forms are ideal geometric solids. . . . He is not recording "type specimens" or specimens of any kind but mathematical properties derived from many examples. . . . Burmester abstracts idealized types from the average of many

forms. . . . Burmester's plate is less a reminder of how actual specimens might look — though it is essential that it still functions in that way — than a non-naturalistic graphic notation in which lengths and angles can be measured directly from the picture.[26]

As such, Burmester's denoised projections of crystals "embody two mutually contradictory ideals," Elkins concludes, "quantitative rigor (which is available only with parallel projection) and perspectival illusion (as if these were crystals that could actually exist and be seen)."[27]

Though taken from different disciplines, Elkins's two examples illustrate the metaphysical mechanisms of "reduction of being to being represented."[28] Most suggestive in Elkins's observation of Burmester's method is the verb "abstract" as an optical operation, which signifies that his crystal drawing is none other than the visual "'construct' of the rational mind, and that its referent becomes the optical projection of a geometric system."[29] Once visually abstracted as such, the acoustic or noisy information in the crystals is "displaced by a pure conceptualization and eidetic logic best communicated [noiselessly] in writing."[30]

It is this exile of sound from the visual that avant-garde poetry parodies through its textual orchestrations of geometric figures, scientific schemata, technical charts, and mathematical notations. The innovative deployments of these visual forms thus perform a formal critique of the visual by way of a structural "repetition and reversal," which "[constitute] an implicit parody of [the forms'] own complicity in illusion."[31] Christian Bök's *Crystallography* resonates almost uncannily, in both concept and methodology, with Elkins's position in *The Domain of Images*. A few pages into the section subtitled "Euclid and His Modern Rivals," for instance, Bök duplicates the image of *Molécules intégrantes* by the Abbé Haüy (fig. 7), whose *Traité de minéralogie* (1799), as Elkins mentioned, marks the division of two large periods in the history of crystallography and helps to formalize the representation of crystals.[32] Bök's text that accompanies this denoised image reads as follows (fig. 8):

A botanist, by chance dropping
calcite shards, beholds them shatter
into regular patterns, every piece
a tiny brick of glass for building,
stack by stack, crystallographic
prison-house: riot cells for souls

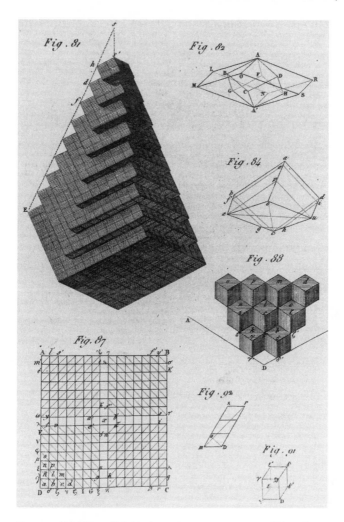

Figure 7. Abbé Haüy, "Molécules intégrantes in a quartzoid" (1822).
From James Elkins, *The Domain of Images* (Ithaca: Cornell University
Press, 1999), 19.

Already cued by a rather out-of-place "botanist" in this context, Bök's parody therein is most powerfully articulated, in part, through Elkins's *The Domain of Images* as its subtext. Haüy's *Molécules intégrantes,* as Elkins makes it clear, represents the idealized visual projection of "fundamental units that combine according to certain laws of *décroissement* to form crystals," and as Bök himself also references briefly in the biography section toward the end of his book, it is part of the search by neoclassicists for "'letters of the alphabet'" or "the geometric building blocks of nature."[33] The objective of this search that Bök alludes to in his text is thus fully explained in that of Elkins:

> When Haüy began, he actually broke large specimens into pieces, so that he could show that cleavage yields only smaller versions of minerals' characteristic shapes. He imagined that if such fragments could be broken and re-broken carefully enough, under the microscope, even the tiniest pieces on the verge of invisibility would have the same form.[34]

From this perspective, Bök's textual display of *Molécules intégrantes* dramatizes a self-reflexive mirror image of "the main movement in the history of crystal illustration: away from haphazard naturalism and toward geometric notation," as Elkins puts it, a neoclassical movement that "stressed schemata over substance, flattened lines over chiaroscuro and depth, and the tabula rasa of pure breathless abstraction over the lush Baroque undergrowth that seemed to be choking visual imagination."[35] In time, crystallography has developed and instituted a "'visual literacy,'" philosophical, aesthetic, as well as methodological, Elkins continues, which "has to be learned" precisely at the sacrifice of acoustic imagination.[36] It is in this sense, perhaps, that Haüy's *Molécules intégrantes* is reseen in Bök's visual poem as "crystallographic / prison-house: riot cells for souls."

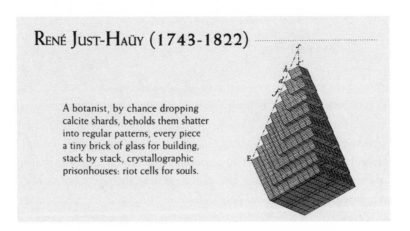

Figure 8. Christian Bök, "René Just-Haüy (1743–1822)." From *Crystallography* (Toronto: Coach House Press, 1994), n.p. Copyright © 1994 by Christian Bök. Reprinted with the permission of Coach House Books.

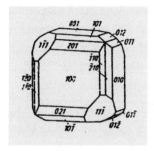

Figure 9. Christian Bök, "Crystal structure with numbers." From *Crystallography* (Toronto: Coach House Press, 1994), n.p. Copyright © 1994 by Christian Bök. Reprinted with the permission of Coach House Books.

Bök then further highlights the denoising nature of crystallography with a map of a crystal in the following section devoted to "W. H. Miller (1801–1880)" (fig. 9). "The map of a crystal is but a series of values, a set of ratios," he comments, "that do not let you see the form so much as show you how to build it into view." Hence a contrast: a noisy "seeing" situated in a concrete experience vis-à-vis a noiseless "view" constructed in an ideational isolation. Sounding a biting sarcasm against the noise-free transparency of crystallographic perception, Bök ends this section with a critical portraiture of crystallographers and their standardized method of drawing perfect crystals: "Crystallographers play connect-the-dots with these galaxies / of thought that emerge from the cloud chambers of a darkroom."

II

"If there is anything to be drawn from previous work in phenomenology, particularly from work concerned with perception," Ihde asserts, "the first result should be to understand that the primordial sense of experience is *global*"; and "For Merleau-Ponty and Heidegger," he specifies further, "the primordial experiences of being embodied or incarnate in a world are, if anything, even more strongly dependent upon the global character of primordial experience," which, more importantly, "is not experienced as being constructed from parts."[37] Against "'sense atomism,'" in which "'beliefs' lie deeply imbedded" and which "infects even the sciences at their 'metaphysical' level," Ihde then postulates "a phenomenological 'empiricism,'" a "style of thinking" that foregrounds "as foundational" a synthetic form in which this global experience occurs: "the object 'primitively' stands before us in all its diversity and richness and unity."[38] It is, stated otherwise, a phenomenological empiricism of interface, of a sound-vision "overlap."[39]

Such an empiricism raises, as its prologue, the question regarding the structural and perceptual mechanisms of the visual that deny this experiential overlap by habitually processing it into separate categories, with sound routinely silenced. By Ihde's account, the visual field has a built-in double structure: the intentional or noematic, and the experiential-attentional or noetic, each with its focus and fringe. Ihde thus outlines this double structure:

> [The] "structure" within visual experience . . . is for phenomenology an international structure. The noematic *core* or area of *focus* of the visual "world" is preliminarily distinguishable from its neomatic *fringe*. Correlatively, the act of attention *is* a focusing (noetic act) which as an experiential structure displays a central awareness which shades off into the barely aware or implicit consciousness which is at the "fringe" of a more explicit or focused attending.[40]

Perceptually, the visual field is organized into three zones of varying degrees of intentional intensity:

> Noematically the appearances of the visual "world" in most ordinary experience display (i), a *focal core,* that which stands out before one, the central "object" or object range of the visual intentionality; (ii), the peripheral fringe, situated in relation to the core but never absent even if not explicitly noted; (ii) shades off to (iii), the *horizon,* which is the "border" or limit of the visual field and its "beyond."
>
> Together (i), focus, and (ii), fringe, make up the totality of the visual field, the totality of explicit to implicit visual *presence.* The horizon (iii) is sensed as a limit to the "opening" which is the visual field, and this sense of limit is the first sense of horizon.[41]

Moreover, the operation of the visual within the visual field is predicated upon a "*ratio,*" as is already addressed implicitly by Elkins and stated explicitly by Bök, a ratio of the intentional to the experiential and, within the intentional, of the core to the fringe, of the explicit to the implicit, of the visible to the invisible, and of silence to noise.[42] With this ratio adjusted and maintained in direct proportion to the demands of telos, the visual demonstrates and asserts its authoritative intentionality by abstracting the world from an experiential realm into an intentional construct, from an acoustic chorus into a silent image, and from a plethora of signifiers into a transcendental signified. Such being the case, "the proximate way in which" sound could become physically manifest "lies at hand in the already exemplified distinctions of a ratio of focus-to-fringe and of the ratio of the explicit-to-the implicit."[43] If this ratio were adjusted otherwise or altered, in other words, one would then experience "a *field state*," in which, "phenomenologically, [one is] attending to nothing-in-particular, and the focal core itself [recedes] toward a limit of disappearance in the *blank stare* of boredom."[44] This field state of blank-stare at nothing-in-particular in turn reveals, by virtue of its optical dilation and defocusing, a phenomenological-experiential world in which sound or noise is heard, allowed in from beyond the visual totality of the core and the fringe, from the edge of the horizon, where it still exists, "whether intended or not," as John Cage has claimed, only in reverse ratio to the visual intensity of a transcendent intentionality.[45] It is a type of phenomenological seeing that sees "something," as John McCumber argues in his reading of Derrida and Plato, "which contains all things and puts eternal essences into the play of Becoming."[46]

Predicated upon a ratio in direct proportion to the effective silencing of sound, the visual operation of these structural and perceptual mechanisms is fully captured and parodied in avant-garde visual poetry. Christian Bök's *Crystallography* is, again, a case in point. In the section subtitled "Piezoelectricity," the poet produces, from left to right across two pages, a set of four images that outline, both metaphorically and literally, the structural and perceptual procedure leading to the visual production of logos out of sound or noise (fig. 10).[47] The subtitle is itself, for instance, already abundantly suggestive, in that "piezoelectricity" presents a phenomenological overlap of sound ("ultrasonic songs") and the visual ("Fireflies"), as is described and invoked in the first column of the text. Consisting of nothing but evenly formed "zi" as the transliteration of the piezoelectric noise, the first image from the left contributes to the suggestiveness of the subtitle further by unfolding a field state, in which the eye attends, indeed, to nothing-in-particular and, concomitantly, its visual focal core is dilated into a ratio-less and, therefore, all-embracing stare; hence a sound-visual overlap.

The second image from the left begins to show some changes, however. Its

```
ziziziziziziziziziziz    zizizizizi•iziziziziz    ZIzizIZIziIZiZiZizizIZ    ziziziziziziziziziziz
iziziziziziziziziziziz    izizizizi• ziziziziz     iziZI * izIZiZIziZIzI     iziziziMEANINGiziziz
ziziziziziziziziziziz    zizizizi • iziziziziz     ZiziZIzIziziZiZi * Zz     zizizCONSTITUTESziziz
iziziziziziziziziziziz    izizizizi • iziziziz      IzizIZiziZ * i IZiZizI    iziziziOURiziziziz
ziziziziziziziziziziz    ziziziziz * iziziziz       zi * IzIZIZiziZIZiziz     ziziziPOTENTIALiziziz
iziziziziziziziziziziz    izizizizi * iziziz        iZizIZiZIzIzIZ * Zizl     izizPIEZOELECTRICziziz
ziziziziziziziziziziz    ziziziziz * iziziz         ZIZIziZi * izIZIziZiz     iziziDISCHARGEiziziz
iziziziziziziziziziziz    izizizizi * zizizi        iziziZiziZiZIZiziZizl     iziziziziziziziziziz
```

Figure 10. Christian Bök, "zizizi . . ." ("Meaning, constitutes our . . ."). From *Crystallography* (Toronto: Coach House Press, 1994), n.p. Copyright © 1994 by Christian Bök. Reprinted with the permission of Coach House Books.

field state is now invaded, split in the middle by the penetration of a string of ever-expanding, bold-faced dots and asterisks, the visual appearances of which are devoid of any sound attributes and resist any acoustic rendering. In addition, described in terms of "flashbulbs," these dots and asterisks introduce a ratio into the field state by way of their "luminosities," which not only "awaken" intention from its state of attending into a "galvanic / life in their embrace," but also "brighten" the entire field state out of its nothing-in-particular by instituting a visual focal core at the center, thus pushing the "zi" noise proportionally toward the fringe and even the horizon.

With the use of vision-invoking words such as "watch," "stars," "asterisks," "ignite," and "television" in the accompanying text, the third image foregrounds the visual and its pervasive infiltration into what used to be the field state. Strategically located in the field, the asterisks now become irresistibly eye-catching by establishing and maintaining a proper ratio vis-à-vis the "zi" noise, each keeping the latter at a certain distance, repelling it into the background, by an illuminated and illuminating space. Derogated as "static jolts," noises now begin to assume an irregular and abnormal form ("iziZI"), and they seem to exist in the peripheral fringe for no other purpose than paying homage to the regularity and the normality of the visual.

From the third image, it is only a short step to arrive at the last one, in which logos ("MEANING / CONSTITUTES / OUR / POTENTIAL / PIEZOELECTRIC / DISCHARGE") is constructed by light for the eye ("Sparks, triboluminescent") out from the middle of noises ("zi," "manual typewriter," "keystroke"), which now fade into virtual silence in face of the imposing, overpowering sight at the center, the sight of word or meaning, that is, which, capable of being absorbed visually and silently, "does not transgress the norms of vision," as McCumber points out, though from a different perspective, "but fulfils them."[48]

As renditions of critical parody, these four images effectively bring into visibility, step by step, the structural and perceptual procedure operated by a ratio whereby an experiential sound-vision overlap is visually abstracted into an intentional vision-sound hierarchy.

III

"Do all things, when *fully* experienced, also sound forth?"[49] To this question by Ihde, the answer is affirmative, as is eloquently articulated in avant-garde visual poetry, which pursues, in addition, another objective: an antireductionist exploration of sound realms in the visual as the site of experiential possibilities yet to be realized. It follows, then, that this exploration finds its forms in the second type of visual configuration: random drawings, obscure forms, fuzzy shapes, and chaotic aggregates, among others. Underlying this exploration is a specifically phenomenological question: Since "sounds are 'first' experienced as sounds *of* things," as Ihde has asserted, what, then, is the sound shape of the visual configurations as such?[50]

In his study of "the shapes of sound," Ihde argues that "at the experiential level where sounds are heard as the sounds of things it is ordinarily possible to distinguish certain *shape-aspects* of those things," and that it is by no means "outrageous" to "*hear shapes*."[51] The example Ihde cites is a children's auditory game, in which one is asked to identify the shape of the object in a box by the sound it makes when the box is shaken and rolled. The result is that "the observer soon finds that it takes little time to identify simple shapes and often the object by its sound," be it that of "a marble" or "a die (of a pair of dice)."[52] In this sense, "the difference of shape has been *heard*," Ihde thus concludes, "and the shape-aspect has been auditorily discriminated."[53] However, sound shapes of things thus heard present a problem.

It is important to note that Ihde's observations and theorizing are based on what he specifies as "ordinary" or "usual daily activities."[54] Conducive to "virtually immediate" identifications of the sound shapes of things in these circumstances is an "auditory field" defined as a "context," which is characterized, more specifically, as "situated," "limited and bounded," and therefore graspable "anticipatorily."[55] In other words, things readily yield their shapes auditorily not so much because they are simple as because they are routinely experienced in a collective and conventional environment and, therefore, familiar, expected, recognizable, and determinable through habitual associations. Although Ihde is right by insisting that "the shape-aspects which are heard . . . must be strictly located in terms of their auditorily proper presentation and not predetermined or pre-limited by an already 'visualist' notion of shape," his own phenomenological approach, as is evidenced in the examples he has cited, does not transcend the contextually predetermined visualist sensibility and its corresponding methodology.[56]

Central to an exploratory rethinking of the sound shape of the visual is, again, the issue of values and ratios that Bök has pointed out earlier in his rereading of crystallography, the conventionally established determinants and coordinates that constitute the "functional difference between vision and audition."[57] Jakobson, for one, thus summarizes the prescriptive values in terms of time and space:

> Both visual and auditory perceptions obviously occur in space and time, but the spatial dimension takes priority for visual signs and the temporal one for auditory signs. A complex visual sign involves a series of simultaneous constituents, while a complex auditory sign consists, as a rule, of serial successive constituents.[58]

Describing such spatiotemporal differences between vision and sound more specifically as "asymmetries" maintained by tradition, Ihde presents them, similarly but more tellingly, by way of a descriptive contrast, which, further accentuated in terms of restricted economy, can be outlined as follows:

Vision: Spatial richness — Temporal poverty
Sound: Spatial poverty — Temporal richness[59]

While vision, differently put, foregrounds a space-dependent "simultaneity" of all constituents for an immediate access and comprehensive grasp through a perceptual-conceptual gestalt of clarity, sound privileges a time-sensitive "successivity" of constituents for an elongated experiential process of becoming. Hence, spacing as the value-ratio index for vision, and temporalizing as that for sound.[60]

To Jakobson's and Ihde's spatiotemporal specifications of sound and vision, McCumber adds an explanation that specifies the metaphysical terms underlying the traditionally determined and sanctioned asymmetries privileging vision over sound. There are, he asserts, "four aspects of vision that have traditionally found their way from the sensory up to the transcendental realm."[61] Of the four aspects, two of them are most pertinent to Jakobson's and Ihde's theorizing of the respective properties of sound and vision. "First, we cannot see the momentary," McCumber writes, "vision requires relatively fixed objects (or, as the Greeks might say, no *horao* without *horizo*: I cannot see without determining)"; it follows that "second, the realm of vision lies homogeneously open to our gaze."[62] By contrast, sound "disappears as it arises," and thus "it is the reverse of stability"; in addition, "sound does not appear as a single unity" but as a multiplicity.[63]

Vision, in other words, is a spatial operation armed with a metaphysical intention, and to see, in this sense, is to frame the fluctuating multitude into a timeless pattern of fixity and stability, to transcend the whirling chaos of noises into an ideally eternal form of silent clarity and transparency. Follow-

Figure 11. Steve McCaffery, "Tissue Text: 'OXO.'" From *Seven Pages Missing, Volume Two: Previously Uncollected Texts, 1968–2000* (Toronto: Coach House Books, 2000), 29. Reprinted with the permission of Coach House Books.

ing its rational mind that believes in an a priori homogeneity, to see is thus to predetermine the ordered shape of the world and to construct it in its corresponding image. Different from vision, sound, however, articulates a trajectory at once temporal and quotidian. To sound, in this view, is to announce the concomitant exit of sound, to render acoustically the fleeting moment of its own physicality. Transient and unstable, sound thus makes manifest audible traces of its varying tracks.

It is against this tradition and its established values that random drawings, obscure forms, fuzzy shapes, and chaotic aggregates make their appearances

Figure 12. Steve McCaffery, "Triple Random Field." From *Seven Pages Missing, Volume Two: Previously Uncollected Texts, 1968–2000* (Toronto: Coach House Books, 2000), 31. Reprinted with the permission of Coach House Books.

in avant-garde poetry as an immanent critique and re-vision. Among other critical objectives, they are intended, philosophically as Theodor Adorno has argued, "to dissolve the rigidity of the temporally and spatially fixed object into a field of tension of the possible and the real," and they do so by rewriting the constitutive value-ratio indexes that have hitherto determined the functional hierarchy of sound and vision.[64] With a textual appearance that resists and frustrates any attempt at either a visual determination or an auditory systematization known to a trained mind, these visual forms point to a world of sound-vision overlap yet to be imagined and articulated. And they begin to explore their own sound shapes by way of a reconfigured interface of spacing and temporalizing that break away from the fixed value-ratio indexes through a temporal expansion and a spatial extension, both grounded in and supported by the philosophy of general economy. As such, the newly created value-ratio index, as is invoked by these forms, finds its expression in "space's becoming-temporal, and time's becoming-spatial."[65]

That being the case, the sound of the shape of the visual is the shape of space in the visual becoming acoustically temporal; it is the shape of time in sound becoming visually spatial (figs. 11–12).

The sound shape of the visual is, then, a phenomenological interface of becoming in a participatory process of fully experiencing the world.

VISUAL EXPERIMENT AND
ORAL PERFORMANCE / BRIAN M. REED

What is the medium of poetry? This might seem an old-fashioned question, but it is also curiously difficult to answer. One can, after all, readily (albeit tentatively) answer the same question in regard to other art forms. What is sculpture? Sculpture involves the disposition of forms in space. What is music? Music is the arrangement of sounds within an interval of time. What is painting? Painting requires the application of pigment to a flat surface. But — what is a poem? Is it something heard? Overheard? Performed? Read silently on the page? Or, as Susan Stewart has argued, is it ultimately corporeal, a bodily rhythm that prompts toes to tap and heads to nod in time?[1] Lack of a clear or self-evident answer to this problem bespeaks a fundamental ambiguity within the field of poetics, namely, what exactly constitutes its object of study.

Lack of clarity on this point entails any number of practical consequences. Here is an instructive example drawn from contemporary Russian poetry, the opening of part 7 of the long poem *Osen' v lazarete nevinnykh sestior* (Autumn in the Lazaretto of the Innocent Sisters, 1977) by the neofuturist writer Elizaveta Mnatsakanova:

Я вернусь	как смеются	я вернусь	как сойдутся	
Я приду	сойдутся	я приду	слепятся слепые	
Я взгяну	сестрицы	я взгяну	глазницы	
я приду	сквозь	я взгяну	сквозь	слепые
я вернусь	пустые	я приду	пустые	пустые
я взгяну	глазницы	я войду	сквозь	глазницы
Взглядом	я рядом	тем взглядом	мертвым взглядом	
Мертвым	тем ядом	белым ядом	я рядом мерным	
тем ядом	я рядом	я рядом	глазницы	

[Ia vernus'	kak smeiutsia	ia vernus'	kak soidutsia	
Ia pridu	soidutsia	ia pridu	slepiatsia slepye	
Ia vzglianu	sestritsy	ia vzglianu	glaznitsy	
ia pridu	skvoz'	ia vzglianu	skvoz'	slepye
ia vernus'	pustye	ia pridu	pustye	pustye
ia vzglianu	glaznitsy	ia voidu	skvoz'	glaznitsy
Vzgliadom	ia riadom	tem vzgliadom	mertvym vzgliadom	
Mertvym	tem iadom	belym iadom	ia riadom mernym	
tem iadom	ia riadom	ia riadom	glaznitsy]²	

Part 7 of Mnatsakanova's poem begins with a slightly unusual page layout. Clumps of words are suspended free-floating within a staggered, gridlike pattern. This odd arrangement, it is important to note, hinders but does not preclude standard Russian reading practice, that is, movement from word to word, left to right, top to bottom of a page. One can, in fact, make out nine distinct and separate lines of verse, the first of which reads, "Ia vernus' kak smeiutsia ia vernus' kak soidutsia" (I will arrive as they laugh I will arrive as they gather). There is important visual confirmation, too, that this is the proper way for a reader to navigate the text. The only capital letters to appear in the opening passage do so flush against the left-hand margin: three capital *Я*'s, a *B,* and an *M.* Since capital letters, in Russian as in English, designate the beginning of a sentence, the implication — especially strong in regard to the three capital *Я*'s — is that we are looking at sentences unfurling left to right across the page in parallel fashion, peculiarly punctuated, true, but probably so for reasons of dramatic effect.

This set of conclusions about the poem are wholly rational. Yet there happens to exist a CD recording of Mnatsakanova reciting *Osen' v lazarete nevinnykh sester* in which she treats the opening of part 7 differently.³ She chooses to read each clump of words individually, top to bottom, before moving on to the next. In other words, as performed, part 7 begins: "Ia vernus' / Ia pridu / Ia vzglianu / kak smeiutsia / soidutsia / sestritsy" (I will return / I will arrive / I will look / as the sisters / laugh / [and] gather). The divergence between what the page suggests and what the poet recites creates a dilemma for a critic. If one wishes to quote the beginning of part 7 in the course of an article, which word order ought to be preferred? Which takes precedence, the written text or the oral performance? Which medium is accorded greater weight?

This kind of scenario arises fairly often when writing poetry criticism.

One has to judge between competing versions of a poem before proceeding with an analysis. Fields such as early modern textual studies, African American studies, and the study of avant-garde writing have proven especially good at elucidating and theorizing the persistently "multimedia" character of the art of poetry, that is, its proclivity for dissemination via a variety of different channels of communication.[4] Such scholarship has not yet, however, had much impact on business as usual in the field of poetics more generally, where a certain set of assumptions about visual-verbal relations remains the norm, what Jacques Derrida long ago diagnosed as phonocentrism.

Since the eighteenth century, most — though by no means all — Western critics and poets have tended to assume, implicitly or explicitly, that a poem, whatever else it might be, can be understood as representing a script for possible oral performance. This way of thinking has important ramifications. When picking up a book of poems, for example, a reader scans a given page and decides what counts and does not count as part of a poem by reference to an imagined scene in which a person reads the text aloud. Things that cannot plausibly or realistically be included in such a reading — page numbers, line numbers, annotations, illustrations, choice of font — are deemed to be extrinsic to the "real" poem. In the process, the concretely visual, that which an actual eye takes in, is effaced or displaced.

Similarly, if somewhat paradoxically, the oral, too, is rendered marginal, in the sense of something physically heard. Any given recitation or performance of a poem is almost always considered to be only one possible realization of a poem under contingent local circumstances. "The poem," as it is cited or analyzed in the course of a conference paper or other scholarly work, typically refers to a script that somehow precedes, and remains uninflected by, the act of reading aloud. The poem has something to do with sound, of course — one can scan it metrically, for instance, or talk about its intonation and tone — but it remains less vocalized than vocalizable, that is, susceptible to entering the everyday soundscape while remaining somehow outside it, or better yet, prior to it. As a script for possible oral performance, then, a poem becomes a quasi-transcendental entity. It escapes the empirical and phenomenal world and becomes accessible more to the intellect and the imagination than to the five senses. As a consequence, the question of what is the medium proper to poetry never really arises or becomes vexatious, since "the poem," as a subject for literary analysis, necessarily precedes any debasing fall into embodiment.

Significantly, the existence of verse that runs counter to this logic is rarely seen as disproving or unsettling it. Rather, poetry that places a pronounced emphasis on its material realizations tends to be labeled inferior, bad, or childish. Avant-garde sound poetry such as Hugo Ball's and slam poetry such as Saul Williams's stray too close to pure oral performance and therefore tend to be greeted with embarrassment by the scholarly establishment.[5] Verse that depends heavily on visual play for its effects is likewise frequently considered superficial or wrongheaded. George Herbert's seventeenth-century pattern poetry, for example, has regularly been dismissed as "false wit," from Joseph Addison down to the present day — as if, by providing images for eyes to appreciate, it perversely refused fulfilling the art's higher calling, crafting imagery for the imagination to view in the mind's internal theater.[6]

A quasi-immaterial text that relates to but precedes speech and that, moreover, subtends an array of evaluative judgments: this way of thinking about poetry offers a classic, point by point illustration of Derrida's idea of phonocentrism. Derrida saw phonocentrism as a fundamental wrong turn within the history of Western thought, and throughout his career he vigorously opposed its insidiousness. In *Of Grammatology* (1967), he famously offered alternative models for poetic composition. Above all, he held up Ezra Pound's poetry as possessing great "historical significance." Pound's long-term "fascination with the Chinese ideogram" led him to break with Western metaphysics by pursuing an "irreducibly graphic poetics."[7] Derrida appears to have had in mind Pound's gradual move toward including Chinese characters in his own verse, exemplified best by the later *Cantos*. The use of this script, or so the argument runs, introduces a stubbornly visual and non-vocalizable stratum to the poetry, thereby blocking the dynamics essential to phonocentric thinking.

In the first line reproduced in figure 1, for instance, a Chinese character meaning "middle" appears between the Italian words "Nel mezzo" and the English phrase "the crystal." This moment is multiply self-referential. The Italian translates as "In the middle." Just as the character consists of a vertical line bisecting a square, so too it splits a line in two — a line, furthermore, that appears in the middle of a canto in the midst of a very long poem. Pound situates a reader where Dante Alighieri did so long ago, "nel mezzo del cammin di nostra vita," in the middle of our life's course, except that Pound characteristically places that "middle" not in a "selva oscura," a dark wood, but in an obscure text. Here we are, arrested amid life's flux, bending over a book. These implications become apparent when visually inspecting canto 100, but how could an oral performance ever convey the same ideas without

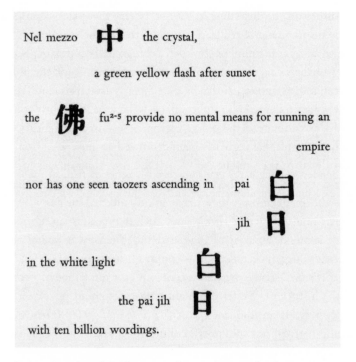

Figure 1. Ezra Pound, "Nel mezzo . . ." From *Canto 100* (738).

an elaborate tedious digression? Writing as something seen trumps its role as something to be read aloud.

Derrida's thoroughgoing opposition to phonocentrism and his identification of phonocentrism with a primal fall in Western thought provide a frame to his comments on Pound in *Of Grammatology* that can easily lead his readers to conclude that the *Cantos* provide a model for radical political praxis. Appeal to the eye, not the ear, and ¡arriba la revolución! Steve McCaffery's early publication *CARNIVAL the second panel* (1977) is exemplary in this regard (see fig. 2). A sprawling sixteen-panel work intended to be assembled and hung on a wall, it combines pell-mell typewritten text with texts transferred by xerography, carbon paper, and other means. Lines and letters occupy a variety of clashing oblique spatial orientations. Overprinting, smudging, blurring, and other effects greatly reduce its legibility, even when viewed up close. In a 1975 introduction McCaffery mentions Pound four times and the *Cantos* twice as inspirations for *CARNIVAL* and its vigorous opposition to speech-based verse.[8] He explains that his visual experiments are calculated to achieve certain ends. First, he wants viewers initially to encounter the piece all at once as a "seen thing," to give them "the privilege of distance onto language as something separate." From this "peak" perspective, they should then begin to perceive that the poem's "conflicts and contradictions are accommodated in a form based more on free flight of its particulars than on rigid component control." And as they begin to attend to the composition's details, they "experience . . . non-narrative language":

> There are no clues to passage for the reader other than the one phrase of Kung's: "make it new," move freely, as the language itself moves, along one and more of the countless reading paths available, through zones of familiar sense into the opaque regions of the unintelligible, and then out again to savour the collision of the language groupings.[9]

In such rhetoric, one encounters the familiar avant-garde equation between formal innovation and an increase in personal (and by extension political) freedom. What makes this restatement news is the accompanying thesis that

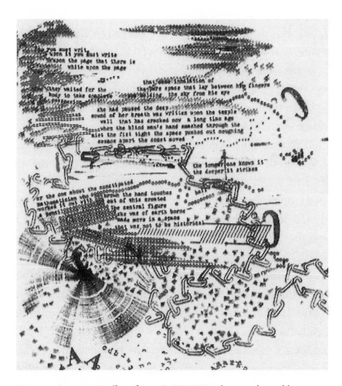

Figure 2. Steve McCaffery, from *CARNIVAL the second panel* (1970–1975). Courtesy of Steve McCaffery.

one gesture in specific, "subordinat[ing] the semantic to visual effects," somehow crucially advances this emancipatory project.[10]

While this kind of utopian response to the Derridean critique of phonocentrism might give rise to fascinating poetry, it nonetheless underestimates the degree to which deconstructive thinking requires not simply inverting a value-laden binary but also unpacking and superseding it. One should try not so much to elevate the visual over the auditory as to undo the crispness of that distinction and in the process render any impulse to assign precedence moot. In this particular case, the deconstructive cause is furthered once one realizes that Derrida's adulatory aside concerning Pound is imprecise and therefore misleading. As Yunte Huang and other critics have noted, Chinese characters are hardly "irreducibly graphic" — if one happens to be an educated literate speaker of Mandarin (or of any other language that employs them as a writing system).[11] The first line in figure 1 can be read aloud with ease by a bilingual speaker for whom the character for "middle" and its Pinyin romanization *zhōng* would represent interchangeable ways of referring to the same Saussurean sound-image.

Pound, too, is fully aware that Chinese characters can be read aloud. Indeed, he wants his readers to appreciate that fact. The three characters in figure 1 that appear after *zhōng* are each carefully paired with phonetic transliterations. These transliterations might be old-fashioned (they follow the Wade-Giles system), and, in the case of "pai" and "jih," they might lack the required tonal markings — in Pinyin *fú* would replace "fu²⁻⁵," *bái* would replace "pai," and *rì* would replace "jih" — but they do create a prominent redundancy, a pairing of two modes of inscription such that even monolingual speakers of English, if alert, ought to recognize that characters possess phonetic values. Ever the pedagogue, Pound goes so far in this passage as to repeat "pai jih" twice alongside the same characters to drive the point home (as well as pairing iteration number two with an English translation, "white light").

None of this implies that Derrida is one hundred percent wrong. As shown earlier, there is visual play in the *Cantos* that cannot be readily performed orally. Read aloud, the verse in figure 1 would lose the rich visual punning on the word "middle." Then there are the paired transliterations and characters. Does one vocalize both, creating a peculiar stutter: "fú fú," "bái bái rì rì"? That would seem ridiculous, yet the alternative is to omit words clearly present on the page. Similarly, how does one recite the last three lines of the passage? If one does choose to read the passage's characters aloud, should it go "in the white bái / the pai jih rì / with ten billion wordlings" — an ordering that preserve normal English left-to-write word progression? Such a rendering, though, would separate the characters *bái* and *rì,* thereby violating their placement on the page in traditional Chinese top-to-bottom word order. Respecting that word order, however, would require a hybrid path across the page, with the left-to-right verses — "in the white light / the pai jih / with ten billion worldlings" — interrupted at some arbitrary point, perhaps during one or the other line break, by the words "bái rì."

In short, though one certainly can read the later *Cantos* aloud, they also inhibit any unreflective or automatic treatment of them as a script for performance. They make overtly troublesome the process of what contemporary media theorists and cultural semioticians call "transmediation," "the act of translating meanings from one sign system to another."[12] One discovers that moving from page to performance inevitably incurs a set of denotative and connotative losses. Such losses, though, are not lamentable fallings-away from an Edenic ur-text. Readers familiar only with the earth-tone-orange New Directions tome are in for quite a surprise if they visit the collection of recordings available on PennSound's Ezra Pound page.[13] There they will discover entirely new, unexpected dimensions to the *Cantos.* The author's intonation, rhythm of delivery, choice of dialect, spontaneous interjections, occasional use of drum accompaniment, pauses for breath, and other performative devices all richly influence the poem's course and progress. And, of course, these aural techniques cannot be readily translated back into print, either. Like visual play on the page, they remain stubbornly medium-specific. Transmediation rarely if ever results in works that correspond in a precise one-to-one fashion since no two media address the same sense or mix of senses in exactly the same way.

Derrida's comments on Pound's *Cantos* are insightful and valuable, once one qualifies them slightly. The Chinese writing system is not in itself "irreducibly graphic," nor does the mere presence of characters in the *Cantos* magically create a breach in Western metaphysics. Rather, Pound purposefully employs them in such a way as to draw attention to an "irreducibly graphic" stratum that any written text could potentially exploit. He does not thereby prove that writing is somehow superior to speech. Rather, he reveals that written texts, like orally performed ones, can accomplish unique ends. This argument could be extended to painting, sculpture, dance, music, or any other artistic medium. They all offer distinct advantages and disadvantages;

authors and artists adapt to (or resist or sometimes outright defy) these don-nées as they seek how best to realize their aesthetic intuitions. Phonocen-trism rests on a false and hierarchical ranking of two out of many possible means of communication.

The field of poetics must come to terms with this principle and its ramifi-cations. A written text and a live performance are not related in the manner of original and copy. One might precede the other chronologically, in which case one can talk about its "transmediation" from one medium to another, but they remain different instantiations of the same work and should be judged separately, on their own terms. A popular poem, such as Allen Ginsberg's *Howl* (1956), might in fact exist in a multiplicity of versions — in print, on audiotape, on videotape, on CD, on DVD, and so forth — that vary widely in quality, utility, and interest, from the classic (the 1955 Six Gallery read-ing) to the banal (amateur recitations on YouTube). All versions, however, must share sufficiently many family resemblances that audiences, after being exposed to one or to a small set, can recognize the others as also belonging to an open-ended series of texts and performances called *Howl* that can be assigned to Ginsberg's name.

This manner of defining a poem — and of ascribing authorship — obvi-ously introduces a host of questions, not least the problem of where one ceases to talk about "versions" and has to start using labels such as "paro-dies," "imitations," and "revisions."[14] Revamping the field of poetics so as to make it truly nonphonocentric will likely require a thorough reassessment of many of the discipline's basic concepts — as well as of its cherished literary-historical narratives. What would a history of Anglo-American modernism look like, for example, that places equal emphasis on performed and pub-lished verse? Would poets such as Vachel Lindsay, whose "higher vaudeville" so impressed W. B. Yeats, and Dylan Thomas — a pioneer in recording and broadcasting verse — end up as central canonical figures? All such matters deserve to be explored much more fully than space here permits. This essay will have to content itself with a simpler task, observing that the problem of transmediation has long been a lively and productive area of inquiry among poets themselves. They have much to teach scholars about opportunities for nonphonocentric criticism, once they learn where to look (and listen).

In the mid-twentieth century, for example, the U.S.-based Black Moun-tain School took advantage of certain advances in typewriter design — most notably the invention of the tab key — to develop a set of easily reproducible visual cues intended to govern the transmediation between oral and written versions of a poem. Essays such as Charles Olson's "Projective Verse" (1950) and Denise Levertov's "Some Notes on Organic Form" (1965) sought to codify the aural equivalents of linebreaks, indentation, punctuation, and word spacing. While reading aloud passages such as the following, Robert Duncan famously resorted to an orchestra conductor's hand gestures to insure adherence to his own elaborate self-imposed canon of rules:

> remember this time   for it returns this betrayal of what we are
>   among the people likewise   armd   camps arise, and
>   *agents provocateurs* keep the source of the trouble alive
>   — in his Hell Cantos he named it
>   "*the slough of unamiable liars,*
>   *bog of stupidities,*
>   *malevolent stupidities, and stupidities*"
>   — we've got it   with new faces.
>   In the highest   this hatred
> doing away with public services as the cost of the government's self-service rises,
> in every domain fighting to destroy the humanities[15]

"My hands keep time and know more than my brain does of measure," as Duncan puts it in a preface to *Ground Work: Before the War* (1984), which then goes on to explain in detail how his typography dictates proper oral delivery.[16] Although the Black Mountain writers are usually remembered for endorsing a speech-based poetics — hence, for instance, Steve McCaffery's explicit "repudiation" of Olson's reliance on "breath" in *CARNIVAL the second panel* — it is significant that their discussions of speech often also concern the minutiae of page layout.[17] Additionally, the Black Mountain School is perhaps best known for the influential "projectivist" look of its free verse, that is, its bold arrangement of phrases and lines suspended in white space. Instead of decisively favoring oral performance over print in the manner of, say, the 1970s Last Poets,[18] the Black Mountain poets can more accurately be said to have aimed for frictionless transmediation. They hoped to minimize the divide between written and spoken versions of a poem. Ideally, having heard a poem recited, one should be able to notate it perfectly, and, having read it on the page, one should be able to recite it as its author intended.

Other poets have taken an opposite path and accentuated the difficulties inherent in transmediation. The post–World War II British poet Bob Cobbing, for one, finds excitement where the Black Mountain poets would perceive sloppy craft, namely, a situation in which readers might not know how to vocalize a text. He delights in increasing confusion, composing works where few if any standard methods for performing a poem apply. *Jade-Sound Poems* (1984) is a representative sample.[19] It contains a sequence of narrow, roughly vertical columns of oversized letters and punctuation. The title suggests that these are "poems" that can be "sounded," and in fact Cobbing frequently employed comparable pieces as scores for avant-garde sound poetry, performed solo or in groups. It is not at all apparent, though, how a person should (or could!) read such verse aloud. Faced with the piece in figure 3, for example, what is one supposed to do with a word that begins with an exclamation point? If it were upside down, one might proceed by analogy with Spanish, but this punctuation mark is right-side up. Does it perhaps indicate a clicking sound, as it would in a southern African name such as N!xau (the star of the film *The Gods Must Be Crazy* [1980])? And what does one do with an unpronounceable consonant cluster like *kxv*? Worse, further down is a mysterious nonletter that looks like the Greek letter lambda. Or is it an upside-down *V*? It visually echoes an earlier *V* — a *V* toward which the eye is drawn by an identical V-shape, above and to the right, that makes up half a *W*. The letter *Y*, too, which appears beneath and to the left, contains another *V*. Once one starts seeing *V*'s and *A*'s it is hard to stop thinking about reflections — or perhaps rotations. The *O* in the center looks suspiciously like a pivot around which the other letters might spin. (That might, after all, explain how the exclamation point ended up at the top of the page instead of at the bottom.) The longer one stares, the more the letters seem to flip and move. One even begins to see words that simply are not there: wow, vow, wok, and the Latin *vox,* meaning "voice." And here one arrives back at the original problem — how to give voice to such a peculiar text. Asked to perform *Jade-Sound Poems* orally, readers are forced to think, reflect, and, above all, look. They are free to invent rules or intuitively improvise moment to moment — which means that no two people are likely to perform *Jade-Sound Poems* in remotely similar ways — but, courtesy of the writing's obdurate resistance to transmediation, they all surely undergo an intense experience of the poetry as a material, tangible artifact, a set of unusual marks on a page. Curiously, then, the process of figuring out how to vocalize Cobbing's texts enriches one's appreciation of them as both a visual and a verbal construct. By impeding transmediation he paradoxically achieves something similar to what the Black Mountain poets accomplish by easing it: an assertion of the close relationship between sight and sound in the act of reading a poem.

A third option is to make the act of transmediation itself the subject of

Figure 3. Bob Cobbing, untitled poem from *Jade-Sound Poems* (1984). Courtesy of Lawrence Upton.

one's work. In *Musica Iconologos* (1993), the Tokyo Fluxus artist Yasunao Tone revisits the problem of the phonetic value of Chinese writing in a way utterly unforeseen by Pound, Derrida, or their respective commentators.[20] He makes classical Chinese verse audible by literalizing the idea that a poem constitutes a script for performance. First, he scanned the relevant poetry into a computer. Then he ran the resulting digital images through software designed to play a musical score. Most human musicians would be flummoxed if presented with such a challenge — imagine a violinist confronted with the characters *zhōng, bái,* and *rì* superimposed on a musical staff and ordered to play them — but computer programs know no better and will follow exactly the same algorithms for translating visuals into audio whether fed the Confucian odes or the Queen of the Night's aria from *Die Zauberflöte* (1791).[21] The end result: intermittent rapid buzzing bursts of frantic electronic noise. While *Musica Iconologos* has an austere beauty well worth savoring in its own right, like many post–World War II process-based pieces its conceptual implications are arguably its most stimulating aspect. Can one truly consider it a "reading" of a group of poems? In what sense? Does this piece qualify as a musical setting of the poems — turning them into "lyrics" of another sort? Is this what Chinese characters "really" sound like? Yasunao

Tone calls into question — and thereby brings into the open so that people can scrutinize — the many assumptions and conventions that guide the performance of more traditional texts.

Twenty-first century poets might have the most to teach literary critics about literary-critical analysis that privileges no one medium in particular. The present age rewards individuals with access to and skill using a range of different means of communications: email, cell phone, text messaging, digital photography, streaming video, podcasting, and so forth. Why limit oneself to publishing a chapbook with a small press when sound files uploaded to the internet can travel further, faster, and cheaper? Nowadays many poets have Web pages that promote the full range of their work, including everything from blogs to poem drafts to webcasts of their latest public readings. Not surprisingly, this broad media literacy has had profound effects on how and what certain authors write. One consequence has been the emergence of figures who define a poem less as a one-off artwork ("I just wrote a poem!") than as a cluster of related works in different media ("hmm, now let's try that again, but let's do it another way!"). Caroline Bergvall's "About Face" (2005), for example, exists in a number of divergent versions, including live performances, live recordings, printed copies, online copies, and published working notes.[22] Kenneth Goldsmith's *Fidget* (2000) is a performance piece, a gallery installation, a book, and an e-poem.[23] Christian Bök's *Eunoia* (2001) is a book, an e-book, an e-poem, and a recording available at UbuWeb.com.[24] Such "cross-platform" writers treat each new medium as a chance to explore how a work might unfold differently under different conditions. When Goldsmith took *Fidget* online, for instance, he decided to have the words move in three dimensions and to make the piece interactive. The occasion of transmediation becomes a spur to innovation. The poem renews itself from instantiation to instantiation.

A few words about one contemporary poet, Sawako Nakayasu, can usefully draw this chapter to a close. On the page, Nakayasu's *So We Have Been Given Time or* (2004) takes as its starting point the tradition of the closet drama. Throughout the long poem appear headings, in all caps, flush left, that recall the stage directions at the start of a dramatic script: CHARACTERS, TIME, PLACE, and so on.[25] Other sorts of words creep in, however, some literary-critical (RESOLUTION, PLOT, CONFLICT), and others intrusively random (BLANKLY, SKIP, EAT).[26] These headings introduce fanciful catalogs of variable length. Nakayasu pokes fun at the idea that a poem represents a script for possible oral performance by providing readers with a text nearly impossible to stage:

CHARACTERS: geography enthusiast, twice removed.

brother, as in your.

or as in oh.

young czech intellectual, female.

estranged or expatriated cousin, male.

young man of marrying age, recent dumpee.

his too-kind mother, a goose.

owner of the voice on the answering machine.

soccer player whiffing a penalty kick.

bartender outside of his natural environment.

innocent spectators.

fish butcher.

man later determined as yang, the active male principle.[27]

"[G]eography enthusiast" here is almost certainly an allusion to Gertrude Stein, author of *Geography and Plays* (1922), whose pieces for theater likewise push the boundaries of theatrical possibility. Nakayasu, like Stein, slyly suggests that the only playhouse capable of staging her artistry is the page itself, the space wherein written language cavorts.

This moral obviously does not translate well into oral performance. *So We Have Been Given Time or* cannot be read aloud continuously word-for-word without blunting the book's medium-specific message. A reading from October 2004 shows Nakayasu's awareness that the poem had to proceed differently to suit the circumstances.[28] She begins working her way through the poem "straight," but, a few minutes in, she switches from English to Japanese. Then she switches back. With increasing rapidity, with dazzling stop-on-a-dime timing, she modulates between English, English-accented Japanese, Japanese-accented English, and Japanese. She thereby highlights something that Pound, in his use of Chinese writing, underplays: the power dynamics involved. In the *Cantos* he has the audacity to present himself as teacher of a language in which he is not proficient, and he presumes that his audience is less proficient than he. (I've had native speakers respond to Pound's Chinese instruction with everything from perplexity to anger to laughter.) As a bilingual immigrant, Nakayasu is acutely sensitive to what it means to speak in front of a U.S. audience. She has abundant experience with the complex ways in which race, gender, language skills, and citizenship status inflect an audience's reception of a speaker's words. Accordingly, she takes a poem about theater and turns it into a virtuosic demonstration of her mastery of the art of oral performance. Moreover, she demonstrates how bilingualism, instead of placing one in a precarious intermediary position, in reality enables entirely new forms of expression. In addition, by deemphasizing the semantic content of the poem in favor of thespian pyrotechnics, she makes it possible for a range of people with differing kinds and degrees of linguistic competency to listen appreciatively. If the print version of *So We Have Been Given Time or* looks back to Steinian modernism, the 2004 reading of the poem has closer affinities with the macaronic postmodern performance poetry of Miguel Algarín and Guillermo Gomez-Peña.

This essay opened with a question: What is the medium of poetry? Contemporary poets such as Bergvall, Bök, Goldsmith, and Nakayasu suggest that there is a better question: What can this medium do for poetry? Language comes to us always already in a mediated form, and poetry is a language-based art with a penchant for reflecting on its channels of communication. The last two decades have seen an unprecedented proliferation of media that are cost-effective enough for a large percentage of the public to make use of them on a regular basis. If critics cease to hold poetry at a quasi-transcendental remove from the material world, they might discover that it offers unparalleled opportunities for coming to grips with the new media ecology. Poets, as they experiment with transmediation, serially bring to light each medium's textures, contours, and inner logic. As ever, antennae of the human race, they feel out the paths for the rest of us to follow.

POSTLUDE: I LOVE SPEECH

KENNETH GOLDSMITH

I am an American poet, and like most Americans, I speak only one language. When asked to publish this piece in an American anthology, I figured that the last thing you, dear reader, needed was more American culture (remember the Clash's "I'm So Bored with the U.S.A."?). Hence, I've decided to write this piece in English, a language that I neither speak nor write.

Most likely, you can't understand a word I'm writing, even though it's your native language. So, we're even: we're both in a situation of not understanding. All we can possibly do is to look at the way these English words sit on this page instead of trying to understand what they mean. And by doing so we are both entering into a new relationship to language that permits us to view the language through the lens of the opaque, the mundane.

For years, I've been working toward a situation like the one we find ourselves in now: one where language is purely formal and concrete; like language itself, this essay is both meaningful and meaningless at the same time. The page is now thick with words posing as language.

I could continue and write the rest of the piece in English but I think you get the point. After this rough beginning, you can better understand what I'm trying to do with my work: to approximate the utopian situation we find ourselves in at the moment, one of willful ignorance.

I LOVE SPEECH

Recordings made of Wittgenstein's *Zettel* in German by an English speaker: a language neither read nor understood, so horribly mispronouncing the words that German speakers who hear it don't recognize it as German.

285

Everyone, absolutely everyone, was tape-recording everyone else. Machinery had already taken over people's sex lives — dildos and all kinds of vibrators — and now it was taking over their social lives, too, with tape recorders and Polaroids. Since I wasn't going out much and was home a lot in the mornings and evenings, I put in a lot of time on the phone gossiping and making trouble and getting ideas from people and trying to figure out what was happening — and taping it all.

The trouble was, it took so long to get a tape transcribed, even when you had somebody working at it full-time. In those days even the typists were making their own tapes.

The beauty of it all is that Cage need do so little — nothing, really — to make this turning of our minds happen. He just opens the window, turns on his tape recorder. Like Thoreau, Cage is a master at simply noticing things.

In 1996, I wrote a book called *Soliloquy* that was every word I spoke and utterance I made for a week, unedited, from the moment I woke up on a Monday morning until the moment I went to bed on Sunday night. When published, it totaled five hundred pages.

Since transcribing the *Soliloquy* tapes, I've never heard language in quite the same way. Sometimes, when someone is speaking to me, I'll stop understanding what they're saying and instead begin to hear the formal qualities of their speech — utterances, stumbling, divergent thoughts, and sounds.

When transposed onto the page, it's an extremely disjunctive text — every bit as disjunctive as any work of high modernism.

It's an ext. . . . . um, an extremely, uh, disjunctive . . . wait, what was I saying? Uh, oh, yeah? What did you . . . ? It's an extre, uh, you know, uh, ex, ext, ah, uh huh . . . work of modernis . . . yeah, OK.

Theater and movies after *Soliloquy* are inevitably disappointing. I now hear the studied and stilted way that the actors speak: Too clean, too directional, less complex than everyday speech.

Real speech, when paid close attention to, forces us to realize how little one needs to do in order to write. Just paying attention to what is right under our noses — framing, transcription, and preservation — is enough.

The rise of appropriation-based literary practices: Suddenly, the familiar or quotidian is made unfamiliar or strange when left semantically intact. No need to blast apart syntax. The New Sentence? The Old Sentence, reframed, is enough.

I LOVE SPEECH

I used to be an artist; then I became a poet; then a writer. Now when asked, I simply refer to myself as a word processor.

There is no museum or bookstore in the world better than our local Staples.

It is the transcription that makes the writing. How does one transcribe a radio broadcast? Since spoken language contains no punctuation, what choices go into the act of transcription? Does one decide to flow the language as a never-ending stream without punctuation or pause, or does one decide to parse it according to standard rules of grammar? David Antin, for example, never uses punctuation whilst transcribing; instead he connotes pauses and inflection, using graphical space between the words.

The necessity of bad transcription: working to make sure that the pages in the book matched the way the high-school typist had transcribed them, right down to the last spelling mistake. I wanted to do a "bad book," just the way I'd done "bad movies" and "bad art," because when you do something exactly wrong, you always turn up something.

The sensuality of copying gigabytes from one drive to another: the whirr of the drive, intellectual matter manifested as sound.

I wish that they would graft an additional device onto the radio — one that would make it possible to record and archive for all time everything that can be communicated by radio. Later generations would then have the chance of seeing with amazement how an entire population, by making it possible to say what they had to say to the whole world, simultaneously made it possible for the whole world to see that they had absolutely nothing to say.

I'm interested in a valueless practice, in quantifying and concretizing the vast amount of "nutritionless" language; I'm also interested in the process itself being equally nutritionless.

Like morality, politics seems an unavoidable condition when we are engaging in the framing of public language and discourse.

Entartete Sprache.

I LOVE SPEECH

I sympathize with the protagonist of a cartoon claiming to have transferred x amount of megabytes, physically exhausted after a day of downloading. The simple act of moving information from one place to another today constitutes a significant cultural act in and of itself. I think it's fair to say that most of us spend hours each day shifting content into different containers. Some of us call this writing.

In the Middle Ages, composers' songs were routinely printed on broadsides and sold on the street for pennies. One minor composer, however, was clever and included beautifully hand-drawn images on his scores. Over the ages, they were framed and preserved, not so much because of the music, but because of how beautiful and distinctive they were as objects. While his peers' music — printed and distributed in the same form but without any decoration — vanished, this composer's scores remain as the only existing examples of the genre. Hence they are now considered musical classics.

The act of listening has now become the act of archiving. We're more interested in accumulation and preservation than we are in what is being collected.

Rabelais tells of a winter battle when it was so cold that the sounds created during the battle instantly froze upon hitting the air, falling to the ground, never reaching the ears of the combatants. When springtime arrived, these long inaudible sounds began to melt randomly, creating a racket by skewing their original temporal sequences of action. It was suggested that some of the frozen sounds be preserved for later use by packing them in oil and straw, when an objection was made: "'Tis a folly to hoard up what we are never like to want, or have always at hand."

The endless cycle of textual fluidity: from imprisonment to emancipation, back to imprisonment, then freed once more. The balance between dormant text warehoused locally and active text in play on the expanded field. Language in play. Language out of play. Language frozen. Language melted.

If every word spoken daily in New York City were somehow to materialize as a snowflake, each day there would be a blizzard.

The gradual accumulation of words; a blizzard of the evanescent.

Language as material, language as process, language as something to be shoveled into a machine and spread across pages, only to be discarded and recycled once again. Language as junk, language as detritus. Nutritionless language, meaningless language, unloved language, everyday speech, illegibility, unreadability, machinistic repetition. Obsessive archiving & cataloging, the debased language of media & advertising; language more concerned with quantity than quality. How much did you say that paragraph weighed?

More interested in a thinkership than in a readership. Readability is the last thing on this poetry's mind.

Sculpting with text.

Data mining.

Sucking on words.

How to proceed after the deconstruction and pulverization of language that is the twentieth century's legacy. Should we continue to pound language into ever smaller bits or should we take some other approach? The need to view language again as a whole — syntactically and grammatically intact — but to acknowledge the cracks in the surface of the reconstructed linguistic vessel. Therefore, in order to proceed, we need to employ a strategy of opposites — unboring boring, uncreative writing, valueless speech — all methods of disorientation used in order to reimagine our normative relationship to language.

Our task is to simply mind the machines.

I LOVE SPEECH

NOTES

Introduction

1. Roman Jakobson, "Linguistics and Poetics," in *Language in Literature,* ed. Krystyna Pomorska and Stephen Rudy (Cambridge: Belknap Press of Harvard University, 1987), 87. See also Andrew Welsh, *Roots of Lyric: Primitive Poetry and Modern Poetics* (Princeton: Princeton University Press, 1978), 3–24 and passim.

2. Harold Bloom, *Agon: Toward a Theory of Revisionism* (New York: Oxford University Press, 1982), 11, my emphasis. Cf. my "Postmodernism and the Impasse of Lyric," in *The Dance of the Intellect: Studies in the Poetry of the Pound Tradition* (Cambridge: Cambridge University Press, 1985), 172–97.

3. Paul de Man, "Lyric and Modernity" (1969), in *Blindness and Insight: Essays in the Rhetoric of Contemporary Criticism,* introduction by Wlad Godzich, 2nd ed.(Minneapolis: University of Minnesota Press, 1983), 182. In the index, under the entry "Lyric," we read "See Poetry."

4. The notable exception is Virginia Jackson's "Who Reads Poetry?" (*PMLA* 123 [January 2008]: 181–87), whose subject is the misguided "historical transformation of many varied poetic genres into the single abstraction of the post-romantic lyric." The rhetorical discourse of Herman Melville's "The Portent," with its impassioned address to a public "you," differs appreciably, Jack-

son argues, from the romantic lyric mode, which is its context.

5. Oren Izenberg, "Poems Out of Our Heads," *The New Lyric Studies, PMLA* 123 (January 2008): 217.

6. Ibid.

7. W. B. Yeats, *The Poems,* ed. Richard J. Finneran (New York: Macmillan, 1989), 154.

8. The most recent, Frost's "Spring Pools," was published in *West-Running Brook* (1928). In his "The Specter of Interdisciplinarity" (188–94), Brent Hayes Edwards lauds the contemporary Martinican poet Monchoachi, but he cites, not any of his poems, but an impassioned Heideggerian speech on poetry dating from 2003. Yet another nineteenth-century poet, Baudelaire, provides Robert Kaufman ("Lyric Commodity Critique," 207–15) with his entry into the question of Marxist aesthetics in Adorno and Benjamin, but Kaufman is not concerned with the particular poems in *Fleurs du mal* themselves. Again, Rei Tarada's summarizing "After the Critique of Lyric" (195–200) focuses on lyric theory rather than specifics and is, not surprisingly, somewhat pessimistic about its future.

9. *The Oxford English Dictionary,* ed. John Simpson and Edmund Weiner, 2nd ed.(Oxford: Oxford University Press, 1989). Cited in the text as *OED.*

10. See James William Johnson, "Lyric," *The New Princeton Encyclopedia of Poetry and Poetics,* ed. Alex Preminger (Princeton: Princeton University Press, 1993), 713–27. Subsequently cited in the text as *PEPP.* This essay, which includes material on lyric from the Sumerians to the present around the world, is a goldmine of information and has an excellent bibliography; cf. C. H. Wang, "Chinese Poetry," *PEPP,* 190–91. The reader is also referred to the related entries "Poetry" by T. V. F. Brogan and "Poetry: Theories of" by M. H. Abrams.

11. *PEPP,* 720.

12. *PEPP,* 714.

13. Alexander Pope, "The Rape of the Lock," in *The Major Works,* ed. Pat Rogers (Oxford: . Oxford University Press, 2006), 86–87.

14. Johnson, "Lyric," 714–15.

15. Ludwig Wittgenstein, *Zettel,* ed. G. E. M. Anscombe and G. H. von Wright, trans. G. E. M. Anscombe (Berkeley: University of California Press, 1970), no. 160.

16. Joseph Shipley terms such words, like "cleave," autantonyms. *The Origin of English Words: A Discursive Dictionary of Indo-European Roots* (Baltimore: Johns Hopkins University Press, 1984), 128.

17. Pope, *Major Works,* 29.

18. Quoted in Jakobson, *Language in Literature,* 81.

19. Jan Mukařovský, "Sound Aspect of Poetic Language," in *On Poetic Language,* trans. and ed. John Burbank and Peter Steiner (Lisse, Netherlands: de Ridder, 1976), 23

20. The literature is extensive, but see, for a starting point, Bohuslav Havránek's *Studie o spisovném jazyce* (Prague: Nakladatelství Československé Akademie Ved, 1963), 11–18 et passim, as well as the excerpt translated as "The Functional Differentiation of the Standard Language," in *A Prague School Reader on Esthetics, Literary Structure, and Style,* ed. and trans. Paul L. Garvin (Washington, DC: Georgetown University Press, 1964), 3–16; Jan Mukařovský, "Standard Language and Poetic Language," in Garvin, 17–3; Roman Jakobson: "The Dominant," trans. Herbert Eagle, in *Readings in Russian Poetics: Formalist and Structuralist Views,* ed. Ladislav Mateika and Krystyna Pomorska (Normal, IL: Dalkey Archive, 2002), 82–87; Jakobson, "Concluding Statement: Linguistics and Poetics," in *Style in Language,* ed. Thomas A. Sebeok (Cambridge: MIT Press, 1960), 350–77; and Julia Kristeva, *Revolution in Poetic Language,* trans. Margaret Waller (New York: Columbia University Press, 1984).

21. Shana Williamson, "The Poetry of Sound," accessed on December 15, 2007, at http://www.termpapersmonthly.com/essays/21769.html.

22. Jakobson, *Language in Literature,* 81.

23. Benjamin Harshav, *Explorations in Poetics* (Stanford: Stanford University Press, 2007), 144 et passim. Cf. Reuven Tsur, *What Makes Sound Patterns Expressive?* (Durham: Duke University Press, 1992). To avoid any possible confusion, let me note that Harshav's essay was originally published under the name Benjamin Hrushovski, "The Meaning of Sound Patterns in Poetry: An Interaction Theory," *Poetics Today* 2, no. 1a (Autumn 1980): 39–56.

24. Alan Galt, *Sound and Sense in the Poetry of Theodor Storm: A Phonological-Statistical Study,* European University Papers, 1, 84 (Frankfurt: Peter Lang, 1973), 1. One might compare Galt's work with Ivan Fónagy's "Communication in Poetry," *Word* 17 (1961): 194–218.

25. Galt, *Sound and Sense,* 4.

26. See, for example, the selections in Jed Rasula and Steve McCaffery's *Imagining Language* (Cambridge: MIT Press, 1998), 362–367.

27. Galt, *Sound and Sense,* 91.

28. Ibid., 94.

29. Ibid., 1.

30. Louis Zukofsky, *"A"* (Baltimore: Johns Hopkins University Press, 1993), 138.

31. Sarah Stickney Ellis, *The Poetry of Life* (Philadelphia: Carey, Lea and Blanchard, 1835), 168.

32. *PEPP,* 804.

33. Ibid., 713.

34. Ibid., 714. Cf. Northrop Frye: "By musical I mean a quality of literature denoting a substantial analogy to, and in many cases an actual influence from, the art of music," "Introduction: Lexis and Melos," in *Sound and Poetry: English Institute Essays, 1956* (New York: Columbia University Press, 1957), ix–xxvii, x–xi.

Susan Stewart, *"Rhyme and Freedom"*

1. G. W. F. Hegel, *Hegel's Aesthetics: Lectures on Fine Art,* trans. T. M. Knox, vol. 2 (Oxford: Oxford University Press, 1998), 1137. Hegel discusses the various advantages of Spanish meters, the French Alexandrine, and German and English meters on p. 1174. The independence of rhyme from language practices is evident in English in the ways a "gendered" system of differences is carried over in the conventions of masculine and feminine word endings in rhyme while it is dropped in the everyday use of articles. By contrast, in the Romance languages a masculine or feminine rhyme can be made by means of a noun of the opposite gender — in English such a difference can be effected only through semantics.

2. *Poetics,* trans. Ingram Bywater, in *The Basic Works of Aristotle,* ed. Richard McKeon (New York: Random House, 1941). "The distinction between historian and poet is not in the one writing prose and the

other verse — you might put the work of Herodotus into verse, and it would still be a species of history; it consists really in this, that the one describes the thing that has been, and the other a kind of thing that might be. Hence poetry is something more philosophic and of graver import than history" (1463–64).

3. Richard Aldington, "Free Verse in England," *Egoist,* September 15, 1914, 351. Donald Wesling's article, "The Prosodies of Free Verse," in *Twentieth-Century Literature in Retrospect,* ed. Reuben Brower (Cambridge: Harvard English Studies, 1971), 155–87, discusses Paul Valéry's claim in *The Art of Poetry* that he was "seized by a desire to throw away rhyme and everything else" and Donald Davie's pronouncement in his introduction to the Manchester edition of *The Poems of Dr. Zhivago* that "in translating rhymed verse the rhyme is the first thing to go" (160–61).

4. Ibid.

5. For a discussion of the heartbeat and rhythm, see Andrzej Szczeklik, *Catharsis: On the Art of Medicine,* trans. Antonia Lloyd-Jones (Chicago: University of Chicago Press, 2005), 55–67.

6. One of the most thoughtful and provocative arguments about such issues of "traditional" and "free" prosody in translation is Yves Bonnefoy's 1979 rejoinder to Joseph Brodsky's contention that strongly metered Russian poetry, such as that of Mandelstam, was ill served by free verse translation. Bonnefoy describes the French alexandrine with its symmetrical halves as particularly suited, as a closed system, to metaphysical and idealized worlds — the Racinian world of "rational and intemporal exchange between the archetypes of the mind." In his translations of Shakespeare, Bonnefoy saw the alexandrine as particularly ill suited, but he also found that following the

Shakespearean line led him to a recurring emphasis on eleven syllables — a pattern of six and five that began freely, without preconception as to meter, and ended quite close to Shakespeare's own. Bonnefoy concludes that this encounter between "the absolute and life" led to a flexible meter that would at times even expand to an alexandrine as "an indication of plenitude." I cite this example because it describes a translation process that is quite close to the composition process with which I began this essay. Yves Bonnefoy, "On the Translation of Form in Poetry," in *Companion to Contemporary World Literature from the Editors of World Literature Today,* ed. Pamela A. Genova (New York: Twayne/Thompson Gale, 2003), 10–11.

7. T. V. F. Broghan, "Rhyme," in *Princeton Encyclopedia of Poetry and Poetics,* ed. Alex Preminger and T. V. F. Brogan (Princeton: Princeton University Press, 1993), 1061. I have relied on this entry throughout this essay.

8. Aldington, "Free Verse in England," 351. Here is another prose version from a recent translation by David Kovacs: "Do you know the nature of our mortal life? I think not. How could you? But listen to me. Death is a debt all mortals must pay, and no man knows for certain whether he will still be living on the morrow. The outcome of our fortune is hid from our eyes, and it lies beyond the scope of any teaching or craft." Euripides, *Cyclops; Alcestis; Medea,* trans. D. Kovacs (Cambridge: Harvard University Press/Loeb Library, 1994), 233.

9. William Harmon, "Rhyme in English Verse: History, Structures, Functions," *Studies in Philology* 84, no. 4 (1987): 365–66. See also Eduard Norden's discussion of *homeoleuton* in *Die Antike Kunstprosa vom VI. jahrhundert v. Chr. bis in die zeit der Renaissance,* 2 vols. (Leipzig: Teubner,

1898), 1: 51f. (in ancient rhetoric) and 2:871f. (in medieval texts and the genesis of rhyme).

10. Helen Fulton, "The Theory of Celtic Influence on the Harley Lyrics," *Modern Philology* 82, no. 3 (1985): 242 and 242n. Fulton's essay argues against an influence of Celtic versification on Middle English lyrics, but, she writes, "the contribution of Irish Poets to Latin verse in the early medieval period, in terms of alliteration, rhyme, consonance, and assonance, undoubtedly produced a verse rich in sound ornamentation, which influenced other Latin composers" (248). For overlapping accentual and syllabic systems in Irish verse, she cites James Travis, *Early Celtic Versecraft: Origin, Development, Diffusion* (Ithaca: Cornell University Press, 1973), 42.

11. Helen Waddell, *Medieval Latin Lyrics* (New York: Henry Holt, 1929), 68. Here is her translation, p. 69:

Day of the king most righteous,
The day is nigh at hand,
The day of wrath and vengeance,
And darkness on the land.

Day of thick clouds and voices,
Of mighty thundering,
A day of narrow anguish
And bitter sorrowing.

The love of women's over,
And ended is desire,
Men's strife with men is quiet,
And the world lusts no more.

12. Caesar, *Gallic Wars* 6.13.

13. The description of Celtic poetry in this section relies upon a series of articles in the *Princeton Encyclopedia of Poetry and Poetics:* Irish poetry; Celtic prosody; Generic rhyme; Indo-European prosody. For a complex system of rhyme analogous to Irish poetics — one that recognizes both external

rhyme (between end syllables of lines) and internal rhyme (within certain clusters of syllables in each line) — see Thomas John Hudak, "Internal Rhyme Patterns in Classical Thai Poetry," *Crossroads* 3, nos. 2–3 (1987): 94–105.

14. Of the fifty-four forms of the verb of first conjugation in Provencal, for example, only nine have the accent on the root; the remaining forty-five have it on the final syllable and hence all forty-five rhyme. See Francis Hueffer, *The Troubadours* (London: Chatto and Windus, 1878), 325, where he discusses further rhyme words as well.

15. Denis de Rougemont's classic study of courtly love and the Tristan myth, *Love in the Western World* (Princeton: Princeton University Press, 1983), argues that the myth reveals a convergence of Celtic and Druid belief with a strain of Zoroastrianism that survived in Manichean thought. He contends that the very structure of Manicheanism is "lyrical" — that is, at once subjective and given to divine possession (61–66). On the basis of a leonine rhyme practice found in both Zoroastrian *Gāthās* and Tertullian's second-century *De judicio Domini,* John W. Drapper argues that Indo-Iranian rhyme practices are the origin not only of rhyming in the West but also of Chinese practices, perhaps through Scythian nomads. These arguments are laid out in two articles, "The Origin of Rhyme," *Revue de Littérature Comparée* 31 (1957): 74–85, where he argues a Chinese origin, and then a correction based on archaeological material indicating that Chinese rhyming followed Persian influence, "The Origin of Rhyme: A Supplement," *Revue de Littérature Comparée* 39 (1965): 452–53. Regardless of the soundness of these historical arguments, we still can see, throughout the West, vestiges of the shamanic power of rhyme in rhyming choruses and

refrains of folk songs and folk stories, just as the incantatory power of rhyme remains evident in any playground.

16. Ezra Pound, *The Spirit of Romance* (New York: New Directions, 1968), 30. Dante's praise is in *De vulgari eloquentia* (2.2).

17. F. R. P. Akehurst's empirical study of restrictions on rhyme words in troubadour verse ("Incantatory Value of Words in the Provençal Troubadours," in *Court and Poet,* ed. Glyn S. Burgess [Liverpool: Cairns, 1981]) underlines an argument made by Robert Guiette that "given the social requirement for discretion, the poet sings not the love which he experiences, but an ideal love": "le thème n'est qu'un prétexte. C'est l'oeuvre formelle, elle-méme, qui est le sujet." "D'une poesie formelle en France au Moyen Age," *Revue des sciences humaines,* n.s., fasc. 54 (1949): 61–69.

18. Aldington, "Free Verse in England," 351.

19. Here is an unrhymed translation by K. Foster and F. Boyd (*Dante's Lyric Poetry* [Oxford: Clarendon Press, 1967]) of the poem as it appears in Dante Alighieri's *Rime* (approx. 1283–1308):

You who are intelligent, consider this vision
and please show its true meaning.
It was like this: a fair woman, in gaining
whose favour my heart takes much pleasure,
made me a gift of a green leafy garland;
and charmingly she did so. And then
I seemed to find myself clothed
in a shift that she had worn.
Then I made so bold as gently to embrace
her. The fair one did not resist, but smiled;
and as she smiled I kissed her repeatedly.
I will not say what followed — she made me
swear not to. And a dead woman
— my mother — was with her.

20. Perhaps groups of "rimatori" and rhymers' clubs are popular throughout literary history because they speak to the social

confederation of poets as a kind of rhyme, or echo chamber, of compatible sounds. The Imagists' identification by a visual phenomenon is far more unusual than the recurrence of groups of rhymers and rhymesters. The term has a derogatory ring based in Aristotle's denigration of "mere verse" that also becomes a badge of modesty — this resonance can be detected in the earliest use of the word in English print: John Dennis's 1719 "But as Poets are not capable, so neither are they impartial Judges. I speak of those who are only Rhimesters" (*OED*). When William Butler Yeats, Ernest Rhys, Lionel Johnson, and others formed the "Rhymers' Club" in London in 1890 their goal was to recite and publish works together that would follow a new aesthetic of becoming closer to speech. A useful contrasting example of poetic confederation and what might be called "dis-federation" is Edward Pen's contention in "Free Verse Movement: Its Reception in Japan and China" (*Tokyo 1991: The Force of Vision,* Proceedings of the International Comparative Literature Association meetings, [Tokyo: University of Tokyo Press, 1995], 61–67) that free verse arose in Japanese poetry as a consequence of the deprofessionalization of the role of the poet.

21. There is an intriguing and uncanny connection between this poem and the argument Allen Grossman makes in his "Summa Lyrica" about the relation of rhyme to the prelinguistic chora of the mother: *"Scholium on rhyme and the mother tongue.* The mother is present wherever in the poem language is specialized toward sound, as in rhyme which arrests the word in the ear, requiring that it delay in the realm of the body, before passing to sensory extinction as mere notation in the brain. Rhyme like all phonic or merely structural repetition

(as in grammatical rhyme) summons to common membership at the level of the species, tending to extinguish difference as transcendence and establish difference at the level of substance. The difference/no difference ambiguity in rhyme functions as the repetition of the sufficient conditions of sensing (the rule of texture), and as the substantiation of the parallel ambiguity at the level of meaning. Sound as silence (rhyme as sensation) articulates silence as sound (the meaning of words and sentences)." Allen Grossman, "Summa Lyrica" in *The Sighted Singer: Two Works on Poetry for Readers and Writers,* by Allen Grossman and Mark Halliday (Baltimore: Johns Hopkins University Press, 1992), 362.

22. John Milton, *Complete Poems and Major Prose,* ed. Merritt Y. Hughes (New York: Odyssey, 1957), 210.

23. It is striking that couplets are dominant even earlier. Andrew Marvell, for example, seems to have had some knowledge of Dante: see Nigel Smith's note to line 62 of "Tom May's Death" in *The Poems of Andrew Marvell* (London: Longman, 2003). In that line he mentions the Guelphs and "Ghib'llines" and refers to the "basket" used to receive votes in Florentine elections. And his travels in Italy in the 1640s may have exposed him to Italian editions of the *Commedia.* Yet there is no use of terza rima in his poetry — he occasionally uses song forms of *abab* and *abcabc,* but the end-lined rhyming couplet dominates his verse.

24. Ralph Waldo Emerson, "The Poet," in *Essays: First and Second Series* (New York: Vintage Books, Library of America, 1990), 229.

25. Reuven Tsur, *What Makes Sound Patterns Expressive?* (Durham: Duke University Press, 1992), 5–35.

26. Emanuel Swedenborg, *An Hieroglyphic Key*

to Natural and Spiritual Mysteries by way of Representations and Correspondences, trans. from the Latin by R. Hindmarsh (London: R. Hindmarsh, 1792), 15. Hindmarsh writes in his preface to this work: "correspondence in general may be defined, the relation subsisting between the essence of a thing and its form, or between the cause and its effect; thus the whole natural world corresponds to the spiritual world; the body of a man, with all its parts corresponds to his soul; and the literal sense of Word corresponds to its spiritual sense." He contrasts this to the arbitrary choices of speakers and writers who are merely using figures and metaphors — it is the interior, intrinsic connection that he emphasizes, in accordance with the doctrines of Swedenborg, concluding that "the language of correspondences is the language of God himself" (3–4). In this sense, the sounds of words are more intrinsic and spiritual than the arbitrary meanings that are conferred upon them by human beings.

Baudelaire's deep interest in the doctrines of Swedenborg is evident even before his "Correspondances" of 1861 in his 1860 essay "Le poème du haschisch," where he writes: "Fourier et Swedenborg, l'un avec ses *analogies,* l'autre avec ses *correspondances,* se sont incarnés dans le végétal et l'animal qui tombent sous votre regard, et, au lieu d'enseigner par la voix, ils vous endoctrinent par la forme et par la couleur." Charles Baudelaire, *Oeuvres complètes,* ed. Y.-g. Le Dantec (Paris: Gallimard, 1961), 376. "Correspondances" itself emphasizes the transposition of odors as strongly as the visual senses: "Les parfums, les couleurs et les sons se répondent." For Swedenborg a theology of the Word underlies rhyme; for Baudelaire correspondences are synaesthetic, but their "longs échos" are effected through the medium of poetic language.

27. Ralph Waldo Emerson, "Swedenborg," in *Representative Men* (Boston: Phillips, Sampson, 1850), 111.

28. In his *Physics,* Aristotle suggests that the maker partly imitates nature and partly carries to completion what nature has left incomplete. *Physics,* trans. R. P. Hardie and R. K. Gaye, in *The Basic Works of Aristotle,* ed. Richard McKeon (New York: Random House, 1941), 236–39 (2.2). And in the *Nicomachean Ethics* he also emphasizes the conceptual origins of art: "all art is concerned with coming into being . . . and considering how something may come into being which is capable of either being or not being and whose origin is in the maker and not in the thing made." *Ethica Nicomachea,* trans. W. D. Ross, in *Basic Works of Aristotle,* 1025 (6.4).

29. See Dante's discussion of rhyming practices by his contemporaries in *De vulgari eloquentia* 2.13.4, 2.12.8, and 2.13.6. Michael Hurley's essay "Interpreting Dante's *Terza Rima,*" *Forum for Modern Language Studies* 41, no. 3 (2005) discusses Dante's adaptation of metaphors from the Florentine wool industry to individual words and phrases (328–30).

30. William Wordsworth, "Preface to Lyrical Ballads and Appendix" (1850 version), in *Selected Prose,* ed. John Hayden (Harmondsworth: Penguin, 1988), 296.

31. Arthur Schopenhauer, *The World as Will and Idea,* book 2, reprinted in *Critical Theory since Plato,* ed. Hazard Adams (New York: Harcourt Brace Jovanovich, 1971), 483.

32. Paul Bauschatz, "Rhyme and the Structure of English Consonants," *English Language and Linguistics* 7 no. 1 (2003): 52.

33. Henri Meschonnic brings this connection forward in "Rhyme and Life," trans. Gabriella Bedetti, *Critical Inquiry* 15, no. 1 (1988): 96: "[Rhyme] participates in

paronomasia. . . . What only its restrictive
identification to a final position masked.
Rhyme cheats the way destiny would cheat
if it played cards. Because it would know
ahead of time. Rhyme knows ahead of
time. . . . Because rhyme is a principle of
listening" (96).

34. This tension between rhyme and syntax
seems inevitable, despite various attempts
by theorists of poetics to contradict it.
Dryden, for example, in his dedication
to his 1664 play *The Rival Ladies* claimed
that rhyme could be successfully included
in "ordinary speaking" so readily, and be
such a helpful aid to memory, that it "has
all the advantages of prose beside its own."
Dedication to the Earl of Orrery, *The
Rival Ladies* (London: W.W. for Henry
Herringman, 1664), 5–7. An illuminating contemporary position on this issue
of poetry's relation to ordinary speaking
is the contemporary French poet Jacques
Roubaud's argument that the free verse
practiced in France in the 1970s had only an
"illusion" of liberty because it had not yet
freed itself from the demands of ordinary
syntax: the freedom of free verse should
be expressed in relation not to metrics but
to the language. See Andrew Eastman,
"Jacques Roubaud et le 'vers libre améric-
ain,'" *Revue Francaise d'Etudes Américaines*
80 (1999): 24.

35. See Ruth Weir, *Language in the Crib* (The
Hague: Mouton, 1966). Clare Kirtley,
Peter Bryant, Morag MacLean, and Lynette
Bradley ("Rhyme, Rime, and the Onset of
Reading," *Journal of Experimental Child
Psychology* 48 [1989]: 224–45) argue that
English-speaking children divide syllables
into opening consonants or consonant
clusters and the remainder (the rhyme).
This predilection may make children more
sensitive to rhyme and lead to height-
ened phonological awareness around the

time of learning to read. In "A Deficit in
Rime Awareness in Children with Down
Syndrome," Margaret Snowing, Charles
Hulme and Robin Mercer discovered that
children with Down syndrome did fairly
well on tests of identifying alliteration but
could not score above chance recognition
in determining end rhymes. *Reading and
Writing: An Interdisciplinary Journal*
15 (2002): 471–95.

36. For a discussion of how nonsense choruses
in lullabies encode the vowel preferences
of the singer's language, see Bess Lomax
Hawes, "Form and Function: Some
Thoughts on the American Lullabye,"
Journal of American Folklore 87 (1974):
140–48.

37. Bruna de Cara and Usha Goswami, "Phonological Neighbourhood Density: Effects
in a Rhyme Awareness Task in Five-Year-
Old Children," *Journal of Child Language*
30 (2003): 697.

38. Marjorie Perloff's essay "The Linear
Fallacy" (*Georgia Review* [Winter 1981]:
855–68) points out that the free verse line
works as poetry only when it involves
"both recurrence and suspension" (866). It
is striking that these principles also characterize rhyme, even in its most "traditional"
uses, and we might ask whether the most
successful free verse, in abjuring rhyme, has
taken on rhyme's most fundamental formal
gestures (which I would rephrase inversely
as suspension and recurrence) without its
particular manifestation in sound.

39. Louis Simpson wrote that "in our time
writing in regular form leads to writing
light verse." If adjacent rhymes occur today
most often in the realm of advertising,
perhaps it is because advertising is designed
to stamp its impression on the wax of
our disbelief. "Irregular Impulses: Some
Remarks on Free Verse," *Ohio Review* 28
(1982): 54–57.

40. T. S. Eliot uses close rhyme and related devices of sound repetition extensively in his "Four Quartets" where, he writes, "My words echo / Thus, in your mind." Close rhyme, and rhymes separated by only one word, appear in: *unseen eyebeam, white light, receipt for deceit, sea anemone, hardly barely, grief into relief, Mars converse, horoscope haruspicate, observe disease, tea leaves, riddle the inevitable, the womb or tomb, daemonic chthonic, budding nor fading, dark lake, flood and drouth, done and been, faces and places, all shall be well.* He also plays with transposed letters in *deliberate hebetude* and the several-times-repeated *dawn wind* and *winter lightning.* The overall effect is one of regeneration by echo.

41. Ian K. Lilly, "On Adjacent and Nonadjacent Russian Rhyme Pairs," *Slavic and East European Journal* 29, no. 2 (1985): 195.

42. At the same time, there is evidence that fifteenth-century scribes, when copying manuscripts, would change words into their own dialects but would rarely change the spelling of a rhyming word — the rhyme thereby was a way of transmitting pronunciation intact. Stefania Maria Maci, "The Language of *Mary Magdalene* of the Bodleian MS Digby 133," *Linguistica e Filologia: Quaderni Del Dipartimento di Linguistica, Universita degli Studi di Bergamo* 10 (1999): 135. For studies of poetic rhymes as a record of dialect pronunciation in American poetry, see Gene Russell, "Dialectal and Phonetic Features of Edward Taylor's Rhymes," *American Literature* 43, no. 2 (1971): 165–80, and Kathryn Anderson McEuen, "Whittier's Rhymes," *American Speech* 20, no. 1 (1945): 51–57.

43. Philip Sidney, *An Apology for Poetry,* ed. Forrest G. Robinson (Indianapolis: Bobbs-Merrill, 1970). Sidney argues famously as well that "verse" serves as a mnemonic (52, 54–55). At the very end of his treatise,

he discusses the differences between English verse and ancient verse on the one hand and French and Italian rhyming practices on the other. He sees English verse as best suited "before any other vulgar language I know" for carrying forward the ancient tradition of the "well-weighed syllable" and the possibilities of rhyme for "the sweet sliding" necessary for musical effects (86).

44. See Kristin Hanson's "Vowel Variation in English Rhyme: A Note on the History of the Rhetoric of Rhymes," in *Studies in the History of the English Language: A Millennial Perspective,* ed. Donka Minkova and Robert Stockwell (Berlin: Mouton de Gruyter; 2002), 215. Hanson is particularly interested in the expressive possibilities of partial rhymes. For an analogous argument about iconic uses of rhyme (as in George Herbert's use of "rhyme" and "chime" in "Deniall" and Dryden's use of "alone," "grown," and "none" to signify negation, see Max Nänny, "Iconic Uses of Rhyme," in *Outside-In-Inside-Out: Iconicity in Language and Literature,* ed. Costantino Maeder, Olga Fischer, and William Herlofsky (Amsterdam: Benjamins, 2005), 195–215. Following Marjorie Perloff's pathbreaking *Rhyme and Meaning in the Poetry of Yeats* (The Hague: Mouton, 1970), Michael McKie's "Semantic Rhyme: A Reappraisal" discusses Yeats's composition process, which often would begin with a prose analysis of a set of rhymes and what could be made of them. *Essays in Criticism* 46, no. 4 (1996): 342–43.

45. Krystina Pomorska, "Semiotic Implications of Rhymes: Pushkin's Poems of the Erzerum Period," *Canadian-American Slavic Studies* 22, nos. 1–4 (1988): 377–81. All the primary rhymes in these poems are of Turkic origin, are feminine, and are placed at the end of the stanza, in the accusative case. Rhyme words end the stanza and end the sentence, for each stanza is a sentence (378). In a suggestive comparison to the subtle changes in action worked by Skelton's rhyming adverbs, Pushkin rejected a popular proscription against using verbs as rhyme words. J. Thomas Shaw, "Parts of Speech in Puškin's Rhymewords and Nonrhymed Endwords," *Slavic and East European Journal* 37, no. 1 (1993): 1–3.

46. See Hurley, "Interpreting Dante's *Terza Rima*," for a discussion of terza rima's pattern as like "the juggler's three-ball cascade" (323).

47. See also the discussion of clapping, ululation, and other ways of marking line endings in Ode S. Ogede, "Oral Performance as Instruction: Aesthetic Strategies in Children's Play Songs from a Nigerian Community," *Children's Literature Association Quarterly* 19, no. 3 (1994): 114–15, and the role of clicks in nursery rhymes used by nursing mothers in China in Geoffrey S. Nathan, "Clicks in a Chinese Nursery Rhyme," *Journal of the International Phonetic Association* 31, no. 2 (2001): 223–28.

48. George Santayana, *Skepticism and Animal Faith* (New York: Charles Scribner, 1923), 153.

Leevi Lehto, "In the Beginning Was Translation"

1. See Charles Bernstein, *Runouden puolustus. Esseitä ja runoja kahdelta vuosituhannelta,* ed. Leevi Lehto (Helsinki: PoEsia 2006), 252–53. Translation published in original in Charles Bernstein, *With Strings* (Chicago: University of Chicago Press, 2001).

2. For a useful discussion of the questions of "materiality" in translation, see Fredrik Hertzberg, *Moving Materialities. On Poetic Materiality and Translation, with Special Reference to Gunnar Björling's Poetry* (Åbo: Åbo Akademi University Press, 2002).

3. See M. H. Abrams, "Keats's Poems: The Material Dimensions," in *The Persistence of Poetry: Bicentennial Essays on Keats,* ed. Robert M. Ryan and Ronald A. Sharp (Amherst: University of Massachusetts Press, 1998), 36–53.

4. Published, in Harry Zohn's 1968 translation, for instance in *The Translation Studies Reader,* ed. Lawrence Venuti (London: Routledge, 2000).

5. Here I'm partially inspired by Andrew Benjamin's discussion, in his *Translation and the Nature of Philosophy* (London: Routledge 1989), on the relation of translation to the concept of tradition: "Existing at a particular point in historical time [the conflicts of interpretation] enact the plurality of tradition. Tradition in this sense is both plural and conflictual. Its unfolding is the unfolding of the conflicts that constitute it.... There is no outside of tradition.... Tradition becomes therefore the generalized site of interpretative differential plurality" (163–64).

6. Friedrich Schleiermacher, "Ueber die verschiedenen Methoden des Uebersetzens" (1813), *Friedrich Schleiermachers sämmtliche Werke,* part 3: *Zur Philosophie,* vol. 2 (Berlin: Reimer, 1838), 207–45.

7. See my essay "Plurifying the Languages of the Trite" for a seminar entitled "Poetry in Time of War and Banality," in Campinas, Sao Paulo, Brazil, April–June 2006, available at http://www.leevilehto.net and http://sibila.com.br/; in Portuguese in *Sibila* 10 (2006); in Norwegian at http://nypoesi.net; in Dutch at http://decontrabas.typepad.com; in Russian in *Говорим пограничная страна — Финнся стихомашина 21. века,* ed. Leevi Lehto (Helsinki: ntamo, 2008); and in Finnish in Leevi Lehto, *Alussa oli kääntäminen* (Turku: Savukeidas, 2008). Also see the

Icelandic poet Eiríkur Örn Norðdahl's fundamental online essay "On the Importance of Destroying a Language (of One's Own)," at his blog at http://www .illiteration.blospot.com. For examples of experimentation in "Barbaric English," see Aki Salmela, *Word in Progress* (Helsinki: ntamo 2007), as well as my own *Lake Onega and Other Poems* (Cambridge, UK: Salt Publishing, 2006).

8. Schleiermacher, "Ueber die verschiedenen Methoden des Uebersetzens."

Yunte Huang, "Chinese Whispers"

1. Frances Wood, *Did Marco Polo Go to China?* (Boulder, CO: Westview Press, 1996), 63.

2. Wikipedia, "Chinese Whispers," August 20, 2007, http://en.wikipedia.org/ wiki/Chinese_whispers.

3. Jacques Attali, *Noise: The Political Economy of Music* (Minneapolis: University of Minnesota Press, 1985), 3.

4. Jerome Rothenberg, *Pre-faces* (New York: New Directions), 76–92. Cf. Steve McCaffery and bpNichol, *Rational Geomancy: The Kids of the Book-Machine* (Vancouver: Talonbooks, 1992), 48.

5. Bronislaw Malinowski, "The Meaning of Meaningless Words and the Coefficient of Weirdness," in *Symposium of the Whole: A Range of Discourse toward an Ethnopoetics,* ed. Jerome Rothenberg and Diane Rothenberg (Berkeley: University of California Press, 1983), 107.

6. Charles Olson, *Collected Prose,* ed. Donald Allen and Benjamin Friedlander (Berkeley: University of California Press, 1997), 156.

7. Ezra Pound, *Cathay* (1915), reprinted in *Poems and Translations,* ed. Richard Sieburth (New York: Library of America, 2003), 252.

8. Marjorie Perloff, *Differentials: Poetry, Poetics, Pedagogy* (Tuscaloosa: University of Alabama Press, 2004), 41.

9. Pound, *Cathay,* 257.

10. Perloff, *Differentials,* 44.

11. Charles Sanders Peirce, "Letters to Lady Welby (1903–1911)," in *Charles Sanders Peirce: Selected Writings,* ed. Philip Wiener (New York: Dover), 391.

12. James N. Baker, "The Presence of the Name: Reading Scripture in an Indonesian Village," in *The Ethnography of Reading,* ed. Jonathan Boyarin (Berkeley: University of California Press, 1993), 98–138.

13. Marco Polo, *The Travels of Marco Polo: The Complete Yule-Courdier Edition,* vol. 1 (New York: Dover), 423–24.

14. Ibid., 171.

15. Ibid., 181.

Rosmarie Waldrop, "Translating the Sound in Poetry: Six Propositions"

1. Ezra Pound, *The Literary Essays* (New York: New Directions, n.d.), 72.

2. Walter Benjamin, "The Task of the Translator," in *Illuminations,* ed. Hannah Arendt, trans. Harry Zohn (New York: Schocken, 1969), 69.

3. Ernst Jandl, *sprechblasen* (Neuwied/Berlin: Luchterhand, 1968), 51.

4. Muriel Kittel in *An Anthology of French Poetry from Nerval to Valéry,* ed. Angel Flores (New York: Doubleday Anchor, 1958), 92.

5. Keith Waldrop, unpublished.

6. Ulf Stolterfoht, *fachsprachen I–IX* (Basel/ Weil am Rhein: Urs Engeler, 1998), II, 6.

7. Paul Blackburn, *Guillem de Poitou, His Eleven Extant Poems* (Mt. Horeb, WI: Perishable Press, 1976), 16.

8. W. D. Snodgrass, *Six Troubadour Songs* (Providence: Burning Deck, 1977), n.p.

Richard Sieburth, "Ensemble discords"

1. John Hollander, *The Untuning of the Sky* (Princeton: Princeton University Press, 1961), 24–25, 42, 45.

2. See James Helgeson, *Harmonie divine et subjectivité poétique chez Maurice Scève* (Geneva: Droz, 2001), 27–38.

3. Ashbery's comments on Scève (which are related to his own Scève-inspired "Fragment" of 1968) are quoted in John Shoptaw, *On the Outside Looking Out: John Ashbery's Poetry* (Cambridge: Harvard University Press, 1994), 111.

4. See Hollander, *Untuning of the Sky,* 26–28.

5. The originals and translations of the *Délie* are quoted from the second edition of my *Emblems of Desire: Selections from the* Délie *of Maurice Scève* (New York: Archipelago Books, 2007).

6. Randle Cotgrave's *Dictionarie of the French and English Tongues* (1611), an essential anatomy of mid-sixteenth-century French, in turn defines the verb *delire* as "to chuse, cull, select, gather, picke out" and *delirer* as "to doat, rave, do things against reason."

7. In his commentaries on Plato's *Timaeus,* Ficino provides perhaps the most influential Renaissance account of the effects of music on the human body, emphasizing the hot gust of *spiritus* that constitutes the "matter" of melody and that in turn circulates its fervor throughout the body. See Cynthia Skenazi, "L'harmonie dans la *Délie:* musique et poésie," in *A Scève Celebration:* Délie, *1554–1994,* ed. Jerry C. Nash (Saratoga: Anma Libri, 1994), 89.

8. According to the *Trésor de la langue française* (Paris: Éditions du CNRS, 1983), 4: 467, the Italian term *intervallo* begins taking on this musical sense in 1546.

9. Hollander, *Untuning of the Sky,* 42.

10. Jerry C. Nash, ed., *Maurice Scève: Concord-*
ance de la Délie, 2 vols. (Chapel Hill: North Carolina Studies in the Romance Languages and Literatures, 1976).

11. Quoted in Skenazi, "L'harmonie dans la *Délie,*" 89. See also Helgeson, *Harmonie divine,* 10–11, 22–25, 105–115, for a fuller discussion of *concordia discors* and an extensive bibliography on the subject.

12. Three poems (D 41, D 82, D 89) were set by composers before the actual publication of the *Délie* and four (D 5, D 131, D 256, D 364) afterward; four of the settings were polyphonic (for four voices), three homophonic. For more detail, see V.-L. Saulnier, "Maurice Scève et la musique," in *Musique et poésie au XVIe siècle* (Paris: Éditions du CNRS, 1954), 89–103.

13. Mireille Huchon, *Louise Labé: Une créature de papier* (Geneva: Droz, 2006). The following quotes from Labé are taken from Huchon's facsimile reproduction of the *Euvres de Louïze Labé Lionnoize* published by Scève's publisher friend Jean de Tournes in 1555.

14. This is by far the most elusive line in the poem. Pierre Bonniffet provides a very suggestive musicological reading

Feignant le ton que plein ... *est la première des notations techniques du sonnet. La technique de la musica ficta consiste à jouer un bémol ou un dièse là où le compositeur n'en a pas indiqué de sa main: c'est une règle non écrite de la musique que les interprètes connaissaient bien. Certaines notes appelaient ce bémol mais comme, en même temps, la stabilité intangible du mode mélodique ecclésiastique — disons, ici, "platonicien" — interdisait théoriquement des altérations accidentelles à la gamme choisie, le musicien ne les inscrivait pas sur son manuscript: à l'interprète de deviner où elles devaient être placées. Le sens du vers 8 s'éclaire ainsi: feindre un ton plein, c'est faire d'un ton entier un intervalle de* seconde diminuée.

Pierre Bonniffet, "Leuth-Persona ou Lut-Personage (M. Scève et L. Labé n'entendent pas le luth de la même façon)," in *Louise Labé, les voix du lyrisme*, ed. Guy Demerson (Paris: Éditions du CNRS, 1990), 256–57.

15. Hollander, *Untuning of the Sky*, 130–31.

16. See Michel Deguy, "L'infini et sa diction ou de la diérèse," *Poétique* 40 (1979): 432–44.

17. Pascal Quignard, *La parole de la* Délie (Paris: Mercure de France, 1974), 65–70.

18. See Hollander, *Untuning of the Sky*, 137, for a discussion of the phenomenon of "sympathic vibration" — the production of a tone by a free string if another one, placed at some distance but tuned to exactly the same frequency, is struck. A 1618 emblem of "Love as Sympathetic Vibration" is reproduced on page 242.

19. For Marot and Scève see Gérard Defaux, ed., *Délie* (Geneva: Droz, 2004), 1: xliv–li. For Petrarch's Rhône and Scève's, see Jacqueline Risset, *L'anagramme du désir* (Paris: Fourbis, 1995), 53–57.

20. Dolet's treatise on punctuation is reprinted in Nina Catach, *L'orthographe française à l'époque de la Renaissance* (Geneva: Droz, 1968), 305–9. My colleague John Hamilton informs me that various musicologists of antiquity introduced what was known as a "komma" — a small interval (about a quarter-tone) — in order to even out or temper the distance between the tonic and the fourth and hence justify some of the inconsistencies in the musical scale (*musica ficta* again?). Later musical theorists from the Renaissance on adopted kommas of varying sizes (barely perceptible intervals such as a quarter-tone, a fifth-tone, a sixth-tone) to align the imperfections of *musica instrumentalis* with the mathematical purity of *musica mundana*. It would be extremely tempting to connect these intervals to Dolet's system of punctuation — except that what we call "comma" he calls "point à queue," and what he calls "comma" we would call a colon (or *deux points*).

Gordana P. Crnković, "The Poetry of Prose, the Unyielding of Sound"

1. Thomas H. Johnson, ed., *The Complete Poems of Emily Dickinson* (Boston: Little, Brown, 1960), 350.

2. I am referring here to Milica Borojević and Ljiljana Jojić's translation, in Nevenka Košutić-Brozović, *Čitanka iz stranih književnosti* II (Zagreb: Školska knjiga, 1976), 230.

3. Note that the title inverts the word order of the original. The language of the novel, which used to be called "srpsko-hrvatski" and "hrvatsko-srpski" ("Serbo-Croatian" and "Croato-Serbian") at the time of its publication, has, following the breakup of Yugoslavia in the early nineties, assumed a number of "separated" names in the region, such as "Bosnian," "Croatian," and "Serbian"; in the near future there may also be the officially proclaimed "Monte Negran" language as well. The area where the speakers of this language (or of these languages) live is historically a volatile and active language area, with constant processes of both mutual differentiation and mutual rapprochement among the various variants of the language that could linguistically still be seen as one, but not unified. Some contemporary linguists hold that there was a more unified language in the past but that centrifugal forces are now taking the separate variants increasingly apart to the point where they may be becoming new different languages; some think that there was and still is a more unified language; some believe that there never has been a more unified language; and some hold a different viewpoint altogether. American

academics seem to be going in the direction of accepting the term "Bosnian, Croatian, Serbian," or "Bosnian/Croatian/Serbian" for all the variants of the language that is seen as one but not unified. For a more detailed discussion of this issue see Ronelle Alexander's *Bosnian, Croatian, Serbian, a Grammar: With Sociolinguistic Commentary* (Madison: University of Wisconsin Press, 2006).

4. See Meša Selimović, *Death and the Dervish,* trans. Bogdan Rakić and Stephen M. Dickey (Evanston, IL: Northwestern University Press, 1996.) All further references are to this edition.

5. Henry R. Cooper Jr., Introduction, in Selimović, *Death and the Dervish,* xv.

6. While the translators comment on their rendering of the Koran verses and on the translation of the "numerous words . . . of Arabic, Turkish, and Persian origin" used in the original, they do not comment on their many choices creating an overall more prosaic text out of the original strongly poetic one, other than stating that *"Death and the Dervish* has its fair share of stylistic and linguistic idiosyncrasies, complicating the task of remaining faithful to the original while producing a fluid translation." "Translators' Note," in Selimović, *Death and the Dervish,* xviii.

7. Selimović, *Death and the Dervish,* 3. In the original:

Bismilahir-rahmanir-rahim!
Pozivam za svjedoka mastionicu i pero i
   ono što
                     se perom piše;
Pozivam za svjedoka nesigurnu tamu
   sumraka
i noć i sve što ona oživi;
Pozivam za svjedoka mjesec kad najedra i
   zoru
                     kad zabijeli;

Pozivam za svjedoka sudnji dan, i dušu što
   sama
                     sebe kori;
Pozivam za svjedoka vrijeme, početak i
   svršetak
svega — da je svaki čovjek uvijek na gubitku.

Meša Selimović, *Derviš i smrt* (Sarajevo: Svjetlost, 1970), 9. All further references are to this edition.

In the absence of a sound recording of the above passage and other quotations from this novel, which should literally be heard in order for one to grasp their sound quality, I am including here a brief pronunciation guide taken from Celia Hawkesworth's 1999 *Colloquial Croatian and Serbian: The Complete Course for Beginners* (London: Routledge, 1999), 5–6 (modified for U.S. pronunciation). Parts of this book can be accessed online, and its passages on pronunciation, stress, and tone may be of help in constructing, to an extent, the sounds of the BCS language. The following is excerpted from the "Table of pronunciation and the alphabets." Hawkesworth uses the Croatian variant in the few cases where versions differ (e.g., Croatian *lijep* and *pjesma* rather than Serbian *lep* and *pesma*), but this table can be of considerable help for getting the approximate sounds of the Bosnian/Croatian/ Serbian language(s). The underlining in the right column communicates to nonspeakers where the stress of the word falls.

A a	*a* in f*a*ther	m*a*ma (mom)
B b	as English *b*	brat (brother)
C c	*ts* in ca*ts*	*o*tac (father)
Č č	*ch* in *ch*urch	čaj (tea)
Ć ć	roughly *tj*	k*u*ća (house)
D d	as English *d*	da (yes)
Dž dž	*J* in *J*ohn	dž*e*mper (sweater)
Đ đ	roughly *dj*	dak (pupil)
E e	*E* in b*e*d	kr*e*vet (bed)

F f	as English *f*	Fotografija
G g	as English *g*	Govoriti (to speak)
H h	*ch* in lo*ch*	hvala (thank you)
I i	*e* in h*e*	ili (or)
J j	*y* in *y*es.	jaje (egg)
K k	as English *k*	kino (cinema)
L l	as English *l*	lijep (beautiful)
Lj lj	*ll* in mi*lli*on	ljubav (love)
M m	as English *m*	molim (please)
N n	as English *n*	ne (no)
Nj nj	*ni* in on*ni*on	konj (horse)
O o	*o* in n*o*t	ovdje (here)
P p	as English *p*	pjesma (song)
R r	Rolled	Roditelji (parents)
S s	*ss* in ble*ss*	sestra (sister)
Š š	*sh* in *sh*y	šljiva (plum)
T t	as English *t*	trg (square)
U u	*oo* in f*oo*d	učiti (to learn)
V v	as English *v*	vino (wine)
Z z	as English *z*	zašto (why)
Ž ž	*s* in plea*s*ure	život (life)

8. "Bismilahir-rahmanir-rahim!" This utterance itself focuses the listener's attention with its three words' successive decreasing of the number of syllables (four-three-two), their almost hypnotic repetition of the *a-i* pattern (*ahir, anir, ahim*), same phonetic material in the trio of *lahir, manir, rahim,* the internal rhyming of *ir* (*bismilahir, rahmanir*), and the alliteration of the syllable *rah* (*rahmanir, rahim*).

9. With its preeminence of sound coupled with its plot's setting in the past and its narrative techniques, *Dervish and Death* strongly invokes a premodern, vaguely medieval era. Carlo Vecce notes that Leonardo da Vinci's "affirmation of the primacy of the eye, which he called the 'window of the soul,' has extraordinary anthropological value since it corresponds to the historical moment in which he lived, when the medieval world was passing into the modern period, a passage marked by the supremacy of visual perception over the senses of hearing and smelling in the representation of a human being's relationship to the natural world. The definition of poetry as 'a painting one hears rather than sees' ... or a 'blind painting' ... refers clearly to the oral quality of a text." Carlo Vecce, "Word and Image in Leonardo's Writings," in *Leonardo da Vinci: Master Draftsman,* ed. Carmen C. Bambach (New York: Metropolitan Museum of Art; New Haven: Yale University Press, 2003), 61. *Dervish and Death* may be seen as going back to such medieval supremacy of hearing over visual perception. The novel's potent sound thus creates an archaic collective and sacred space: "Orality is naturally collective, directed at a specific audience, reaching all members of an audience at the same time, and adapted to the actual circumstances of its reception. Hearing is a sense that unifies sounds into a sensory bundle that is then internalized by the listener. The phenomenology of sound gives value to the interior: it penetrates deeply; it tends to coalesce. Sacred writings that preserve the original, spoken quality of an utterance, even in its written form, seek to preserve this quality." Ibid.

10. For instance, instead of using "I begin my story for nothing, without ... ," one could use "I begin this story of mine, for nothing, without. ... " This alternative translation would recreate the weighty and slower rhythm of the original by preserving the basic organization of the sentence, the larger cluster of words and the ensuing rhetorical emphasis on "my story" (*ovu moju priču,* literally "this my story," which could be rendered as "this story of mine," not as merely "my story"), and the separateness of and the emphasis on "for nothing."

11. For example, *zapis* and *zapisana* could be rendered as "a write-up" and "written" (*pisati,* appearing as a root in both words,

means "to write"), rather than "record" and "chronicled" (or, if a "write-up" sounds awkward, one could use "writing"); *moj o meni* could be translated as "mine about myself," rather than just "of myself." In addition, a more exact preservation of the meaning of the original words in translation would help the overall workings of the sound. Although increased accuracy of a word-by-word translation would not directly affect the sound the way the above-mentioned aspects would, it would make clearer the semantics of the sentence and the resulting relationship of this semantics to the sound. For example, one of the possible meanings of the word *korist* is indeed "benefit," but the word sounds harsher than that in BCS, closer to its more stern possibilities of "advantage" or "profit" (with the word *blagodat* being a more benevolent "benefit"). It is "profit *and* reason," not "profit *or* reason." *Muka* may mean "anxiety," but "anxiety" is closer to *tjeskoba* and refers to a more vague and milder subjective state: *muka* with reference to a "conversation with oneself" would point more to the difficult or even tormenting or painful toil of talking to oneself and keeping that conversation going through, as it were, a very dense medium of inner resistance. In short, it seems that *muka* may be better rendered here by "torment," "toil," or even "suffering." *Daleka nada* is a "faraway hope" or "far hope," not a "vague hope"; it is one "account" ("the account"), not the plural of "all accounts"; and the paper "waits," not "lies in front of me" (there is no "in front of me" in the original, only "waits like a challenge").. The translation that may recreate the original better could perhaps start with a draft that looks something like this:

I begin this story of mine, for nothing, without profit for myself and for the others, from a need stronger than profit and reason, so that a writing of mine about myself remains, the written toil of a conversation with oneself, with the faraway hope that some solution will be found when the account is settled, if it is, when I leave a trail of ink on this paper that waits like a challenge.

12. The opening sentence of *Dervish and Death*'s narrative could thus also be read and heard as a poetic utterance that talks about the ultimate things, about why someone tells a story ("for nothing"), about telling that can neither be subsumed under the goals of profit or utility (narrative, psychological, social, political, theoretical, historical, or any other) nor classified under reason (anything that we already know, understand, and can recognize). This sentence can now be heard as being about the telling itself that stems from a need that is physical and unstoppable, like thirst or hunger, the telling that wants — needs — to leave a trail of itself, in writing, behind itself, so that some unnamable, ultimate account may be settled, perhaps, when the challenge of silence, of the empty paper that merely "waits," is answered — if it ever is — by the hand that puts down the sounds of ink.

13. Ernst Robert Curtius, *European Literature and the Latin Middle Ages,* trans. Willard R. Trask (Princeton: Princeton University Press, 1990), 151. Curtius writes:

Dictamen prosaicum *is artistic prose. But* "plain" prose (sermo simplex) *naturally remains the normal vehicle for letters and for chronicle, history, science, and hagiography. There is also rhymed prose . . . and finally, mixed prose — that is, texts in which prose alternates with verse inserts. Such texts are called* prosimetra. *In addition, there are metrical and rhythmical poetry.*

But the picture becomes yet more complex through the introduction of the rhythmical cadence into artistic prose. Antique artistic prose had followed metrical laws (that is, based on syllabic quantity) in its cadences. In late Antiquity, the metrical cadence becomes a rhythmical (accentual) cadence, to which the name "cursus" was applied. From the eighth century the cursus degenerated. At the end of the eleventh century the Papal Curia revived it, taking as point of departure the epistolary style of Leo the Great — hence the terms "leoninus cursus" and "leonitas." These in turn furnished the name for the hexameter with internal rhyme ("versus leonini") which became so popular. That starting from cursus leoninus it was possible to arrive at the designation of a hexameter with internal rhyme is further support for our observation that in the Middle Ages the terminologies of poetry and prose easily interchange. Ibid.

14. The three-syllable question in the first line of the dialogue is followed by a longer four-syllable answer in the second line (sounding longer than that because of the two parts); the third line is again a short three-syllable question, and the fourth line is the longest eight-syllable answer.

15. Here, the replication of "about the brother" is preserved, and the close succession of "about," "aye," "about," and "alive" reiterates the long *a* sound and creates some of the internal echoing (of *je*) present in the original. This version has also a regular alteration of short and long(er) lines.

16. The repeated phrase *ruke su mi* (my hands are) in the original is followed by successively longer realizations of language and sound: a two-syllable trochee (*šuplje*, -u) in the first clause, a three-syllable dactyl (*radosne*, -uu) in the second one, and then two dactyls (*lude i nemoćne*, -uu -uu) in the third.

17. In other words, "my hands are hollow, my

hands are full of joy, my hands are crazy and powerless" should be heard together with, and as the clashing opposite of, the preceding descent into silence of "We give food once. Only. Mornings."

18. The original says not "my hands were" but rather "my hands are" (*ruke su mi*), and then this three-times repeated present ("my hands are") is followed in the same sentence with the past tense, "[they] pressed" (*pritisnule su*). The sound of the repeated present — "my hands are" — is very different from the sound of the only-once-mentioned past ("my hands were"); one hears differently "my hands are hollow, my hands are full of joy, my hands are crazy and powerless, they pressed . . . " and "my hands were unsteady, joyous, crazy and weak; they pressed. . . . " The sound of the first utterance is the sound of the present that is both in the process of unfolding and in the process of being named in disbelief — my hands are becoming full of joy at the same moment when I discover and describe them as full of joy; both the unbelievable yet tangible reality and the language of it are happening at the same moment, now, and the sound of this *now* is increasingly louder, exalted, rising against its own almost complete silencing. The second phrase ("my hands were unsteady, joyous, crazy and weak; they pressed . . . ") warrants a slower, calmer reading of the past, of the things that were once and are gone now, a storytelling reading as opposed to a dramatic one.

The original punctuation should also be preserved in order to recreate the assertive and forward-thrusting sound: the original uses only commas, whereas the translation introduces a semicolon, which is actually needed after that long catalogue of successive epithets created by the translation ("my hands were unsteady, joyous, crazy and weak; they . . . "). In addition, the recreation of the original sound would also be helped by the preservation of the original less literal adjectives: the hands are not "unsteady" and "weak" but rather "hollow" (*šuplje*) and "powerless" (*nemoćne*). One reads and hears the original phrase that has hands that are "hollow," "joyous," "crazy," and "powerless" differently from the phrase we get in translation, in which the hands are "unsteady," "joyous," "crazy," and "weak." The phrase "hollow [hands]" may indicate hands that are unsteady, but "unsteady hands" replaces the original metaphor with a concrete adjective; "powerless" may relate to the hands that are actually merely "weak," but the two adjectives interact with their subject in different ways and thus sound different. In combination with the emphasized rhythm of the original sentence, its partially non-literal language helps create a sound that we hear and receive as different from, more poetic than that of the more "down to the earth" prose of the translation.

19. Infinitives in Bosnian/Croatian/Serbian end in either *ti* or *ći*. Selimović's choice to use eight infinitives consistently ending in *ti* would seem to be related to the creation of a desired sound effect.

20. The original, for example, does not have the clausal connection "which would," which creates, in the translation, a brand-new relation in "a graveyard without any markers, *which would* not remind anyone of anything." Also, it is not "so that an *abstract* human thought would be *all* that was left," but rather "so that a *naked* human thought remains . . . ," and it is not "*even* the river" but a simpler "and the river," which does not make any hierarchical distinction between the river and other things that are to be stopped (birds, mills, etc.) but, on the contrary, asserts their equality in the chain of asked-for destruction.

21. On one side, Hegel posits the supremacy of philosophy over art on account of philosophy's higher (highest) realization of historically self-realizing Absolute Spirit, which, pregnant with knowledge it incorporated and transcended from the world of pure logic, science, law and morality, and finally art and religion, ultimately comes to itself only in philosophy. On the other side are Nietzsche and Marx, for example, or in more recent times a number of contemporary Anglo-American philosophers. Opposing Hegel's idealism ("for Hegel the *essence of man — man —* equals *self-consciousness*"), Marx includes in the "*human* relations to the world — seeing, hearing, smelling, tasting, feeling, thinking, being aware," etc., and writes that "thus man is affirmed in the objective world not only in the act of thinking, but with *all* his senses" (all italics in original). See Karl Marx, *Economic and Philosophic Manuscripts of 1844,* in *Marx-Engels Reader,* ed. Robert C. Tucker, 2nd ed. (New York: W. W. Norton, 1978), 113, 87, 88. Regarding recent Anglo-American philosophy, see Gerald L. Bruns's *Tragic Thoughts at the End of Philosophy* (Evanston, IL: Northwestern University Press, 1999).

22. Curtius, *European Literature and the Latin Middle Ages,* 204.

23. Ibid., 203, quoting *Odyssey* 17.518 and 11.334.

Nancy Perloff, "Sound Poetry and the Musical Avant-Garde"

1. On sound and speech in lyric and on lyric and music, see Susan Stewart, "Letter on Sound," in *Close Listening: Poetry and the Performed Word,* ed. Charles Bernstein (New York: Oxford University Press), 29. Note that for sound poetry, "all sounds" means all those produced by the human voice.

2. How abstract, how pure can sound ever be? Bob Cobbing writes that "the tape-recorder's treatment of the voice teaches the human new tricks of rhythm and tone, power and subtlety. We are in a position to claim a poetry which is musical and abstract; but however hard we try to do so can we escape our intellect? In the poetry of pure sound, yes … " See Cobbing, "Some Statements on Sound Poetry," in *Sound Poetry: A Catalogue,* ed. Steve McCaffery and bpNichol (Toronto: Underwhich Editions, 1978), 39.

3. See McCaffery and bpNichol, *Sound Poetry,* 6ff.

4. Richard H. Hoppin, *Medieval Music* (New York: W.W. Norton, 1978), 57–60.

5. For this reference to the "entire field of sound," see John Cage, "The Future of Music: Credo," in *Silence: Lecture and Writings by John Cage* (Hanover, NH: Wesleyan University Press, 1973), 4.

6. McCaffery describes the audiopoems of Henri Chopin, which, in their deconstruction of the word into 'vocal micro-particulars,' represent a "fundamental break with western poetics." See *Sound Poetry,* 11. The sound poetry shaped by these inventions, especially the tape recorder, constitutes his third phase.

7. *Collected Works of Velimir Khlebnikov,* vol. 1, *Letters and Theoretical Writings,* trans. Paul Schmidt, ed. Charlotte Douglas (Cambridge: Harvard University Press, 1987), 394.

8. Cage, "Future of Music," 6.

9. McCaffery and bpNichol, *Sound Poetry,* 7.

10. *Collected Works of Velimir Khlebnikov,* 370. James H. Billington calls Khlebnikov's *zaum'* "a new and essentially musical language beyond the mind." See *The Icon and the Axe: An Interpretive History of Russian Culture* (New York: Vintage Books, 1970), 476.

11. Translation by Gary Kern in *Snake Train:*

Poetry and Prose (Ann Arbor: Ardis, 1976), vii. For original Cyrillic, see figure 1.

12. See Marjorie Perloff's analysis in *Twenty-first-Century Modernism: The "New" Poetics* (Oxford: Blackwell, 2002), 139–41.

13. Alexei Kruchenykh, "Declaration of the Word as Such," in *Russian Futurism through Its Manifestoes: 1912 — 1928,* ed. Anna Lawton (Ithaca: Cornell University Press, 1988), 67.

14. Craig Dworkin, "To Destroy Language," *Textual Practice* 18, no. 2 (2004): 187.

15. Kruchenykh, "New Ways of the Word," in Lawton, *Russian Futurism through Its Manifestoes,* 72.

16. Kruchenykh, "Declaration of Transrational Language," in Lawton, *Russian Futurism through Its Manifestoes,* 183.

17. Unpublished translation by Allison Pultz with Gerald Janecek for the exhibition *Tango with Cows: Book Art of the Russian Avant-Garde, 1910–1917,* Getty Research Institute Gallery, November 18, 2008–April 19, 2009. For original Cyrillic, see figure 2.

18. Pultz clarified Kruchenykh's use of stress both to disrupt the pattern of rhyming suffixes and to signal the difference between spoken and written Russian.

19. Unpublished translation by Pultz with Gerald Janecek, for the exhibition *Tango with Cows: Book Art of the Russian Avant-Garde, 1910–1917.*

20. See JoAnne Paradise and Annette Leddy, exhibition brochure for *A Tumultuous Assembly: Visual Poems of the Italian Futurists,* Getty Research Institute Gallery, August 1, 2006–January 7, 2007. My discussion of "Après la Marne" has benefited from Annette Leddy's explications of some of the typographic and sonic implications of the poem.

21. Quoted in McCaffery, "From Phonic to Sonic: The Emergence of the Audio-Poem," in *Sound States: Innovative Poetics* *and Acoustical Technologies,* ed. Adalaide Morris (Chapel Hill: University of North Carolina Press, 1997), 150.

22. An exception is Richard Huelsenbeck, who critiqued the sound poetry of Hugo Ball and fellow Dadaists by saying, "The dissection of words into sounds is contrary to the purpose of language and applies musical principles to an independent realm whose symbolism is aimed at a logical comprehension of one's environment . . . the value of language depends on comprehensibility rather than musicality." Quoted by Susan Stewart, "Letter on Sound," in Morris, *Sound States,* 47.

23. See documents accompanying the *Ursonate* recordings on Ubu Sound.

24. The Getty Research Institute owns the only extant copy of this handmade booklet, which represents one of the earliest instances of Schwitters's postwar reception in Europe.

25. Performance instruction in the score of the *Ursonate,* my translation. See Friedhelm Lach, *Kurt Schwitters: Das literarische Werk,* vol. 1, *Lyrik* (Cologne: M. DuMont Schauberg, 1973), 227.

26. For a discussion of Satie's anti-impressionism and his role in leading a small group of French composers (François Poulenc, Darius Milhaud, Georges Auric) to endorse popular entertainment, see my *Art and the Everyday: Popular Entertainment and the Circle of Erik Satie* (Oxford: Clarendon, 1991), 1–18.

27. Nancy Perloff, *Art and the Everyday,* 143–46.

28. Marinetti wrote his manifesto on the Variety Theatre in 1913.

29. Quoted by Glenn Watkins in *Soundings: Music in the Twentieth Century* (New York: Schirmer, 1988), 236. Craig Dworkin pointed out to me that the first sentence of Russolo's statement is uncannily prophetic of the Russian Suprematist Kazimir Malevich's pronouncement "I have destroyed the ring of the horizon and escaped the circle of things." My discussion of futurist music draws upon *Soundings,* 236–40.

30. Cage, *Silence,* 71.

31. Ibid., 71, 78, 80, 81, 84.

32. For this revised dating of Cage's lecture, which scholars have previously thought took place in 1937 or 1938, see Leta E. Miller, "Henry Cowell and John Cage: Intersections and Influences, 1933–1941," *Journal of the American Musicological Society* 59 (2006): 92. Miller identifies Russolo's *L'arte dei rumori"* as a principal influence on this lecture.

33. Cage, *Silence,* 3–6.

34. Ibid., 5.

35. One of Cage's main reasons for eulogizing Satie was the French composer's use of rhythmic structures as a point of departure in his compositions.

36. One performer plays at the keyboard while a second performer applies a metal rod firmly on the strings (harmonics). Slow slides of the rod away from or toward the center of the string's length produce ascending and descending siren-like sounds. The player at the keyboard sometimes sweeps a gong beater across the bass strings.

37. See *François Dufrêne: Affichiste Poeta Sonoro, Affichiste Poète Sonore, Affichiste Sound Poet,* introduction by Joao Fernandes, Museu de Arte Contemporânea de Serralves (Serralves: Fundação de Serralves, 2007), 15–16.

Steve McCaffery, "Cacophony, Abstraction, and Potentiality"

1. Ball himself supplies the evidence for Barzun's and Divoire's precedence in his summary of the first cabaret at his new club. "And, at Mr Tristan Tzara's instiga-

tion, Messrs Tzara, Huelsenbeck and Janco performed (for the very first time in Zurich and in the whole world) simultaneous verses from Messrs Henri Barzun and Fernand Divoire, as well as a simultaneous poem of his own composition" (Hugo Ball, "Cabaret Voltaire," trans. Christina Mills in *The Dada Reader: A Critical Anthology,* ed. Dawn Ades [Chicago: University of Chicago Press, 2006], 20). In actual fact Barzun's *Chants Simultanés* were first performed in 1912. This essay relies heavily upon quotations from Ball's diary, published posthumously as *Flight out of Time,* for precisely the same reason as Ball's fellow Dadaist Hans Richter:

I shall often quote from Ball's diaries, because I know of no better source of evidence on the moral and philosophical origins of the Dada revolt which started at the Cabaret Voltaire. It is entirely possible that any or all of the other Dadaists . . . went through the same inner development, but no one but Ball left a record of these inner conflicts. And no one achieved, even in fragmentary form, such precise formulations as Ball, the poet and thinker.

Richter, *Dada: art and anti-art,* trans. David Britt (New York: Abrams, 1965), 14–15. That said, *Flight out of Time* presents an interpretative challenge in being both compiled retroactively and published posthumously. Based upon his personal diary entries between 1910 and 1921, they were revised by Ball starting in 1924 (after the emotions and incidents described had settled into a reflective distance), and *Die Flucht aus der Zeit* was finally published in 1927. A second edition appeared in 1946 with a foreword by Ball's wife Emmy Ball-Hennings. It is important to emphasize the fact that *Die Flucht aus der Zeit* was assembled from the controlling, executive viewpoint of Ball's new conversion to Ca-

tholicism (a point stressed by Wilhelm Michel in his "Der Refraktär und sein Wort" in *Der Kunstwart* 42 [October 1928]: 1). For the earlier Ball, of Zurich, God is not dead but reified in the profiteering plunder of German capitalism and its supporting ideological state apparatus, including religion. Ball had already launched a scathing attack on the conflation of Christianity and capitalism in his pre-Dada poem "Der Henker" (The Hangman), where Christ is born as "the god of Gold" and lives as "the god of lustful greed" (*der Christenheit Götzplunder*)(quoted in Gerhardt Edward Steinke, *The Life and Work of Hugo Ball Founder of Dadaism* [The Hague: Mouton, 1967], 79).

2. See Dick Higgins, *Horizons: The Poetics and Theory of the Intermedia* (Carbondale: Southern Illinois University Press, 1984).

3. Hugo Ball, *Flight out of Time. A Dada Diary,* ed. John Elderfield, trans. Ann Raimes (New York: Viking Press, 1974), 57.

4. Ibid., 57. T. J. Demos interprets the poem politically as an attack on military authority and, while noting that the theme of homelessness articulates onto the poem's use of multiple and mutually invasive languages, fails to note in this an important antecedent to both *The Waste Land* and *Finnegans Wake.* See T. J. Demos, "Zurich Dada: The Aesthetics of Exile," in *The Dada Seminars,* ed. Leah Dickerman (Washington, DC: Distributed Art Publishers, 2005), 7–29. Although the poem clearly alludes to the Great War (then in progress), I do not concur with Demos's interpretation but see instead a more local cause, a veritable "inn" joke. Huelsenbeck recalls that the Cabaret Voltaire took over the premises of the former Cabaret Pantagruel at Spiegelgasse 1, a century-old building, owned at the time by the ex-sailor Jan Ephraim "now berthed in Zurich"

(Richard Huelsenbeck, *Memoirs of a Dada Drummer,* ed. Hans J. Kleinschmidt, trans. Joachim Neugroschel [New York: Viking Press, 1974], 4).

5. It seems Huelsenbeck incorporated genuine language following a felicitous discussion with the proprietor of the Cabaret Voltaire, Jan Ephraim, who was familiar with the South Pacific and African coasts where he had acquired knowledge of some authentic African songs. Ephraim supplied Huelsenbeck with this brief passage:

Trabadya La Modjere
Magamore Magagere
Trabadja Bono

Huelsenbeck, *Memoirs,* 8–9. According to Huelsenbeck, when his authentic Negro poems were presented at the Cabaret Voltaire "the audience thought they were wonderful" (ibid., 9). Why Huelsenbeck refers to them in the plural is somewhat puzzling, as the only example he records is the four lines above. Moreover, evidence from Ball indicates that Huelsenbeck performed only two such songs on March 30. A Maori song "Toto Vaco" was included, however, in his 1920 anthology *Dada Almanach* and was probably supplied to him by Ephraim.

6. Morgenstern's pithy description of his song, and both poems (in their entirety), are reprinted in *Imagining Language,* ed. Jed Rasula and Steve McCaffery (Cambridge: MIT Press, 1998), 104, 105. Scheerbart's poem first appeared in his 1900 novel *Ein Eisenbahnroman, ich liebe dich* (A Railway Novel, I Love You). While both poems utilize question and exclamation marks, Morgenstern complicates a purely phonetic reading by adding unreadable "passages," such as a semicolon enclosed in brackets, "(;)" and an empty space within square parentheses: "[ ]." It is interesting to note that Morgenstern's own spiritual and mystical

propensities (he was strongly influenced by Rudolph Steiner's theosophical thinking) cannily accord with those of Ball. I discuss Scheerbart's poem "Kikakoku" in relation to Ball's own "gadji beri bimba" in *Prior to Meaning: The Protosemantic and Poetics* (Evanston: Northwestern University Press, 2001), 166–67.

7. Ball, *Flight,* 70.

8. Ibid., 9. Ball volunteered to enlist in the German army but was turned down because of ill health. He did, however, personally travel to observe the war in Belgium, and his reactions are discussed subsequently in this essay.

9. Ibid., 16. Yeats's plans for revising Irish theater along the lines of Japanese Noh theater leads him to remark in 1916: "The human voice can only become louder by being less articulate, by discovering some new musical sort of roar and scream." Introduction to *Certain Noble Plays of Japan* (Churchtown, Dundrum: Cuala Press, 1916), iii–iv. This remarkable congruence of Yeats's emerging theatrical theories and Ball's attraction to eastern dramaturgy and such Zurich Dada manifestations as the *Lautgedicht* remains to be researched.

10. The influence of Kandinsky's dramatic theories on Ball's thinking on expressionist theater is well known (see Ball, *Flight,* 7–10; Huelsenbeck, *Memoirs,* xvi.). However, Kandinsky also seems a palpable theoretical force behind the *Lautgedicht* (especially the materialization of the phonic for spiritual ends), as this passage from his "On the Question of Form" evinces. "Matter is a kind of larder from which the spirit chooses what is *necessary* for itself, much as a cook would. . . . Sound, therefore, is the soul of form, which only comes alive through sound and which works from the inside out" (Wassily Kandinsky in *The Blaue Reiter Almanac,* ed. Wassily Kandin-

sky and Franz Marc, New Documentary Edition by Klaus Lankheit [New York: Viking, 1974], 147, 149).

11. Matthew S. Witkovsky, "Chronology," *Dada* (Washington, DC: Distributed Art Publishers, 2005), 421.

12. Ball had previously been involved in radical publishing ventures. Prior to his flight to Zurich he had published in Franz Pfemfert's left-wing periodical *Die Aktion* and had himself founded in October 1913, with his companion Hans Leybold, the short-lived *Revolution.* Ball quotes the French historian Florian Parmentier, who links the crisis in independent creative existence to a collusion between democracy and journalism, a collusion whose origin Ball traces back to Rousseau. Independence is stifled by the false need for consensual acceptance "because democracy denies the writer the means of existence, because it encourages the monstrous tyranny of journalists" (Ball, *Flight,* 26).

13. Ibid., 3–4.

14. Ibid., 4. On Ball's antagonism to the printing press, it may be of interest to note that the Italian futurist Giacomo Balla wrote "Onomatopoeic Noise Poem for the Printing Press" two years prior to Ball's sound poems. Fortunato Depero also wrote "Canzone Rumorista" (noise song) in the same year as Ball's *Lautgedichte* was conceived. Ball was certainly aware of Italian futurism, having received a copy of *Parole in Libertà* from Marinetti himself (see Ball, *Flight,* 25), and his own assessment of that movement opens up for Ball into a broader problematic: "There is no language anymore" (ibid., 25). Cocteau draws attention to the didactic values to be drawn from the machine on grounds thoroughly consonant with futurist poetics: "it is a weakness not to comprehend the beauty of the machine. The fault lies in depicting machines instead

of taking from them a lesson in rhythm, in stripping away the superfluous" (Jean Cocteau, quoted in Edith Sitwell, *A Poet's Notebook* [Boston: Little, Brown, 1950], 184–85).

15. Ball, *Flight,* 10–11, 22.

16. Ibid., 71. Ball's dissatisfaction with journalistic language dates to well before this famous proclamation. In July 1915 he laments: "the word has been abandoned, it used to dwell among us. The word has become commodity. The word should be left alone. The world has lost all dignity" (ibid., 26).

17. See Huelsenbeck, *Memoirs,* xxvii, and Raoul Hausmann, *Am Anfang war Dada* (Steinbach/Giessen: Anabas-Verlag Günther Kämpf, 1972), 39–42.

18. Ball, *Flight,* 49.

19. Ball's avowal of idiosyncrasy and his belief in the basic individuality of human beings lead him to reject philosophical abstraction: "abstract idealism is itself only a cliché. Living beings are never identical and never act identically, unless they are trained and prepared for the Procrustean bed of culture" (ibid., 47). It is important not to confuse his repudiation of abstract idealism with aesthetic abstraction, which Ball believes is the necessary movement of all art from representational to nonrepresentational form. For Ball's ruminations on the beneficial retreat of art from figuration, see Ball, *Flight,* 55. On these grounds I believe it correct for Hans Richter to characterize the *Lautgedichte* as abstract phonetic poetry.

20. Ball, *Flight,* 68.

21. Jeffrey T. Schnapp, "Introduction: Ball and Hammer" in *Ball and Hammer: Hugo Ball's Tenderenda the Fantast,* ed. Jeffrey T. Schnapp (New Haven: Yale University Press, 2002), 4.

22. Ball, *Flight,* 68.

23. For more on this relation, see my chapter "The Elsewhere of Meaning," on the *Jappements* of Claude Gauvreau, in *North of Intention: Critical Essays 1973–1986* (New York: Roof Books, 1986), 170–77.

24. Arthur Symons writes of Verlaine that "words serve him with so absolute a negation that he can write *Romances sans Paroles*— songs without words, in which scarcely a sense of the interference of human speech remains" (Arthur Symons, from *The Symbolist Movement in French Literature*, quoted in Sitwell, *A Poet's Notebook*, 228).

25. Doesburg published his "lettersoundconstructs" under the pseudonym of I. K. Bonset. An example can be found in Rasula and McCaffery, *Imagining Language*, 14. Hausman's poem can be found in Willard Bohn, ed., *The Dada Market: An Anthology of Poetry* (Carbondale: Southern Illinois University Press, 1993), 97.

26. Ball, *Flight*, 71. Ball's "Elefanten Karawane" is accessible under the tile "Karawane" in Bohn, *Dada Market*, 36. My version in the epigraph restores the original title and removes the typographical varieties that are a striking feature of the 1917 version.

27. It is thus surprising to find Worringer absent from the seminal anthology *Symposium of the Whole: A Range of Discourse toward an Ethnopoetics*, ed. Jerome Rothenberg and Diane Rothenberg (Berkeley: University of California Press, 1983).

28. See Sander Gilman, "The Mad Man as Artist: Medicine, History, and Degenerate Art," *Journal of Contemporary History* 20, no. 4 (October 1986): 575–97. Leah Dickerman also claims Lombroso's theories as precursory to Dada (see Dickerman, *Dada Seminars*, 29–30).

29. It is a well-known fact that several Dadaists (Arp, Huelsenbeck, Tzara) avoided or delayed military conscription by convincingly feigning their insanity (Dickerman, *Dada Seminars*, 23, 40 n. 67).

30. Ball, *Flight*, 75.

31. Ibid., 70.

32. Ball's propensity to self-representation results in numerous fascinating equations. The fate of Ball the poet is the fate of Germany (Ball, *Flight*, 30); he reckons his life script is the same as the biblical Daniel's (ibid., 34) and at other times the same as Stephen the protomartyr (ibid., 49). G. E. Steinke however quotes passages from two of Ball's adolescent poems that indicate "a capacity for being seized and carried away by forces greater than himself" (Steinke, *Life and Work of Hugo Ball*, 23).

33. Ball, *Flight*, 49.

34. Ibid., 29. Benjamin traces a parallel trajectory of the phonic in the career of the Viennese poet-satirist Karl Krauss, noting it to be a dissolution of the instrumental word into "a merely animal voice" (Walter Benjamin, *Reflections: Essays, Aphorisms, Autobiographical Writings*, trans. Edmund Jephcott [New York: Schocken Books, 1986], 264).

35. Ball, *Flight*, 220–21.

36. Schnapp, *Ball and Hammer*, 13.

37. Ball, *Flight*, 221.

38. Ibid., 96, 99. This defense of the individual — outside democracy or community — attunes with Tzara's own reflections on the socio-emotive origins of Dada. "So DADA was born of a desire for independence, of a distrust of the community." Tristan Tzara, *Approximate Man and Other Writings*, trans. Mary Ann Caws (Boston: Black Widow Press, 2005), 125.

39. Ball, *Flight*, 210.

40. Tzara, for his part, will remove the *d*'s in DADA to form his new independent movement of "Aaism" (*Approximate Man*, 115).

Christian Bök, "When Cyborgs Versify"

1. Hugo Ball, *Flight Out of Time: A Dada Diary*, ed. John Elderfield, trans. Ann Raimes (New York: Viking Press, 1974), 71. Ball adds that if this alchemy does not suffice, "we must even give up the word too, to keep for poetry its . . . holiest refuge" (71). Alexei Kruchenykh, "New Ways of the Word (The Language of the Future, Death to Symbolism)," in *Russian Futurism through Its Manifestoes, 1912–1928,* ed. Anna Lawton (Ithaca: Cornell University Press, 1988), 70. Kruchenykh remarks that before the poetic invention of '*zaum* "everything [was] done to suffocate the primordial feeling of our native language" — to which he adds: "up to the present the word has been shackled . . . by its *subordination to rational thought*" (70). Schwitters remarks that, after the poetic invention of *Merz,* "art is a primordial concept, exalted as a godhead, inexplicable as life, indefinable and pointless" — to which he adds (with a hint of irony): "I pity nonsense, because until now it has been so neglected in the making of art." Kurt Schwitters, "From *Merz*," in *PPPPPP: Poems, Performances, Pieces, Proses, Plays, Poetics,* ed. Jerome Rothenberg and Pierre Joris (Philadelphia: Temple University Press, 1993), 215.

2. Raoul Hausmann has indeed influenced much of the phonematic repertoire of *Die Ursonate:* for example, the phrase "fmsbwtözäu / pggiv" (from his poster of 1918) provides many of the themes for the rondos of the first movement of *Die Ursonate.* Moreover, the title of his poem "Lanke trr gll" provides the theme for the scherzo in the third movement; the title of his poem "Grimm glimm gnimm bimbimm" provides the theme for the presto, early in the fourth movement; and the title of his

poem "Priimiitittiii" provides the theme for the cadenza, later in the fourth movement.

3. Readers who might wish to compare recordings of *Die Ursonate,* as performed by Kurt Schwitters and Christian Bök respectively, can do so online: http://www.ubu.com/sound/schwitters.html and www.ubu.com/sound/bok.html.

4. F. T. Marinetti, "Technical Manifesto of Futurist Literature," in *Let's Murder the Moonshine: Selected Writings,* ed. R. W. Flint, trans. R. W. Flint and Arthur A. Coppatelli (Los Angeles: Sun and Moon Press, 1991), 95; and "Multiplied Man and the Reign of the Machine," ibid., 100.

5. Marinetti, "Electrical War (A Futurist Vision-Hypothesis)," in Flint, *Let's Murder the Moonshine,* 113.

6. Marinetti, "Geometric and Mechanical Splendour and the Numerical Sensibility," in Flint, *Let's Murder the Moonshine,* 106.

7. F. T. Marinetti, "Technical Manifesto of Futurist Literature," in Flint, *Let's Murder the Moonshine,* 96.

8. William S. Burroughs, *The Ticket That Exploded* (New York: Grove Press, 1967), 163. Burroughs calls upon his readers to purge themselves of all thought by delegating the internal dialogue of their minds to tape recorders: "Get it out of your heads and into the machines. Stop talking stop arguing. Let the machines talk and argue" (163).

9. Henri Chopin, "*Poésie Sonore:* Open Letter to Aphonic Musicians 1967," in *Sound Poetry: A Catalogue,* ed. Steve McCaffery and bpNichol (Toronto: Underwhich Editions, 1978), 48. Bp Nichol, for example, has expressed the kind of Luddite opinion that typifies the naysayers of Chopin (even though bpNichol has himself experimented with the use of a magnetophone in the course of his career) : "I eschew the tape recorder because it's a machine, it's not the human voice" — to which he adds: "I

find the sound too mechanical." bpNichol, "Interview: With Caroline Bayard and Jack David," in *The Critical Writings of bpNichol,* ed. Roy Miki (Vancouver: Talonbooks, 2002), 182, 183.

10. Paul Dutton, "Beyond Doo-Wop, or How I Came to Realize That Hank Williams Is Avant-Garde: On Free-Voice Singing," *Musicworks* 54 (1992): 15.

11. Bob Holman, "An Interview with Bob Holman," *Cecil Vortex* (March 15, 2007) http://cecilvortex.com/swath/2007/03/15/an_interview_with_bob_holman.html.

12. Paul D. Miller, *Rhythm Science* (New York: MIT Press, 2004), 56.

13. Walter Benjamin, "The Work of Art in the Age of Mechanical Reproduction," in *Illuminations,* ed. Hannah Arendt, trans. Harry Zohn (New York: Schocken, 1969), 242. Benjamin argues that, in the modern milieu of globalized capitalism, "all efforts to render politics aesthetic culminate in one thing: war" (241).

14. Readers who might wish to hear recordings of these excerpts from *The Cyborg Opera* can do so online at PENNsound, http://www.writing.upenn.edu/pennsound/x/Bok.html.

Charles Bernstein, "Hearing Voices"

1. Leslie Scalapino, *Considering how exaggerated music is* (Berkeley: North Point, 1982); John Ashbery, *Girls on the Run* (New York: Farrar, Straus, and Giroux, 1999).

2. Kenneth Goldsmith, "Kenneth Goldsmith Sings Theory," accessed at http://writing.upenn.edu/pennsound/x/Goldsmith.html.

3. Play on T. S. Eliot's title; see note 11 below.

4. Caroline Bergvall, "Shorter Chaucer Tales," accessed at http://writing.upenn.edu/pennsound/x/Bergvall.html. Jack Spicer,

"A Textbook of Poetry," from *Heads of the Town up to the Aether,* in *The Collected Books of Jack Spicer,* ed. Robin Blaser (Santa Barbara: Black Sparrow Press, 1980), 178.

5. PennSound (http://writing.upenn.edu/pennsound) is a Web archive of downloadable poetry readings, which I founded with Al Filreis in January 2005.

6. David Antin, "a private occasion in a public space," in *Talking at the Boundaries* (New York: New Directions, 1976).

7. Reuven Tsur, *"Kubla Khan" — Poetic Structure, Hypnotic Quality, and Cognitive Style* (Amsterdam/Philadelphia: John Benjamins, 2006). See especially chapter 1, "'Kubla Khan' and the Implied Critic's Decision Style." Tsur provides waveform analysis of pitch, amplitude, and intonation in chapter 4, "Vox Humana: Performing 'Kubla Khan.'"

8. Tsur, *"Kubla Khan,"* 18.

9. Ludwig Wittgenstein, *Philosophical Investigations,* trans. G. E. M. Anscombe (New York: Macmillan, 1958), part 2. George Lakoff, *Moral Politics: How Liberals and Conservatives Think* (Chicago: University of Chicago Press, 2002).

10. Louis Zukofsky, *Selected Poems,* ed. Charles Bernstein (New York: Library of America, 2006), 8.

11. T. S Eliot, "The Waste Land," sound recording, accessed at http://town.hall.org/Archives/radio/IMS/Harper Audio/011894_harp_ITH.html.

12. Ezra Pound, *Pound's Cavalcanti: An Edition of the Translations, Notes, and Essays,* ed. David Anderson (Princeton: Princeton University Press: 1983), 171.

13. Zukofsky, *Selected Poems,* 152. You can hear my performance of the poem at http://writing.upenn.edu/ezurl/5/ and Zukofsky's at http://writing.upenn.edu/ezurl/6.

Hélène Aji, "Impossible Reversibilities"

1. Kristine Stiles, "Performance," in *Critical Terms for Art History,* ed. Robert S. Nelson and Richard Schiff (Chicago: University of Chicago Press, 2003), 76.

2. Jackson Mac Low, "Jackson Mac Low — An Interview Conducted by Barry Alpert, The Bronx, New York, April 6, 1974 (revised Jan.–Feb. 1975 by JML)," *Vort* 8 (1975): 6–7.

3. Eric Mottram, "Compositions of the Magus: The Art of JML," *Vort* 8 (1975): 85.

4. To give points of comparison, Vito Acconci starts experimental work that can be related to Mac Low's in the late 1960s and early 1970s. Mac Low starts working "procedurally" around 1954 (see Mac Low letter to Nick Piombino posted on http://epc .buffalo.edu/authors/maclow/piombino. html, accessed October 31, 2007).

5. See Jackson Mac Low, "Make Your Own System! (1990)," *Jackson Mac Low Papers (MSS 180),* New Poetry Archive, Mandeville Special Collections, Geisel Library, University of California, San Diego, box 67, folder 28.

6. Performance of Jackson Mac Low's "Is That Wool Hat my Hat?" http://www.beautymarsh.com/about/ISTHATWOOL HAT.mp3, accessed October 30, 2007.

7. Mac Low, "Jackson Mac Low — An Interview Conducted by Barry Alpert," 5.

8. See Marjorie Perloff, *Poetry On and Off the Page: Essays for Emergent Occasions* (Evanston: Northwestern University Press, 1998).

9. See Craig Dworkin, *Reading the Illegible* (Evanston: Northwestern University Press, 2003), 50–65.

10. Jackson Mac Low, *Doings: Assorted Performance Pieces, 1955–2002* (New York: Granary Books, 2005), 64–68.

11. Charles Bernstein, "Jackson at Home," in *Content's Dream: Essays, 1975 — 1984,* by Charles Bernstein (Los Angeles: Sun & Moon, 1986), 257.

12. Jackson Mac Low and Anne Tardos, "Four Vocabulary Gathas in Memoriam Armand Schwerner, 1999," in Mac Low, *Doings,* audio piece no. 07, 2:43.

13. Jackson Mac Low and Anne Tardos in *Doings,* 249.

14. Jackson Mac Low and others, "A Vocabulary for Sharon Belle Mattlin, 1973," in *Doings,* audio piece no. 09, 5:21.

15. Jackson Mac Low, *Representative Works, 1938–1985* (New York: Roof, 1986), 170–75.

16. Giorgio Agamben, *Remnants of Auschwitz (Quel Che Resta di Auschwitz),* trans. Daniel Heller-Roazen (New York: Zone Books, 2000).

17. Mac Low, "Jackson Mac Low — An Interview Conducted by Barry Alpert," 14.

Craig Dworkin, "The Stutter of Form"

Sincere thanks to Marjorie Perloff for the invitation to present the talk that became the kernel of this essay; Christian Bök for always knowing where the most interesting poetry is; Jordan Scott, Derek Beaulieu, and Ryan Fitzpatrick for the generous access to materials; Christof Migone, Brandon LaBelle, Shelley Jackson, and Elisabeth Joyce for inspired and inspiring writing and correspondence; and — most of all — Michael Davidson, for setting an impeccable example. All translations mine unless otherwise indicated.

1. Herman Melville, "Billy Budd, Sailor," in *Billy Budd, Sailor and Other Stories,* ed. Frederick Busch (New York: Penguin, 1986), 302.

2. Ludwig Wittgenstein, *Philosophical Inves-*

tigations, trans. G. E. M. Anscombe, 3rd ed. (New York: Macmillan, 1968), 193.

3. Gilles Deleuze, "He Stuttered," in *Essays Critical and Clinical*, trans. Daniel W. Smith and Michael A. Greco (Minneapolis: University of Minnesota Press, 1997), 107, emphasis in the original. Such a writer, Deleuze continues, "makes the language itself scream, stutter, stammer, or murmur" (110). For Deleuze, the value of such extremity is clear: "for when an author is content with an external marker that leaves the *form of expression* intact ('he stuttered. . . . '), its efficacy will be poorly understood unless there is a corresponding *form of content*" (108; parentheses and ellipses in original).

4. Ibid., 113; ellipsis and emphases in original.

5. Alvin Lucier, *Reflections: Interviews, Scores, Writings* (Cologne: MusikTexte, 1995), 322.

6. Ibid., 23.

7. Alvin Lucier, *I Am Sitting in a Room*, Lovely Music 1013, recorded 1980.

8. In the earlier recording, initial *r* and *n* sounds also lead to a pronounced stammer.

9. For those keeping score, the technical specifications of that inscriptive relay, according to the publisher, included a "Nagra tape recorder with an Electro-Voice 635 dynamic microphone and played back on one channel of a Revox A77 tape recorder, Dynaco amplifier and a KLH Model Six loudspeaker" (Lovely Music 1013). For more on the theory of inscriptive relay, see Friedrich Kittler, *Discourse Networks 1800/1900*, trans. Michael Metteer with Chris Cullens (Stanford: Stanford University Press, 1992).

10. Christof Migone, "Sonic Somatic: Performances of the Unsound Body" (Ph.D. diss., New York University, 2007), 183. One critic has characterized Lucier's statement of his intention as "either disingenuous or deluded" (Edward Strickland, *Minimalism:*

Origins [Bloomington: Indiana University Press, 1993], 199); the degree of Lucier's earnestness and naïveté can perhaps be better gauged by his contemporaneous *The Only Talking Machine of Its Kind in the World*, which is scored

for any stutterer, stammerer, lisper, person with faulty or halting speech, regional dialect or foreign accent or any other anxious speaker who believes in the healing power of sound. The speaker talks to an audience through a public address system for long enough to reveal the peculiarities of his speech; his friends set up a tape-delay system, tapped from the PA, and the speaker continues talking "until any anxiety about his speech is relieved or it becomes clear that the tape-delay system is relieved or it becomes clear that the tape-delay system is failing and will continue to fail to bring this about"

Quoted in Michael Nyman, *Experimental Music: Cage and Beyond*, 2nd ed. (Cambridge: Cambridge University Press, 1999), 109.

11. Stuart Kendall, review of Catherine Brun's *Pierre Guyotat: Essai biographique*, in *SubStance* 34, no. 3 (2005): 136. The closest English-language equivalents to Guyotat's sexualized violation of literary form might be William Burroughs, Kathy Acker, and Dennis Cooper.

12. Pierre Guyotat, *Prostitution* (Paris: Gallimard, 1975), 9.

13. Pierre Guyotat, *Prostitution: An Excerpt*, trans. Bruce Benderson (New York: Red Dust, 1995), 9.

14. A stage version of *Tombeau* was performed at the Théâtre National in Chaillot in 1981, accompanied by music by George Aperghis, whose work — on the borders of modern composition and sound poetry — often involves the stuttered manipulation of voice.

15. Roland Barthes, "Ce qu'il advient au Signifiant," in *Œuvres Complètes: livres, textes, entretiens, 1968–1971,* revised edition edited by Éric Marty (Paris: Seuil, 2002), 609.

16. Ibid.

17. Cf. Catherine Brun, *Pierre Guyotat: Essai biographique* (Paris: Editions Léo Scheer, 2005), 292.

18. Walter Benjamin, *Selected Writings,* vol.1, *1913–1926,* ed. Marcus Bullock and Michael W. Jennings (Cambridge: Harvard University Press, 1996).

19. Ibid., 259.

20. Ibid., 260.

21. Pierre Guyotat, *Explications* (Paris: Éditions Léo Scheer, 2000), 164.

22. Kendall, review of Catherine Brun's *Pierre Guyotat: Essai Biographique,* 137.

23. Guyotat, *Explications,* 56–57.

24. Ibid., 29, 165. Susan Howe, "The Difficulties Inter-View," with Tom Beckett, *The Difficulties* 3, no. 2 (1989): 18, emphasis added. Guyotat elaborates on the relation of literary rhythm and everyday language:

*Quand je parle du rythme, je ne parle pas de ce qu'un "écrivain" pourrait faire, par exemple, avec ce qu'on nomme le "langage de tous les jours"—à quoi bon écrire si c'est pour reproduire le langage de tous les jours?—.
. . . Je parle du rythme qui fait faire des sacrifices, qui impose qu'on saccage, un peu, beaucoup, la "belle langue," la belle langue française, pour lui rendre son éloquence profonde; et l'éloquence ne sort, ne vient que de ce qu'on nomme.*
[*When I speak of rhythm, I do not speak about what a "writer" could do, for example, with what is called "everyday language"—why write if it reproduces everyday language?— . . . I speak of rhythm that effects sacrifices, that imposes itself, wreaks a little havoc or even really ravages the "beautiful language," the beautiful French language,*

*in order to return its profound eloquence to it; and eloquence issues, comes only from what one names.] (*Explications, *40)*

25. See Guyotat, *Explications,* 35–36, 63. Cf. "J'écris maintenant," in *Vivre* (Paris: Denoël, Collection L'infini, 1984).

26. Pierre Guyotat, *Littérature interdite* (Paris: Gallimard, 1972), 127.

27. It may be that all of Guyotat's unsettling content, his socially unacceptable depictions of bodily activities, is intimately related to the stutter. The stutter describes the intersection between the interiority of the private body and the exteriorized interpellation of that body in public space. Christof Migone underscores the social context necessary for the stutter to register: "as phonetist Marie-Claude Pfauwadel asserts, stuttering requires at least two to be manifest." Marie-Claude Pfauwadel, *Être Bègue* (Paris: Le hameau/retz, 1986): 181; quoted in Migone, "Sonic Somatic," 156. The stutter is the uninsured collision between the individual's intimate bodily mechanism of utterance and the socially forged psychological pressures and discomforts that are both the stutter's cause and effect. For a reading of poetry as a reaction to the social regime of fluency, see Tim Trengove Jones: "Larkin's Stammer," in *Essays in Criticism* 50 (1990): 322–38.

28. Guyotat, *Littérature interdite,* 98. Guyotat frequently recalls his stutter, writing, for instance: "J'ai aussi, pendant très longtemps, dans ma première enfance, et même mon adolescence, beaucoup bégayé. . . . c'était une difficulté, voire un impossibilité à produire certaines phrases, certains démarrages de phrase" (I also, for a very long time, during my childhood and even my adolescence, often stuttered . . . it was a difficulty, even an impossibility to produce certain sentences, certain beginnings of sentences) (*Explications*, 40). The logic of the stutter, with its simultaneous excess and insufficiency, recalls Michel de Certeau's understanding of glossolalia, which is characterized in his account by incompleted beginning and repetitions. Michel de Certeau, "Vocal Utopias: Glossolalias," *Representations* 56 (Fall 1996): 38, 40; cf. 41. For a slightly different understanding of the excess of the stutter, enumerated under the sign of Georges Bataille, see Christof Migone on the "remainder remaining entirely beyond control" ("A Lexicon of False Starts and Failed Advances," in *Writing Aloud: The Sonics of Language* [Los Angeles: Errant Bodies, 2001], 174), and Brandon LaBelle, "Word of Mouth: Christof Migone's Little Manias," *Sound Voice Perform* [L. A.: Errant Bodies, Critical Ear Series] 2 (2005): 14.

29. That squirt is both figurative and literal. Guyotat, infamously, masturbates while writing, and as the 1995 exhibition of some of Guyotat's manuscript pages attests (Cabinet Gallery, London), his writing sheets are dampened and stained as a result. His onanistic habit would be of little more than prurient interest, except that it corroborates the association between writing and written in his work, both in the ways I am arguing here and in his own claim that "my work is not writing; it's a secretion" (quoted in Bruce Benderson, translator's introduction to Guyotat, *Prostitution*, 4).

30. See Guyotat, *Explications*, 58–59. *Prostitution* was published by Gallimard (Paris) in 1975 and issued in a revised edition in 1987. See also Marc Shell, "Animals That Talk; or, Stutter," *Differences: A Journal of Feminist Cultural Studies* 15, no. 1 (2004): 84.

31. Before being published by Coach House Press, *blert* appeared (under the same title) in chapbooks from No Press and MODL Press, as well as in two online collections:

Drunken Boat, no. 8, special issue, "Canadian Strange," ed. Sina Queyras, http://www.drunkenboat.com/db8/canadian strange.html, and *nyposei* 2 (2006), special issue, "Språkbeherskelse," http://www.nypoesi.net/tidsskrift/206/?tekst=0.

32. Bruce Andrews, "Blueier Blue," *2nd Avenue Poetry*, vol. 1 (http://www.2ndavepoetry.com); "Fixed Stars 1," *Lip Service* (Toronto: Coach House Press, 2001), 299; "Dizzyistics," *Eco Poetics* 1 (Winter 2001): 10.

33. Scott describes the project in his dissertation: "In *blert* . . . I have extracted elements of my own stutter and fused those elements with vocabulary from medical studies on the subject as well as theoretical inquiries into the formation of language." "Blort, Jam, Rejoice: Towards a Poetics of the Stutter" (Ph.D. diss., University of Calgary, 2006), 15.

34. Deleuze, "He Stuttered," 111.

35. Roman Jakobson, "Linguistics and Poetics," in *Style in Language,* ed. Thomas A. Sebeok (Cambridge: MIT Press, 1960), 373.

36. Derek Beaulieu, "Refusing the Prairie: Radicality and Urbanity in Calgarian Poetics," *nypoesi* 2 (2006).

37. The association is further corroborated when the lines "tectonic carpals" and "cairn as carpal" pair the geological and the anatomical.

38. Paul Valéry, *Tel Quel II,* "Rhumbs," *Pléiade II* (Paris: Gallimard, 1960), 637. Allen S. Weiss makes a similar connection in his definition of "stammer," *Sound Voice Perform,* 30.

39. Cf. Guyotat's invocation of Demosthenes' stutter, *Explications,* 40.

40. Peter Quartermain, *Disjunctive Poetics: From Gertrude Stein and Louis Zukofsky to Susan Howe* (Cambridge: Cambridge University Press, 1992), 3.

41. Michael Davidson, "Concerto for the Left Hand: Disability (in the) Arts,"

PMLA 120, no. 2 (2005): 615, column 2.
For a Derridean reading of the poetics of
circumlocution and revision understood as
stuttering, see Federico Bonaddio, "Sensing
the Stutter: a Stammerer's Perception of
Lorca," *Neopphilolgus* 82 (1988): 53–62.

42. Davidson, "Concerto," 616, column 2.

43. Michael Davidson, "Missing Larry:
The Poetics of Disability in the Work of
Larry Eigner," *Concerto for the Left Hand,
Disability and the Defamiliar Body* (Ann
Arbor: University of Michigan Press,
2008), 116–41.

Rubén Gallo, "Jean Cocteau's Radio Poetry"

1. Carlos Noriega Hope, "Notas del director,"
El Universal Ilustrado 308 (April 5, 1923): 11.

2. Rubén Gallo, "Radio," in *Mexican Modernity: The Avant-Garde and the Technological Revolution* (Cambridge: MIT Press,
2005).

3. Qtd. in Maxime Scheinfegel, "Orphée ou
les Temps de la Voix" in *Le cinéma de Jean
Cocteau, suivi de Hommage à Jean Marais,*
ed. Christian Rolot et al. (Montpellier:
Université Paul Valéry, 1994), 108.

4. Aurélie Luneau, *Radio Londres: Les voix de
la liberté (1940–1944)* (Paris: Perrin, 2005).

5. *Jean Cocteau: The Art of Cinema,* ed. André
Bernard and Claude Gauteur, trans. Robin
Buss (London: Marion Boyars, 1992), 156.

6. André Breton, *Manifestoes of Surrealism,*
trans. Richard Seaver and Helen Lane
(Ann Arbor: University of Michigan Press,
1969), 37–38.

7. Walter A. Strauss, "Jean Cocteau: The
Difficulty of Being Orpheus," in *Reviewing
Orpheus: Essays on the Cinema and Art of
Jean Cocteau,* ed. Cornelia A. Tsakiridou
(Lewisburg: Bucknell University Press,
1997), 32–33.

8. Breton, *Manifestoes of Surrealism,* 27–28.

9. Peter Read, "L'oiseau qui chantait à l'oreille
de Cocteau, ou les métamorphoses d'une
petite phrase," *Que vlo-ve? Bulletin international des études sur Apollinaire,* 2nd series,
25 (January–March 1998): 23–24.

10. Willard Bohn, "Un oiseau chante," *Que
vlo-ve?* 2nd ser., 23 (July–September 1987):
24–25.

11. Rudolf Arnheim, *Radio* (London: Faber
and Faber, 1936), 232.

12. Georges Duhamel, *Defense of Letters* (New
York: Graystone Press, 1939), 30, 35.

13. Bertolt Brecht, "The Radio as an Apparatus
of Communication," in *Radiotext(e),* ed.
Neil Strauss (New York: Semiotext(e),
1993), 15–17.

14. Kurt Tucholsky, "Radio Censorship"
(1928), *The Weimar Republic Sourcebook,*
ed. Anton Kaes et al. (Berkeley: University
of California Press, 1994), 603.

15. *Jean Cocteau: The Art of Cinema,* 62.

16. Ibid.

17. Ibid.

18. Ibid.

19. Radio France Internationale, "Marcel
Proust dans tous ses états," Institut National
de l'Audiovisuel, DL R 20070226 RFI 12.

20. Françoise Haffner, "La voix de Cocteau
dans ses films," in Rolot et al., *Le cinéma de
Jean Cocteau,* 45.

21. For a discussion of radio imagery in
"Lettre-Océan," see Gallo, "Radio."

22. Read, "L'oiseau qui chantait à l'oreille de
Cocteau," 26.

23. Jean Cocteau, *Opium. Journal d'une désin-
toxication* (Paris: Stock, 1930), 176.

24. Kenneth Goldsmith, "Paragraphs on Conceptual Writing," *Open Letter: A Canadian
Journal of Writing and Theory* 12, no. 7
(2005): 108–11. Craig Dworkin, introduction to Ubuweb Anthology of Conceptual
Writing at http://www.ubu.com/concept/.

25. Read suggests that Cocteau had mixed
feelings about his relation to Apollinaire:

"Dans le filme d'Orphée, l'attitude de Cocteau face à l'œuvre d'Apollinaire, représentée par ce verre unique, est un mélange de crainte et d'admiration extrème, comme s'il avait peur d'être ensorcelé par un appel irrésistible. Il confirme lui-même cette attitude en 1954 lorsqu'il écrit encore sur Apollinaire: "Pas une chanson qu'il fredonnait en écrivant, pas une tache qui tombait de sa plume, qui ne collaborassent à un charme, dans le sens médiéval du terme." Read, "L'oiseau qui chantait à l'oreille de Cocteau," 26.

Antonio Sergio Bessa, *"Sound as Subject"*

1. Décio Pignatari, "Poesia concreta: organização" [Concrete poetry: organization], in *Teoria da poesia concreta–Textos críticos e manifestos, 1950–1960,* by Augusto de Campos, Décio Pignatari, and Haroldo de Campos, 2nd ed. (São Paulo: Livraria Duas Cidades, 1975), 86. (Unless otherwise noted, all translations are by the author.) Coincidentally, Mário de Andrade, in *Pequena história da música* [Short history of music], lists the "composer" Ezra Pound in the same breath as Webern: "Also in trios, quartets and quintets a most interesting generation has bloomed, employing the most unusual and curious group of soloists (Kurt Weill, Falla, Ezra Pound, and Anton Webern)." Augusto de Campos concludes that Andrade might have heard of the performance of *Le Testament* at the Salle Pleyel in 1926. Augusto de Campos, *Música de invenção* (São Paulo: Editora Perspectiva, 1998), 27.

2. Decio Pignatiari, in Augusto de Campos et al., *Teoria da poesia concreta,* 87.

3. Ibid., 48.

4. The interplay of visual and sonic values is also one of Flora Süssekind's concerns in her essay "(Quase audível) — Nota sobre 'ão'" [(Almost audible) — Note on 'ão']. In it, Süssekind quotes from a rare 1971 interview with bossa nova singer and songwriter João Gilberto, in which he claims that "when I sing, I think of a light-filled and open space where I will place my sounds; it's as if I were writing on a blank sheet of paper" (in the original, "Quando eu canto, penso num espaço claro e aberto onde vou colocar meus sons, é como se eu estivesse escrevendo num pedaço de papel em branco"). Commenting on this passage, Süssekind adds that "it is, then, on another plane, that of the graphic space, of the letter, and not in the phonic materiality itself, that the vocal image is constructed. It is through vision that we perceive what is directed to the ear, as Barthes has suggested in commenting on acoustic images." (É, pois, num outro plano, o do espaço gráfico, o da letra, e não em sua própria materialidade fônica, que se procura construir, aí, a imagem vocal. 'É através da visão que sera percebido aquilo que é dirigido ao ouvido,' se poderia dizer, nesse sentido, seguindo comentário de Barthes sobre imagens acústicas.) Flora Süssekind and Júlio Castañon Guimarães, eds., *Sobre Augusto de Campos* (Rio de Janeiro: 7 Letras, 2004), 153.

5. Rodrigo Naves, "Minha relação com a tradição é musical," in *Metalinguagem & outras metas,* by Haroldo de Campos, 4th ed. (São Paulo: Editora Perspectiva, 1992), 257–58.

6. Ferdinand de Saussure, *Course in General Linguistics,* trans. with an introduction and notes by Wade Baskin (New York: McGraw-Hill, 1966), 66.

7. Luís A. Milanese, "Poesia e música," in Haroldo de Campos, *Metalinguagem & outras metas,* 285.

8. Augusto de Campos et al., *Teoria da poesia concreta,* 15.

9. Glenn Gould, mimeograph distributed with program for New Music Associates concert, Toronto, October 3, 1953 (rescheduled to January 9, 1954), http://www.uv.es/~calaforr/Webern/gould.htm. Gould, a musician with a profound understanding of the complexities of twentieth-century music, also commented on the visual aspects of Webern's music, and in his 1974 article "Korngold and the Crisis of the Piano Sonata," in *The Glenn Gould Reader,* ed. Tim Page (New York: Knopf, 1984), he describes Webern's mature work as "occupied with Mondrian-like geometric concerns" (200). Mondrian's paintings were also one of de Campos's inspirations for Poetamenos, as acknowledged by the author in an interview from 1998: "Music is for me an indispensable 'nutrient of impulse.' Since poetry, as Pound says, is closer to music and the visual arts than literature itself, I find it natural that it is thus. Without Webern, Mondrian and Malevitch I couldn't have formulated 'Poetamenos' (which also owes to Mallarmé, Pound, Joyce and Cummings)." (A música é para mim uma 'nutrição de impulso' indispensável. Como a poesia, no dizer de Pound, está mais próxima da música e das artes plásticas do que da própria literatura, acho natural que assim seja. Sem Webern, Mondrian e Maliévitch, eu não teria formulado o 'Poetamenos' [também devedor, é óbvio, de Mallarmé, Pound, Joyce e Cummings].) *Cult* (1998): 7.

10. This diagram, which Webern used as the basis for his Concerto, op. 24, and which was ultimately inscribed on his gravestone, can be translated as "Arepo, the harvester, holds the wheels at work," and there is much speculation as to what it really represents.

11. In his 1934 *Concerto for Nine Instruments,* for example, all the pitch material is derived only from the three-note series B-B<flat>-D and its three mirror forms (retrograde, inversion, retrograde inversion).

12. Augusto de Campos, *Música de Invenção,* 96.

13. Ibid., 95.

14. Augusto de Campos, *Balanço da bossa e outras bossas* (São Paulo: Editora Perspectiva, 2003), 213.

15. In John Hollander's *The Figure of Echo* (Berkeley: University of California Press, 1981), we find the expression "imago vocis," which the author explains thus: "This phrase ... comes from the fairly literal Latin use of *imago,* or sometimes *imago vocis,* for echo. It precedes, rather than tropes, our primarily visual use of the word image" (11n). I thank Fernando Pérez-Vilallón for bringing to my attention Hollander's notion of the acoustic image, a subject of central interest in the poetics of concretism.

16. In a reminiscence of Alban Berg, Adorno mentions that composer's "unmistakable gift for the visual arts" and how his commitment to music was "almost accidental." He adds that Berg "retained much of his sense of the visual, most noticeably in the calligraphic appearance of his full scores," and conjectures that his propensity "for mirror and retrograde formations may, apart from the twelve-tone technique, be related to the visual dimension of his responses; musical retrograde patterns are anti-temporal, they organize music as if it were an intrinsic simultaneity. It is probably incorrect to attribute those technical procedures solely to the twelve-tone technique; they are derived not only from the microstructure of the rows, but also from the overall plan, as if from a basic outline, and as such they contain an element of indifference toward succession, something like a disposition toward musical saturation."

Theodor W. Adorno, *Alban Berg — Master of the Smallest Link* (Cambridge: Cambridge University Press, 1991), 14.

17. A literal translation reads, "A sound that does not sound/in the air that is not/almost as a person." At its most basic level, the poem "Pessoa" plays off the sonority of the Portuguese word *pessoa* (person), the suffix of which, *soa*, is homonymous to *soa* (the third-person singular of the verb *soar*, "to sound"). Augusto de Campos's gesture is to suggest that inside each individual (*pessoa*) a sound (*soa*) resonates. The etymology of the word *pessoa*, from the Latin *persona*, suggests the act of "sounding through a mask" in a play. Coincidentally, the Latin term, *personae*, was used as the title of Ezra Pound's 1909 collection of poetry.

18. Eduardo Sterzi, "Todos os sons, sem som," in Süssekind and Guimarães, *Sobre Augusto de Campos,* 105.

19. Ibid., 107.

20. It can perhaps be argued that this shift was part of an international phenomenon, since innovations related to the projection of voice in bossa nova shared a sense of kinship with musicians like Chet Baker, for instance, and even Fred Astaire. The *canto-falado* style subsequently found near-perfect vehicles in two films by Jacques Demy, done in collaboration with the composer Michel Legrand: *Les parapluies de Cherbourg* (1964) and *Les demoiselles de Rochefort* (1967).

21. Walter Garcia, *Bim Bom–A Contradição sem conflitos de João Gilberto* (São Paulo: Editora Paz e Terra, 1999), 81–82.

22. The role of the machine in concrete poetry is addressed by Haroldo de Campos in "Poesia concreta — Linguagem — Comunicação," in Augusto de Campos et al., *Teoria da poesia concreta,* 70. In English: "Concrete Poetry — Language — Communica-

tion," trans. A. S. Bessa, in *Novas — Selected Writing of Haroldo de Campos* (Evanston: Northwestern University Press, 2007).

23. Garcia, *Bim Bom,* 122.

24. Ibid., 126.

25. Ibid., 127.

26. Ibid., 171.

27. Cf. the final poem in "Bestiário — para fagote e esôfago," in Augusto de Campos, *Poesia 1949–1979* (São Paulo: Ateliê Editorial, 2000), 89: "and/this/the/official/cate/gory/of the/bard/with/whom/ — soon he's dead — /the/august/bust/fair enough/embattles."

28. Gary Tomlinson, *Metaphysical Song* (Princeton: Princeton University Press, 1999), 47.

29. Sterzi, "Todos os sons," 112.

30. The influence on Augusto de Campos of Rodrigues's songbook, and of the work of other composers and poets, still remains to be fully appraised. In *Balanço da bossa,* Augusto de Campos dedicated three essays to this great composer, including a complete discography.

31. Augusto de Campos, *Balanço da bossa,* 315–16.

32. Augusto de Campos's admiration for Lupicínio Rodrigues is cleverly memorialized in his translation of John Donne's "The Apparition," in which he uses a famous line by Rodrigues ("nos braços de um outro qualquer") as a solution for Donne's "And thee, feigned vestal, in worse arms shall see." For a detailed reading of de Campos's unorthodox "recreations" of Donne, see Ana Helena Souza, "'A urdidura subjacente': Recriações de poemas de John Donne," in Süssekind and Guimarães, *Sobre Augusto de Campos,* 268–84.

33. Augusto de Campos, *Balanço da bossa,* 222–23.

34. The popular music movement known as Tropicália that appeared in Brazil around 1968 has often been considered a

direct development of the concretist and neo-concretist aesthetics. The title of the movement is borrowed from an installation work by Hélio Oiticica produced the previous year. Singer and songwriter Caetano Veloso, one of the movement's chief proponents, fostered a lifelong relationship with both de Campos brothers, often collaborating musically.

35. Prominent among these references are an anonymous Provençal song from Galicia and lines from Luís de Camões ("Esperança de um só dia" [Hope of a Single Day]), as well as from the Parnassian poet Luis Guimarães Junior ("Oh, se me lembro, e quanto" [Oh, Do I Recall It, and How]).

36. In a French anthology of de Campos's work (Augusto de Campos, *Anthologie — Despoesia* [Paris: Al Dante, 2002], 16–29), Jacques Donguy performs a formidable "unpacking" of the word mutation going on in *Poetamenos*. In the section that follows, I use many of Donguy's solutions, as well as information given to me directly by Augusto de Campos.

37. The beginning of de Campos's poem is a rearrangement of the first lines of "Canção do figueiral" (Song of the Fig Orchard), a Provençal song from Galicia that celebrates the rescue of six young women captured by Moors. The original song starts thus: "No figueiral figueiredo, e no figueiral entrei" (In the fig orchard, in the fig orchard I entered). Cf. Marques da Cruz, *História da Literatura* (São Paulo: Editora Cia. Melhoramentos, 1924).

38. Both expressions are complicated creations that contain very little trace of Portuguese. Donguy writes that "exampl'eu" is "un néologisme latinisé, au sens de 'ouvrir vers l'extérieur,'" while "'fêmoras' est une autre creation à partir du latin 'femina,' 'femme' et 'femora,' 'femur.'" De Campos, *Anthologie,* 20. It's worth noting that the Latin root

ampl- is also present in *amplexus* (embrace). This convoluted line would thus suggest an inversion of the biblical account of the creation of Eve.

39. In the line "dedat illa(grypho)," de Campos deconstructs the Portuguese verb *datilografar* (typewrite) in order to insert his beloved's name within his poetic practice. It could be said that the "ghost" (or presence) of Lygia haunts his writing: *grypho* can be read as both "glyph" and "griffin."

40. The portmanteau "estesse" (composed of two demonstrative pronouns with a subtle difference: *este* [this] and *esse* [this]) can concomitantly be (mis)read as "ecstasy."

41. Camões's sonnet "Sete Anos De Pastor" refers to the biblical story of Jacob, who labored seven years in order to marry Rachel.

Sete anos de pastor Jacó servia
Labão, pai de Raquel, serrana bela;
mas não servia ao pai, servia a ela, e a ela
só por prêmio pretendia.
Os dias, na esperança de um só dia,
passava, contentando-se com vê-la;
porém o pai, usando de cautela,
em lugar de Raquel lhe dava Lia.
Vendo o triste pastor que com enganos
lhe fora assim negada a sua pastora,
começa de servir outros sete anos,
dizendo: — Mais servira, se não fora
para tão longo amor tão curta a vida.

Near the end of the poem, the family name of the beloved, Azeredo, echoes "figueiredo" in the second poem. The word *azeredo* indicates an orchard of *azeiros* (Prunus lusitanica), a tree of the Rosaceae family. Most Portuguese family names are inspired by nature, and according to the legend around *Canção do figueiral,* the youthful hero took the name Figueiredo after freeing the maidens from the Moors.

42. Apropos of "Lygia fingers," Donguy writes, "Idéogramme lyrique de la féminité et de

la félinité, avec la syllabe 'ly' qui assume le caractère d'une cellule thématique." Augusto de Campos, *Anthologie-Despoesia,* 8.

43. Elaborating on the "signification of the relation of Pan or the natural world with a voice," Hollander quotes the following passage from Francis Bacon's *De dignitate et augmentis scientarum:* "For the world .enjoys itself, and in itself all things that are. . . . The world itself can have no loves or any want (being content with itself) unless it be of *discourse.* Such is the nymph Echo, a thing not substantial but only a voice; or if it be more of the exact and delicate kind, *Syringa,* — when the words and voices are regulated and modulated by numbers, whether poetical or oratorical. But it is well devised that of all words and voices Echo alone should be chosen for the world's wife, for that is the true philosophy which echoes most faithfully the voices of the world itself, and is written as it were at the world's own dictation, being nothing else than the image and reflection thereof, to which it adds nothing of its own, but only iterates and gives it back." Hollander adds: "This marriage is one of nature to the true poetry of natural philosophy, the marriage for which he himself claims, in the *Novum organum,* to be writing the spousal verse or epithalamium." Hollander, *Figure of Echo,* 10.

44. Translation by Augusto de Campos and Antonio Sergio Bessa.

45. Marjorie Perloff, *Differentials — Poetry, Poetics, Pedagogy* (Tuscaloosa: University of Alabama Press, 2004), 41–42.

46. Ibid., 45.

Johanna Drucker, "Not Sound"

1. Paul Saenger, *Space Between Words: The Space of Silent Reading* (Stanford: Stanford University Press, 1997), 5–17. This reference came to my attention through the work of Laura Mandell, cited below.

2. Laura Mandell, "What Is the Matter? Or What Literary Theory Neither Hears Nor Sees," *New Literary History* 38, no. 4 (2007): 755–78.

3. Ibid., 759.

4. Ibid.

5. Ibid.

6. Saenger, *Space between Words.*

7. Saenger, *Space between Words,* in Mandell, "What Is the Matter?" 759.

Ming-Qian Ma, "The Sound Shape of the Visual"

1. See Ferdinand de Saussure, *Course in General Linguistics* (New York: McGraw-Hill, 1959), 66.

2. James Elkins, *The Domain of Images* (Ithaca: Cornell University Press, 1999), 11, 13.

3. Howard Nemerov, "On Poetry and Painting, with a Thought of Music," in *The Language of Images,* ed. W. J. T. Mitchell (Chicago: University of Chicago Press, 1980), 9, 10. Nemerov's observation here refers to poetry and painting in the mimetic tradition and situates them in the context of "the solemnity of the museum" (9). It nevertheless represents, rather ironically, an unspoken and yet widely accepted approach to these images in the texts of avant-garde poetry of innovation, an approach that is inclined to take these visual features at their face value and to promptly dismiss them as such.

4. The last appositional phrase is a paraphrase of the title of a study by P. Christopher Smith: "From Acoustics to Optics: The Rise of the Metaphysical and the Demise of the Melodic in Aristotle's *Poetics,*" in

Sites of Vision: The Discursive Construction of Sight in the History of Philosophy, ed. David Michael Levin (Cambridge: MIT Press, 1997), 69. For his detailed argument, see pages 69–91.

5. Roman Jakobson, *Language in Literature,* ed. Krystyna Pomorska and Stephen Rudy (Cambridge: Belknap Press of Harvard University Press, 1987), 466. Critical studies regarding the structural and perceptual relations between visual and the auditory signs have been hitherto rather limited, confined primarily within such disciplines as language studies, both literary and linguistic, and film studies. In other disciplines such as music studies and media studies, which include digital studies and the studies of acoustic technologies of various kinds, sound and the visual are treated, more often than not, separately, each in relation to language rather than to the other. Pursuing a set of critical issues and problems similar to those with which the above-mentioned studies have concerned themselves from the perspectives of either vision or sound, this essay focuses, instead, on the sound-visual relation as is manifested in variously nonlinguistic, graphic forms in the texts of contemporary avant-garde poetry.

6. As a major component of poststructuralist thinking championed, among many others, by Jacques Derrida and Michel Foucault, the scholarship on the critique of ocularcentrism is rich and extensive. For a comprehensive, historical overview of this issue, see Martin Jay, *Downcast Eyes: The Denigration of Vision in Twentieth-Century French Thought* (Berkeley: University of California Press, 1993). For more detailed rethinking of vision from diverse philosophical and theoretical perspectives, there are two important anthologies of critical essays, both edited by David Michael

Levin: *Modernity and the Hegemony of Vision* (Berkeley: University of California Press, 1993) and *Sites of Vision: The Discursive Construction of Sight in the History of Philosophy* (Cambridge: MIT Press, 1997).

7. Don Ihde, *Listening and Voice: A Phenomenology of Sound* (Athens: Ohio University Press, 1976), 14, 9, emphasis in the original. Unless otherwise noted, all emphases are in the original.

8. Foregrounding experiential over metaphysical content, Ihde defines "existential possibilities" further by making a distinction between his term and other types of possibilities in the history of philosophy. He writes: "But because there is also a need for a preliminary and at first schematic outline of existential possibilities, it may be necessary to differentiate them from the more familiar 'logical possibilities' of contemporary philosophy. Existential possibilities form a particular type of possibility in the investigation of an actual dimension of human experience" (Ihde, *Listening and Voice,* 30).

9. Ibid., 15, 14.

10. Nemerov, "On Poetry and Painting," 10.

11. Ihde, *Listening and Voice,* 9.

12. Ibid., 111. Ihde makes this statement with some qualifications: "Silence belongs to the syncopation of experience in which what is seen seems silent while what is not seen may sound. In this one could almost say that silence is a 'visual category.'" When understood in the context of his overall argument, however, his use of the phrase "syncopation of experience" effectively disqualifies his original qualification indicated by his expression "one could almost say." Michel Chion, *Audio-Vision: Sound on Screen,* ed. and trans. Claudia Gorbman, foreword by Walter Murch (New York: Columbia University Press, 1994), xxvi.

Although Chion's field of research is film studies, with his theory of the audiovisual relationship contextualized exclusively in this book in a cinematic kinetics, his understanding and theorizing of the sound-visual relation are usefully applicable beyond film studies.

13. Ihde, *Listening and Voice,* 111. It is important to point out here that Ihde's theorizing of silence and its status of relativity to thing is rooted in the tradition of Husserlian phenomenology and the concept of intention. He writes, "In Husserlian terms, silence belongs to the 'empty intention,' the aim of intentionality which is co-present in every intention but which is the 'infinite' side of intentionality that does not find fulfillment. There is a 'depth' to things which is revealed secretly in all ordinary experience, but which often remains covered over in the ease with which we take something for granted" (111). For a critique of Husserl and his concept of intention, see Theodor W. Adorno, *Against Epistemology: A Metacritique,* trans. Willis Domingo (Cambridge: MIT Press, 1982). Chion, *Audio-Vision,* 5. In a very illuminating way, Chion defines "added value" more specifically as follows: "By *added value* I mean the expressive and informative value with which a sound enriches a given image so as to create the definite impression, in the immediate or remembered experience one has of it, that this information or expression 'naturally' comes from what is seen, and is already contained in the image itself. Added value is what gives the (eminently incorrect) impression that sound is unnecessary, that sound merely duplicates a meaning which in reality it brings about, either all on its own or by discrepancies between it and the image" (5).

14. Jakobson, *Language in Literature,* 470. Jakobson credits George MacKay with

the use of this "good expression." For the context in which the reference is made, see page 470.

15. Walter Murch, Preface, in Chion, *Audio-Vision,* vii, viii. This is a summary paraphrase of Murch's description. For his original and more specific wording in the context of Chion's argument, see these two pages.

16. Michel Serres, *Hermes: Literature, Science, Philosophy,* ed. Josué V. Harari and David F. Bell, Post-face by Ilya Prigogine and Isabelle Stengers (Baltimore: Johns Hopkins University Press, 1982), 68.

17. James Elkins, *The Domain of Images* (Ithaca: Cornell University Press, 1999). Elkins's study is not a critique of the ocularcentric tradition. Rather, it is a revisionist rethinking that attempts primarily to expand the discipline of art history by arguing for an aesthetic affinity between scientific and artistic images. Regardless of the differences in criteria, for instance, "the 'two cultures'" of science and art "are virtually indistinguishable," he contends, especially "in terms of the attention scientists lavish on creating, manipulating, and presenting images" (10, 11). However, Elkins's historical and genealogical approach in his study of images effectively provides convincing evidences that testify to the privileging of vision over sound and its development over time.

18. Elkins, *Domain of Images,* 10.
19. Ibid., 10, 11.
20. Ibid., 11.
21. Ibid., 11.
22. Ibid., 15.
23. Ibid., 15.
24. Ibid., 15.
25. Ibid., 17.
26. Ibid., 15–17.
27. Ibid., 17.
28. Levin, introduction, in *Modernity and the Hegemony of Vision,* 5.

29. Ibid., 10.
30. Smith, "From Acoustics to Optics," 84.
31. Henry Louis Gates Jr., *Figures in Black: Words, Signs, and the "Racial" Self* (New York: Oxford University Press, 1987), 240.
32. Christian Bök, *Crystallography* (Toronto: Coach House Press, 1994). This poetry book is not paginated. Henceforth no endnotes will be used when it is referenced. The same image appears in Elkins's book (19).
33. Elkins, *Domain of Images,* 18.
34. Ibid., 18. Although Elkins points out that "at times the search also took a more radical turn, with the discovery of elementary forms that do not resemble the structures they combine to form," and that "Haüy also thought along counterintuitive lines," the results are ultimately predicated on "a more abstract, mathematical mode of analysis" (18, 20).
35. Ibid., 17, 18.
36. Ibid., 23.
37. Ihde, *Listening and Voice,* 43.
38. Ibid., 43, 17, 44. As is indicated by his rhetoric, Ihde's understanding of this global experience and its form of experiential synthesis is qualified as "primordial," "in its first naïveté," and happening "at the first level," "primitively" (43, 44). Such an understanding implies, then, a later and higher level of experiencing the world where sense data will be processed differently. The result, as is evidenced to some degree even in Ihde's own theorizing, is a return, however subtle or implicit, to none other than the sense atomism whereby sound and the visual are still approached separately. As much as this is the case, Ihde's position here is useful, as it acknowledges a form of experience prior to the phenomenological reduction.
39. Ibid., 49. According to Ihde, sound overlaps "with moving beings," an idea that has received increasing elaboration in recent years, especially in film studies, and the audio-visual overlap is only partial. For more detailed explanation by Ihde, see his chapter 4, "The Auditory Dimension," 49–55. While much of the argument concerning the sound-visual relation in this essay is made in light of Ihde's theory and articulated in his useful terminology, it departs from his position on several issues, and particularly on that of the sound-visual overlap here.
40. Ibid., 38.
41. Ibid., 39.
42. Ibid., 40.
43. Ibid., 44.
44. Ibid., 40.
45. John Cage, *Silence* (Hanover, NH: Wesleyan University Press, 1961), 8. For a fascinating study of the persistence of sound in the writings of metaphysics, see Smith, "From Acoustics to Optics."
46. John McCumber, "Derrida and the Closure of Vision," in Levin, *Modernity and the Hegemony of Vision,* 239.
47. Although this essay focuses on the use of extralinguistic signs in its argument, as specified at the beginning, and although the example here seems to be a language-based, letteristic one, it can be argued that these images present not so much a letteristic rendering as a transliteration, whereby to delineate, in the most physical way possible, the procedure in which sound fades into the intense light of logos.
48. McCumber, "Derrida and the Closure of Vision," 237. McCumber's statement quoted here has a different context in his essay, which is his reading of Derrida reading Hegel and Husserl, and in which he equates "word" to "sound." When read from a non-Derridean perspective, however, McCumber's statement makes a valid and pertinent point regarding this

particular poetry text under analysis here. For more details of McCumber's reading, see pages 234–251, especially 237.

49. Ihde, *Listening and Voice,* 55.

50. Ibid., 59.

51. Ibid., 56, 60, 61.

52. Ibid., 61.

53. Ibid., 61.

54. Ibid., 40.

55. Ibid., 61, 72. For more detailed elaborations on this topic, see chap. 6, "The Auditory Field," 72–83.

56. Ihde, *Listening and Voice,* 61.

57. Jakobson, *Language in Literature,* 467.

58. Ibid., 469.

59. Ihde, *Listening and Voice,* 65.

60. Jakobson, *Language in Literature,* 470. The two by now rather familiar terms "spacing" and "temporalizing" are borrowed from Jacques Derrida and his book *Speech and Phenomena and Other Essays on Husserl's Theory of Signs* (Evanston: Northwestern University Press, 1973), 130. Rather than highlighting their deconstructive associations, they are used here with a Deleuzian spin, emphasizing the notion of becoming.

61. McCumber, "Derrida and the Closure of Vision," 242.

62. Ibid.

63. Ibid., 243, 244.

64. Theodor Adorno, "Sociology and Empirical Research," in *The Positivist Dispute in German Sociology* (London: Heineman, 1981), 69.

65. Derrida, *Speech and Phenomena,* 136.

Brian M. Reed, "Visual Experiment and Oral Performance"

1. Susan Stewart, *Poetry and the Fate of the Senses* (Chicago: University of Chicago Press, 2002), chap. 3, "Voice and Possession."

2. Elisabeth Netzkowa [Elizaveta Mnatsakanova], *Osen' v lazarete nevinnykh sest'or: Rekviem v semi chast'akh* (Vienna: Grandits-Team, 2004), 18.

3. Elisabeth Netzkowa [Elizaveta Mnatsakanova] (text) and Wolfgang Musil (music), *Osen' v lazarete nevinnykh sest'or: Rekviem v semi chast'akh* (Vienna: Grandits-Team, 2004).

4. See, e.g., *Close Listening: Poetry and the Performed Word,* ed. Charles Bernstein (New York: Oxford University Press, 1998); *Crisis in Editing: Texts of the English Renaissance,* ed. Randall McLeod (New York: AMS, 1994); Meta DuEwa Jones, "Jazz Prosodies: Orality and Textuality," *Callaloo* 25, no. 1 (2002): 66–91, and "Listening to What the Ear Demands: Langston Hughes and His Critics," *Callaloo* 24, no.4 (2002): 1145–75; Fred Moten, *In the Break: The Aesthetics of the Black Radical Tradition* (Minneapolis: University of Minnesota Press, 2003); Bruce R. Smith, "Hearing Green: Logomarginality in Hamlet," *Early Modern Literary Studies* 7, no. 1 (May 2001), http://extra.shu.ac.uk/emls/07–1/logomarg/intro.htm; *Sound States: Innovative Poetics and Acoustical Technologies,* ed. Adalaide Morris (Chapel Hill: University of North Carolina Press, 1997).

5. On the "divide over merit" between "academic poetry," on the one side, and slam and hip hop poetries, on the other, see Saul Williams, Interview, *Callaloo* 29, no. 3 (2006): 735.

6. Joseph Addison, *Spectator* no. 58 (May 7, 1711).

7. Jacques Derrida, *Of Grammatology,* trans. Gayatri Chakravorty Spivak (Baltimore: Johns Hopkins University Press, 1976), 91–92.

8. Steve McCaffery, *Seven Pages Missing,* vol. 1, *Selected Texts 1969–1999* (Toronto: Coach House Books, 2000), 445–46.

9. Ibid., 446.

10. Marjorie Perloff, "Inner Tension / In Attention: Steve McCaffery's Book Art," *Visible Language* 25, nos. 2–3 (1992): 178. This paragraph, it is important to note, tells only one episode in a much longer story. McCaffery's poetics have evolved substantially since the mid-1970s. Ibid., 177–78, 180–81, 183–84, and 186–87. A 1999 reading of *CARNIVAL the second panel* is a measure of how far he has traveled: he treats the text as an incitement to oral performance, not as a challenge to speech's primacy. A recording is available at http://writing. upenn.edu/pennsound/x/McCaffery.html (accessed July 5, 2007).

11. For an illuminating account of the "deeply rooted Western conception of 'pictorial' Chinese," with special attention to Ernest Fenollosa and Ezra Pound, see Yunte Huang, *Transpacific Displacement: Ethnography, Translation, and Intertextual Travel in Twentieth-Century American Literature* (Berkeley: University of California Press, 2002), 73–75.

12. Marjorie Siegel, "More Than Words: The Generative Power of Transmediation for Learning," *Canadian Journal of Education* 20, no. 4 (1995): 455.

13. The PennSound web page, edited by Richard Sieburth, is titled "Pound's Collected Poetry Recordings" and can be found at http://writing.upenn.edu/penn sound/x/Pound.html (accessed July 4, 2007). The site contains readings from twenty-seven different cantos, thirteen of them written after World War II, when Pound's use of Chinese characters greatly accelerated.

14. For an instructive presentation of this problem, see Joseph Grigely, *Textualterity: Art, Theory, and Textual Criticism* (Ann Arbor: University of Michigan Press, 1995), 98–101.

15. Robert Duncan, *Ground Work: Before the War / In the Dark* (New York: New Directions Press, 2006), 36.

16. Ibid., p. 3.

17. McCaffery, *Seven Missing Pages,* 447.

18. The Last Poets is a group of African American poets and musicians who recorded four influential spoken word albums in the early 1970s. Its members have included Jalaluddin Mansur Nuriddin, Umar Bin Hassan, Suliaman El-Hadi, and Abiodun Oyewole.

19. Bob Cobbing, *Jade-Sound Poems* (London: Writers Forum, 1984), no pagination.

20. Yasunao Tone, *Musica Iconologos,* Lovely Music CD 3041.

21. See John Cage's *Song Books: Solos for Voice 3–92* (New York: Henmar Press, 1970) for a work that does in fact present performers with comparable challenges: to "play" a portrait of Henry David Thoreau (the fifth solo) and a profile of Marcel Duchamp (the sixty-fifth solo). Tone's *Musica Iconologos* is in dialogue with these and other Cagean experiments with the relationship between graphical notation and live performance.

22. On her PennSound web page, Bergvall notes the origins of "About Face": "This text started as a performance for the Liminal Institute Festival in Berlin in 1999. I had just had a painful tooth pulled out and could read neither very clearly nor very fast. Tape players with German and English conversations on the text were circulated among the audience. It took 45 minutes to perform the materials. For its 2nd showing at Bard College, I speeded up the tapes, transcribed the snaps of half-heard materials, and integrated these to the performing voice." On the same site one will also find a 2002 recording of a live reading at Devon, UK, http://writing .upenn.edu/ pennsound/x/Bergvall.html. Another recording is available: "About Face, Part 1," UbuWeb, http://www.ubu .com/sound/mo_cd2.html. For online text

versions, see "from *About Face* (ongoing),"
British Poetry Center, http://www.soton
.ac.uk/~bepc/poems/bergvall_1.htm and
"About Face (opening section)," *Electronic Poetry Review* 6 (September 2003),
http://www.epoetry.org/issues/issue6/text/
poems/cb1.htm. For its publication in a
book, see *Fig: Goan Atom 2* (Cambridge,
UK: Salt Publishing, 2005), 31–48. For
performance instructions, working notes,
and accompanying illustrations, see "Piece
in Progress: About Face (*Goan Atom, 2*),"
How2 1, no. 6 (2001), http://www.asu.edu/
pipercwcenter/how2journal/archive/
online_archive/v1_6_2001/current/
in-conference/bergvall.html. All online
sources accessed July 14, 2007.

23. *Fidget* began as a live performance commissioned by the Whitney Museum of
American Art (June 16, 1998). The gallery
installation at Printed Matter in New York
City lasted from June to September 1998.
Subsequently, it was published as a book
(Toronto: Coach House Books, 2000). For
the e-poem version, see Kenneth Goldsmith and Clem Paulsen, "Fidget Applet,"
Stadium, http://www.stadiumweb.com/
fidget/fidget.html. A complete recording

of *Fidget* was made at the WFMU studios,
Jersey City, New Jersey, during 2004–5
and is available at Goldsmith's page at
PennSound, http://www.writing.upenn
.edu/pennsound/x/Goldsmith.html. All
online sources accessed July 14, 2007.

24. Christian Bök's *Eunoia* is available both
as a book (Toronto: Coach House Books,
2001) and as an e-book (http://www
.chbooks.com/archives/online_books/
eunoia/text.html). A 2002 recording of
Eunoia is available at UbuWeb, http://
www.ubu.com/sound/bok.html. Two
2001 readings from *Eunoia* are available
at PennSound, http://writing.upenn
.edu/pennsound/x/Bok.html. For the
interactive e-poem version, see Bök and
Brian Kim Stefans, "eunoia: chapter e (for
rené crevel)," UbuWeb, http://www.ubu
.com/contemp/bok/eunoia_final.html. All
online sources accessed July 14, 2007.

25. Sawako Nakayasu, *So We Have Been Given
Time or* (Amherst: Verse, 2004), 1–2.

26. Ibid., 13–15 and 20–21.

27. Ibid., 1.

28. A recording of this reading is available at
http://www.factorial.org/sn/online.html
(accessed July 5, 2007).

CONTRIBUTORS

HÉLÈNE AJI is a professor of American literature at the Université de Maine in France. In addition to a number of articles on modernist and contemporary American poetry, she is the author of *Ezra Pound et William Carlos Williams: Pour une poétique américaine* (2001), *William Carlos Williams: Un plan d'action* (2004), and a book-length essay on Ford Madox Ford's *The Good Soldier* (2005). Recently she edited the "Poetry and Autobiography" issue of the online journal *EREA* (http://www.e-rea.org).

CHARLES BERNSTEIN is the Donald T. Regan Professor of English and comparative literature at the University of Pennsylvania and is the author of many books, including *Blind Witness: Three American Operas* (2008), *Shadowtime* (2005), *Republics of Reality: 1975–1995* (2000), *Content's Dream: Essays 1975–1984* (1986), *Controlling Interests* (1980), *My Way: Speeches and Poems* (1999), *With Strings* (2001), and *Girly Man* (2006), the latter three published by the University of Chicago Press.

ANTONIO SERGIO BESSA is the director of curatorial and education programs at the Bronx Museum, the author of *Oyvind Fahlstrom: The Art of Writing* (2008), and co-editor of *Novas — Selected Writings of Haroldo de Campos* (2006). A former editor of the avant-garde journal *Zingmagazine,* he has translated Susan Howe's *Pierce Arrow* into Portuguese (São Paulo: Lumme Editor, 2008), as well as selected works by Augusto de Campos, Haroldo de Campos, and Waly Salomão into English.

CHRISTIAN BÖK is a professor of English at the University of Calgary (Canada) and the author of *Crystallography* (1994), a "pataphysical encyclopedia," and *Eunoia* (2001), a leading work of experimental literature; he has performed his sound works and lectured around the world.

GORDANA P. CRNKOVIĆ, a native of Zagreb, is a professor of Slavic and comparative literature at the University of Washington, Seattle. She is the author of *Imagined Dialogues: Eastern European Literature in Conversation with American and English Literature* (1999), as well as many essays on East-West aesthetic and cultural interaction. She has also written extensively on the work of John Cage and on contemporary film.

JOHANNA DRUCKER is the Bernard and Martin Breslauer Professor of Bibliography in the Department of Information Studies at the University of California, Los Angeles. She has published extensively on the history of written forms, typography, design, and visual poetics. In addition to her scholarly work, Drucker is known internationally as a book artist and experimental visual poet. Her recent books include *Graphic Design History: A Critical Guide,* with Emily McVarish (2008), *Testament of Women* (2006), and *Sweet Dreams: Contemporary Art and Complicity* (2005), the latter published by the University of Chicago Press.

CRAIG DWORKIN is a professor of English at the University of Utah. Among his most recent publications are *Language to Cover a Page: The Early Writings of Vito Acconci* (2006); *Parse* (2008); and *The Consequence of Innovation: Twenty-First-Century Poetics* (2008).

RUBÉN GALLO is a professor of Latin American literature at Princeton University, where he directs the Program in Latin American Studies. He is the author of *Mexican Modernity: The Avant-Garde and the Technological Revolution* (2005) and *New Tendencies in Mexican Art* (2004). He is also the editor of *The Mexico City Reader* (2004) and is currently completing a new book tentatively entitled "Freud in Mexico: The Neuroses of Modernity."

KENNETH GOLDSMITH teaches writing at the University of Pennsylvania, where he is also a senior editor of PennSound, an online poetry archive. He is the author of ten books of poetry, founding editor of the online archive UbuWeb (ubu.com), and the editor of *I'll Be Your Mirror: The Selected Andy Warhol Interviews,* which was the basis for an opera, *Trans-Warhol,* that premiered in Geneva in March 2007. Goldsmith is also the host of a weekly radio show on New York City's WFMU.

SUSAN HOWE'S most recent collection of poems is *Souls of the Labadie Tract* (2007). Her critical works include *My Emily Dickinson* and *The Birth-mark: Unsettling the Wilderness in American Literary History.* Two CDs in collaboration with the musician/composer David Grubbs, *Thiefth* and *Souls of the Labadie Tract,* were released (on the Blue Chopsticks label) in 2005 and 2007, respectively. Until her retirement in 2007, Howe was the Samuel P. Capen Chair in Poetry and the Humanities at the State University of New York, Buffalo.

YUNTE HUANG is a professor of English at the University of California, Santa Barbara, and the author of *Transpacific Imaginations* (2008) and *Transpacific Displacement* (2002). He is also the author of a book of poems entitled *Cribs* (2005).

LEEVI LEHTO is a Finnish poet, editor, publisher, programmer, and translator of a.o., Louis Althusser, Gilles Deleuze, George Orwell, Stephen King, Ian McEwan, John Keats, John Ashbery, and Charles Bernstein. His translation of James Joyce's *Ulysses* into Finnish is forthcoming. Lehto is also known for his experiments in digital poetry, such as the Google Poem Generator, and his sound work can be accessed at the online poetry archive PennSound (http://writing.upenn.edu/pennsound/x/Lehto .html). He has published poetry, fiction, and nonfiction, including *Lake Onega and Other Poems* (2006), and a volume of essays in Finnish titled *Alussa oli kääntäminen* (2008).

MING-QIAN MA is a professor of English at the State University of New York, Buffalo. He is the author of *Poetry as Re-Reading: American Avant-Garde Poetry and the Poetics of Counter-Method* (2008) as well as many essays on modernist and postmodernist poetics.

STEVE MCCAFFERY is the David Gray Chair of Poetry and Letters at the State University of New York, Buffalo. The author of more than twenty-five volumes of poetry and criticism, he is also a solo practitioner of sound poetry and a longtime member of the sound-performance ensemble Four Horsemen. His critical works include *Prior to Meaning: The Protosemantic and Poetics* (2001), *North of Intention* (1986), and (with Jed Rasula) *Imagining Language* (1998).

MARJORIE PERLOFF recently retired from the Sadie D. Patek Chair of Humanities at Stanford University and is currently Scholar-in-Residence at the University of Southern California. She is the author of many books on poetry and poetics that include discussion of sound, ranging from *Rhyme and Meaning in the Poetry of Yeats* (1970) to *The Futurist Moment* (1986), *Radical Artifice* (1992), and *Wittgenstein's Ladder* (1996), all three published by the University of Chicago Press, as well as a memoir, *The Vienna Paradox,* from New Directions (1994).

NANCY PERLOFF is curator of modern and contemporary collections at the Getty Research Institute, Los Angeles. She is the author of *Art and the Everyday: Popular Entertainment and the Circle of Erik Satie* (1991) and co-editor (with Brian Reed) of *Situating El Lissitzky: Berlin, Vitebsk, Moscow* (2003). Her most recent exhibitions are *Tango with Cows: Book Art of the Russian Avant-Garde, 1910–1917* (2008–9) and *Sea Tails: A Video Collaboration* (2004), based on a recreation of David Tudor's only video work.

BRIAN M. REED is a professor of English at the University of Washington, Seattle. He is the author of the book *Hart Crane: After His Lights* (2006) and the coeditor (with Nancy Perloff) of *Situating El Lissitzky: Berlin, Vitebsk, Moscow* (2003). He has also published articles on visual-verbal relations, on poetry and recorded sound, and on such modern and postmodern writers as John Ashbery, Susan Howe, Ezra Pound, Tom Raworth, and Rosmarie Waldrop.

JACQUES ROUBAUD, professor emeritus of mathematics at the University of Paris X (Nanterre), is one of France's leading poets and novelists and one of the founders of Oulipo in 1966. His many books translated into English include *Some Thing Black* (1990) and *The Plurality of Worlds of Lewis* (1995), both translated by Rosmarie Waldrop, and, most recently, *The Form of a City Changes Faster, Alas, Than the Human Heart* (2006), translated by Keith and Rosmarie Waldrop. Roubaud's *La vieillesse d'Alexandre* (1978) is one of the seminal studies of the development of metrics in French poetry.

RICHARD SIEBURTH is a professor of French and comparative literature at New York University. He is the author of *Emblems of Desire: Selections from the* Délie *of Maurice Scève* (2002; revised 2007). His other translations include works by Friedrich Hölderlin, Walter Benjamin, Gershom Scholem, Gérard de Nerval, Michel Leiris, Henri Michaux, and Antonin Artaud.

SUSAN STEWART, a former MacArthur Fellow and a Chancellor of the Academy of American Poets, is the Annan Professor of English at Princeton University and is the author of five books of poems, including, most recently, *Columbarium* (2003), which won the 2003 National Book Critics Circle Award, and *Red Rover* (2008). Her many prose works include *On Longing* (1984), *Poetry and the Fate of the Senses* (2002), and *The Open Studio: Essays on Art and Aesthetics* (2005). Her co-translations include Euripides' *Andromache* (2001) and *TriQuarterly 127: Contemporary Italian Poetry* (2007), and she is the translator of *Love Lessons: Selected Poems of Alda Merini* (2009).

YOKO TAWADA, born in Tokyo, has made her home in Germany since 1982. She has published widely in both Japanese and German — poetry, fiction, essays, and criticism — and has been a guest professor at many universities. Her books in English translation include *The Bridegroom Was a Dog* (1998), *Where Europe Begins* (2002), and *Facing the Bridge* (2007). Her most recent book in German is a meditation on language entitled *Sprachpolizei und Spielpolyglotte* (2007).

ROSMARIE WALDROP'S recent poetry books are *Curves to the Apple* (2006), *Blindsight* (2003), and *Love, Like Pronouns* (2003). She is also the author of a collection of essays entitled *Dissonance (if you are interested)* (2005). Her translation of Ulf Stolterfoht's *Lingos I–IX* (2007) was awarded the PEN Award for Poetry in Translation in 2008.

INDEX